SEE!
Urban Transformation
in Southeastern Europe

ERSTE Foundation Series
Volume 2

SEE!
Urban Transformation in Southeastern Europe

Edited by Kai Vöckler

LIT

Content

Archis SEE network

www.seenetwork.org

MOLDOVA
UKRAINE
ROMANIA
ATU – Association for Urban Transition
Zeppelin Association
FRONTAL
Bucharest
ADAPTations1
Sofia
BULGARIA
Archis Interventions_Istanbul
Istanbul
TURKEY
Archis Intervention_Cyprus
Nicosia / Lefkosa
CYPRUS
Dipkarpaz / Rizokarpaso

RESTORAN
EURO
Jagnjetina sa ražnja Sač
1 km
BOSNA I HERCEGOVINA JE SADA MIRNA I SIGURNA
Vrijeme je da se okrenemo budućnosti!

Preface, or Do We Need a Publication on Urban Transformation in Southeastern Europe?

Kai Vöckler

Since the end of communism in southeastern Europe and the war that led to the breakup of Yugoslavia, a substantial amount of construction activity has taken root across the region, resulting in a completely new type of urbanization. This is a typical development in post-conflict states in transition, where the weakness or total lack of institutional structures makes regulating building activity problematic, as has happened in Prishtina, Belgrade, Tirana, and Famagusta/Gazimağusa. The erratic sprawl of makeshift buildings is a product of the urban crisis that has shaped the region since its post-socialist transformations and wars. At the same time these urban changes highlight a new typology that is completely independent of regional particularities. They are, in fact, an expression of the developments taking place across wide sections of society—developments that tie up investments to a large extent. Their specific forms are the result of an interdependence of spaces linked by a media-based world of images, migratory movements, and cash flow.

Turbo Urbanism

The original meaning of the word "turbo," as the acceleration or increase of a motor's performance, finds its counterpart in the concept of "turbo culture," with its exaggerations, excesses, inordinateness, and random amalgamation of both local and global ornamentation. The symbolic significance of the irregular, the random, and the accidental particularly refers to the actual informal nature of this cultural expression. Informality and apparent randomness (the rules have not been canonized) are symbolically related by the city and its architecture to the world. Its architectural language quietly implies a certain worldwide phenomenon: the "informalization" of urban space as a result of neoliberal capitalism. Summed up by the buzzword "turbo capitalism" (Edward Luttwak), this development is characterized by an economy focused purely on efficiency and the maximization of profit on a global scale, accompanied by the dismantling of national regulations, with the aim of eventually completely relinquishing state governance. The creation of "informality" is consistent with this deregulation, especially in the working sector, which struggles to adapt to the new circumstances.

One thing that all of these countries have in common is that, after the collapse of the socialist systems, they underwent a phase in which they transformed from planned economies to market economies. This phase took place under conditions dictated by a globalized economy and the financial capital coming from around the world. Of course, it had a dramatic effect on everyday life and development in the cities. Besides democratization, the paradigm for this socio-political transformation involved the speediest possible privatization and liberalization of the market. In most cases, the result was a weakening of the state's ability to regulate and oversee the market. In particular, an overly confident belief in market forces ignored the non-economic factors that are just as important to a functioning community. This led to "turbo urbanism," the informalization of urban space that results from unfettered neo-liberal capitalism and all of its concomitant phenomena. Cities were overwhelmed by new construction booms, ranging from questionable investment projects in downtown areas to large quantities of informal, private housing developments, generally on the urban periphery. Characteristically, these booms occurred with weak city oversight, or even an outright lack of regulation. Community property was privatized—something that was happening everywhere in Eastern Europe—and the new owners were mostly left to fend for themselves. Governments quickly unburdened themselves of their social responsibilities. On top of this development came the European Union integration attempts, with some countries aiming to join, as Slovenia, Bulgaria, and Romania eventually did. At the core of the integration agreements is the unrestrained mobility of people, goods, capital, and services—a freedom that has led to completely new conditions for mobility and urban development.

The Impact of Migration and Remittances

In addition, the wars in the 1990s that came with the break-up of Yugoslavia unleashed political conflicts, some of which remain unresolved to this day. Another example is the almost total collapse of Albania after the implosion of the "pyramid schemes" in 1997; the lack of government oversight had catastrophic financial consequences, mostly for small investors, and also led to mass emigration. The effects of this have not yet been sufficiently analyzed; for instance, high numbers of migrant workers—up to one-third of the population in some countries—invest in houses for their families, but do not themselves live there. And, as statistics also show, countless family budgets rely on remittances of money from relatives in the diaspora. In proportion to the entire economic development of each country, these remittances can make up a considerable percentage of a country's gross domestic product (GDP). A good example is Kosovo: after the end of the war in 1999, about one hundred thousand Kosovar refugees were forced to return from the diaspora. However, it is estimated that about four hundred thousand Kosovars legally reside in OECD nations—more than one-fifth of the entire population of Kosovo. If we add the numerous illegal migrant workers from Kosovo, it becomes clear how closely Kosovo is connected to all of Europe. Since the unemployment rate in Kosovo is over forty percent and the country has the highest birth rate in Europe, as well as the worst economic statistics in the region, Kosovo is still dependent upon remittances from migrant workers. European Union policy is to close the borders to Kosovar migrants and to donate large sums for development. This policy seems highly questionable, since these sums could be earned by migrant workers. The IMF estimates that up until 2008 remittances amounted to approximately 2.4 billion euros, while international developmental aid totaled only 2 billion euros.

"Informal" Building

After the collapse of the socialist system, southeastern European architects and urbanists were confronted with a wave of building, most of it informal. "Informal" construction was essentially caused by the changed political situation. The new situation led inhabitants to begin a great many building projects. In addition, there were large numbers of immigrants from rural areas, as well as working migrants returning from western countries, and refugees (practically the biggest group in the western Balkans). This resulted in a lack of housing, which was a big problem, even under socialism. It also meant that there were good prospects of profiting from this demand, despite the economically precarious situation.

At the same time the existing legal framework was insufficient or inchoate. Also, weak, incipient governmental institutions were unable to adequately enforce laws and regulations. Sometimes they were incapable of enforcing them at all. Therefore, construction projects could only be "informal"—or, as we have mainly witnessed, planning policies were incapable of producing master plans. Planning was random, provisional, and haphazard. A lack of engagement on the part of responsible government agencies led to difficulties, as the different case studies show.

The Future of the European City?

To understand the current situation in southeastern Europe, it is essential to be aware of how to evaluate "formal" and "informal" structures. It cannot be denied that the many problems require that the state intervene, to protect the common welfare. Alarmists may be heard claiming that the situation in Tirana, Belgrade, and Sofia is simply a result of consistent deregulation, and they are warning that such developments could soon be seen throughout western European cities, in view of the increasing retreat of communal governance and the emergence of so-called public-private partnerships focused mainly on financial interests. All too hastily, the planning management's position is adopted. Examples show that uncontrolled and unrestricted town planning is a result of political and social crisis, and its problems should not be attributed to the failures of local management and politicians alone. Urban development is a social process—its product is not only the result of the intentions of all participants, but also of the instruments of power that account for their influence and economic success. The situation in most cities in the Balkans cannot be compared to that of western European cities. While western European urban development is essentially structured by economic interests and communal planning within a highly formalized framework, in southeastern Europe it is, to a large extent, led by family organizations and shaped by a patronage economy. In this respect, we are dealing with a distinctive type of urbanization—one that can be found progressing in its own, specific way in other places across the region, such as Athens. This is why it is necessary to come up with a combination of governmental and social controls, which could form the basis for successful regulation. This kind of negotiation needs to find its own form. A western European notion of planning cannot simply be transferred. Planning strategies are needed that do not aspire to autocratic or bureaucratic solutions, but instead address the population directly—a population that must collectively agree on the future of its own commonwealth.

Archis Interventions in Southeastern Europe

Here is where the Archis Interventions project begins. The aim of Archis Interventions, a community-based, non-profit offshoot of Archis (also the publisher of *Volume* magazine), is to support cities by supplying ideas and concepts that will help to revitalize public space and renew faith in public dialogue. Local partners play the main roles in the process, since they are the ones requesting intervention in the development of their city.[1] Archis Interventions' activities in southeastern Europe began in 2005, when the author and his Kosovar colleagues founded a local branch in Prishtina (Archis Interventions/Prishtina). Against this backdrop, Archis Interventions began expanding its activities across southeastern Europe.[2] A network of independent urban initiatives and organizations in southeastern Europe was launched in 2008 by Kai Vöckler, in cooperation with Srdjan Jovanović Weiss—and is still growing. In almost all larger cities in southeastern Europe there exist independent urban initiatives that use their expert knowledge and experience to defend the interests of civic stakeholders. Such initiatives often work in isolation from one another or have only limited opportunities to participate in international urban discourse on new urban development and planning methods and concepts. The aim of the Archis

1 Documented on www.archis.org.

2 See www.seenetwork.org. The Archis Interventions project in southeastern Europe is supported by the ERSTE Foundation.

Interventions SEE network is to network regionally, develop international cooperation projects, share past experience, transfer relevant knowledge, and last, but not least, strengthen local initiatives by embedding them in supra-regional networks. By 2010 the network had been extended to include the countries that emerged from the former Yugoslavia, as well as to Albania, Bulgaria, Romania, Turkey, and Cyprus. Professionals from all over the region have been involved in different local projects. And the initiatives' work has been presented in international exhibitions (e.g., the *Balkanology* exhibition at the Swiss Architecture Museum (2008), the Architecture Center Vienna (2009), and the National Museum of Contemporary Art in Bucharest (2010)—as well as at conferences, and in local and international media.

Perspectives of Urbanism

Unquestionably, urban development has its own characteristics in each part of the region. Also, this selection deliberately refrains from attempting to communicate a presentation of urban development that is applicable to the region as a whole. Instead, selected examples from different locations reveal the new types of influences on architecture and urban development, while critically examining the potential for improvement through architectural and urbanist measures. Therefore, the publication begins with reflections on the perspectives of urbanism, followed by a second section, introducing selected initiatives and Civil Society Organizations from the region through interviews about the role of the architect in the conflict-ridden field of urban transformation. This will give the reader an understanding for the different approaches taken by these initiatives, as well as for their experiences and perspectives, with regard to the local urban developments in which they intervene.

The third section of the publication is about post-conflict development in cities that have experienced war, and how the conflict is spatially embedded in so-called divided cities, such as Mostar (Bosnia-Herzegovina), Mitrovica (Kosovo), Nicosia, Pyla, and Dip Karpaz (Cyprus). A comparative study about creating a new communication sphere in the form of community centers or public forums, in order to overcome the division of each city, reflects on their perspectives. Also, the importance of reinventing public space and collecting public memories is shown through the example of project done in Mostar. A specific problem of post-conflict development—the increase of population caused by the return of refugees to a city, and its aftermath, the unregulated and informal building boom—is shown in the example of Prishtina. Different strategies to influence the situation, e.g., doing media campaigns and public debates, developing a concept for the legalization of informal settlements, and implementing it to improve the future prospects of the city of Prishtina will be presented, accompanied by interviews about the situations in Mitrovica, Mostar, and Nicosia. A project focusing on the situation in rural sites, using the village of Dipkarpaz/ Risokarpaso in North Cyprus as an example, shows how villagers deal with the division in their everyday lives.

The fourth section shows how the breakdown of the socialist system and the implementation of a market economy affected urban development. The problem of maintaining privatized socialist housing estates, and the strategies developed to improve communication between homeowners and the local governmental administration are presented through economic concepts and urban and architectural strategies in Bucharest. Added to this are projects regarding urban transformation in Skopje. A specific problem affecting all of Europe is the so-called "integration" of Roma people, most of whom have lived in their respective cities for generations. Examples and different strategies are presented. Besides this, the breakdown of the socialist system also led to boom in constructing buildings for religious usages. In the case of the former Yugoslavia, this was also part of the creation of a "national identity," as examples from Bosnia-Herzegovina, Croatia, and Serbia will show.

Do We Need a Publication on Urban Transformation in Southeastern Europe?

A close reading of the book will show the reader that, beyond obvious differences, the cities in the region have common problems, from the necessary rehabilitation of the socialist housing sector, the integration of informal settlements, to the necessity of creating new spaces for communication, in cases of post-conflict development. Yet, first and foremost, it demonstrates the importance of local civic engagement, as governmental bodies are challenged beyond their capacity by these problems, regardless of cause. Some of the studies, interventions, and projects presented were initiated by Archis Interventions, while others were developed independently by local initiatives and activists. The aim of this publication is to give local activists—most of them architects and urbanists—greater visibility in the international urban discourse, by inviting them to present their activities and their ways of intervening in urban development, in order to have a positive influence on the city's future perspectives. They can teach us the lessons that need to be learned.

The article is based on previous publications: Balkanology - Neue Architektur und urbane Phänomene in Südosteuropa / Balkanology – New Architecture and Urban Phenomena in Southeastern Europe, Schweizerisches Architekturmuseum & Kai Vöckler, eds.; SAM no. 6, 2008; and Kai Vöckler, Prishtina is Everywhere, Turbo Urbanism: the Aftermath of a Crisis, Amsterdam: Archis, 2008 (published in German by Parthas, Berlin).

Perspectives of Urbanism

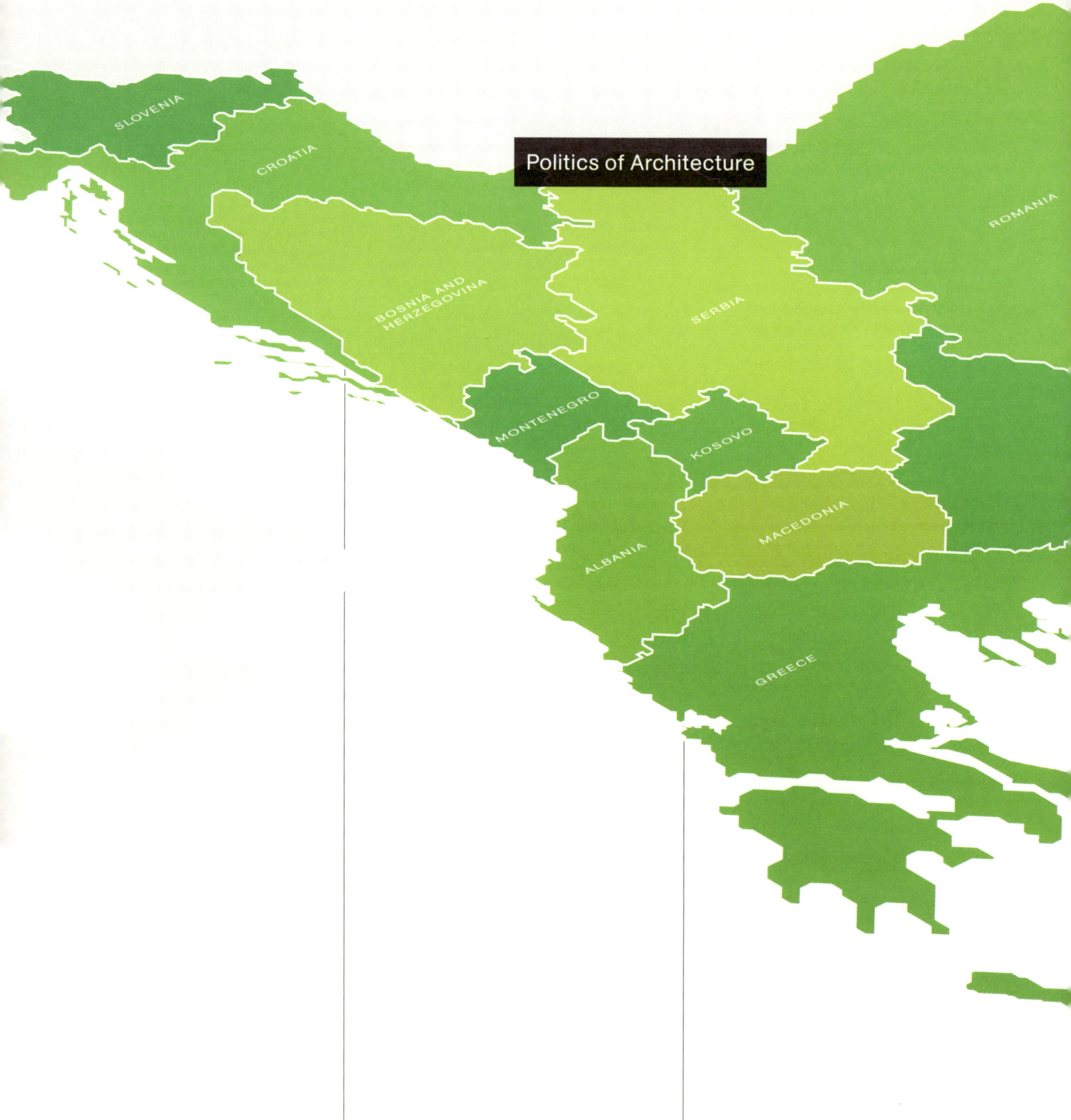

Politics of Architecture

UWYH - Use What You Have
Towards an Urbanism of Opportunities

Margins of Modernity
On the Institutional Crisis in Post-socialist Urban Planning

Politics of Architecture

Kai Vöckler

Social and political problems materialize in cities, but since every city's population is confronted with these problems and must examine how they develop, there is also a chance to influence residents' view of the future positively, in ways that go beyond the provision of basic necessities. The pivotal meaning of the city as an agent for political and social change becomes particularly obvious in a post-conflict situation. In this case, a city's development takes place under mostly unsafe, unstable conditions, and it is essentially defenseless against the global mechanisms of political and economic events. This kind of city is scarred by conflicts; it is the expression of the crises in which the city finds itself.

Cities that have to regenerate themselves after a conflict always have a recurring, similar problem: the exchange of population segments that occurs when many residents flee a city during periods of armed conflict. Often, many of these people do not return to their homes, for a variety of reasons: they may have better prospects elsewhere, or the political situation in their homeland may have altered so much that they are not interested in returning. Often, the conflicts have not been solved, but have instead become embedded in the city itself—the numerous divided cities around the world—from Belfast to Nicosia, Mostar to Beirut—are evidence of this. In addition, many people migrate to cities from rural areas. The result is that existing communities dissolve, and new neighborhoods are rapidly assembled. The people in them did not know each other previously, and have little to do with the city and its history. And in the case of rural immigrants, they are often not familiar with city life, which requires people to live closely together with many other different types of people. Living conditions are precarious, production has to be set up again, business has to develop, and jobs are scarce. Government institutions have to be rebuilt and do not function well; the political situation is unstable; corruption is everywhere. Most crucial though, is the fact that, because of the rural immigrants and the return of refugees after a conflict, the population of a city will grow a great deal in a very short period of time. Cities like Prishtina or Kabul tripled or even quintupled their populations within a few years after military interventions. This results in an unregulated, informal boom in construction, since the demand for living space increases dramatically. Not only does the reconstruction of the city—the rebuilding of ruins—make its

mark on a post-conflict situation, but the construction of new buildings also has a significant effect. Political power vacuums at the national level, along with the absence of self-monitoring in the civilian population, generate uncontrolled forces, which can seriously damage these cities' chances for recovery. For this reason, it is necessary to scrutinize the aid and planning strategies we have used, and intensify the search for possible alternatives.[1] One fact that often goes unrecognized is that social and political structures are shaped to a great degree by the way a city is developed. This raises the question of how the expertise of architects and planners can be utilized, not only to overcome the consequences of a crisis, but also to avoid more conflict in the future. What would an "architecture of peace" look like?

Housing construction is strategically important. Housing is the basis for survival in war or other catastrophic situations, since it guarantees a minimum of safety and protection. And it is the key to urban development. It is not only of great economic significance, but it also helps to constitute new types of social interaction, which have the immediate ability to help institutions begin functioning again. It incorporates economic, social, and political capital. From the way a city is rebuilt, one can see how its inhabitants relate to their future prospects. Still—just like the process of rebuilding urban structures that have been destroyed during armed conflict—the construction of housing, the restoration of architectural legacies, or the expansion of industrial and commercial buildings are not merely questions of architecture or urban planning.

1 See Sultan Barakat, ed., *After the Conflict: Reconstruction and Development in the Aftermath of War*, London, New York 2005; Gerd Junne, Willemijn Verkoren, eds., *Postconflict Development: Meeting New Challenges*, Boulder, London 2005; Kai Vöckler, *Prishtina is Everywhere. Turbo Urbanism: the Aftermath of a Crisis*, Amsterdam 2008; Jon Calame, Esther Charlesworth, *Divided Cities: Belfast, Beirut, Jerusalem, Mostar, and Nicosia*, Philadelphia 2009.

Political and economic interdependencies are embedded in these issues. Architects and urban planners have to find their own positions in relation to this complicated association of intertwining forces.

In recent years, the importance of the international community in managing local conflicts has increased considerably. Banding together international aid organizations, the international community not only contributes a great deal to the regulation of conflicts, but also to the restoration of political, social, and cultural institutions. Even when the primary task is to provide basic necessities—such as water, electricity, streets, and public transportation—rebuilding a city's infrastructure means that all of the decisions and steps taken in the process will profoundly influence the further development of the city. Thus, the urban transformations initiated by global players in very diverse regions around the world often follow the same pattern. However, there are an increasing number of problems: first, it is becoming ever more difficult to discern who is involved, and second, large organizations such as the UN, the OECD, and the World Bank, along with countless NGOs, are unable to coordinate their efforts. In addition, these organizations are frequently in indirect competition with each other for political sway; their financial backing is opaque, there is no legal oversight of their actions, and, last, but not least, there are individuals employed in these organizations who are involved in outright criminal activities, and they often get away scot-free. It has become urgently necessary to subject the methods and procedures of the international aid community to critical scrutiny.[2]

2 See Regina Bittner, Wilfried Hackenbroich, Kai Vöckler, eds., *UN Urbanism. Post-conflict cities Mostar Kabul*, Berlin 2010; Linda Polman, *War Games: The Story of Aid and War in Modern Times*, London, New York 2010.

Global governance and NGO activities

In a post-conflict situation, the process of rebuilding a city and restoring acceptable living conditions must be adapted as soon as possible to a specific situation, which is marked by a great deal of ambiguity and insecurity. Most aid and development programs aim to establish new forms of good governance, which often simply imitate the political structures of the donor countries and usually try to apply generally unquestioned notions of a "civil society" to the situation at hand.[3] Hence, normalization strategies around the globe operate with images and concepts—from historical reconstruction to the idea of capacity building. However, despite all of the good intentions, these strategies disregard the realities of these cities. Ideas and concepts, such as "freedom and democracy," are exported, even though most of the time, they are mere euphemisms, used to cover up the introduction of the same capitalist principles of property and market economies that dominate the donor nations. Even the term "human rights" is regarded as a political norm that should be valid everywhere, and the fact that human rights have a history, as well as a changeable definition, is overlooked. To spell it out, so as not to be misunderstood: of course, human rights are highly desirable and worth defending, but they do not represent a neutral system of values. Rather, they are always permeated by political claims and ought to be negotiated and adapted to suit local conditions. Briefly stated, too little consideration is given to the special circumstances of local political situations, and frequently, there is little knowledge of local culture and society.

The result is a kind of "donor speak," whose goal is to align everything with the political aims of the donor; this language is spoken by all of the members of local initiatives, as well as by those working for international organizations. Unfortunately, this is not a phantasm, but a political reality, and every plan in the crisis situation has to adjust to it. Donors are accountable to their own countries, and have to consider the political situations there, too. Consequently, it is all the more necessary to create a context for planning in crisis situations, and make sure that the goals of the plan reflect the local

3 See John E. Trent, *Modernizing the United Nations System: Civil Society's Role in Moving from International Relations to Global Governance*, Farmington Hills, Opladen, 2007.

situation and are suitably appropriate. It is imperative that local political, cultural, and social conditions be considered in the process. Through urban planning, overlapping problems in the development of the society as a whole can be dealt with, and models for solutions can be concocted. However, this means that the "architecture of peace" must have a clear understanding of the specific form of local political governance that arises in a post-conflict situation, and it also has to reflect upon its own position in relation to that.

Numerous recent global conferences—for example, the 1992 World Environmental Conference in Rio de Janeiro, the 1996 HABITAT II in Istanbul, the 1999 URBAN 21 in Berlin, and the 2010 World Urban Forum in Rio de Janeiro—have all rehabilitated planning, in terms of influencing and managing social processes. Widely implemented by global players, such as the World Bank in the 1980s, the predominant neoliberal ideology and its efforts to minimize state influence has proved crisis-prone and increased the drive to reconfigure state structures and develop new forms of planning. This strategy, christened "good governance," directly addresses urban agglomeration as the focal point of social transformation, referring to a development that has become increasingly apparent over the last two decades: in conjunction with the significant expansion of cross-border exchange, new transnational structures have also arisen, and they express a new kind of relationship between the local and the global.

This is associated with profound alterations in the concept of statehood itself, as well as in planning, for it is no longer the hierarchic and centralistic state that comprises the center of politics and controls development, when it comes to comprehensive planning. Governmental action instead distinguishes itself in various areas. The state now tends to play the roles of moderator and coordinator between the international and local levels. Non-governmental players are increasingly involved in decision-making and implementation processes, this being the aim of the term "governance." Governance is defined as the sum of all possible options, within which public and private institutions and organizations are constantly regulating their common affairs in order to coordinate their interests and facilitate cooperative action.[4] Within this structure, there are active balances of power that are worthy of special attention.

Along with the cross-border expansion of communications, transportation, and information systems, the intensification of economic relationships in the global market, and the internationalization of production and labor conditions, new forms of political regulation have arisen on a global scale. First attempts at a kind of global governance have been carried out by NATO, the IMF, the OECD, and the United Nations, more or less successfully. They act on an international level, wherever there is a lack of formal democratic institutions. They are the protagonists in post-conflict situations, since they are the organs of the international community, which is supposed to guarantee reconstruction, as well as integration into the global market and the international community of nations. They frequently replace missing state institutions, or participate to a large degree in their formation (nation building). Here, the international NGOs are important correctives. Evidence of this is the almost dramatic increase in the numbers of international NGOs that have begun operating in post-conflict situations in recent decades. However, their role within the current form of political regulation (policy regime) is also problematic and ought to be critically examined. Are they simply one component of a dominant political and regulatory system, or do they represent the interests of local civil societies?

Non-governmental organizations are, according to the general definition, civil society organizations that do not represent the state. They are supposed to be financially and organizationally independent of state apparatuses and private business, and they should not be involved in the pursuit of commercial interests, but the interests of

4 Ulrich Brand, "Stadt als runder Tisch: Zum neuen Leitbild 'Global' oder 'Good Governance,'" HYPERLINK "http://www.bmgev.de/themen/urban21/brand" www.bmgev.de/themen/urban21/brand. See also Michael Zürn, "Regieren im Zeitalter der Denationalisierung," in: Claus Leggewie, Richard Münch, eds., *Politik im 21. Jahrhundert*, Frankfurt am Main 2001.

the community, instead.[5] Ideally, the work of NGOs should conform to the following description:

- they represent interests that have no voice in existing political structures (political advocacy)
- they identify problems and topics, and include them in political negotiations and decision-making processes on both the local and international level (agenda setting)
- they mobilize factual expertise and knowledge in order to solve or debate topics in public
- they develop projects that are not undertaken by state and supra-state players, or else carry them out when governments or the international community cannot do so for organizational or political reasons

Their potential lies in their scientific, technical, or even political expertise, as well as in the fact that they are very familiar with the problems in their field and the local structures. This assumes, of course, that an international NGO cooperates with local, civil society organizations, so that they can successfully adapt their strategies to the local political, social, and cultural context. One important component in the success of their work is their ability to mobilize the public on both international and local levels, in order to further the goals of the interests formulated. If they can do this, they can make essential contributions to the processes of reaching the compromises and consensus necessary to political decision-making, and thus play an important role as mediators, since they are pursuing neither commercial nor wider political interests.

Reality, however, has a somewhat different appearance: very few NGOs can finance themselves through donations, and therefore, they are highly dependent upon the financial support of governments, international governmental organizations (such as the EU), and their semi-public organizations. For financial support, the only other alternative is to turn to private foundations, such as the Aga Kahn's, or George Soros', or foundations financed by international corporations.[6] Therefore, NGOs are forced to adapt their approaches, to accommodate the goals and programs set forth by their financial supporters. In addition, professionalizing their work force also means paying their employees, which leads to a factual constraint: they have to compromise their own programs, in order to conform to the donor's agenda. Over time, NGO "companies" have arisen, which are frequently only guided by self-interest. And the staffs of international NGOs are also part of the elite corps of managers and functionaries whom Mary Kaldor calls the "cosmopolitans"—a community of like-minded, well-educated experts, who work for the United Nations, one of the international or non-governmental organizations, or for foreign investors (who also count local experts as part of their membership). This, too, is a new form of global domination, which Kaldor describes as the "new divide." On one side are the generally impecunious local residents and migrants, who are seeking a place in the new urban communities, and on the other side are the global citizens and their allies—the local elite, most of whom have been educated abroad.[7] Yet another difficulty is that NGOs specialize in specific topics, and this often prevents them from understanding an overarching complex of problems, which would require a correspondingly comprehensive policy. Last, but not least, is the NGO's own, non-elected (and therefore undemocratic) position within the political negotiation process. In practice, all of this often results in a condescending, paternalistic way of working.

Accordingly, the policies of NGOs operating in post-conflict situations should be critically examined, but they should also be allowed to develop further. An important step toward reinforcing their position enough to resist donors, gain independence from them, and to find their own place within the political regulatory system, is to strengthen their contacts with each other and organize more among themselves, so that, ultimately, they can become institutionalized on an international level and form a political counterweight. Independent, international collaborations and associations would then also help them to formulate comprehensive political goals. This also means, however, that they have to

5 See Ulrich Brand, Alex Demirovic, Christoph Görg, Joachim Hirsch, eds., *Nichtregierungsorganisationen in der Transformation des Staates*, Münster 2001.

6 Archis Interventions' activities in Southeastern Europe have been mainly supported by ERSTE Foundation. ERSTE Foundation is the main shareholder of ERSTE Group (the savings bank). See HYPERLINK "http://www.erstestiftung.org" www.erstestiftung.org

7 Mary Kaldor, "Cosmopolitanism Versus Nationalism: The New Divide?," in: Richard Caplan, John Feffer, eds., *Europe's New Nationalism: States and Minorities in Conflict*, New York, Oxford 1996.

develop new forms of democratic politics. New, more transparent, and therefore more open ways must be found to select and represent topics and content, as well as to develop decision-making processes. It is always evident that an "intervention" from the outside is only successful when there is collaboration with local groups and support for political self-determination. This means that there must be more effort made to integrate non-governmental organizations and other civil society groups into the international system, and to increase their presence on the scene. The search for new ways must begin.

Architects and planners as "agents of change"

Architecture and urban planning only have disciplinary perspective when they consider themselves part of this overall political system—that is to say, of "governance." They must also come up with a new planning strategy that can contextualize itself within various social situations and simultaneously prepare new contexts for participants in society.[8] Should one employ the contextualization necessary in order to plan (for that, too, can be considered a political project), fundamental principles consequently arise. This is strategic, in the sense that it must react to various social and cultural contexts, while mediating between the special needs of individual social groups and the international power structure and its mechanisms. Yet it must also be cooperative, in as much as it provides, in its own turn, various participants with new contexts, in order to open up these spaces, whose effects go beyond local (and national) contexts. In this sense, planning must be communicative, because participants can only be mobilized through dialogue. This dialogue is not just local, however; it must also be conducted at an international level.

Planners and architects have a seductive perspective of the city from above, which can block the view of how the city should be used, as well as the view of the social relationships and political power relations inscribed in its spaces. Space is not neutral. Accordingly, neither is the position of the architect or planner; there is no such thing as "architecture for architecture's sake," nor is there any such thing as a "neutral" plan. Every plan is the result of negotiation and power relations, and these things are expressed through the plan. When architects and planners regard themselves as "agents of change," and try to intervene positively in city development, then they need to realize that they will need political "patronage." This support, however, should not be based in opaque relationships and closed-door agreements; rather, it should be transparent and open. Only then would it also be possible to address the programs set forth by other political factions, and to include them in the negotiation process. This requires a delicate tightrope walk in the political arena, which has to be undertaken by all independent groups whenever they attempt to intervene in the urban space. On one hand, one of their essential tasks is to articulate the interests of excluded segments of the population and to scrutinize the process of developing the city by mobilizing the public. On the other hand, they have to position themselves within the negotiation process, and, accordingly, be ready to cooperate or compromise with other political forces. In short, they have to have the ability to criticize the predominant political situation, while being part of it at the same time. This is because critique and public debate alone are not enough, even though they are perquisites for a successful intervention—for if sustainable change is indeed going to come about, then it is always brought about by assertive action; hence, it is a question of power. The regulation of city development cannot be left up to society's self-regulation and customary law, especially not in post-conflict situations. Accordingly, it is directly linked to the ability of state organs to act assertively, because they have a monopoly on the legitimate use of force. However, no plan, no regulation, no urban development strategy can be carried out if there is no consensus in the society itself about the meaning and purpose of the plan. Yet, even here, limitations have to be set: when organs of the state (and the international institutions and organizations that support them) offer only repression and corruption, then they also have no legitimation. Even when they carry out measures through the threat of force, a critical distance must be maintained. But it is naïve to believe that an "architecture of peace" can exist independently of an "architecture of power."

Non-governmental organizations in post-conflict situations must adapt their approach to the local context and thus, only limited generalizations can be made. However, it is possible to propose some fundamental principles for discussion:

- reflect upon and communicate one's own position
- do not pursue any commercial interests
- address different interest groups, in order to incorporate them over the long term
- gather various interests together for projects that require groups to cooperate in order to carry them out
- balance collaborations; advantages and profits must be shared equally
- create transparency: goals and procedures should be openly discussed in public
- create room for negotiation, open up perspectives, mobilize knowledge and place it at everyone's disposal
- plan and design the process; structure it through dialogue and keep it open

Correspondingly, the three fundamental pillars of the work are: (1) communication, (2) cooperation, and (3) shaping the process. What does this mean, specifically, for architects and planners who want to intervene in urban development? They should think less about a project, and more about the process of conceiving projects, especially at first. And, as an aside, they should not assume that their project will necessarily wind up in a plan or as a building. As the saying goes, "when you have a hammer, every problem looks like a nail." From the standpoint of the architect, every problem becomes a construction project. Frequently, however, an urban problem can also be solved by other means: a space can be revitalized through public debate, by using it for something else, or else through an economic strategy or regulation, to name just a few examples. That means, when figuring out projects in a post-conflict situation, it always helps to ask a few basic questions:

- Where: where is the space? Where are there spaces that are not disputed and controversial, but "neutral"?
- What: is it possible to create a new space, which will open up new perspectives?

8 See Nikolaus Kuhnert, Anh-Linh Ngo, 'Governance', *Archplus* 173 (May 2005)

- Why: who needs it; who will profit from it? Who are the partners involved in the process? Is it in the interest of the public welfare?

- How: what tools and strategies are needed, in order to create this space? How can collaborations be established, and how can the process be shaped?

Flexible planning

In post-conflict situations, the obvious failure of city government and the international organizations, which are together responsible for city development, can be traced back to a problematic understanding of planning and the role of the expert. Undeniably, plans are needed in order to structure and regulate the city's development. However, in the traditional top-down approach that is part of hierarchically structured planning—from the strategic master plan, to land zoning, to regulated building plans—there are already a number of troublesome aspects, which are not really taken into consideration. The main problem is the extremely tedious process that often drags out over several years: by the time it comes to an end, reality has already outpaced it. Also, the city is regarded as a coherent form—an object to be shaped and designed. The fact that the city has an active, constantly changing form is ignored. Of course, it is necessary that there be goals in planning, and that planning be a regulated force in urban development, but it is an ongoing process that needs to be flexible whenever circumstances change. This is the paradox of urban planning: on one hand, it establishes and fixes things, but on the other, it also has to be flexible. Accordingly, a plan needs to envision the vagaries of the future, and this can only happen when planning itself is regarded as a process. It has to take into consideration the fact that the city is more than just a form to be structured. Rather, it is the product of deeds performed by different actors, and among the protagonists is the city administration. In turn, the actors are guided by norms and values that can be used as orientation points. In this respect, the challenge for planners is to develop ways to cooperate with various actors—ways that are suited to the specific political and social circumstances. In this sense, planning is always political, too.

If the traditional model of urban planning is rejected, then new forms of cooperation and processes of negotiation between private parties and governmental institutions need to be developed. Master plans that attempt to treat complex layers of political and economic problems in the same way (comprehensive planning) are of no significance. Instead, it is necessary to develop processual, participatory, and hence, communications-based types of plans (collaborative planning). For this kind of flexible planning, it is crucial that new ways of collaborating be permitted. However, these kinds of cooperative efforts should remain transparent, especially transparent enough to be monitored by the public. Therefore, the forces of civil society should be encouraged to participate; they need to be regarded as an important corrective to the planning process. The key to all of this is communication: public debate had to be stimulated, with the assistance of local media. Public campaigns should also stimulate active participation and provide opportunities for people to get involved.

Within the conflict-ridden system of international politics (localized through governmental structures), a globalized market and civil society projects—developed in cooperation with local, independent urban initiatives—could develop new kinds of cooperative and communicative planning, which will help to support the society's weak civil powers in particular. Thus, positioning within this new framework of governance is of crucial significance, because if an intervention is to succeed, then it has to develop relationships with government institutions and the civil sector alike. The independent, non-governmental, non-commercial initiatives formed by professionals play an important part here, because not only do architects and urban planners bring their expertise to the table, but they frequently also act as both initiator and mediator, employing empowerment strategies to facilitate or influence urban developments.

The article was previously published in Volume 26, 2010.

Margins of Modernity

On the Institutional Crisis in Post-socialist Urban Planning

Marko Sančanin

Even though urban development has always been closely connected to the real estate industry, it would be an act of historical hypocrisy to claim that the recent economic crisis is the only reason for bad urban planning. The crisis of modern planning became apparent much earlier and it has been going for decades. Even during the most heroic times of modernism, the crisis was always somewhere around the corner. Maybe the intrinsic failure of planning was hidden; it evaded discussion, because it testified to the crisis of the modern project as such. For modernist governments, architectural plans were always a representational screen, but it became apparent by the end of the 1960s that they were only a blueprint masking the power and hegemony of the elites of modern society (regardless of whether the government's program was socialist or capitalist). This inability of architects to see the development of their discipline from historical and political perspectives[1] is probably the most important cause for present-day confusion about the architect's role in society and (especially if he or she is practicing urban planning) his or her inability to understand the complex contingencies of today's urban governance. In that sense, today's economic crisis is pretty irrelevant.

In the post-socialist Balkans, the lack of memory has a long, uninterrupted tradition and is not just particular to architects). After socialism, the collective amnesia and the culture of (re)constructing the past—along with ethnic fundamentalism, which pushed the states of ex-Yugoslavia to go their separate ways—continued in the same fashion as before. If they have not been completely erased from language, written history, or cultural production, traces of the socialist past are constantly under assault. Ironically, now, when it has become obvious that reinventing national identities has failed to produce livable social conditions, the absence of memory has become a cognitive obstacle to understanding today's social reality.

Instead of supporting a constructed and static notion of historical narratives, there should be a different approach. An active historiographical practice, a socially situated activity that is in dialogue and in discursive tension with both past and present, is more appropriate. It is a combination of some kind of forensic activity (forensic, because one has to scrutinize a body that is seemingly dead, i.e., socialist modernism) and observing the social chemistry of elements, which, after being separated, continued to function, albeit in a different way. This is precisely what is missing in today's urban discourse and practice: an almost technical knowledge that could articulate the direct link between what is known as socialist urban planning and its contemporary remains. In making this link, it is inevitable that the technology of urban planning that be primarily dealt with. More than simply analyzing master plans and zoning principles, it would be better to scratch the surface of blueprints to scrutinize the language governing nomenclature and the institutional system. This text should be read as an invitation to acquire this forensic technique for both the recent socialist past and the contemporary, post-socialist present. It is also an oblique attempt to redirect the critical attention of architects to the *terrains vagues* of urban territory, which in odd ways, unite the failures of urbanism of both the socialist period and its post-socialist stage, opening up a view from the other side of modernity and urban control.

1 It was Manfredo Tafuri who first rendered this critique with a compelling clarity. In his *Towards a Critique of Architectural Ideology* (1969), he completely unmasked architectural modernism and literally accused architects of political backwardness and historical naivety.

Socialist urbanism

At the beginning of the socialist stage, Yugoslav architects and urban planners, unlike their Western colleagues, were not directly tied to market tendencies. Instead, they were highly dependent on political circumstances, because socialist modernism was "happily" married to state ideology. More than being an active agent of political and cultural critique, architecture was a representational screen for the system—an image of a successful, socialist model of a non-aligned Yugoslavia. Political nomenclature transmitted this image toward both sides of the Iron Curtain. Today we have to admit that the lack of professional independence actually had its good side. Until the beginning of the 1970s, the progressive tendencies of political and cultural reforms incubated architectural discourse and practice with fresh ideas based on the concept of social justice and models of governance through self-management. Therefore, the architecture of social utopia had its ideological foundations (particularly important for urban planning, as the abolition of private ownership and land expropriation enabled modernist urban schemes), while economic prosperity opened up space for outstanding architectural innovations. This is important, because governmental and non-governmental corporate forms that dealt with planning (university departments, governmental departments and institutes, self-managed companies—a socialist version of business enterprise, etc.) developed without historical antecedents (the profession of urban planning barely existed before World War II, so it was practically invented during the socialist era).

One should be aware that there has always been a (creative) tension between professional planners and politicians. Professional urban institutes at first operated as parts of municipalities, but during the 1960s and '70s they separated, claiming their independence from political decisions on both local and federal levels. Those independent entities provided services to municipalities and federal units, but tried to keep political influence outside of the planning studio. They invested efforts in continuous capacity building (education of employees, publishing books and magazines, and promoting new tendencies in urban planning—including models of civic participation).

Unfortunately, the period did not last long enough to yield a coherent discourse and a tradition of independent urban planning. When the deficiencies of the Yugoslavian model started to show, architectural discourse began losing its reformatory capacity. After bureaucratic claims and demands took precedence in the 1980s, the culture of critique and moral authority was even more diminished, and their purposes frustrated to varying degrees. Aside from different forms of state control, market oriented tendencies started to weaken the architectural discourse and social agency as well. This is particularly important to understand, while at the same time connecting the socialist past with contemporary political and economic circumstances. The fact is that the self-managed, socialist society in Yugoslavia was a product of continuous changes and adjustments between the models of a state economy and a free market economy. The greatest shift—and probably the crucial phase—occurred after the big constitutional changes in the mid-1960s. Afterward, in the mid-1970s, during the late phase of socialist self-management, the patterns for organizing labor, the inflation of popular culture, the bureaucratization of government, and a strong shift toward the market, with its attendant development of politically influential techno-elites, created social

Although the *Keneta* neighborhood (formerly a swamp in the Adriatic coastal city of Durres, Albania) is built on a regular land division, drainage canals were the basis for the subdivision of the land, so a serious lack of the most basic communal standards (water, sewage, and electricity) makes housing conditions barely livable.

Kozari Bok is one of the biggest and oldest informal settlements situated in Zagreb's eastern industrial zone. Typical of abrupt industrialization and urbanization of the 1950s and '60s, informal settlements inhabited by workers started to cluster in the vicinity of factories. In 2004 Platforma 9,81 – Institute for Research in Architecture started a project titled *Superprivate* with the aim of investigating the housing and lifestyles of suburban areas in post-socialist cities.

Until the 1990s, suburbanization of Split was mainly due to industrialization. After the big political changes in the 1990s the city became a migration hub for political and economic refugees from Bosnia. The city perimeter exploded, resulting in an unprecedented encounter between the informal building enterprises of migrants and small building companies. A parallel city (without legal status or basic communal standards) has grown up on land zoned for agriculture. In the absence of public, educational, and cultural facilities—apart from concrete cathedrals, which testified to a renaissance of traditional values—everything was improvised: from DIY sewage systems to garages turned into kindergartens. Project *Supeprivate* did a comparative analysis between the dwelling habits and communal practices of the tenants of socialist multi-family apartment buildings and the new suburban inhabitants.

conditions that comparable to post-Fordist society. Respectively, there was also a comparable influence on urban planning.

In essence, there weren't many differences. Architectural practice became a receptacle to be emptied and filled as party policy or the market dictated. The proof is that artistic and technological experiments appeared in western and ex-Yugoslavian architecture almost simultaneously, as acts of dissent toward reality, and replacing active social engagement. Urban planners were thus reduced to being some kind of highly skilled delivery boy, dealing with the technology of planning. This technology was closely connected to the instrumentals of planning protocols and language. It is possible to trace how the language of planning turned into a kind of meta-language that was applicable irrespective of context. The irony is that it actually became a kind of planning diglossia, which, in spite of its formal purity, had different meanings in different situations, respective of political or financial power.

What is left over from socialist modernism are half-realized urban schemes that only mimic successful urban design. The notion that utopian urban schemes would produce utopian social conditions failed to live up to its promise. Our heritage is not modernity, but is only made up of physical objects that are tokens of modernity. In spite of astonishing architectural achievements, the urban environment is the product of modernized artifacts, without structural or institutional modernization. Architects and planners often show regret for unrealized competition entries or unfinished urban schemes, but what they really miss is the fulfillment of the big promise that architecture and planning would evolve in professionally independent and democratic practice. This lack of structural modernization and political culture, combined with market tendencies from the last stage of socialism, was the point of departure for post-socialist urban planning.

Transition

Transience is a dynamic quality. To understand it you have to move along and observe the process, not its formal side effects. Even though the transitional 1990s brought about the whole repertoire of new forms of urban planning, economic or cultural and political shifts were far more important. It is also crucial to pay attention to what didn't change. To some extent the 1990s were shockingly, violently new, but below the deck of the planning "machine," some parts didn't change at all. The transitional landscape of planning institutions is a bricolage of rusty parts that still (pretend to) function, and refurbished or new imported parts that (pretend to) function better. They operate in multiple layers and it is not always easy to tell one from another, especially if old nomenclature takes on a totally new agenda, or when old language takes on a different meaning that eludes interpretation outside of a political or financial key.

Ljubomir Bratić gave an excellent reading of institutional transformations in post socialism: "We can easily see continutity of institutions. Instutional bonds stayed connected but they changed direction of their sociopolitical, cultural and economic activity. Institutions became instruments that anybody can operate because the old instructions for use are lost and new vocabulary invented."[2] This anomie of professional vocabulary, the free interpretation of social norms and the respective diglossia of planning protocols greatly affected urban planning, because previous legal documents, like master plans and physical plans, became obsolete, while building permits were issued arbitrarily from case to case. The master plan stopped being an instrument for long-term public development strategy and became a dynamic map on which political and economic interests were projected during election periods.

After going through lists of employees in urban departments and ministries, it is easy to conclude that technical and executive governance never really changed; however, you will also find old names in newly privatized companies. The fact is that highly ranked executives stayed the same and continued operating through a closed network of private alliances. What changed radically is their performance. Not only did ex-socialist urban bureaucrats become zealous advocates of neoliberalism, but they also formed an extra-institutional layer of governance with and within different forms of neoliberal power (investors, banks, media). The ideological arrow of post-socialist planning institutions has turned upside down: instead of social programs for professional support, urbanization, and infrastructural development for the benefit of the community, the tendency is to support short-term, feasible projects that serve particular interests.[3] Today's concept of urban governance operates as an odd symbiosis of old forms of management under the control of state politics and the global financial market. Zagreb is a good example, because in the last ten years big investments were made in the city and city governance was characterized by financialization (the city issued short-term bonds, indebting its citizens without giving them the opportunity to vote on the issue) and the corporatization of public services (all city services are united under one corporation which, while trying to run city as a business enterprise, is becoming less dependent on public opinion and more on the shares that international banks have in urban development business). The city is hardly guided by a coherent vision or long-term strategy, under legal scrutiny or civic participation. Therefore, newly planned and built investment schemes do not result in social change, but only add to more of the same.

Instead of being surprised, we should finally understand that the nomenclature flipped its agenda so easily, and the language of planning became the instrument of particular interests, because the tendency was already inherent in the concepts of socialist modernism. None of this would have gone as smoothly if there had not been structural weaknesses in planning technology, which were already apparent forty years ago. Somehow it all comes back to the instrumental rationality of modern society and the fact that urban plan was nothing more than an organizational pattern employed by the state or free market capitalism.

But what about the *terrains vagues* of urbanization that resisted the orthodoxies of urban control and accumulated urban and cultural paradoxes instead? In a time of the general dissolution of the architectural discourse and obvious planning mistakes, it might prove useful at least to pay attention to urban territory that covers a much bigger urban area and is commonly labeled as suburban, marginal, or peripheral. Is there anything to learn from the margins of the modernist project?

2 Ljubomir Bratić, "On the Transformation of the Elite at European East" http://transform.eipcp.net/transversal/0208/bratic/sr

3 Once I was at a meeting with Zagreb's chief urban development strategist. I was surprised that he didn't have a big master plan on the wall, which was pretty common during socialist times. Instead, he had a huge, blank topographic map of the city featuring the fabric of construction. The map was covered in yellow stickers with the telephone numbers of potential investors. Later I realized that, within the logic of short-term development, when a city is struggling to pay off its debts, it is more useful to know about the appetite of potential investors than about urban regulations.

Margins of modernity

First of all, the mechanisms of development on the urban periphery changed in a way that differed from that of the representational showcase of the modern city center. To be more accurate, it changed slowly and/or under different dynamics. It changed slowly because, since, aside from the interests of the cultural, financial, or political elites, nobody could care less what is happening there. Therefore, the periphery rarely becomes part of any grand scheme of revitalization or improvement (unless improvement means demolishing the periphery to build expansive offices and apartment buildings).

When the periphery did change rapidly (illegal building boom and similar phenomena), its economy still did not change. Small investments in private homes and family enterprise were never intended to build according to modern urban standards, just housing. Therefore, the main objection to periphery—that it is not a proper city—mainly is due to the lack of communal amenities and infrastructure like schools, kindergarten, or sewage disposal systems.

In comparison with the modern city, the periphery does looks like urban chaos. Very often it is illegal on paper. Its cultural authenticity is based on clichés, which still resonate soundly with the ethnic-religious fundamentalism of the 1990s. All in all, seeing it from the outside, through a modernist lens, it is a form of deep regression. However, one should be cautious about labeling marginality, especially from the Balkan perspective, since the colonial regimes of knowledge within which such entities as "the West," "the Balkans," or the Second World are also the product of a modern reading of history. Paraphrasing Chakrabarty on history, modernity remains the sovereign, theoretical subject of all cultures. There is a peculiar way in which all other cultures tend to become variations on a master narrative that could be called "the western modernity." In this sense, any peripheral modernity is in a position of subalternity. One can only articulate subaltern-peripheral modernity in the name of Modernity itself.[4]

Ironically, maybe the most interesting phenomena of today's urbanity are far removed from the interests of professional urbanists and their elite institutions. It is at the *terrains vagues* of urban planning—in neighborhoods of low- and mid-rise, human scale, resilient, and endlessly adaptable semi-legal housing—where the greatest contradictions of any planned city always accumulate. At the margins of Croatian, Serbian, or Albanian cities there are material testaments that urbanization as a planned and controlled activity does have its twin reality.

However the freshly improvised vitality of these neighborhoods is interesting primarily for its social potential, not for its formal inventions, which are exhibited all over art galleries. It is the capillary social power and potential for communal micro-policies that make them extremely valuable, especially because there already are examples of grassroots civil initiatives that operate as micro-political governing bodies. Out of a natural solidarity, based on a combination of existential interests, neighborly love, and cultural clichés, inhabitants of those areas gather to build sewage systems and erect garages for community homes. In a time of complete erosion of the political culture in the center, this could potentially mean the rebirth of authentic, direct democracy on the periphery.

Maybe what we are witnessing is not a kind of delayed, undeveloped, or unfinished modernity, but rather, the fact that urban margins are becoming examples of another kind of modernity that should be considered an integral part of international modernity per se, because it is most inherent in it.

4 Dispesh Chakrabarty, *Provincializing Europe: Postcolonial Thought and Historical Difference* (Princeton: Princeton University Press 2000, p. 27).

UWYH - Use What You Have

Towards an Urbanism of Opportunities

Wilfried Hackenbroich

Most cities in Southeastern Europe (SEE) follow the global trends of urban planning, a fact-based, top-down urban development strategy. Using projects done in collaboration with Archis Interventions and local planners for Prishtina in Kosovo and Bucharest in Romania as examples, I would like to show an alternative path to urban planning: UWYH - Use What You Have - Urbanism of Opportunities.

Today increasing urbanization and changing social practices are addressed in two separate urban discourses. The existing dichotomy between careful, socio-political, urban approaches versus fact-based, economically driven urban developments has widened over the last decade. The urgent need to house millions of people around the world has led to replications of simple urban models and global typologies. Shopping malls, office towers, airports, and repetitive types of housing are the elements of new or expanding cities, regardless of their actual problems and potentials. While urban planners, architects, and artists have rediscovered the city through small-scale interventions and local participation, large-scale urban developments are incapable of incorporating qualities that characterize urban life. Alternative culture spaces, creative spaces, nondescript spaces, flexible and shared spaces are required, in order to generate urban qualities beyond utilitarian needs.

UWYH - Use What You Have explores the potential of associating contemporary urban planning strategies with local conditions and participants. Top-down planning strategies need to be complemented by local forces, issues, and activities that will cope with the contemporary urban problems that manifest under our complex social and political conditions. Conversely, bottom-up strategies need to be framed so that they can inform and guide urban planning approaches and provide sustainable improvement to our cities. The question today is not a technical matter of how to "build" a city—it is a cultural, social, and political question of how to structure urban life.

The top-down planning approach had a long tradition prior to the founding of C.I.A.M.,[1] yet the work of C.I.A.M. laid the foundation for a fact-based, rational approach to urban planning, resulting in a kind of almost Fordist production of cities. Radical neglect and the substitution of different social practices have triggered a counter move by Team 10:[2] adopting daily activities as paradigms for urban and architectural developments. Team 10's practice of urbanism and architecture has followed "as found" design strategies, being more rooted in actual urban and architectural circumstances than Modernist movements are. Many contemporary, bottom-up projects can be traced back to Team 10 and their thinking. UWYH incorporates this bottom-up approach and extrapolates the planning process by integrating top-down planning strategies.

UWYH's urban planning discourse consists of different combinations of key strategies employed in the project for Prishtina, Kosovo, and Bucharest, Romania. The following five strategies frame the intentions and goals of the discourse.

Strategic Typologies/Zones

concentrate urban transformation in specific zones or typologies that will have a catalytic effect on the surrounding urban environment.

Strategic Planning

employs established planning strategies with social, political, or cultural goals, including utilitarian needs, but also going beyond them.

Strategic Participation

employs local inhabitants as urban producers, critics, and consumers. They are the engines of urbanity and need urban planners, architects, or designers to provide spaces in which to realize opportunities.

Strategic Legislation

takes advantage of ways to change, amend, or add laws and regulations to achieve social, political, or cultural goals.

Strategic Accumulation

allows a bottom-up process, where a number of events, activities or spaces amass, either over time or in different locations, and create a critical momentum to make the project successful.

These five strategies provide the core of action for "UWYH - Use What You Have." For any of these strategies to be successful, the project needs a precise urban, social, cultural and political analysis in order to identify problems, potential, and the forces driving the particular urban situation.

Legalization of Informal Buildings, Prishtina (Kosovo) 2006–2011[3]

Production of informal buildings since 1999 has led to excessive urban problems in Prishtina. Today, more than 75% of the buildings in Prishtina have been built without any type of permit. This bottom-up building production has been paralleled by the top-down design of regulatory plans for the main areas of Prishtina. These plans only incorporate legal buildings and were obsolete by the time they were drawn. After the war in 1999 the private sector catered to the housing shortage by constructing informal buildings, while the city of Prishtina has stimulated the development of global typologies through a strategic plan, which incorporates a high-rise zone for offices, hotels, and shopping malls. While this top-down planning strategy was underway, we started our work to legalize the informal buildings in 2005, with the goal of bridging the gap between the city's top-down urban developments and the inhabitants' bottom-up construction projects.

On our first encounter with the urban system of Prishtina, it became evident that most buildings did not conform to existing building regulations. Under these regulations, most buildings had to be demolished or substantially rebuilt, turning most parts of the city into a blank slate. Surely, destroying capital and burdening the majority of inhabitants could not be the solution. Instead, we decided to use what the city had and explore the opportunities provided by the existing situation.

The strategies we employed included strategic legalization as the main incentive; strategic typologies comprising an analytical framework and basis for strategic legalization; strategic participation as a tool for communication and inclusion; and

1 Congrès internationaux d'architecture moderne – C.I.A.M. (International Congresses of Modern Architecture). From 1928 to 1959 this group of architects and urban planners conducted conferences around the world to develop and explore the Modernist movement.
2 Team 10 was a group of architects responsible for the organization of the 10th th C.I.A.M. congress in 1956. The members of this group had already taken a critical position toward C.I.A.M. at the 9th conference and initiated the dissolution of C.I.A.M. In the following years the group expanded and is known for its alternative urban and architectural approach.
3 Team: Archis Interventions / Prishtina (Florina Jerliu, Visar Geci, Vlora Navakazi), Archis Interventions/SEE (Kai Vöckler, Thilo Fuchs), Hackenbroich Architekten (Wilfried Hackenbroich)

finally, strategic planning, to provide a direction for development in the city of Prishtina and to integrate legalized buildings into the official urban planning process.

To understand Prishtina's urban system, we employed strategic typologies as an analytical tool to identify prototypical problems of the informal buildings and to develop a framework for adequate action. We singled out major typologies, such as the informal suburban housing built according to building regulations, but without construction permits with a total lack of public infrastructure. Inner city buildings exceeded by far the maximum floor area, had limited fire escape routes, were set too close to neighboring buildings, in many cases, the buildings covered more than ninety percent of the plot. Instead of paring back the size of the buildings, we strove for a regulatory solution that would ensure security and quality of life, with minimal building alterations. Informal roof extensions on socialist housing blocks also exceeded the maximum permissible floor area, but even more cleverly, exceeded the structural capacity of the original building. As far as this type of building was concerned, it was evident that safety and structure had to be re-evaluated.

The typological approach enabled us to understand the given situation, as well as the principles required in order to develop initial solutions to the major problems and define characteristics that ought to be preserved.

In order to legalize the informal housing stock in Prishtina, we had to include strategic legislation and develop legal guidelines for solving the existing urban and building problems. In our *Manual for Legalization* we developed simplified building regulations with graphics of the requirements for the building. Legalisation provided benefits and incurred obligations for both the owner and the city, and also made it possible to address urban issues. We developed a simple equation: through legalization, owners were assured of their ownership and had to pay property and land taxes, while the city garnered more tax revenues and had to provide adequate public infrastructure. The manual became the basis for the legalization law in 2010 and is now officially on the books.

Implementing the manual meant more than dealing with the legal aspects. To make this transformation successful, a broad swath of stakeholders in the city had to be persuaded to accept it. We used strategic participation to generate two-way communication involving local authorities, professionals, academics, property owners, and the general public. Tools for communication included expanding building capacity through student projects and workshops; professional awareness through an international conference, public awareness through newspapers and other publications; nationwide awareness through a TV show produced exclusively to support the legalization process and increase local participation through public discussions, and workshops with the various owners.

Legalizing the informal buildings solved the problems generated by the bottom-up building activities. Nevertheless, these buildings were still disconnected from the top-down urban planning of the city's strategic plan and regulatory plans. Since the legalization process retained most of the informal buildings, the regulatory plans needed substantial revision, in order to integrate the buildings constructed in the previous dozen years. By making the informal buildings part of the future planning, legalization actually turned informal building activities into a form of participatory urbanism.

The regulatory plans were developed separately, and the strategic plan did not provide an urban and economic vision for the city, which made the urban planning of Prishtina questionable. To ensure that the regulatory plans were revised to include effective and sustainable strategies from the bottom up *and* top down, it became necessary to apply strategic planning and define the direction of city development on economic, social, urban, and cultural levels.

Strategic planning was our last project phase and again we applied the logic of UWYH by using what was already planned and built, as well as understanding what was really needed to stimulate the city and make the existing planning relevant.

The city of Prishtina has little potential to generate future development. The city is of little value to tourism, and has only a few international businesses, mostly regional trade, and a high unemployment rate. Still, sixty percent of the population in Prishtina is under the age of 25, and combined with the established state university and the increasing number of private universities, there is evidently huge potential for the city's future. Additionally, as the capital of Kosovo, Prishtina stands for national identity and history, important aspects essential to future development.

In order to relate the main issues of youth, history, national identity, education, and economy in a dynamic way, we developed three strategic typologies. These typologies are placed at crucial points in the inner city to form a network of otherwise unrelated places. Programmatically, these typologies facilitate exchanges and relationships among youth, history, national identity, education, and economy. To achieve this kind of exchange, the main incentive must be to support non-academic education and youth entrepreneurship. Typologies included housing for young entrepreneurs and students with minimally equipped apartments and collective functions; the incubator, enabling entrepreneurship by offering small office spaces, information services, collective office functions, and financial support; and finally, the public community center, offering education outside the academic realm via a news and information center, along with a café and a small exhibition and performance space. In terms of space, these typologies are points of attraction and enhance exchanges in the city center, while at the same time forming a bridge to neighboring districts of the city.

These three typologies work on social, educational, cultural, and economic levels to bring the city's youth into a position where they can participate in and contribute to the economic development of the city and stimulate growth of local businesses and investments, independent of global capital. This growth will eventually make top-down planning of global typologies valuable to local business, and therefore it will also become sustainable.

Throughout the different stages of the project we synchronised and empowered independent urban and economic developments in the city. By following the discourse of UWYH, we needed only minimal investments to achieve maximum effects.

Magic Blocks – Behind the Concrete Curtain

Bucharest, Romania 2009–2010[4]

The urban fabric of Bucharest is strongly influenced by the socialist housing block, as are the majority of post-socialist cities. But in Bucharest's case, the housing blocks were not only built on a kind of tabula rasa, they were also built along the existing boulevards. Apartment blocks, eight to twelve stories high, entirely transformed the existing fabric of one- to two-story houses. The slab buildings were like a concrete curtain, framing large areas of low-density housing and giving the boulevards a dense, urban appearance, while protecting the green, suburban setting behind them.

Today, socialist collective housing is privatized and low-density housing is intact and highly valued. In the process of privatization, only individual apartments changed ownership, while the land remained city property, leaving a no-man's-land of public space between the buildings. The city of Bucharest still is incapable of maintaining or developing this no-man's-land. The devastation of these areas is accelerated by the unrelated juxtaposition of high-rise apartments and low-density housing. Bucharest has focused its attention on planning the city center from the top-down, major infrastructure, and new commercial centers involving global types of structures, such as high-rise offices, shopping malls, and hotels. In 2007, after the global financial crisis, it became evident that this development had tied the city to global forces, leaving the existing local potential behind.

When we started our investigation in 2007, in cooperation with Archis Interventions and local planners, the city ran a façade renovation program, offering thermal insulation and plastic windows for socialist housing blocks. Minimal improvements had been made along the boulevards, and private property owners had renovated their houses. The public space behind the concrete curtains remained untouched and derelict. A substantial part of Bucharest suffers from this condition, and we decided to develop a prototypical solution for this condition along the Calea Mosilor.

4 Team: Zeppelin (Cosmina Goagea, Constantin Goagea, Ştefan Ghenciulescu), Point 4 (Justin Baroncea, Carmen Popescu), Archis Interventions/ SEE (Kai Vöckler), Hackenbroich Architekten (Wilfried Hackenbroich)

Within the context of UWYH we used strategic typologies to identify prototypical situations; we also developed strategic zones to frame strategic legislation to address development problems, strategic planning to reconfigure and reprogram the abandoned spaces, and *strategic participation* for research, communication, and initiation. Our goal was to go beyond the simple beautification of public space in order to reactivate the abandoned areas behind the slab buildings.

Through strategic typologies, we identified particular sets of problems for five prototypical situations. Besides the individual solutions each of them needed, a common factor in all of the areas was that private properties facing the residual space were underdeveloped. Consequently, we developed strategic zones of two kinds: an intervention zone, where planning was needed; and a buffer zone, where private investment was necessary. Private investment was stimulated through strategic legislation, allowing higher building density in the buffer zone. The intervention zone was transformed to improve public spaces for the apartments and to provide high-quality conditions for private investments. Looking at the buffer zone in relation to the entire city, it has the potential to become a huge development area. Its proximity to Bucharest's main roads ensures good accessibility to the buffer zone from most of the city. Furthermore, an active buffer zone absorbs the existing development pressure in low-density areas, providing them with protection from existing and destructive building activities.

In order to resolve the various problems of each prototypical situation, we used strategic planning to reorganize and reprogram the open spaces and usages in the intervention zone. We introduced distinctions between public and semi-public spaces, reorganizing existing activities and injecting new activities. Shortcomings, such as neighborhood parking problems, lack of social infrastructure, limited accessibility, and dilapidated public spaces, were also addressed in the planning, leading to economically interesting possibilities for developments in the buffer zone.

In the next step of the project, we used strategic participation to raise awareness in the professional field by producing an exhibition. To address the local public in the neighborhood and to test our strategic planning, we realized a set of small-scale interventions, which explored re-programming and re-organizing abandoned spaces. With minimal means, we were able to engage the inhabitants, received valuable feedback, and paved the way for a prototypical project, so that we could realize our strategies on a larger scale. This step has yet to be taken, but it should trigger a transformation of the concrete curtains throughout Bucharest.

The UWYH discourse is not a substitute for existing urban planning strategies; it is a guiding principle for employing strategies and tools as efficiently as possible, offering a much-needed expansion of existing practice. UWYH connects projects to local conditions and solves gridlock problems. It stimulates local activity, so that it can be effective in the local and global contexts alike.

While top-down projects demand extensive financial resources and political power to position them in the market, the UWYH strategies are effective with minimal resources. Acceptance by users and markets is far higher, and stimulation of the local market leads to sustainable, lasting developments. The combination of top-down and bottom-up urban strategies maximizes benefits for the city. Global capital, international business, and international urban practices can be incorporated into the city, while promoting local participants and businesses. When it comes to building urban environments, UWYH represents a crucial discourse.

Why Do We Need Architects and Urbanists?

Civil Society, Urban Transformation and the Role of the Expert

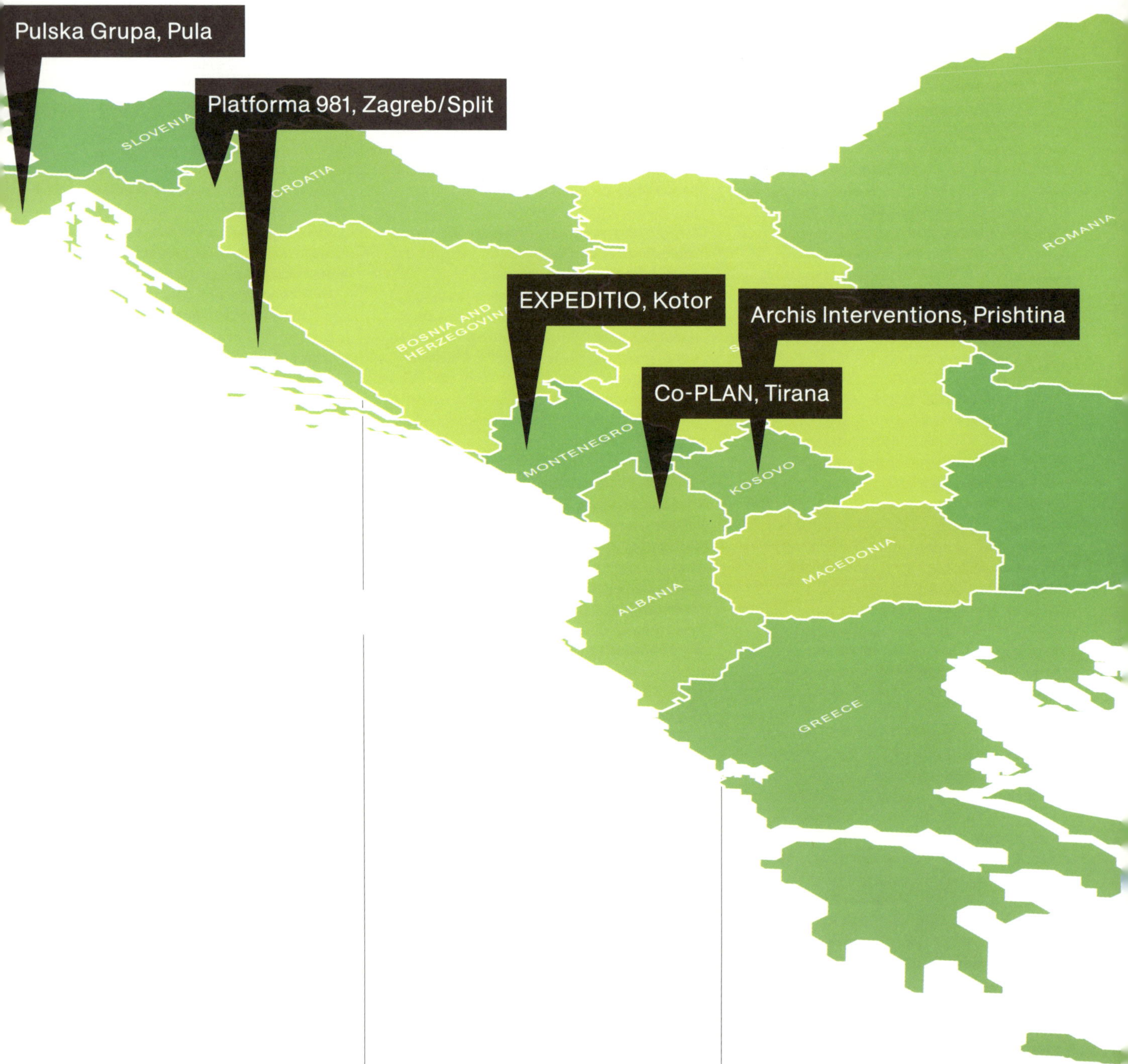

Zeppelin, Bucharest
MOLDOVA
BULGARIA
TURKEY
CYPRUS

Platforma 9,81

Institute for Research in Architecture

Zagreb and Split, Croatia
www.platforma981.hr

INTERVIEW

with Marko Sančanin, Dinko Peračić, Miranda Veljačić

How was the political and social situation in your country and specifically in your city, when you and your colleagues started the initiative?

The initial point and conceptual kick-off came from anxiety that we felt already as students. It was a pretty abstract anxiety, but nevertheless, we felt it had to do with the missing link between the urban reality of bigger cities (Zagreb, Split, Rijeka) and what was thought in architectural school. That's how we made up joke about the 9,81 (little "g" of gravity constant) in our name. It was a joke about the system of architectural education and architectural discourse in general that basically taught us laws that practically did not exist outside the school. It was as if someone was telling you that you could fly, while there are forces of gravity whose existence nobody would admit to. Forces like political transformations, the inability of urban regulations to deal with new economic realities, radical cultural shifts in housing lifestyles and everyday practices, transformation of the public sphere, and so on. Even though we tried to learn our lessons, read all of the articles in polished design magazines, and listened carefully to what older colleagues from the architectural society were saying, our architectural knowledge melted away like ice-cream the minute we stepped out onto the street or opened the daily papers.

At the beginning of 1990s the scene was pretty closed, but the real problems started when it began opening up to contemporary influences without any critical distance. It was a time when architectural debate moved toward the concept of "second modernity" and "super modernity," which was mainly introduced by Dutch authors. The Croatian architectural scene was strongly influenced by figures like Herman Hertzberger or later Rem Koolhaas, and the young generations that developed in OMA's incubator. Unfortunately, Croatian architects always read foreign contemporaries on a formal level. Without the opportunity to apply ideas to local conditions, reflections were rare and did not take society into consideration. That is why our practice was always more discursive than formal or material. We opened up space for communication for those "other" discourses, so they could come together and be heard. It was an open space, a flat platform. At the very beginning we were organizers of this discursive practice, more hosts than producers. It took us about three years to start producing ourselves. I guess the production was impossible until we articulated what it meant to perform architecture, and we had to realize that architectural effects could be achieved through very unusual practices that sometimes had nothing to do with design as we know it today.

What is your main reason for forming an initiative/organization? What do you want to achieve with it? Who is your target group?

I guess we wanted to imagine a space for freedom, where we could practice ideas outside of the clichés and norms of architectural practice as we knew it. I also think the reason was to escape the "feeling lonely" syndrome that all of us, as individuals, felt in the world of architecture, which started losing critical voices, where everything became possible and everything was turning into its complete opposite and nobody minded. Platforma 9,81 was a space where we could invite others to join us. We tried to leave it as open as we could—not only because we wanted others to join, but also because we needed space for ourselves.

Seeing it from today's perspective, I really think it was a semi-conscious political act, because pretty soon (after we stopped being just a bunch of students gathering in the attic of the faculty building) we decided to take on an organizational shape that formed clear ideological assumptions about the relationship between architecture and society, about citizens' rights and spatial justice, about the whole renaissance idea of authorship, the architect as universal man, etc. At the time we were all students, so many of our activities started spreading among the student population and the young architects' scene. We resisted the establishment, and of course, the young population liked it. Today our target is the general public. When it comes to projects that we do with neighborhoods, then we focus on those micro-situations.

With whom do you work, who supports you? How are your relationships to governmental bodies and the private commercial sector?

We rarely work with the private and commercial sector, and until recently we worked almost exclusively on projects that were funded by either governmental or foreign foundations. Finally, we managed to establish partnerships with local municipalities, so we have a couple of extensive urban studies and design projects in our portfolio. The most practical projects are done for civil initiatives and organizations, which are our most faithful partners. It is not a client-architect relationship in the strict sense, because we basically work together in all phases, and the process of learning goes both ways.

What can we learn for the future from your experience? What is your advice to architects, planners, and others who are dealing with urban development? How do you see the role of the expert?

Our work is constantly changing. It is hardly possible to transfer operative technical knowledge from situation to situation, because we are never working alone. We have many collaborators, and each time there is a new social contingent and new actors in space. Nevertheless, there are few foundational points in our work.

We do active and socially engaged research of transitional phenomena, which have corresponding implications for territory. It is impossible to develop an architectural discourse without constantly mapping urban situations—primarily because, for an architect, it is crucial to understand the different interests and antagonisms that shape today's urbanity. Second, we are devoted to the concept of spatial justice, which is still a pretty vague conglomerate of topics, like even distribution of land and resources, civil participation in architectural design and urban policies, and environmentally intelligent and socially sustainable urbanization.

Third, we do obsessive research into new types of communal spaces. We think that the rapid transformation of the public sphere and the weakening of political culture require that there be spaces for new, authentic, and contemporary social experiences.

PORTRAIT

Location: Zagreb, Croatia
Foundation year: 1998
Structure: non-profit organization
Members: architects

Focus: exploring spatial and urban implications of shifting political, economic, and cultural identities; developing new methods in architectural practice, using cross-disciplinary educational and research networks. The organization promotes new urban research techniques and activism through public events, mass media and educational programs.

Approach: spatial implications of contemporary public and cultural spaces (Invisible Zagreb); transformations of physical structure of the public domain and collective housing typologies (SuperPrivate); urban phenomena of tourist development on Adriatic coast (Tourist Transformations); cultural inter-disciplinary and tactical networking (Zagreb Cultural Capital of Europe 3000); models of participatory urban planning and bottom-up development at seven locations on the Adriatic coast (Croatian Archipelago – New Light Houses), strategic urban planning and development studies for local municipalities.

Zagreb 2000

Set-up for a Zagreb salon of young artists: the organizers wanted to change the usual linear set-up, so the whole exhibition was moved outside of the museum. It was decided to use 16,000 square meters of a fair pavilion in a part of town with no cultural facilities. The set-up was built from the wrecked machinery of bankrupt building companies and industrial containers bombed as they traveled through Bosnia. Construction components were transported by the Croatian military and the whole process of organizing the exhibition turned into a negotiation between artists and military bureaucrats.

The main idea behind the set-up was to use a big, air-conditioned space for producing a temporary cultural biotope, mixing art with independent urban culture.

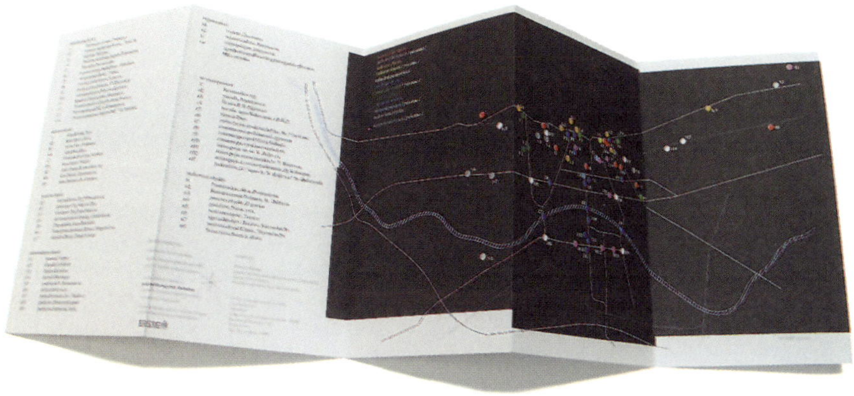

Invisible Zagreb was operating as an “illegal non-profit real estate” agency, having more data about public ownership than the municipality. The map of Invisible Zagreb: 66 locations, approximately 1.4 million square meters.

Invisible Zagreb

Invisible Zagreb is a project whose goal is to investigate the spatial implications of contemporary culture and the empowering effects of architectural knowledge when made available for public use and free interpretation. The project addresses suppressed political aspects of urban planning. Spatial implications of cultural policy are examined through the possibility of physical planning and actual inhabiting of the city. This activity is particularly present at places and zones marked on the Invisible Zagreb Map. The map indicates places that are now devoid of their former social functions, thus opening up possibilities for negotiating new functions as community places. By temporarily occupying these places, Invisible Zagreb is enabling the non-institutional cultural scene to claim new sites for cultural production.

Organizing cultural events in empty spaces

Labin – Underground City

Labin – Underground City was an extensive strategic development platform created through research, architecture, urban programming and design, facilitation work, urban negotiation, cultural programming, consultancy, and administrative support. Client was the Municipality of Labin, an Istrian coal-mining city that was once a center of the largest network of coal mines in the region. Within three years, more than 200 km of underground coal-mine infrastructure, with its respective above-ground ground facilities, became the focal point of the project, which involved redirecting development toward new tourist technologies, and the development of cultural heritage through innovative cultural practices and local production.
The project was initiated as part of the Croatian Archipelago – New Light Houses, which started in 2005, a partnership between the Berlage Institute and the Croatian Association of Architects. Platforma 9,81 coordinated NGO activity at seven locations on the Adriatic coast.

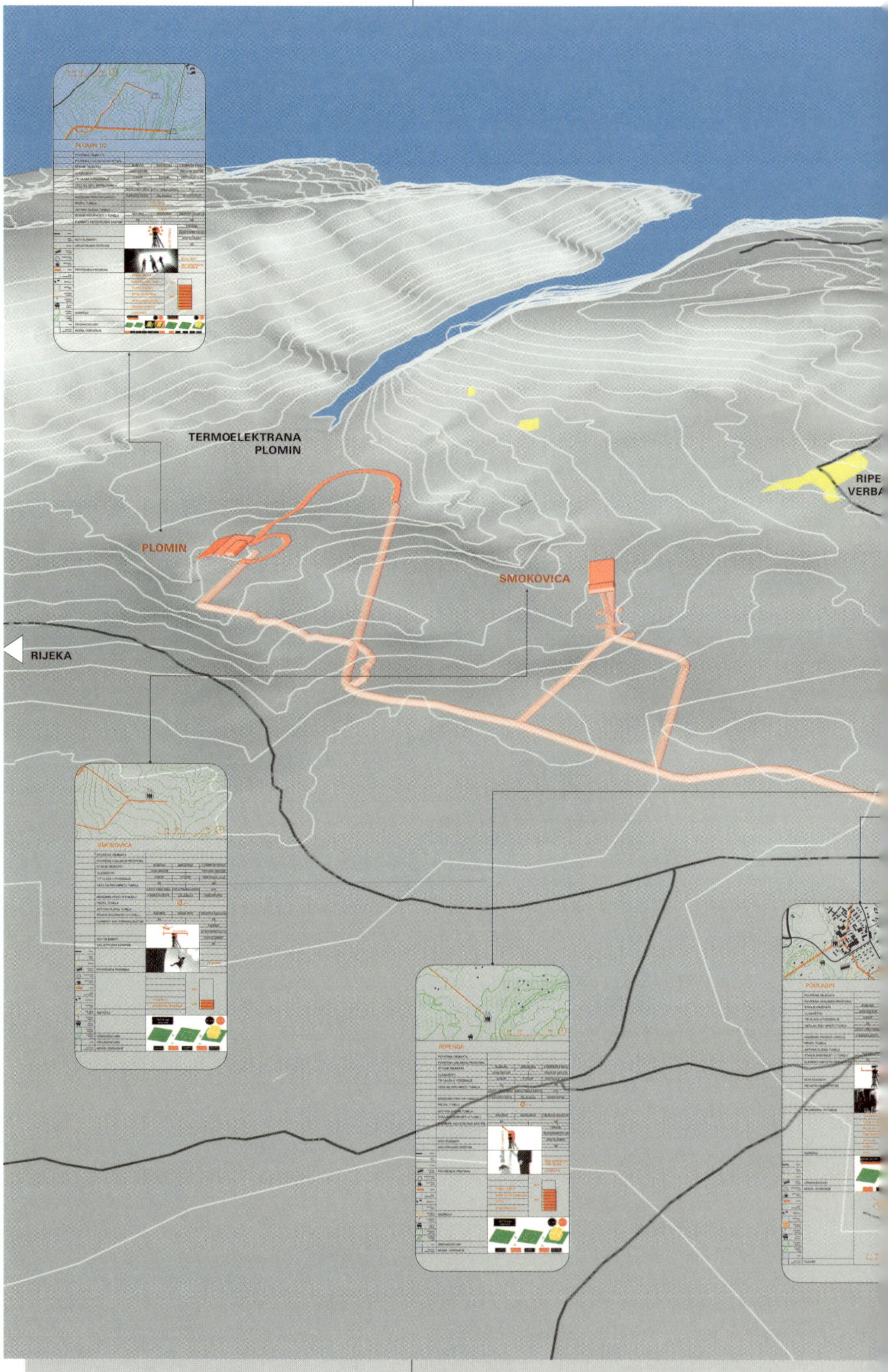

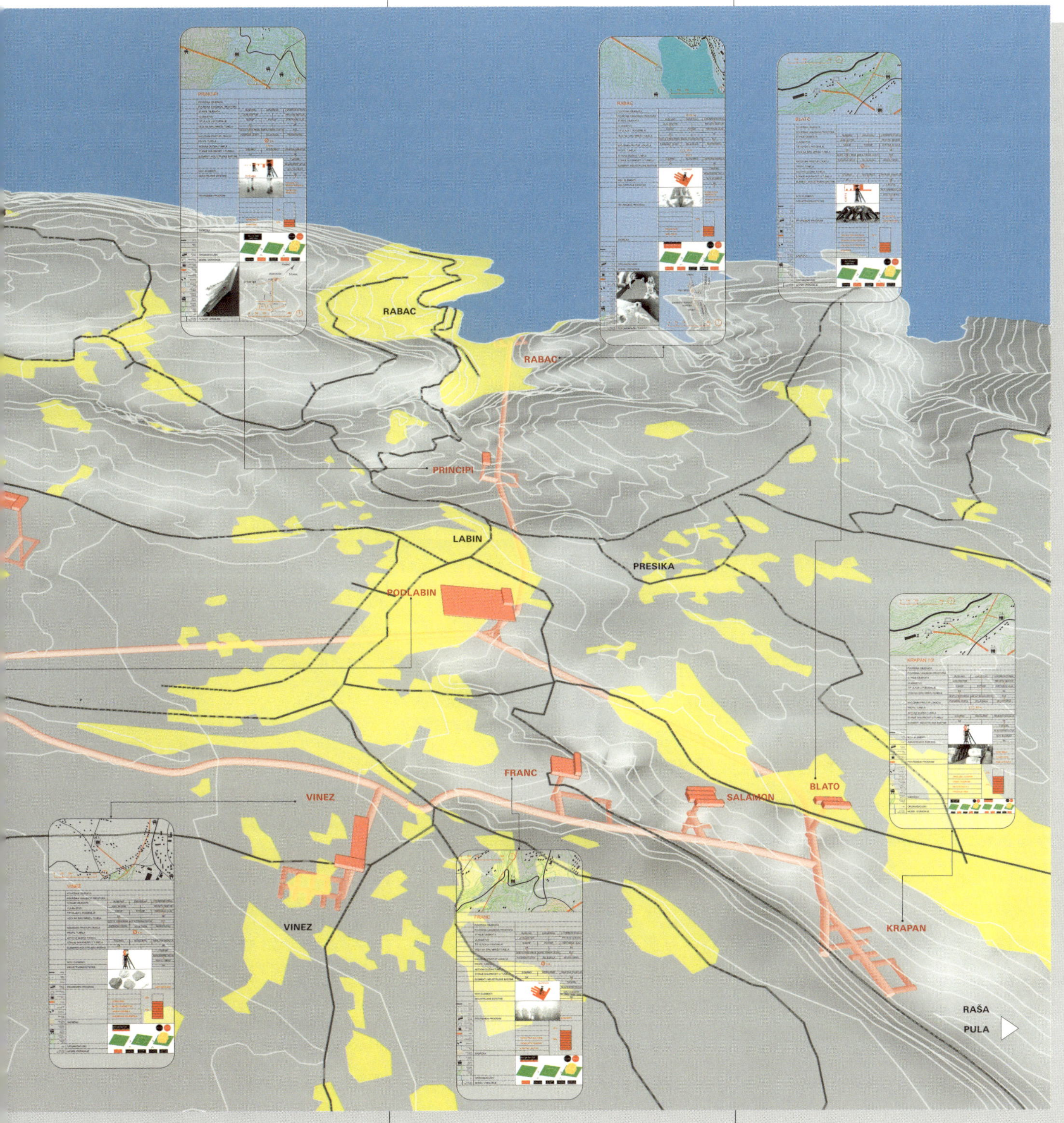
RABAC
RABAC
PRINCIPI
LABIN
PRESIKA
PODLABIN
FRANC
VINEZ
SALAMON
BLATO
VINEZ
KRAPAN
RAŠA
PULA

Archis Interventions / Prishtina

Prishtina, Kosovo
www.seenetwork.org

INTERVIEW

with Florina Jerliu

How was the political and social situation in your country and specifically in your city, when you and your colleagues started the initiative?

The Archis Interventions initiatives in Prishtina commenced in late 2006—that is, about seven years after the war in Kosovo. At that time, Prishtina had already almost doubled in terms of its population, and its urban boundaries expended accordingly. Although the new state institutions, and hence, the local administration in Prishtina, were put in place together with the international bodies responsible for Kosovo's reconstruction and democratization per se, the postwar transition has proven to be complex, long, and not always successful; one of the failures of the governing bodies (local institutions and UNMIK) on the local level during the last decade was the disregard for urban transformation, which ran wild, coupled with mismanagement in city planning. Although the new master plan for Prishtina was adopted in 2004 (that is, four years after this transformation had begun), unguided urban development remained unchecked. Furthermore, the city administration was not efficient in delivering the urban regulatory plans that were supposed to be derived from the 2004 plan, and their prime purpose became the issuance of building permits, rather than urban regulation. Hence, parts of Prishtina yet not covered by such plans were developing simultaneously. New buildings erected without building permits in these areas would be constantly ignored in the planning process. By 2006, about 75% of Prishtina's territory was considered to have developed illegally. Illegal buildings became a reality that one could not ignore, and their integration into the planning process became inevitable.

What is your main reason for forming an initiative/organization? What do you want to achieve with it? Who is your target group?

It was the very moment that we identified back in 2006, when our initiative went into operation. Even though two years had passed since the adoption of the master plan for Prishtina (namely, the "Strategic Plan: Urban Development of Prishtina 2004–2020+"), the planning process was segmental and slow, while builders were way too mobilized, fast, impatient, and in many cases, negligent about laws and regulations. Having acknowledged this, we aimed to disclose and disseminate the magnitude and nature of the illegal building problems, and to initiate a new turning point in the planning process, by dealing directly with the problem, rather than ignoring it and hoping that the plans themselves, whenever they might be adopted over the years, would "erase" buildings erected without permits, and fix the urban space in Prishtina. Archis Interventions/Prishtina's main goal is therefore to intervene in the process of city planning, as well as to mediate between the city's public institutions and private interests.

With whom do you work, who supports you? How are your relationships to governmental bodies and the private commercial sector?

We work closely with the Municipality of Prishtina, and this enables us to devise strategies and propose plans and project timelines, which must be approved by the local administration, on one hand, and on the other hand, by our local, regional, and international experts, who participate in our joint workshops. This cooperation ensures a wider dissemination of our initiative throughout local governmental bodies and the commercial sector in Prishtina.

Our activities basically consist of workshops, and the production of workshops results in a variety of study papers and guidelines; we have been continuously supported by ERSTE Foundation, ECF, FES, and the Municipality of Prishtina.

What can we learn for the future from your experience? What is your advice to architects and planners, and others who are dealing with urban development? How do you see the role of the expert?

After the war, architects and planners, like the majority of other professionals in Kosovo, were finally free to develop their businesses and seek better incomes. Therefore, job opportunities with low salaries in institutions were generally not attractive. As a result, newly formed institutions ended up with rather low professional capabilities on one hand, and on the other hand, experts—who tended to act individually through their businesses—failed to consolidate and act as a factor by providing their expertise from outside the institutions. The lesson that one might learn from this situation is that, ideally, experts should directly engage in decision-making institutions, although this mission is very work-intensive and sometimes not rewarding in terms of individual, short-term benefits. Also, engagement in associations is vital in terms of ensuring that an environment for professional standards be put in place.

In the case of Prishtina, the combination of these two scenarios would have most probably led to better planning and management of urban space, in contrast to what we observe today. However, there is one other scenario, which we—Archis Interventions/Prishtina—brought in: a model of how to work in transitional processes of urban development, which has proven successful over the long run. Ultimately, it means that there must be competent groups of experts, and new agendas need to be introduced in an environment of cooperation and mutual understanding and recognition, involving all parties in the urban development process.

PORTRAIT

Location: Prishtina, Kosovo
Foundation year: 2005
Structure: non-profit NGO

Members: architects, urban planners, and urbanists
www.seenetwork.org

Archis Interventions and Kosavar architects and town planners began their cooperation in Prishtina in 2005 by co-founding a local NGO.

Focus: Following deployment of KFOR troops in Kosovo in 1999, a boom in unregulated construction set in and the population of Prishtina tripled within a very short time. Indeed, it was impossible to obtain a building permit at all until 2006. Such illegal building activity ultimately destroyed large areas of the city—some seventy-five percent of its original urban structure was deformed. Amateur building ventures have given rise to considerable public safety issues and social conflict. In addition, they have radically limited access to what were previously public spaces, and seriously overtaxed the already inadequate urban infrastructure and public amenities.

Aim: To develop a concept to legalize those buildings erected illegally since 1999 as well as a concept that will bring urban development in line with adequate standards, and to formulate a pilot project as well.

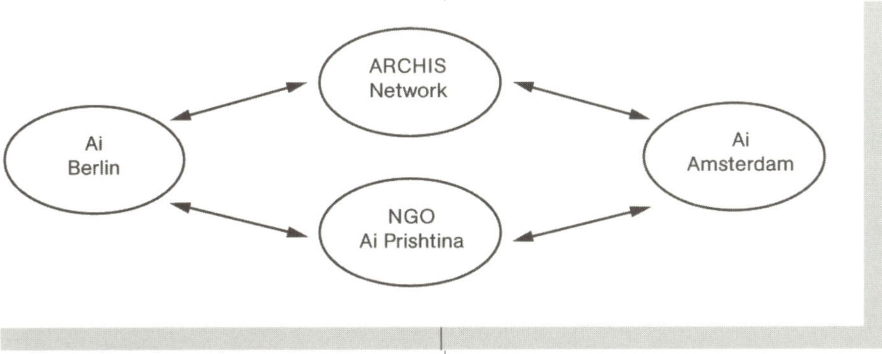

Approach: To analyze existing structures in the city and develop solutions to current problems. To formulate a communications strategy and thereby involve various local media, as a means to foster public debate and mobilize local policymakers. To develop an implementation strategy in cooperation with the local administration and politicians.

Achievements to date (2011):
Following a public debate held in Prishtina, urban development became the crucial issue in the run-up to mayoral elections. The legalization concept formulated in cooperation with the city administration laid the groundwork for a resolution on legalization made by the Municipality of Prishtina (City Council) in July 2009, which provoked public debate and positive media feedback. A TV series dealing with legalization issues launched at the same time as the new legislation was adopted. An urban vision was drafted. Local professionals and politicians were encouraged to participate in public discussions. The issue was integrated into international urban discourse.

Cooperation: Municipality of Prishtina

Collaborators: Hackenbroich Architekten (Berlin), Co-PLAN (Tirana)

Archis Interventions in Prishtina Documentary film by Luise Donschen, August 2009

The film documents the activities of Archis Interventions/Prishtina in 2009. Kai Vöckler, program director of Archis Interventions/Southeastern Europe, explains the main principles of the Archis strategy in the region. Archis Interventions/ Prishtina organized a workshop on illegal construction in Prishtina in March 2009, with the aim of developing a strategic concept (a manual), which would enable institutions to respond to the ongoing process of dealing with informal building. Florina Jerliu, co-founder of Archis Interventions/Prishtina, explains the most important aspects of this issue. A public campaign designed by Archis Interventions/Prishtina will accompany the process of regulating informal construction (including legalization of existing buildings), which is scheduled to begin in January 2010. Public presentations and a media campaign—including an eight-part TV series produced in collaboration with Pixels Productions, Prishtina—will raise public awareness of aspects such as safety regulations, the need for public infrastructures and amenities, and the impact of informal building on the community—and will hopefully help to eradicate informal building.

The film documents the production of the first episode of the TV series, as explained by Visar Geci, co-founder of Archis Interventions/Prishtina and a renowned TV star in Kosovo. The film ends with a statement by Dr. Isa Mustafa, the Mayor of Prishtina, regarding the forthcoming legalization process and the workshop organized in October in collaboration with Archis Interventions, the aim of which was to develop an "Urban Vision for Prishtina".

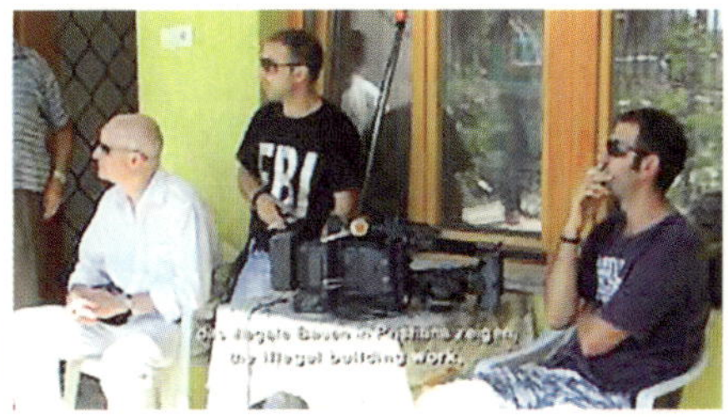

EXPEDITIO Center for Sustainable Spatial Development

Kotor, Montenegro
www.expeditio.org

INTERVIEW

with Aleksandra Kapetanović, Biljana Gligorić and Tatjana Rajić

How was the political and social situation in your country and specifically in your city, when you and your colleagues started the initiative?

The winter/spring of 1996–1997 was a time of dramatic change in the former Federal Republic of Yugoslavia. During that period, university students from across the country took part in the six-month-long students' protests against the regime of then Serbian President Slobodan Milosevic. Inspired by the positive energy of these demonstrations, six of us, students in our final year at the University of Belgrade's Faculty of Architecture, came together to found a non-governmental organization, EXPEDITIO. We believed that we could not practice our profession without taking an active part in creating change. It was the moment to shape our society.

What is your main reason for forming an initiative/organization? What do you want to achieve with it? Who is your target group?

EXPEDITIO is dedicated to improving the architecture and planning in Montenegro and the region. Over the last fourteen years, EXPEDITIO has promoted sustainable development in Montenegro and throughout the Balkan region. We advocated for development that takes into account the needs of local people instead of just the interests of private companies. To further this mission, EXPEDITIO conducts research and studies, workshops, and public advocacy in the fields of architecture, cultural heritage, urban planning, and green building. EXPEDITIO also works to increase cooperation among citizens, non-governmental organizations (NGOs), and the public and private sectors. EXPEDITIO also participates in the South East European Heritage Network (SEEH), an association of non-governmental organizations in the Balkan region dedicated to cultural heritage protection.

Our target groups are various: architects and professionals in spatial planning, civil engineering, students, local and state institutions, youth, etc.

With whom do you work, who supports you?

EXPEDITIO has an extensive network of local and international collaborators in different fields. We cooperate with non-governmental organizations from Montenegro, former Yugoslav countries, South East Europe, the Mediterranean region, Western Europe, as well as some other parts of the world (the USA, Canada, and Singapore, for example). So far, numerous local and international donors have supported our work (Municipality of Kotor, Ministry for Spatial Planning and Environment of Montenegro, Ministry of Tourism of Montenegro, Ministry of Culture, Sports and Media of Montenegro, Parliament of Montenegro, Rockefeller Brothers Fund, the EU Delegation of the European Union to Montenegro, European Agency for Reconstruction, the EU European Movement in Serbia - European Integration Fund, UNDP, USAID/ORT, Map, USAID/IRD, SIDA - Swedish International Development Cooperation Agency, FOSI - Foundation Open Society Institute, Regional Environmental Center for Central and Eastern Europe (REC), Cultural Heritage without Borders (CHwB), European Cultural Foundation (ECF), PHILIA - Association of Multiethnic Cities of Southeast Europe, and The Embassy of Netherlands in Belgrade.

How are your relationships to governmental bodies and the private commercial sector?

We cooperate with various municipalities and governmental bodies in Montenegro. We have collaborated with the municipalities of Kotor, Tivat, and Herceg Novi in several projects so far. We submit comments and take part in public hearings related to different local and national planning and strategic documents that are drawn up. A representative of EXPEDITIO has often been a member of working groups formed by the Ministry of Culture of Montenegro responsible for conducting studies for several built heritage sites in Montenegro (Preliminary Technical Assessment – PTA- for the reconstruction and renovation of the Winter Palace of King Nikola in Rijeka Crnojevića; PTA for three fortresses on Skadar Lake). Another representative is a member and vice president of the National Council for Sustainable Development of Montenegro. EXPEDITIO has been engaged by the Ministry for Spatial Planning and Environment to prepare, in cooperation with ATLAS TV from Podgorica, a series of 35 short TV programs focusing on the topic of "My Town-My Home." The programs aim at raising awareness among the citizens of Montenegro for the principles of sustainable development, in as far as they concern living in towns. EXPEDITIO has successfully cooperated with the Office for Sustainable Development.

What can we learn for the future from your experience? What is your advice to architects, planners, and others who are dealing with urban development? How do you see the role of the expert?

EXPEDITIO was formed in specific circumstances, when we were not able to practice our profession in the way we thought right, because the entire social environment was in a chaotic situation. That is why our developmental path is the result of specific social conditions. Experience has taught us that today an architect can have a role that goes beyond the traditional notion of this profession, i.e. that he/she can have an educational and awareness-raising position and be an active factor in social changes.

PORTRAIT

Location: Kotor, Montenegro
Foundation year: 1997
Structure: non-profit NGO

Members: founded by architects; five full-time employed; 400 members

Focus: encouraging sustainable spatial development, as well as enhancing urban and rural areas in Montenegro through activity in the fields of architecture, urban planning, town planning, environmental protection, and civil sector development.

Approach: promotion of sustainable development, green building, modern trends in architecture, urban and town planning; organization of scientific, expert, and research projects (publications, workshops, work camps, campaigns, exhibitions, round-tables, discussions, lectures, seminars).

The area of Montenegro, covering only 13,812 square kilometers and with about

680,000 inhabitants, is characterized by exceptional natural values, diverse natural phenomena, and layers of cultural heritage. However, current processes in Montenegro bring about uncontrolled changes in space and the fast transformation of the cultural landscape, influenced by different factors, among which are: the lack of development strategy, a rapid and large influx of capital and investments, an inappropriate planning system, and inadequate construction/ architecture. However, it is characteristic of Montenegro that its non-governmental sector is active; civil engagement/public participation becomes important in the ongoing processes; different projects, campaigns, reactions in media, petitions, public discussions, and appeals are made by local NGOs and supported by foreign organizations.

Billboard of the campaign 'Look Around – Think About Space' placed in front of the parliament in Montenegro.

Exhibition of the photo competition, intended for citizens of Montenegro, on the topic 'The most beautiful and the most unattractive view of my town'.

Restoration work camps in Perast.

Perast projects

We can say that Perast, a town in Boka Kotorska and one of the most charismatic sites in Montenegro, is responsible for the creation of EXPEDITIO. Although EXPEDITIO has carried out numerous projects related to other localities in Boka Kotorska and a wider area, many people still recognize us by our first projects conducted in Perast.

Impressed by the town's beauty and the strength of its spirit, and aware of the threats that the town is exposed to, we organized a student summer school of architecture in Perast in 1997. This was the first project-expedition that we conducted. The town inspired us and it resulted in a publication and exhibition on Perast entitled *Three Hundred Years of Solitude.*

This was followed by an international architectural workshop on the topic of "Revitalization of the Town of Perast," which was another step further on the path first taken with the research conducted the previous year.

After that, our work extended to creating an urban project on Perast, organizing exhibitions and conducting numerous smaller projects aimed at promoting Perast and raising awareness about its values. We also organized three volunteer restoration work camps in Perast.
EXPEDITIO helped a local organization, the Society of Friends of Perast, to recommence its activities. Today, they are one of important initiators of various activities in the town.

Pulska Grupa

Pula, Croatia
www.praksa.hr

INTERVIEW

How was the political and social situation in your country and specifically in your city, when you and your colleagues started the initiative?

We started working as a group in 2005 in Pula, a town on the Croatian coast. At that time Croatia was going through a transition from a nationalist regime to a capitalist one. This was especially visible in the coastal area, where the revival of tourism brought about many processes of privatization of land (which some in Croatia call the second privatization, after industry, which was the first). We observed a few major scandals at that time, like the one in Barbariga, where the political authorities sold the coastal land in a non-transparent deal, which is still under investigation in what is well-known as the "hypo bank affair."
Since the process of privatizing common land looked like it would not stop, and at some point it started to become a serious threat to our home town of Pula, we understood that it was necessary to act. So we organized a workshop with students of architecture from Venice, Ljubljana, and Zagreb. It took place in one of the deserted military locations, which was, according to the land use plan of that time, supposed to become a gated community resort. We wanted to start our engagement with a creative process of urban planning, working together with citizens, while struggling at the same time against the privatization of the land.

What is your main reason for forming an initiative/organization? What do you want to achieve with it? Who is your target group?

We have two major target groups. The first comprises citizens of Pula engaged in resisting privatization, especially the ones active at problematic sites, the ones who are squatting and occupying public land, and who transform it for the common good, instead of turning it into private property. To work with this target group, we organized a civil movement that publishes its own newspaper and organizes protests and actions in town.

The second target group is made up of architects and urbanists in Croatia and from around the world, to whom we communicate our proposal, which competes with the exclusive visions of the oligarchy. Guided by different principles, we gathered some of our European colleagues at the Post Capitalist City Conference in 2009 in Pula. We tried to expose a few things concerning the profession—one is the unjust process of spatial planning in capitalism; the other is the precarious situation of the profession itself. As far as this last issue is concerned, we managed to take over the regional association of architects, with the aim of transforming this organization into a solidarity group within the architectural profession itself.

With whom do you work, who supports you? How are your relationships to governmental bodies and the private commercial sector?

We commonly work with our fellow citizens and colleagues from around the globe who share the same approaches and values. From the beginning we were organized as a non-formal group and we financed ourselves through our own commitments. A few months ago we established a cooperative called Praksa, which is the first architectural cooperative in Croatia. We are trying to establish economic and professional relations through it on a direct democratic level, and take these values into the economic sphere. Our relations with governmental bodies are antagonistic. They discredit our professional skills and participative will, and we discredit their governmental role and monopoly of power. We blame a few persons who are currently occupying executive positions of power for being directly responsible for privatizing common resources.
We don't have any unique relationships with the private commercial sector, but do work with private enterprises on occasion.

What can we learn for the future from your experience? What is your advice to architects, planners, and others who are dealing with urban development? How do you see the role of the expert?

We can maybe share what we have learned through our practice. When we started our group we thought about two types of spaces—public and private. While the private is managed by private bodies, the public sphere is managed by public bodies, like the municipality or state. So we went to representatives of public institutions to negotiate, and we realized we had nothing to negotiate, since public institutions regarded this space as their space—the space of citizens' representatives, and not the space of citizens themselves. Then we understood that a third space exists, which is neither public nor private, but common, and citizens can manage it directly, on a democratic foundation, independently of political representatives. The second thing we learned is that this doesn't come by itself; you need to fight for it. So now we can communicate with friends in Madrid, Barcelona, Cairo, and Athens who are right now struggling in public squares to achieve exactly this. And it precisely in these public squares, populated by the resistance, that we see experts playing a role.

PORTRAIT

The Pulska grupa is an informal initiative from Pula, Croatia, which has been active since 2006, when it organized a student workshop at Katarina, a former military zone in Pula. The workshop led to conflict on the local political scene, because its results, published in a book titled *Katarina 06 – Opening Pula`s Coast,* confronted official municipal and state plans. Since then the group has produced publications, and organized conferences, lectures, demonstrations, and exhibitions to agitate in public against official urbanism in Pula and throughout Croatia. The group's latest event, a conference entitled Post-capitalist City was held in August 2009 in Pula`s autonomous zones.

Plan Mediterraneo

1. MARLERA – *polikampanja*

If the water infrastructure on Marlera were used to support agriculture instead of golf courses, this land would no longer be on the brink of ruination. Marlera's infrastructure can be altered to accommodate a full production cycle—growing, storage, sorting, frozen storage, packing, and vending on the hypermarket premises. Once this integral transformation has been brought about, the *kampanja* (field) can evolve into *polykampanja*.

2. BARBARIGA – *hyperstancija*

Existing *stancijas* (farmsteads) were converted to villas to be used as second homes or summer residences. Lack of traditional agricultural sites has made it necessary to seek out better settings for cattle breeding, vineyards, and olive groves. Such space is available in the former military zones. Now that automation has been introduced into traditional processes, the stancija is subdivided into several specialized, connected facilities—transforming it into a hyperstancija.

3. FERIJALNO – *komunal*

The intensive transformation of agrarian manufacturing systems in the region could cause cultural changes in Pula. Public land, organized like this, becomes a *komunal* (common land)—land that anyone can cultivate and use. As an alternative to expensive and isolated resort areas, the town should create affordable tourist accommodations on public land—where the citizen-farmer meets the traveler-explorer.

4. LEVAN – re-reef

Isolation—one of the main characteristics of an island—is an advantage in some sectors of the economy, for example, for recycling factories. Non-recyclable waste would be deposited as landfill near an island to create new islets and reefs. Eventually it would become an artificial archipelago that can be utilized for recreational purposes, for example, as a nautical resort.

5. PUNTA CRISTO – self-organized harbor facility (SHF)

SHF is an independent association that operates from ports. The harbor's main characteristic is its flexible infrastructure—pontoons with cranes that move between coasts and arriving ships.

6. SVETICA – *superbaraka*

Superbaraka is a superstructure for so-called illegal builders—a 120-meter-high concrete skeleton with 16 plateaus, 710 meters long, equipped only with bearing walls, plumbing, and electricity. In this case there is no sense in distinguishing between legal and illegal buildings, but only between useful and useless buildings!

7. KATARINA – Center for Post-capitalist Cultures (CPC)

CPC is a vision of the type of urbanism that could emerge in the near future—taking into account that the current crisis within the capitalist system portends the none-too-distant end of the neo-liberal doctrine. Discovering a typology for a new social organization will be the utmost challenge for twenty-first-century architecture.

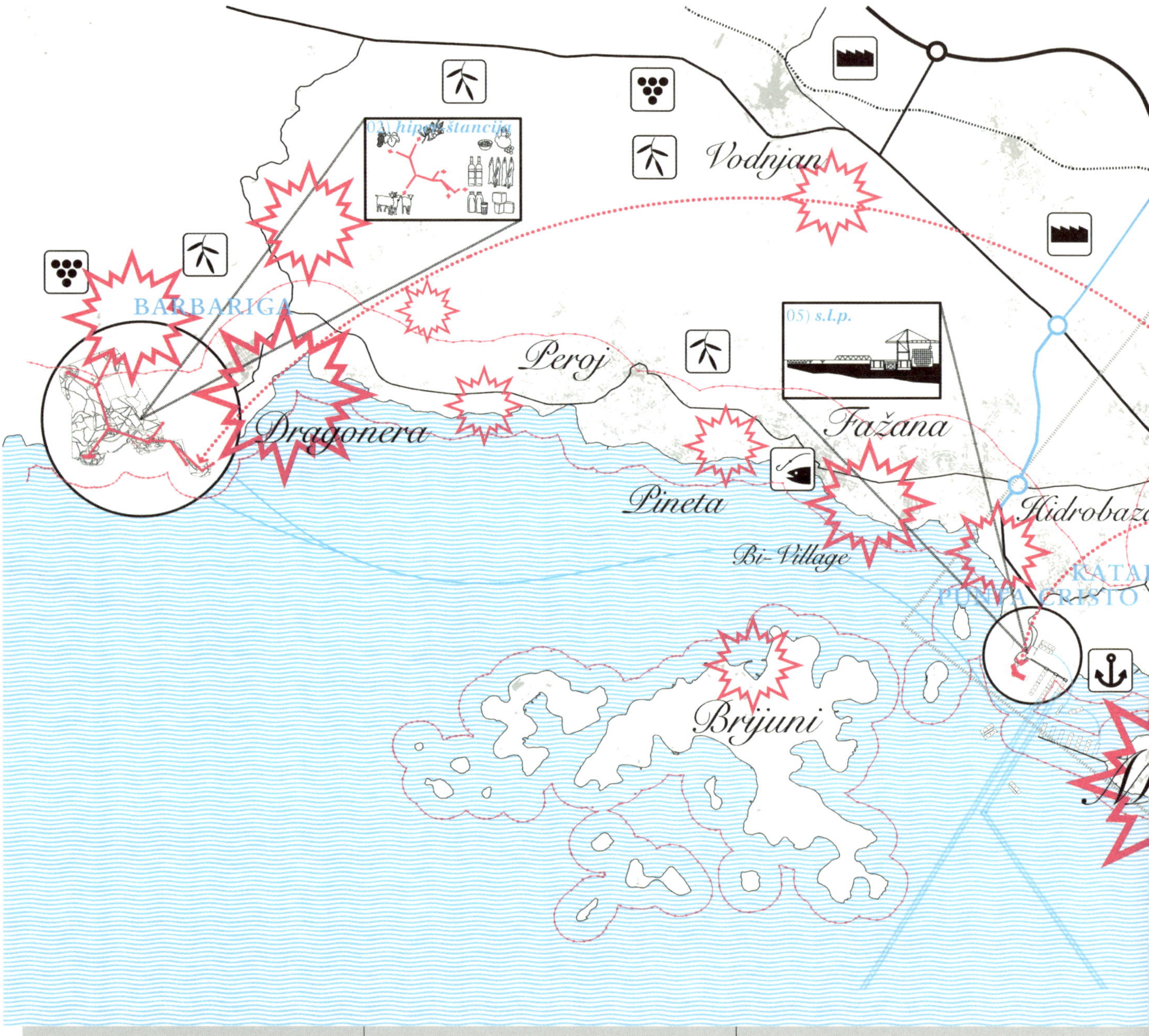

Southern Istria was codified for the first time as a map system in the mid-nineteenth century. The fortified military area of Pula extended from Barbariga in the north to Marlera in the south. When the investors who comb the Mediterranean in search of untouched sites became interested in abandoned military landscapes, that area of southern Istria was codified for the second time.

A second map depicting southern Istria—produced in 2006 by the Brijuni Rivijera Corporation—was a spatial program map. But before Brijuni Rivijera developed its concept, and before the former military areas became attractive, it hosted a series of programs and interventions, such as cultural festivals, concerts, parties, and celebrations. The Media Mediterranea festival delineates an invisible map of the seven locations that hosted happenings in the last ten years. Almost from the beginning, the festival used the former Karlo Rojc barracks in Pula as a base for its educational activities and exhibitions. On the last night of the festival, most of the activities were transferred to the respective abandoned military zones at the edge of town.

The strategy for these happenings involved making use of what was available: a generator for electricity as an energy source, part of a building used as a DJ's table and stage, and a sound system and video projector connected to a computer. All these elements can be classified as portable infrastructure. Urban planning could also employ portable infrastructure as a tool. If it is true that whoever controls the infrastructure controls the territory, then we need our own infrastructure!

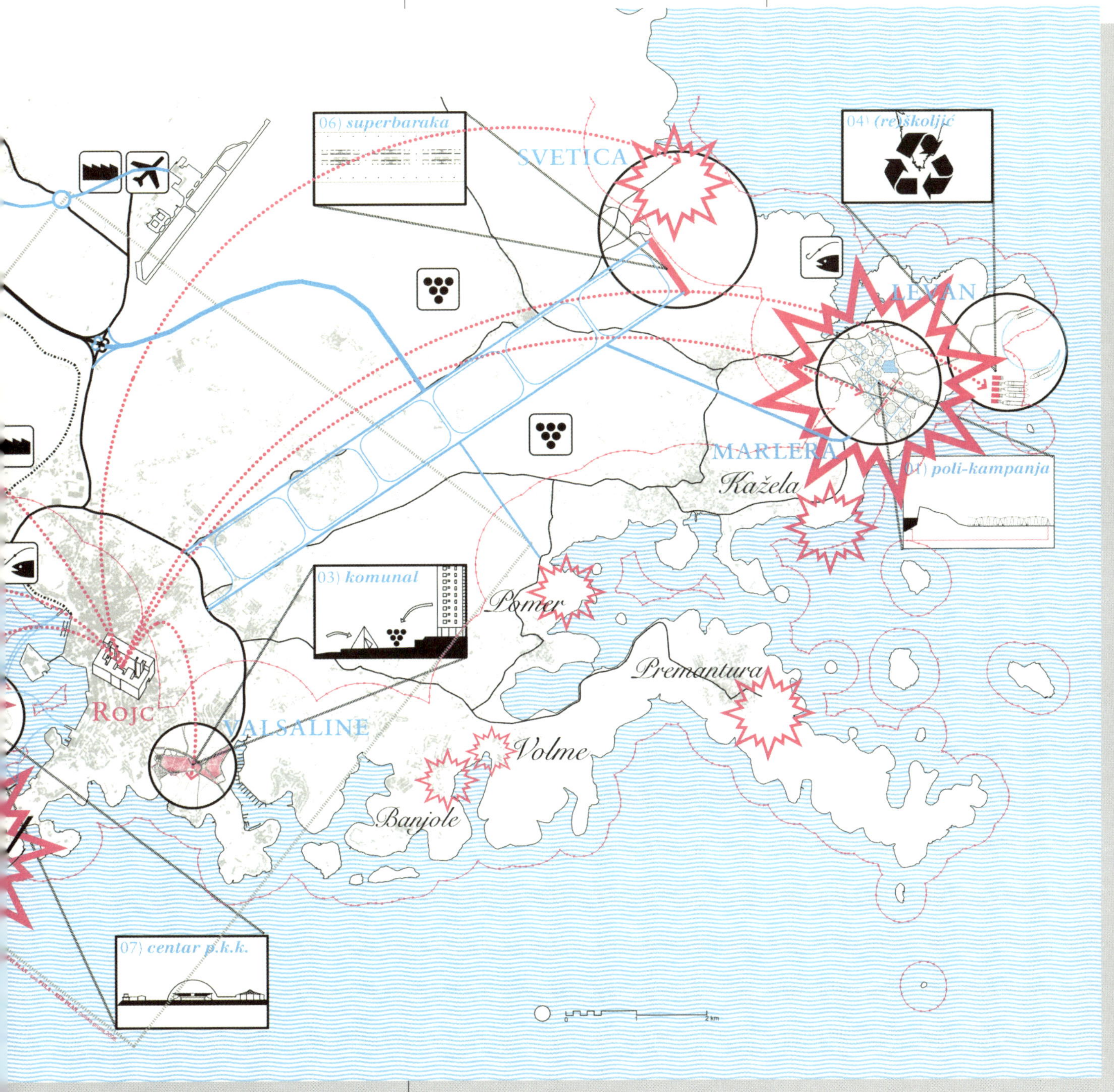

In seven locations in southern Istria portable infrastructure is already in use, but the potential to create a new, independent infrastructure hasn't been realized yet. This story is inspired by the desire to create a third map of southern Istria, one that is on a par with the military and tourist maps: the Plan Mediterraneo map.

Plan Mediterraneo

- **zaštićeni obalni pojas** / protected coastal area
- **pruga** / railroad
- **istarski ipsilon** / Y fast road
- **postojeće ceste** / existing road
- **nove ceste** / new road
- **novi morski pravci (lokalni)** / new sea ways (local)
- **novi morski pravci (globalni)**/ new sea ways (global)
- **novi objekti** / new objects
- **Media Mediterranea festival**
- **konflikt uzrokovan turističkom namjenom** / spatial conflict caused by tourism

Zeppelin Association

Bucharest, Romania
www.e-zeppelin.ro
www.zeppelin-magazine.net

INTERVIEW

with Stefan Ghenciulescu, Cosmina Goagea, Constantin Goagea

How was the political and social situation in your country and specifically in your city, when you and your colleagues started the initiative?

We grew up under Communism and were educated as architects after 1990. Our professional life was (and is) marked by both rapid change and frozen situations, by the chaos and opportunities of a never-ending "transition." Construction and consumption were rather scarce in the 1990s and exploded after 2000. Bucharest, the capital of a very centralized country, concentrates and intensifies changes: one million more cars and one million fewer trees in the last twenty years, ultra-liberalism, impotent planning, a destruction of the heritage that almost matches the totalitarian era of the 1980s; but also the strongest development and westernization in the country and a lot of energy.

What is your main reason for forming an initiative/organization? What do you want to achieve with it? Who is your target group?

We actually started doing things and the organization came later. A group of young architects, some of them partners in a start-up architecture office, began an internet-based architecture magazine in the late 1990s. We were then invited by the Union of Romanian Architects to resuscitate its publication, *Arhitectura* magazine (this was definitely a "Wild East" opportunity). After 2001, the core team, Constantin, Cosmina, and Stefan developed the magazine into an international publication, while working as architects at the same time. At one moment we felt that we could do more than just the magazine, and started organizing exhibitions and conferences, then publishing architecture books. Then came the alternative projects for public space and the practice-based research.

A couple of years ago, we decided to found an NGO, called Zeppelin, in order to bring all of these initiatives under the same umbrella. *Zeppelin* is now also the name of the magazine. The main objectives are to promote good and responsible architecture (mainly from Southeastern Europe, including Romania, but also innovative and alternative approaches from all over the world) through the magazine, conferences and exhibitions; to discuss post-socialist territorial development; and to promote good practice in Romania and good Romanian practice outside of the country. Additionally, we are trying to develop a theoretical practice and real interventions.

The target groups are, therefore, diverse: a mainly professional public for the magazine in Romania and Europe; but we'd like to think that our research and interventions mainly address users—the inhabitants of the cities we work in.

With whom do you work, who supports you? How are your relationships to governmental bodies and the private commercial sector?

We are increasingly working in networks—with partners in Romania (especially our friend Justin Baroncea, a partner in Point4 architecture office) or foreign ones (Archis Interventions mainly, and other organizations from Central and Eastern Europe).

Our philosophy is to integrate all of our different activities and expertise. On a complex project, for instance, involving research, projects, interventions, an exhibition, and a publication—our entire magazine team, from architects, to marketing or PR people and graphic designers, is at work.

Besides, doing a lot of different things means that you can get funding from a lot of different sources. The magazine is mainly financed by advertising. As a cultural and professional publication, we also get project-based support–from state institutions or professional organizations. The same two sources also sustain our cultural and research projects.

While we get along very well with the private commercial sector, we are still too slow at building up partnerships with administrative bodies.

What can we learn for the future from your experience? What is your advice to architects, planners, and others who are dealing with urban development? How do you see the role of the expert?

We would advocate an activity based on overview, multiplicity, and flexibility. Starting from a core activity (in our case, the magazine), where you increasingly become an expert and can build-up a structure, you can go on to develop and integrate a multitude of other jobs. Secondly, we strongly believe in theoretical practice; especially in our part of the world, criticism and research should be done using a "hands-on" approach. On the other side, a practice without theory will, at some point, succumb to compromise and excessive pragmatism. Thirdly, it's about openness: networking and overcoming the strictly national context are essential. And finally, as architects and planners, we think that we have to emphasize our traditional role as coordinators and facilitators. We all tend to be more and more excluded from the real creation of the city, and our insistence on our role as "artists" shifts us increasingly into the marginal position of beautifiers (including urban designers). We should try to remain indispensable, as the ones that bring all the actors together, while retaining a perspective on culture and space, as well as the ability to synthesize an overview.

PORTRAIT

Zeppelin Association is an NGO, based in Bucharest and founded in 2008, by architects Constantin Goagea, Cosmina Goagea, and Stefan Ghenciulescu. The three partners have been working together since 1998. Over time, they have gathered a team of around twelve people—architects, marketing and PR experts, and graphic designers—and they work in permanent or project-based partnerships with other organizations and architectural offices (mainly Point 4 in Bucharest). They also work as practicing architects and Stefan Ghenciulescu teaches at the University of Architecture in Bucharest.

The association's essential goals are to promote good practice in architecture and urbanism, to develop research and to propose and implement alternative projects for public space, dwelling rehabilitation, and cultural and social infrastructure.

Zeppelin magazine

This international architecture magazine, with articles in Romanian and English, has been published since 1999. Up to issue ninety (December 2010), it appeared under the name *Arhitectura*, through a commission of the Union of Romanian Architects, but as an editorially and financially strictly independent publication. In January 2011 the magazine began appearing under the name *Zeppelin*.
Zeppelin magazine publishes both Romanian and foreign materials, with a strong emphasis on the region (Central and Southeastern Europe), young architects, social and sustainable architecture, innovation, the creative use of low budgets, and critical attitudes.

Zeppelin Nights

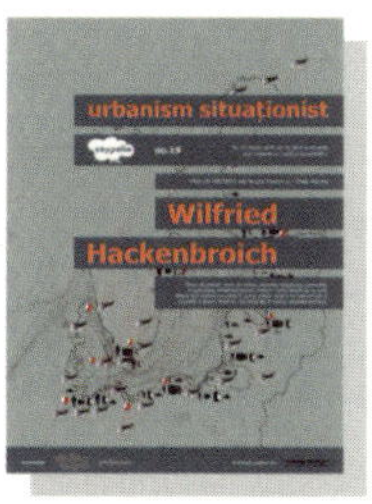

The team has been organizing architectural conferences and debates since 2004. In 2008 Zeppelin Nights became a series of conferences (an average of ten per year, sometimes with more presentations for each event). Established or up-and-coming Romanian and international architects and designers present their practice or research topics in front of audiences that reach up to three or four hundred participants.

Exhibitions

The Zeppelin team has organized more than twenty exhibitions in Romania and abroad, either on its own or with others. Some of the most important have been *Remix! Fragments of a Country* (The Romanian pavilion at the Venice Biennale in 2006), exhibitions organized under the auspices of the Bucharest Architecture Biennial (organization of the 2004, 2006, 2008, and 2010 events), *Jukebox City. Bucharest Today/Histories and Architecture* (Barcelona 2007), exhibitions about the *Magic Blocks* project (see below) in Berlin and Bucharest, the Romanian contribution (in partnership) to the *Balkanology* exhibition, etc.

Research & other publications

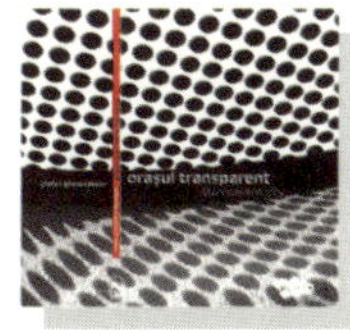

Besides the magazine, and the occasional development of its themes, there is increasing research and publishing activity, with topics ranging from modern and contemporary architectural and urban history, to post-socialist territorial developments in Romania and the Balkans, contemporary tendencies, etc. Besides the catalogues of some of the exhibitions cited above, one could cite *Zeppelin Laborator 01* (2010), *American Avantgarde* (2010, author Cosmin Caciuc), *Transparent City. On Limits & Dwelling in Bucharest* (2009, author: Stefan Ghenciulescu). In 2011 there was the launching of *Urban Report,* a regional platform and cross-cultural research project about contemporary urban phenomena and architecture in Southeastern Europe. The project was a collaboration between Zeppelin, Bina (Serbia), KEK (Hungary), Transformatori and SAW (Bulgaria) and includes input from several other organizations and researchers. The results of the cooperation are published on line (www.urbanreport.ro), in print form, and as DVDs. Since 2012, *Urban Report* has been integrated as a section of Zeppelin magazine.

Alternative projects

Since 2008 we have developed strategies, proposals, and interventions for problematic situations in the post-totalitarian development of the Romanian territory. They bring together research and architectural and urban practice, are developed together with other organizations, and usually do not originate with an actual commission, but from the assessment of essential problems and typological answers. This activity combines top-down and bottom-up approaches, and its main goals range from critical reflection and provocative action to producing models and, eventually, real designs and the realization of operations. One of the most important programs is "Magic Blocks," an ongoing set of studies and projects for socialist collective housing (see the article in this issue). Several past and ongoing projects deal with propositions for public space, recycled urban furniture, urban interventions, etc.

Planning between Vacuum and Energy

The Case of Co-PLAN in Tirana, Albania

www.co-plan.org

Besnik Aliaj

After two decades of almost complete freedom in Albania, immediately following five decades of an authoritarian regime, there is a clear need for a new, realistic concept—in the form of urban and regional planning tools—to guide the development of the physical world. Albania is located on the Adriatic Sea in Southeastern Europe. It shares a common border with Greece, Italy, Montenegro, Kosovo, and Macedonia. Albania has 3.5 million inhabitants, and 1,000,000 have recently emigranted to EU countries and North America. These figures do not include Albanian-speaking communities in neighboring countries. Albania's total surface area is about 28,000 square kilometers (comparable in size to Holland, Costa Rica, or South Korea). Tirana, the capital city, currently has a population of more than 700,000, while the Tirana-Durres metropolitan region has more than 1,000,000 inhabitants. Albania has a long and colorful history. Eastern Orthodox, Roman Catholic, and other religious communities have coexisted here peacefully for centuries. Although the country is now open and easily accessible, it is still largely unknown, even to many Europeans, due to its past. Why such "mystery"? During the second half of the twentieth century, Albania—which, over the centuries, has been under Roman, Slavic, and Ottoman rule and subsequently endured a centralized economy—experienced a harsh regime and futile self-isolation. The people of Albania were denied private property, freedom of religion, and freedom of movement. The ideology behind it was neither communist nor capitalist, but instead a nearly feudal system, "neither eastern, nor western": by the end of the 1980s the country was at the brink of a national humanitarian crisis. Now Albania is a parliamentary republic committed to democracy and a market economy. Despite its rocky start in the 1990s, the economy was relatively stabilized by 2000 and now leads the region. The authorities have wide public support for full integration into the European Union and NATO. Together with countries like Croatia and Montenegro, Albania has one of the ten-fastest growing tourism sectors. During the last decade the overall economy has grown at an average of six percent per annum, while, despite the global crisis, inflation has averaged three percent.

Tirana, a planning laboratory

With policies discouraging urban settlement, Albania was one of the most rural societies in Europe (twenty percent of the population lived in the country in the late 1940s, and thirty-five percent by the late 1980s)—but in less than two decades, it was transformed into an urban society: almost sixty percent of the population now lives in cities. According to the National Institute of Statistics (INSTAT), urbanization and migration rates in Tirana increased dramatically by the early 1990s from seven to nine percent per annum, while authorities were caught off guard by the enormous pressure exerted by individual initiatives. Since 1989 Tirana has more than doubled in area, and the population has tripled. In addition, it is merging with Durres, the country's main port city, as well as with the newly developed informal peripheries.

Imagine a society, which had endured strict planning tenets, suddenly veering toward a mentality in which there is almost no room for planning at all. So, despite the boom of formal investments, more than 500,000 extralegal properties and businesses have also mushroomed in the country, mostly in the capital region and coastal areas. The Albanian government and UNDP estimate the value of this property at nearly thirteen-billion euros, which is four times greater than the international aid given to Albania during the transition, nine times the direct foreign investments, and nine times the non-gold national reserves (the actual national GDP is about ten billion euros).

One third of the country's population now lives in the Tirana metropolitan region. Co-PLAN claims that if this trend continues at this rate, in fifteen to twenty years it will probably be home to about two-thirds of the overall population—at significant cost to society and the environment. In fact, these demographic shifts are already placing a great strain on Tirana, which is not only the most vibrant city in Albanian-speaking territories, but also one of the most promising emerging urban economies in the Balkans. It is also an extremely interesting planning "laboratory" in its own right.

Albania has indeed made progress in many areas, but, for example, is still in the process of addressing restitution problems, setting up sustainable information systems, reforming urban and environmental planning systems, and fighting corruption and informality. However, it is precisely these fast-and-furious features that have elicited the astonishing transformation. Albania and Tirana offer a unique perspective for urban planning and development, and as a repository of boundless energy, deserve to be explored, analyzed, and studied.

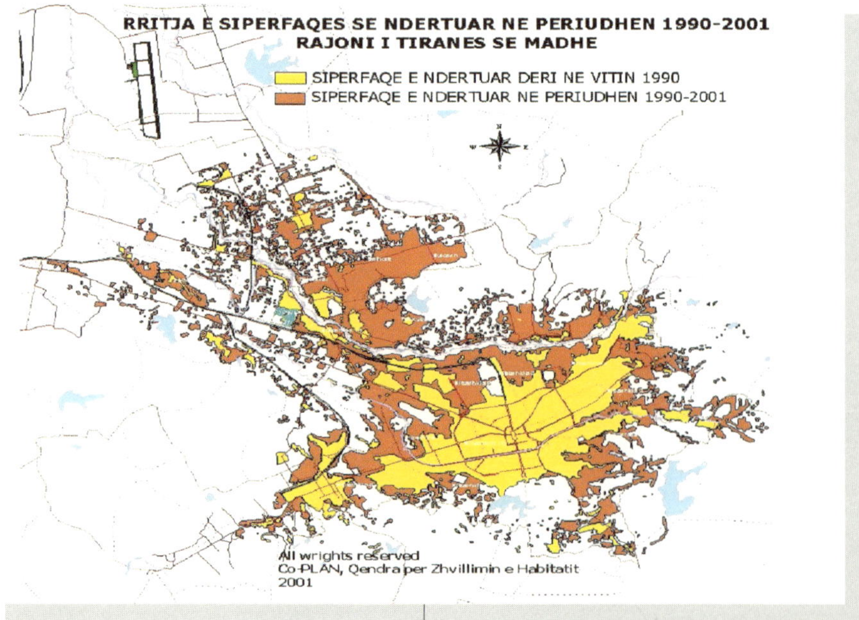

Urban Development 1990–2001

Tirana's bright colors, part of a city-beautification process

Tirana is a city in which the grandiose, delusional urban "dreams" of a local monarch (Zog of Albania) and of a dictator (Benito Mussolini), come face-to-face with those of an authoritarian communist leader (Enver Hoxha). It is a blend of planning from the perspectives of both a centralized and a market economy, while at the same time, it reflects planning that has occurred in an institutional vacuum and amid chaotic human energy. It mixes top-down and bottom-up planning, as well as extreme order and total freedom. It is a city in which formal and informal planning co-exist and compete with one another. Tirana was home to a "forbidden" neighborhood that was off-limits to all but the communist authorities, and then was suddenly transformed into a downtown entertainment district. The ingredients are all there, mixed together with the current enthusiasm, inspired by freedom of movement and private initiatives, and culminating in a sensual urban cocktail.
It is fair to say that emotions run high with respect to planning in Tirana, and the authorities and society as a whole are struggling to cope with them. But Tirana is also well-known for its creative and charismatic municipal governance. It has gained widespread acclaim for the brightly painted façades that were part of a city beautification process, as well as for its international Art Biennale. Tirana is also known for its latest international urban design/planning and architectural competitions. The municipality and its former mayor, Edi Rama, have received several international awards, including the UN's "Mayorship of the World" for the improvement of life in the city. The newly elected mayor, Lulezim Basha, is also committed to serious, city-scale, urban projects, including city parks and rail transport systems.

Co-PLAN and POLIS University

The need for a new concept of realistic architecture and city planning in Albania is being addressed by Co-PLAN and POLIS University. U_POLIS has created a new alternative university in Albania and the surrounding region, serving the field of architecture and urban planning. Indeed, POLIS was established based on the experiences and values of Co-PLAN's Institute for Habitat Development, a pioneering non-government organization in the field of urban planning in Albania.
It intends to establish a critical mass and expertise to effect change in this field in Albania. Indeed, city planning is underrepresented at other schools in Albania. And the public university's program tends more toward urban design. As a result, despite the fact that it is a young university, U_POLIS is a leading institution. It responds pragmatically to the educational and research needs in Albania and Kosovo, and in a second phase, it will, in all likelihood, be active in Montenegro, Macedonia, Bosnia-Herzegovina, and Serbia. POLIS intends to contribute to national and regional development by offering education and research in architecture, as well as in urban and regional planning, through international exchange programs.

As delineated above, for almost fifteen years Co-PLAN's Institute for Habitat Development (www.co-plan.org) has been at the forefront of Albania and Kosovo's research and practice in the field of urban design, planning, and development. Co-PLAN received support from various local communities, authorities, and international donors, while developing several pioneering urban projects in Albania. It has received international recognition and awards, including from the World Bank and UNDP Best Practices. In 2003 Co-PLAN and the Municipality of Tirana organized the European Conference on Housing and Urban Development, entitled "Making Cities Work," on behalf of ENHR (European Network of Housing Research), as well as numerous national and regional workshops, seminars, and sensitizing campaigns. In 2005 Co-PLAN submitted a platform with recommendations for reforming the national planning system, including formalization of informal settlements, to the Albanian Parliament. Through legislation the platform was adopted to a large degree. Currently, Co-PLAN has joined U_POLIS's research department and involves students and academic staff in practical exercises.

Co-PLAN's cumulative experience can be summarized in three main stages:
1. Establishment of organization; first urban upgrading programs.
2. Consolidation of organization and models; replication at wider scale.
3. Impacting society and policy-making; dissemination of knowledge.

The first phase originated in the early 1990s and lasted until the Kosovo conflict began. During this stage, support from Dutch organizations (both governmental and NGOs) was instrumental in the organization's establishment and its capacity building. Co-PLAN introduced the first urban upgrade program at Lapraka, an informal neighborhood in Tirana. Over the course of about seven years, in order to lead neighborhood participatory planning processes, a local CBO was identified and strengthened. This involved opening three km of roads and public space, as well as setting up a community center with social, health, and educational facilities. A plan submitted to the local authorities was approved and a memorandum of understanding for cooperation between local CBO and municipality-guided public investments in the infrastructure (water, sewage, power, roads and garbage

collection). In 1998 it was selected as Best Practice by UN-Habitat. The project was later replicated on a larger scale in the informal settlements of Bathore (Kamza 2002) and Keneta Durres (2003–6; supported by the Austrian government), as well as in the formal areas of Tirana and other cities. It also led to a large-scale, urban land-management program initiated by the Albanian government (supported by the World Bank). During the second stage, from 2000 to 2006, Co-PLAN adjusted its course toward assisting communities and local authorities in Albania to prepare bottom-up urban visions and plans (strategic, action, and regulatory). This includes planning exercises and processes in the municipalities of Kamza, Kruja, Elbasan, Fier, Durres, Tirana, Librazhd, Peshkopi, Fush-Kruje, Vau-Dejes, Koplik, Kukes, Fush Arrez, Berat, Lushnje (Albania), Mitrovica, Junik (Kosovo), etc. The most important program initiated during this phase is "EGUG – Enabling Good Urban Governance." It focuses on the cities Elbasan and Fier, and is supported by the Dutch government. Participatory planning processes were followed by participatory budgeting exercises that led, in turn, to efficient social and infrastructure investments in these cities. Such examples have become references for a new city planning philosophy in Albania. Since 2005, Co-PLAN has also been committed to influencing policy-making in Albania. During this third phase, Co-PLAN drafted a political-technical platform on reforming the territorial planning and property system in Albania and submitted it to the Albanian Parliament. Issues of formalization and integration of informal settlements were also included. Certain aspects of such platforms have been adopted through legislation. Co-PLAN is also currently working toward adapting Albania's laws in accordance with the European Union's requirements. As mentioned above, the establishment of POLIS University was another Co-PLAN initiative, whose goal is to create a critical mass of expertise and knowledge transfer, with the intent of bringing changes to Albania in this sector.

Some of the main lessons drawn from Co-PLAN experience are:
The role of NGOs and CBOs in channeling local city planning processes during stages of early development for post-traumatic and transitional economies is often to instigate change. International experiences should be adjusted, by taking the local context—particularly the owners of local initiatives—into account. When international governmental organizations and NGOs promote local development, especially in situations in which governmental structures are weak, the best results are attained by relying on local structures, and in absence of such structures, on key individuals who tend to build sustainable local institutions. Successful development and planning are only possible when local authorities are involved in the discussions, particularly when they have clear ownership of development visions, accompanied by concrete participation of other local stakeholders. Successful planning processes do not come about without taking into consideration politics and political interests. It is not even fair to say that planners must be 'neutral' in the political game. Planning could also be viewed as public politics. The challenge is to determine how to match local political and economic interests with those of the people and communities, and maintain the professional and intellectual ethics of planners and architects. There will be no 'happy ending' to the planning, if the systems in place are not adapted to incorporate strategic, human-capacity development actions. Therefore, education is a prerequisite to establishing a critical mass of expertise at the local government level, which will hopefully produce positive changes and sustainable institutions. In our endeavors to build sustainable physical, social, and economic city centers, the people, communities, businesses, and authorities involved will have to decide whether to view each other as partners or adversaries. The first option is complex, costly, and difficult in the short term, but sustainable in the long term, while the second will engender endless conflict. At present, much of mankind suffers from inefficient governance, corruption, and lack of access to the decision-making process. This has produced a large extralegal economy, the analysis of which could provide insight into improving the authorities' performance. The extralegal sector is stratified, ranging from criminal activity to a "light grey" economy, and if these different structures are analyzed in detail, special policies could be applied to bring people with low incomes into the formal sector and to combat criminal activity.

Previously published in Hintergrund, 17, Viennese Architectural Congress Balkanology, 45/2010

PORTRAIT

Location: Tirana, Albania
Foundation year: 1995
Structure: non-profit NGO
Members: architects and planners

Focus: sustainable urban and regional development; improvement of low-income neighborhoods

Approach: enabling good governance, developing civil society and empowering community participation, urban and regional management, municipal/environmental management, organizational institutional development, empowering local governments to implement decentralization policies; supporting civil society for institutional strengthening, influencing local and national policy as well as social and economic developments

Keneta project, Durrës

Steps toward the urban rehabilitation and integration of communities in the informal area of Keneta was implemented during May 2004–June 2008 on a selected pilot area of 50 hectares, supported by funds from the Austrian government. The project aimed at integrating the newly created "informal" community into the formal structures of Durres Municipality, by focusing on three key processes: legalization of the informal settlement, infrastructure investments for neighborhood upgrading, and participatory planning.

Providing technical assistance in the legalization process was crucial to successful project implementation, because it was important to respond in a timely way to the needs of the local community, while at the same time being aligned with national governmental initiatives. The project took residents through the process of declaring claim to buildings, which is a critical step for setting up the territorial database. Due to the political dynamics of the legalization process, 75% of the declaration procedures were completed, as compared to 50% across the country.

Apart from providing on-the-spot support for local residents, technical assistance was given to local and regional legalization units, in setting-up and using the database of informal buildings, preparing design briefs, and drawing the boundaries of informal settlements, which are still politically and administratively sensitive issues. Preparation of a design brief, followed by the local area plan using the participatory approach was another strength underlying the success of the integration process. The whole process was conceptualized as a way of communicating and exchanging ideas, while reconciling the needs of the various stakeholders—the municipality and the local community. Throughout the process, Co-PLAN provided professional guidance, while serving as a mediator to bridge the gap between the local government and its constituencies. Co-PLAN, local officials, and community representatives, working as a team, laid down standards and prepared simple sketches, aiming to introduce concepts and practices for the area's public space and service facilities, striving to transform the area from a dormitory-like settlement to a city neighborhood.

An extended communication strategy underlined the whole participatory process. Not only did community representatives participate in designing the plan, but each and every resident of the area was also consulted, thus ensuring transparency and, first and foremost, local ownership.

Infrastructure investments for upgrading the pilot area constituted an important tool for bridging the gap between the community and city hall, thus increasing mutual trust and making cooperation in planning and legalization process effective. Projects were identified and selected jointly through an extensive consultation process; they were also co-financed. This partnership constituted a major project achievement, because it produced a model of public-private partnership and attracted further public investment in the area.

Getting the community involved in the upgrading program was a component of the project, as well as a basic fundamental principle behind the planning and place-making process. It was and still is critical to develop a realistic neighborhood plan that will account for social aspects and community needs, and be implemented through capacity building for the community-based organization and vulnerable groups. While local officials manage urban realities for the people, these people should represent their own interests in the local authorities — through community work — to ensure that their needs are addressed properly.

Long-term efforts were made and an immeasurable amount of energy was spent to bring stakeholders into this arena of cooperation, which produces realistic and useful products, while creating synergies with parallel and upper initiatives. The pilot area became very attractive for further significant public investments. The Albanian government picked up on Co-PLAN's previous experience with community planning, the integration of informal settlements, and the progress of the process in Keneta in order to stir efforts to draft a new law on legalization, while delineating the pilot model to be replicated across the country.

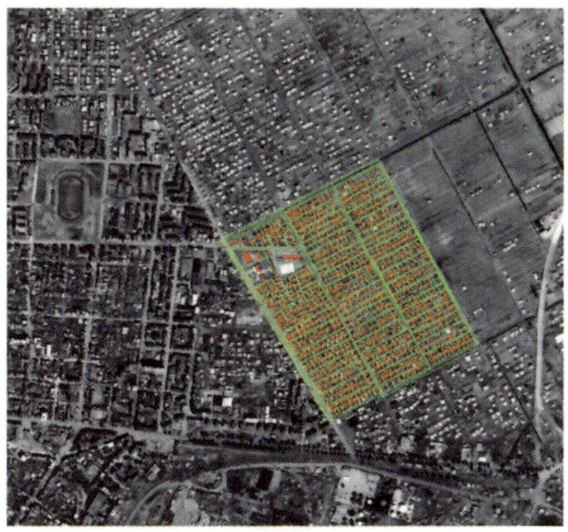

Tirana's fast-and-furious transformation

Road improvement

New Building – Old Building

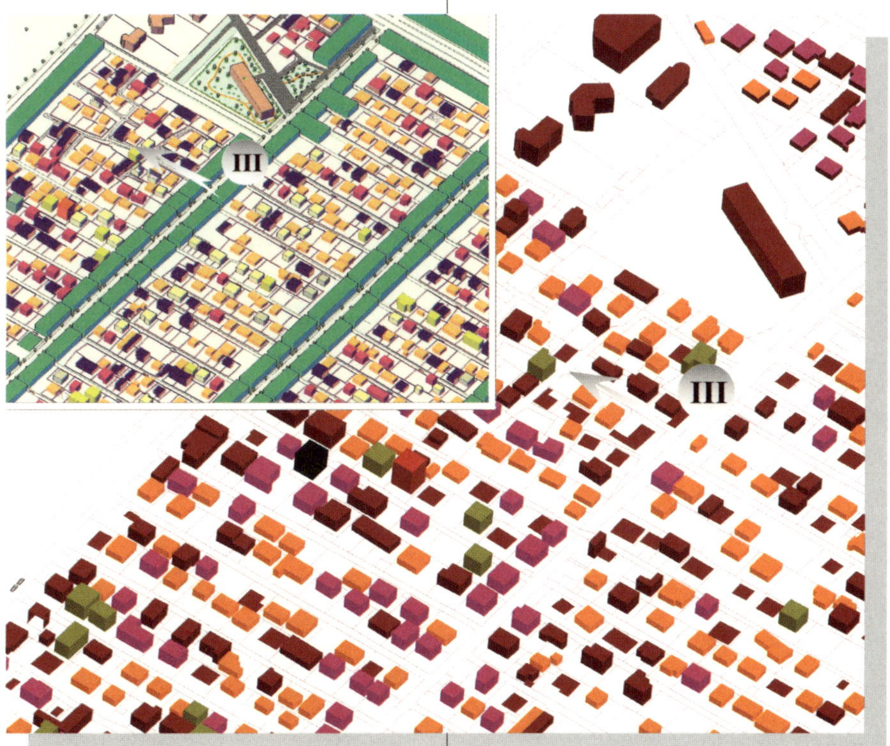

Building Albania

Photos: Kai Vöckler

UFO UNIVERSITY

Post-Conflict Urban Development in Bosnia-Herzegovina, Kosovo and Cyprus

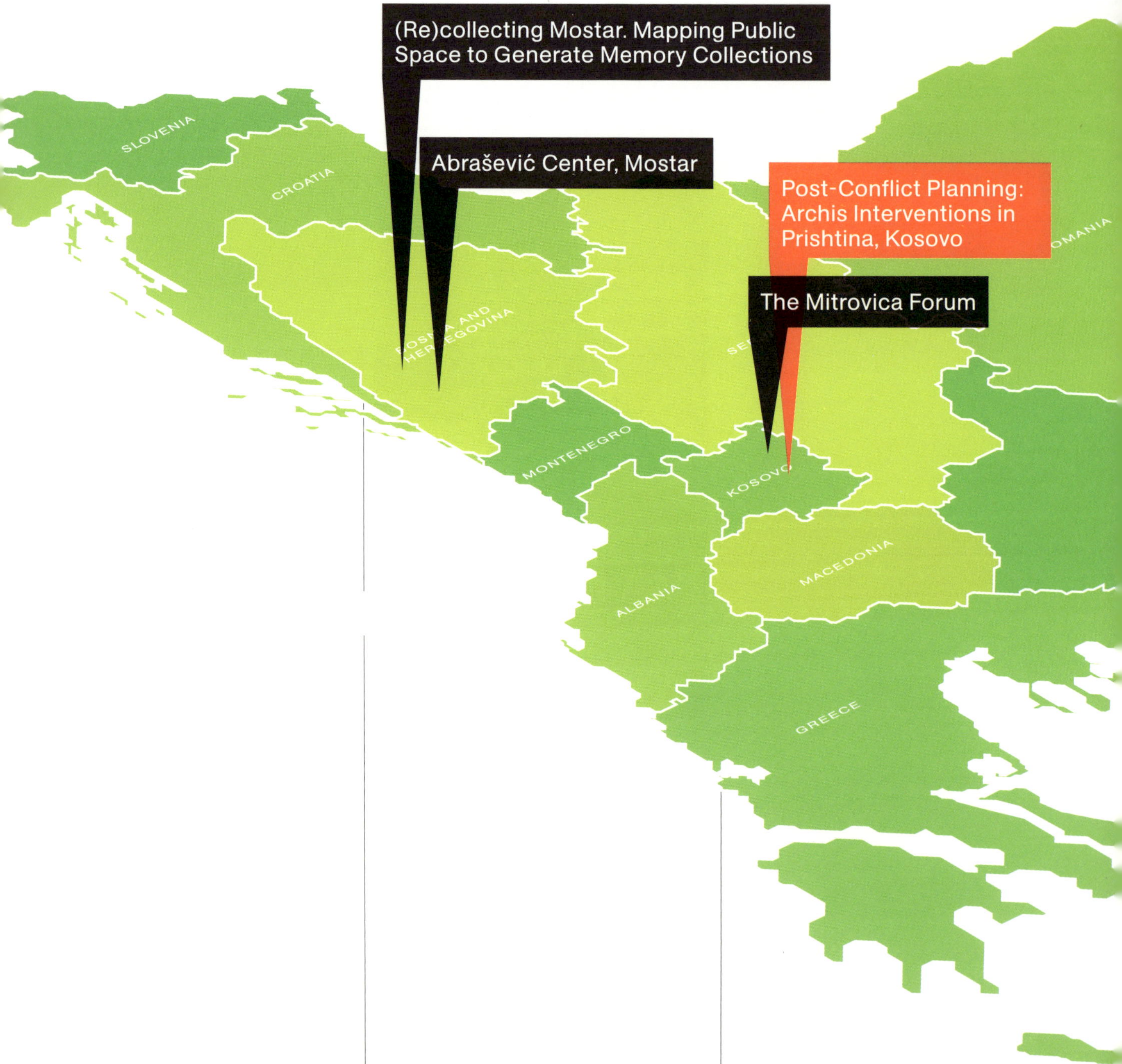

Project by Archis Interventions

MOLDOVA
Divided Cities and Building Dialogue: Community Centers in Mostar, Mitrovica and Nicosia
BULGARIA
TURKEY
Toward a Third Space: Dipkarpaz/Rizokarpaso
H4C – Home for Cooperation, Cyprus
The Pyla Master Plan Project
CYPRUS

Post-Conflict Planning: Archis Interventions in Prishtina, Kosovo

Florina Jerliu, Wilfried Hackenbroich, Kai Vöckler in collaboration with Visar Geci, Vlora Navakazi, Thilo Fuchs

After the NATO-led, international KFOR intervention ended the war between the Serbian military and the Kosovo-Albanian liberation army in 1999, a building boom began in Prishtina. The majority population, made up of Kosovo-Albanians, immediately started erecting urgently needed housing, while, at the same time, the real estate market became one of the most profitable branches of business, due to the enormous lack of both residential and commercial space. Demand intensified when the rural population began streaming into the city, along with Kosovo refugees being repatriated by western European nations. Within a brief period of time, Prishtina doubled its population, resulting in the speedy rebuilding of the city. Those who did not participate in the construction boom were the socially disadvantaged, who had neither land nor money, and the minority population of Kosovo-Serbs, who, faced with a new power structure, were not interested in investing in real estate. Even though Prishtina had not suffered much damage during the war, about seventy-five percent of the city's existing structures—and with them, their historical legacy—were demolished. In addition, all of this construction activity was illegal, due to the breakdown of local government: until 2005 it was practically impossible to get a construction permit, even if one wanted to. Note that all of this occurred under the administration of the United Nations (UNMIK, the United Nations Mission in Kosovo), which did not really regard its main task to be the regulation of urban development for the good of the city, but instead focused on introducing concentrated market economy structures. Of course, institutional structures had to be rebuilt, and there were no fundamental documents (such as a land registry, for instance) to secure the legal system, but still, one wonders why the international community, as represented by the UN mission (whose power was ensured by the KFOR troops), was incapable of setting at least minimum standards for construction. The consequences were grave: not only is most of old Prishtina gone, but public squares are neglected, the infrastructure is totally overwhelmed, and almost everywhere there are blatant safety violations, such as blocked or missing emergency exits; insufficient, overburdened structures—where, for instance, load-bearing walls have been removed in order to enlarge rooms—or single-family houses have been erected on the roofs of five-story apartment buildings from the socialist era. Not least among the difficulties are the social conflicts that have arisen, because neighbors have blocked each other's entrances, or even put up new buildings a hand's width away from a neighbor's living-room window. In short, Prishtina has serious problems in terms of safety for both people and buildings; it has social problems as a result of rebuilding of the city, and it has a problem providing basic infrastructure and services. So, anyone who wants to know why planning is necessary and sensible ought to visit Prishtina today.

The task in Prishtina was, first, to analyze the phenomenon and then to make it comprehensible. In order to do this, we collaborated with Archis Interventions in 2006 to produce a workshop in which selected situations were analyzed and then organized according to type. The various situations were charted and mapped, in order to make it clear how extensive the rebuilding of the city actually was. Parallel to this, we worked out an overall strategic concept, which allowed for a combination of various strategies: aside from the urban-architectural strategy, this affected communications, support from the Archis network, the inclusion of different interest groups in a model project, and the support of local institutions and organizations. These parallel strategies were pursued from the start. First of all, it was necessary to communicate the information about the newly founded, local NGO, as well as the analysis of the situation and the strategic concept. We were able to do this in an international setting, when the project was publicized in Volume 11 in spring 2007; we also presented the project at a number of different conferences on the theme, some of which were organized by the European Union and the UN Habitat. Followed in 2008 by the publication *Prishtina is Everywhere. Turbo Urbanism: the Aftermath of a Crisis* by Kai Vöckler, which documented and reflected the work of Archis Interventions in Prishtina up until that time, as well as the presentation of the work in the Balkonology exhibition at the Swiss Architecture Museum in Basel the same year.

This immediately led to reports appearing in local media, which, in turn, resulted in greater public interest. We were able to take advantage of this when we organized a student workshop, which became a public presentation during the mayoral election

in December 2007. The students took selected situations and developed possible future scenarios for them, which they then visualized in various ways. The visuals made it clear what would happen if the city were simply to continue development as before. The overall study and the concept for intervention convinced the new mayor of Prishtina, Dr. Isa Mustafa, who took our recommendations and made them part of his governance program. The cofounder of AI Prishtina, Florina Jerliu, became his official advisor, and the municipality's consultant on urban issues for Archis Interventions for years to come. The altered political situation, along with the great interest in change shown, not only by the politicians responsible, but also by a large portion of the population, made it possible for us to further develop our concept, and some of it has already been realized. In 2009, for instance, we collaborated with city administrators and the ministry for urban planning to create a "Manual on the Legalization of Structures Built without Building Permits." The manual set up basic minimal standards that would make it possible to legalize existing structures, and contained a concept for carrying out this highly complex process. In July 2009 the City Council used the fundamentals of this concept to pass a resolution to start the legalization process. Furthermore, we worked out a preliminary concept for a set of guiding principles for architecture. At the same time, we produced a television show about illegal construction, which was broadcast in 2011 when the legalization process had begun.

Besides this, it seemed to be very necessary not only to work on improving the existing situation, but also to propose a future perspective for the city. Therefore, the study "Prishtina – Dynamic City," which has its basis in a workshop, develops possible key themes and their spatial relevance as a proposal for discussion of the future of the city and its society. Planning needs visions,

but this should not be a utopian sort of planning. It pursues realistic goals that can be achieved over the long term. Accordingly, these visions must be coupled with key projects that are possible to carry out. This method, which is commonly accepted in contemporary planning, needs to be adapted to the specific social and political context. Here, too, a local urban initiative comprised of experts—such as Archis Interventions in Prishtina—is playing an important role, by intervening in the process of urban development and establishing a different method of planning.

But things are not that easy. Although aware that the process of legalization is a very complex one, and that its success depends on executing steps within given time frames as agreed and subsequently stipulated in the regulation for legalization, municipal officials can still hardly be moved to give up their 'slow mode' attitude and fragmented approach to the problem, which they have shaped over the last decade. First of all, because meeting deadlines—from drafting urban plans required by law to responding to building requests, and implementing municipal projects—has been the weakest side of the Planning Department, since not a single planning official has been punished for misconduct/mismanagement so far. This situation has been aggravated even more by the new planning director, appointed in early 2010, who is failing to manage the already complex situation, and concurrently, to fulfill the promises made by the mayor of Prishtina during the electoral campaign in late 2009, that is: the efficient and effective process of planning, and the issuing of as many building permits as possible, as fast possible. Secondly, the process of legalization—also promised by the mayor—has started, and this is an achievement for him in political terms, despite the fact that the 'technical issues' of the process are not being pursued.

This sort of 'commodity' was transposed in the Planning Department and is directly reflected in the work of the Legalization Sector of the Municipality of Prishtina, both in conceptual and practical terms. Hence, while the revised plans—which were due soon after the registration of illegal buildings (through self-declaration) in early 2011—are not even being considered by the Planning Department yet, the Legalization Sector, on the other side, is proceeding with the process by issuing conditions for legalization based on the (technical) manual, without knowing whether certain buildings ought to comply with any of plans: the existing or the revised ones! In due course, legalization permits will eventually be issued. Thus, because the plans have not been revised, any legalization of illegal buildings in the areas covered by regulatory plans will legally violate the existing plans. In other words, innocent citizens whose houses or adjoining spaces were violated by illegal builders may suffer for a second time the consequences of obeying the law. This situation may escalate into an eventual revolt.

In order to avoid this, Archis Interventions Prishtina organized a workshop in 2011 entitled "Legalization Permit Versus Planning Permit," identified to what extent the illegal buildings violated regulatory plans, and provided concepts for the application of standard rules and possible development.

On a broader scale, we are at the point where we are working on more actions that might have an effect on the public, as well as on a potential model project, which would make it possible to apply a new process for coordinating some sort of agreement between the various interest groups and our goals. What many representatives of international and local organizations thought was impossible in 2005 is now coming to fruition: the situation will be improved for the general good of society. To do all of this, however, we need architects and planners, who want a change and who are willing to work on behalf on their city: they can be regarded as agents of change.

Archis Interventions and Kosovar architects and town planners began their cooperation in Prishtina in 2005 by co-founding a local NGO. Collaborators were Hackenbroich Architekten (Berlin) and Co-PLAN (Tirana). The legalization concept and the study on the future development of Prishtina were developed in cooperation with the Municipality of Prishtina.

Case Studies: Identifying Key Typologies

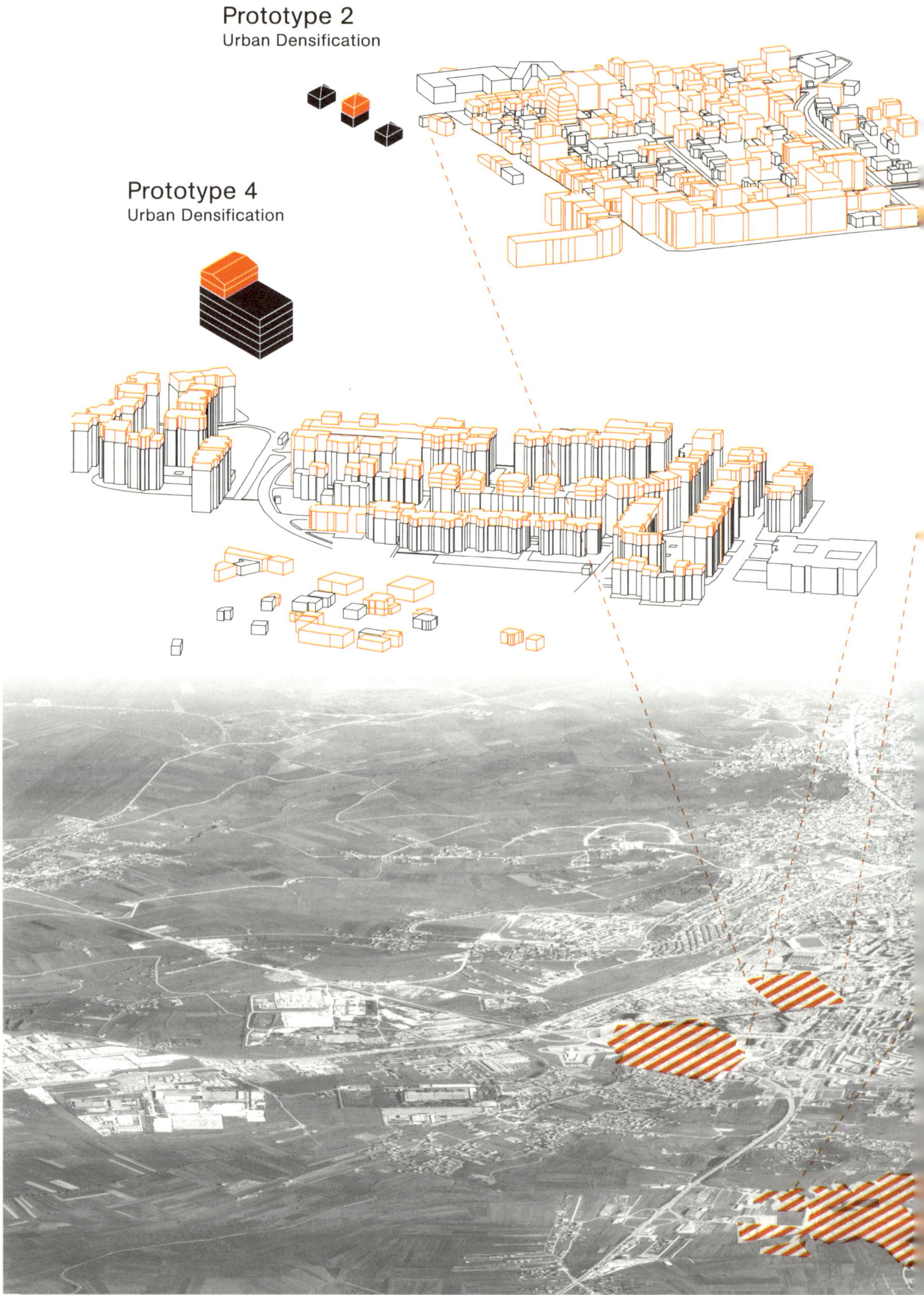

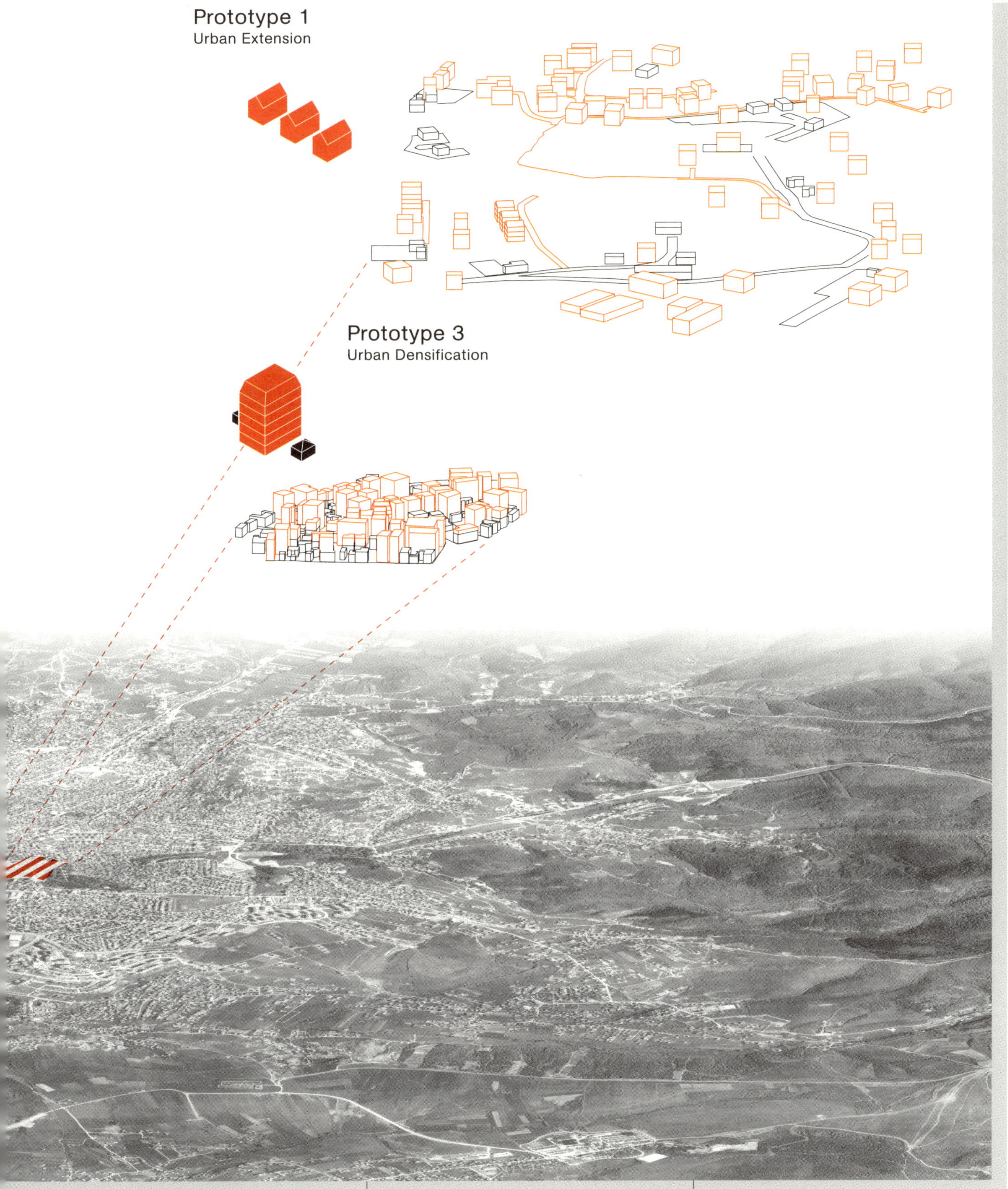
Prototype 1
Urban Extension
Prototype 3
Urban Densification

Case Studies: Identifying Key Typologies

Prototype 1 Urban Extension

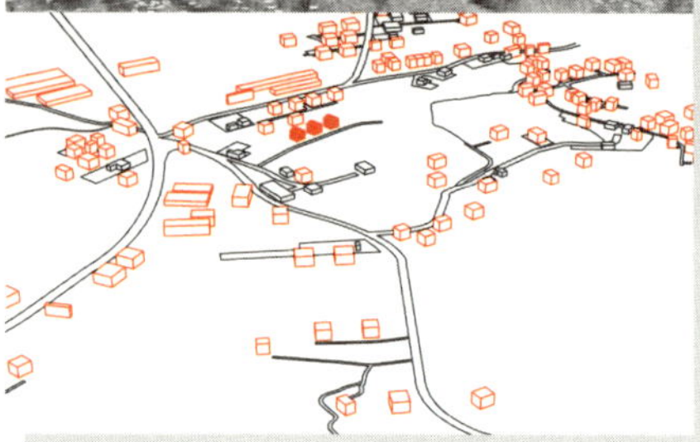

Single-family homes for own use, outskirts. Individual family-based development. The owners are part of the community

Legal Situation/Status of Ownership No dispute about land ownership, the building owners own the land. The land is generally owned or bought by builders (land register entry). Permission is generally not applied for or granted. Generally, neighbors know one another and ask one another before the land is sold, a tradition which is vanishing.

Safety Construction is based on estimates and experience, but not on calculations. The structural members are usually over-dimensioned, and construction is generally executed by construction companies. Fire escape routes are still possible.

Infrastructure Sewage is handled individually. Some households are illegally connected to the public sewage network. Some neighborhoods have jointly applied for connection to the public sewage network. Property access is via unpaved roads. No public transportation system exists. Public amenities are generally lacking, and private amenities are increasingly organized by individuals themselves.

Stakeholders Private individuals.

Growth The UDP Strategic Plan foresees only apartment houses with a minimum of 4–10 stories; the growth of single-family homes is not supported.

TASKS

Architectural Scale:

Improvement Legalizing the informal buildings and obtaining permits. Improvement of building infrastructure and /or adaptation of the informal buildings to recent regulations (regulatory plans).

Channeling Raise awareness of architectural design, aesthetic and functional needs.

Urban Scale:

Improvement Development of collective infrastructure such as water supply and sewage, road network and social amenities.

Channeling Assist in the development of new plans for neighborhoods. Encourage participation of the citizens in the planning process. Improvements on the neighborhood scale. Initiate sustainable processes. Raise awareness of urban design, aesthetic and functional needs.

Prototype 2 Urban Densification

Enlarged buildings for own use, inside the city. Individual development, the owner is part of the neighborhood community.

Legal Situation/Status of Ownership There is no dispute about land ownership; the building owners own the land. In many cases, a permit for a single-family house with a ground floor, first floor and roof was issued, but the final building exceeds the maximum gross floor size for the site and the number of floors allowed. Several land owners work together with an investor to put up a new building, and each land owner gets a share of the final building according to the value of his land.

Safety Construction is not sustainable due to the use of cheap or low-quality materials. Fire safety is limited due to missing or blocked escape routes, insufficient fire walls and insufficient fire protection to neighbors.

Infrastructure Overload of sewage and electricity systems due to extensive overbuilding. Under-serviced garbage collection due to extensive densification. Energy efficiency is not considered at all; thermal insulation is rarely used. The surviving social infrastructure of the city is used. The mostly legal connections to the water, sanitation and electricity networks produce extensive usage pressure on existing capacities.

Stakeholders Families, investors and developers.

Growth Demand for this type of housing development is still rising.

TASKS

Architectural Scale:

Improvement Improve structural safety, specifically the condition of the ground. Legalization and/or redevelopment of the informal buildings and permit acquisition especially for fire escapes, accessibility, parking infrastructure, safety, hygiene and energy efficiency.

Channeling Encourage the process to adapt the buildings to the regulatory plan.

Urban Scale:

Improvement Adjust extreme densification. Transform the negative effects, such as blocked views or light. Negotiate the social dimension in order to avoid conflict. Improvements impact the urban surroundings.

Channeling Address community and raise awareness of security, safety, hygiene and energy efficiency standards. Generate consensus on scale adjustment and the distances between buildings. Learn about owners' interests. Inform them about the consequences of enlarging their homes. Provide advisory board to prevent future urban development mistakes in order to protect the urban fabric and historical buildings.

Prototype 3
Urban Densification

Enlarged buildings not for own use (rental apartments, commercial spaces). Investors (not building for own use) and developers who are not part of the neighborhood community.

Legal Situation/Status of Ownership Recently, developers have started to buy and develop land for pure profit. The apartments are sold or rented. In some cases, the apartments are sold before the building is finished to co-finance construction. Planning permission status: most projects of this type have a building permit, and the buildings are constructed according to the regulatory plans.

Safety Construction is not sustainable due to the use of cheap or low-quality materials. Fire safety is limited due to missing or blocked escape routes, insufficient fire walls and insufficient fire protection to neighbors.

Infrastructure Overload of sewage and electricity systems due to extensive overbuilding. Responsibility rests with the city administration. Due to extensive densification, garbage collection is under-serviced. Energy efficiency is not considered at all; thermal insulation is not used. The surviving social infrastructure of the city is used. Legal connections to the existing water, sanitation and electricity networks produce extensive usage pressure on existing capacities.

Stakeholders Investors and developers.

Growth Rising demand for this type of housing development.

TASKS

Architectural Scale:

Improvement Reduction of building size. Reinstall sidewalks and necessary distances between the buildings.

Channeling Raise public awareness of the negative architectural consequences. Inform users and enable them to be more critical of construction in order to encourage a change in building standards.

Urban Scale:

Channeling Develop minimum apartment size standards and design-related organizational principles.

Prototype 4
Urban Densification

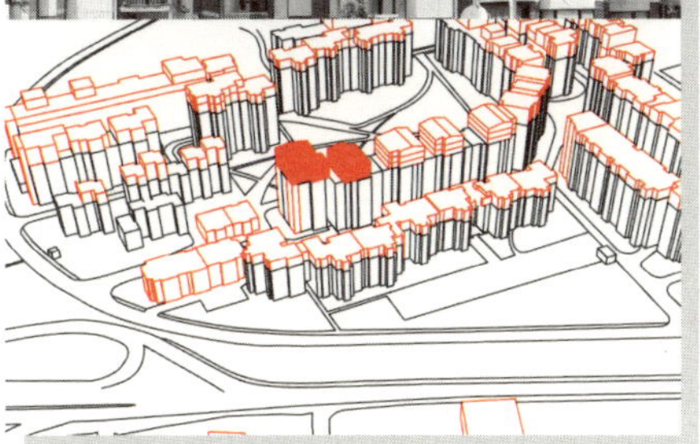

Urban parasites (extensions, annexes, roof extensions and cuts into buildings; houses on roofs). Individual developments; the owners are part of the neighborhood community.

Legal Situation/Status of Ownership Roof extensions are often semi-legal, with basic permits which are exceeded. The municipality supports the transformation of flat roofs into pitched roofs, and therefore raising the roof by one floor is permitted. Many, however, raise their roofs by two, three or even four floors. Often, entire houses are built on the roofs of privatized communal buildings. The owners bought the apartments individually, and the roof becomes the common property of the apartment owners. When roof renovation is needed the apartment owners on the top floors usually opt to raise the roof on their own initiative, saving the community the costs of renovation. Small, individual and hidden extensions to apartment buildings are mostly illegal and carried out without permits, and are often not coordinated with other owners. Renovations to ground floors are mostly carried out with permits for a change of use, but later, load-bearing structures are often taken out or modified. Basements are then often utilized for various purposes, and their ownership is often disputed.

Safety Serious safety problems are created by structural changes to the ground floor and basements due to the removal of supporting walls. This safety risk is increased by the additional load of the roof extensions. Even if concrete perimeter beams are built on the existing building, the roof extensions do not have any vertical connection to the main load-bearing walls. Most buildings not older than 20 years are able to take the additional load of a two-story roof extension, but even that is often exceeded. Emergency escapes are ensured by connecting to existing escape routes.

Infrastructure Except for a few unprofessional connections to the existing sewage system, there are hardly any hygiene problems. Often, owners apply for and get an official connection to the sewage system. Permission to connect to the sewage system is generally granted, even for building extensions carried out without permits, due to bureaucratic inefficiencies. Access to the extensions is provided by the existing access routes.

Stakeholders Mostly families and private apartment owners. For ground floor extensions, shops are bought and used by individuals. Basements are used by individuals.

Growth Development will most likely continue until all flat roofs are converted and extended, and the ground floors and basements are transformed into nonresidential spaces.

TASKS

Architectural Scale

Improvement Improve structural safety of buildings in line with the buildings' transformation. Legalization and/or redevelopment of the informal structures and acquisition of permits, especially for fire escapes, accessibility and safety.

Channeling Provide knowledge about adequate building materials, technical standards and functional needs.

Urban Scale

Improvement Eliminate access via public land, such as staircases on sidewalks.

Channeling Impart an awareness of how to improve the roofscape

Strategic Concept

The strategic concept developed in 2006 (see Volume 11) combined different approaches to achieve public awareness and impart a sensibility for environmental qualities and architectural values. It addresses different participants, local as well as international, and was designed to bridge the gap between them. An important aspect was the combination of a communication strategy (including the production of a TV show) with a support strategy (encouraging students), a participatory strategy (activation of local knowledge), a networking strategy (integration in the Archis network), and last, but not least, an architectural strategy (developing the manual and starting a model project). Actually, most of these strategies were successfully implemented.

Spring 2007

Completed
in progress
to be done

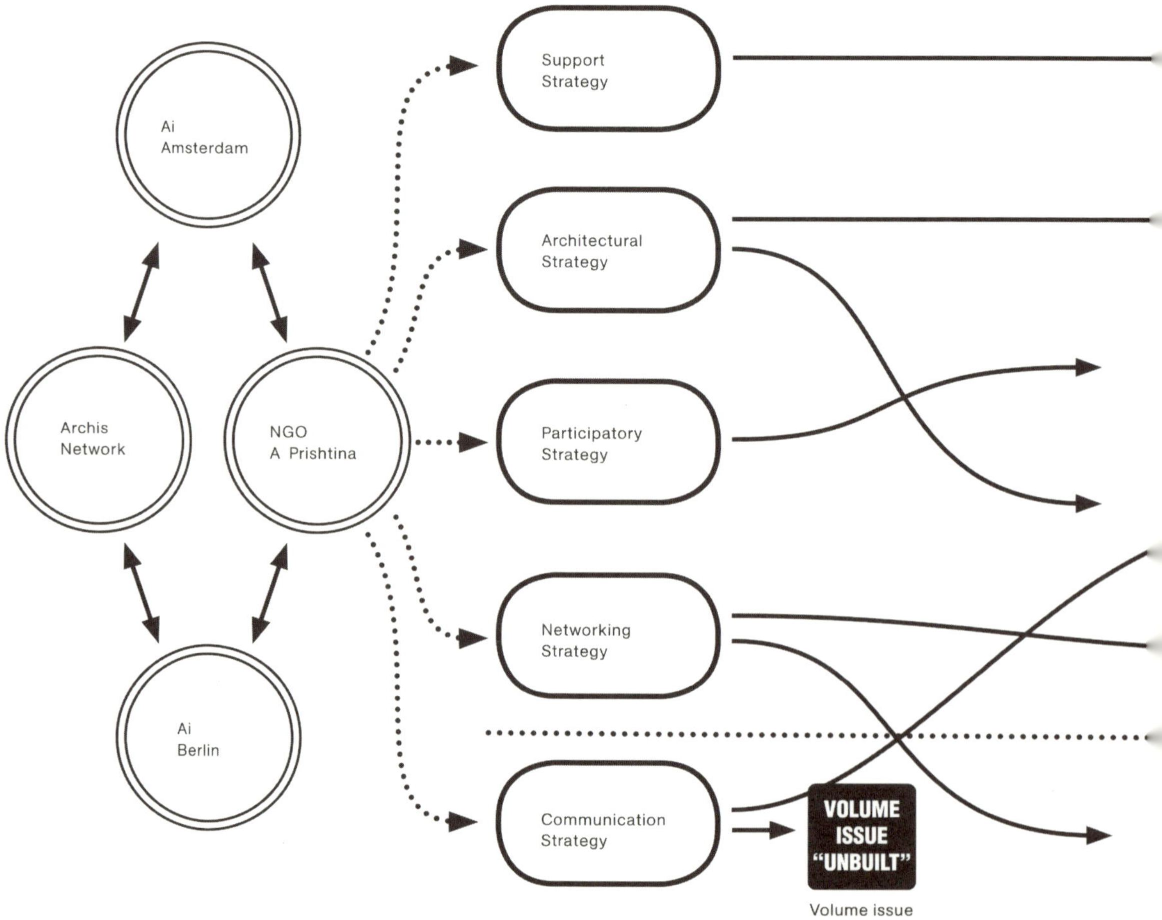

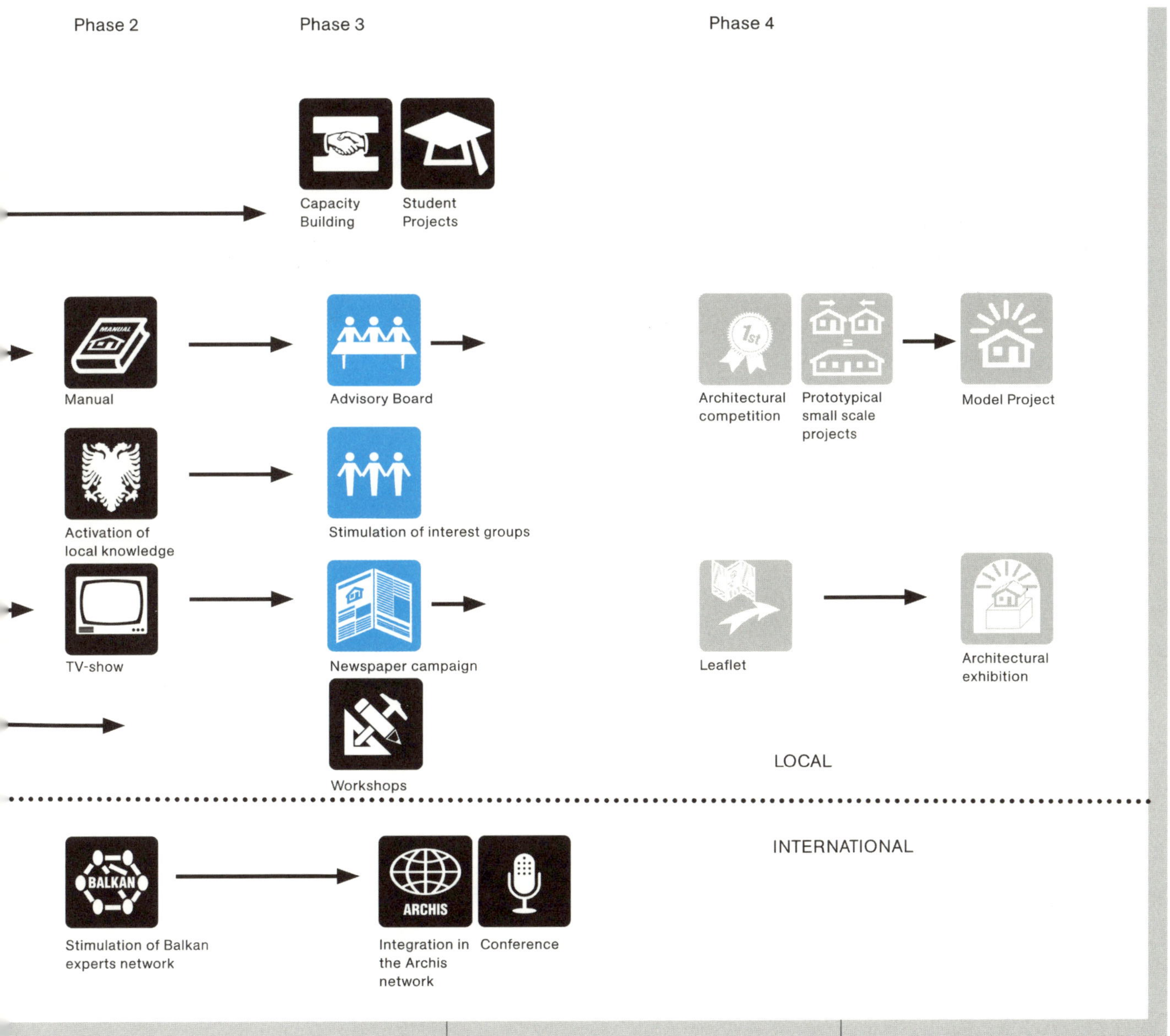
Phase 2
Phase 3
Phase 4
Capacity Building
Student Projects
Manual
Advisory Board
Architectural competition
Prototypical small scale projects
Model Project
Activation of local knowledge
Stimulation of interest groups
TV-show
Newspaper campaign
Leaflet
Architectural exhibition
Workshops
LOCAL
INTERNATIONAL
BALKAN
Stimulation of Balkan experts network
ARCHIS
Integration in the Archis network
Conference

Manual on the Legalization of Structures Built without a Construction Permit

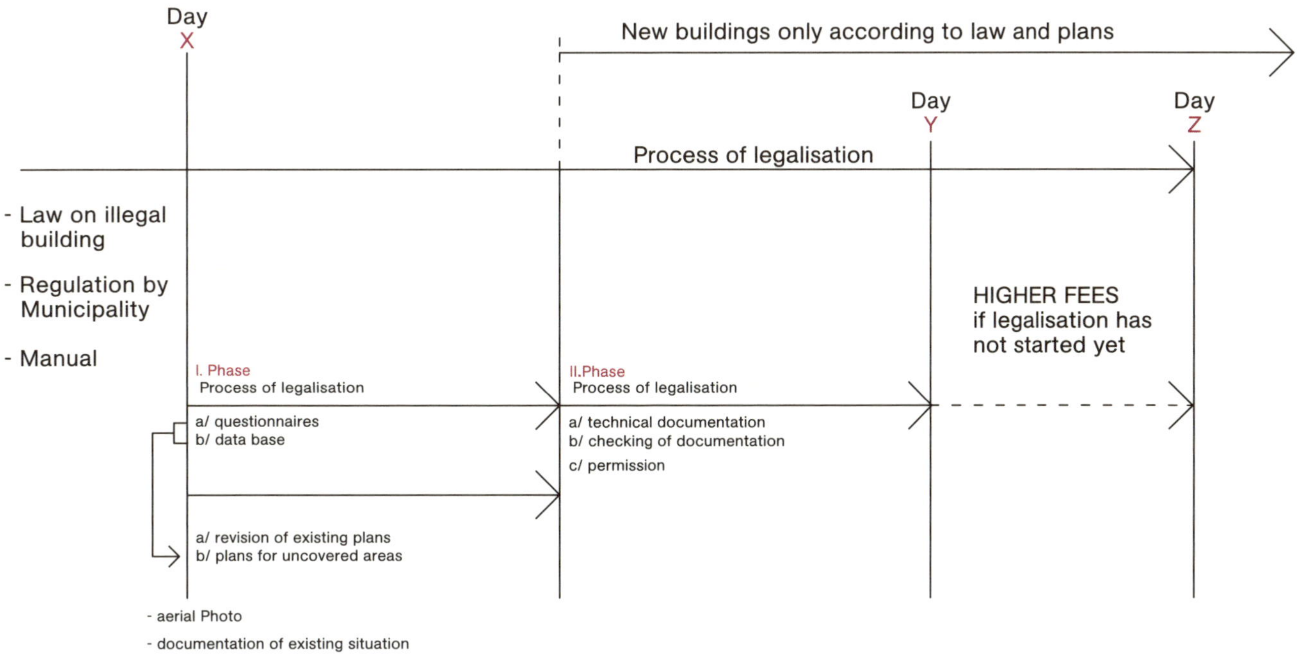

The concept for a manual and recommendations for the legalization process

The first step in developing an implementation strategy was a workshop in which experts were brought together to develop a manual that explains the principles (relating to security, infrastructural networks, social aspects, etc.) necessary to improve the present situation. The manual was conceived in cooperation with international and local experts, including representatives of the municipality, the Institute for Spatial Planning of Kosovo, and other official organizations. The workshop participants developed joint recommendations and strategies on how to act in the near future, and jointly formulated provisos for the manual. They consider this an important step toward bringing major policymakers into closer contact and cooperation, with regard to the legalization issue.

ESSENTIALS

- Legalization is a ONE TIME process
- Day "X" (the start of legalization) is announced 24HRS before
- After Day "X" a FUNCTIONING system for issuing planning permits must be in place
- Buildings constructed after Day "X" shall NOT BE LEGALIZED
- Day "Z" is THE END of the legalization process.
- After Day "Z" only URBAN PLANNING CRITERIA shall apply.

Public debate and resolution of the Prishtina City Council

A public debate on the regulation for legalization of structures built without a construction permit and the manual for legalization of structures built without a construction permit took place in Prishtina on July 2 and 3, 2009. On the basis of the strategic concept presented in the manual, the City Council passed a resolution to start the legalization process after the mayoral election, which took place at the end of 2009. The legalization process started in October 2010.

Download the "Manual on the Legalization of Structures Built without a Construction Permit" at: www.seenetwork.org

1.1. Security Aspect

A / Escape routes

Escape routes are an absolute necessity to rescue residents in the case of fire or other disasters. Escape routes have to be existing, marked and accessible (not blocked). In case of buildings with no direct access to the street, an escape route through the neighbors' lot has to be accessible, also for the purpose of intervention by the fire brigade.

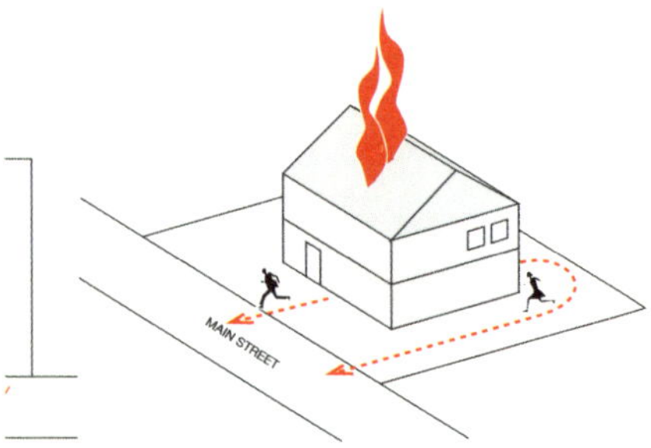

1.1. Security Aspect

A / Escape routes

Minimal Standard:

a) Each building should have direct access to a public road

b) In case of not having direct access to a public road, agreement of use of the right to passage with the neighbor should be reached.

c) if agreement is reached, passage for pedestrian should be minimum 1.0 meter wide and the length of the passage from the building to the main street should be not more than 100 meters

d) In order for the passage to have the character of the secondary street, it should be minimum 3.0 m wide for a one-way street, or minimum 5.5 m for a two-way street.

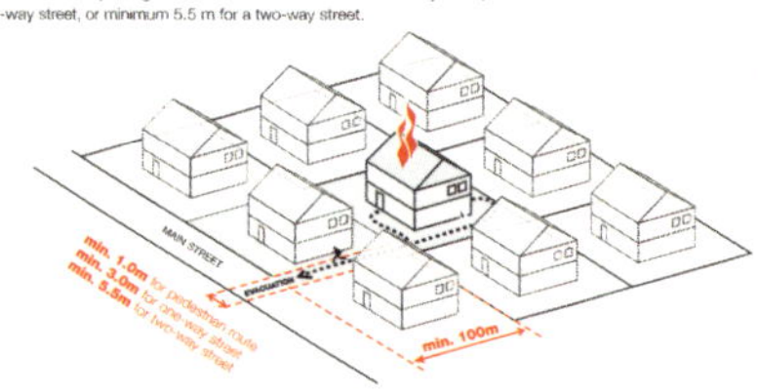

1.1. Security Aspect

B / Minimal distance - Fire protection

In case of fire, a minimal distance between buildings protects the neighbors building. (that is, if fire emerges in a building, it easily captures the neighboring building if minimal distance is not applied).

Minimal Standard:

a) if the building is on the plot line:
- windows, doors, balconies or other openings are not allowed in the bordering wall;
- the roof is not allowed to extend over the wall the roof should end with attic.

b) if the building is up to 1.0 meter distance from the neighboring building:
- windows are not allowed;
- balconies are not allowed;
- the roof is not allowed to extend over the plot line;
- fence or other blocking structure between two neighboring buildings is not allowed

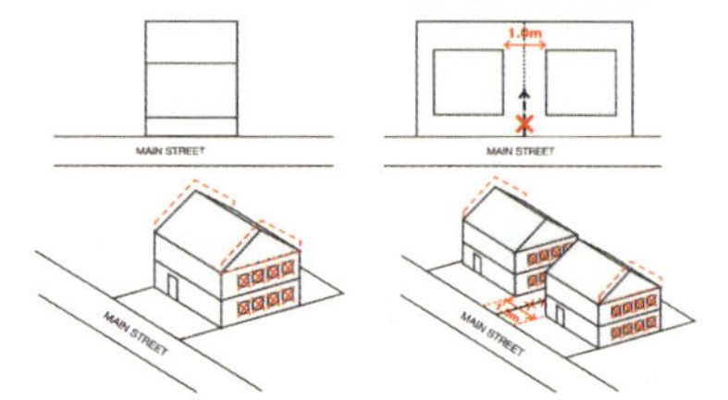

1.1. Security Aspect

B / Minimal distance - Fire protection

Minimal Standard:

c) if the building is from 1.0 - 3.0 meters from the plot line:
- only windows of bathrooms and staircases are allowed
- other windows may be allowed if there is an agreement from the neighbor stating that, in case of fire the responsibility for the damages caused to their buildings and other neighboring structures lies within the parties agreed.

d) if the building is more 3.0 meters from the plot line, the planning criteria are applied.

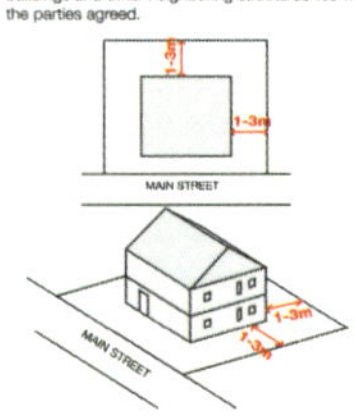

1.2. Social Aspect

A / Relation between neighbors

A1 / Blocking views (view, lighting)

A2 / Occupation of neighbor's plot

B / Relation between individual and the neighborhood

B1 / Occupation of public space

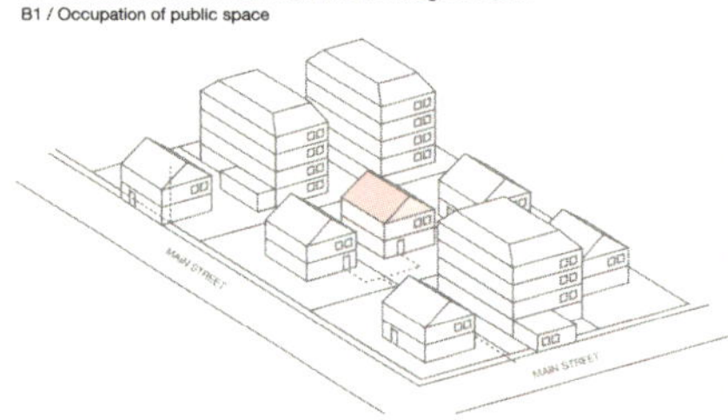

1.2. Social Aspect

A / Relation between neighbors

Conflicts between neighbor's results mostly out of the blocking of view (view, insulation) by building too narrow to the neighbor's building, or out of the occupation of a neighbor's plot. A negotiation between neighbors in case of such problems is also basis for the legalizations of a building.

A1 / Blocking views (view, lighting)

Minimal Standard:

a) The building should not block the primary view of other buildings. The neighbor whose primary view is blocked, has the right to complain against the applicants for legalization permit.

b) Blocking of the primary view is considered when:
- building with max 450 sqm applying for legalization is in a distance less than 3.0 meters from the plot line of the neighbor's parcel, who has a building with max 450 sqm);
- building with max 450 sqm applying for legalization is in a distance less than 5.5 meters from the bordering wall of the neighboring building with over 450 sqm which has openings other than windows of bathrooms and staircases;

c) In case of blocking, the building can be legalized if agreed by the neighbor whose front facade is blocked;

d) In case there is no agreement, the blocking building needs to be cut back to create the due distance.

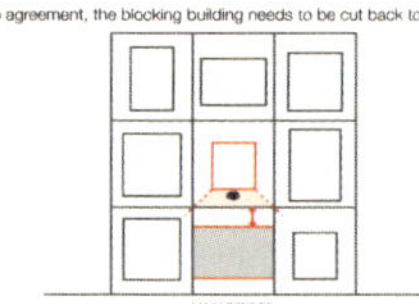

1.2. Social Aspect

B / Relation between individual and the neighborhood:

B1 / Occupation of public space

The occupation of public space (street side, green spaces, open spaces reserved for the recreation or other usages of the whole neighborhood and the whole community) raises in big problems for the whole city. These situations are unacceptable and buildings shall be demolished if built in special preserved zones such are:
- **protected areas,**
- **historic center,**
- **natural resources,**
- **areas, subject to urban planning implementation, especially of neighborhood's primary streets.**

In other cases, the Municipality may decide the form for legalization.

Minimal Standard:

a) building needs to be on its own plot.

b) in case the building occupies public ground, the building or a part of it, built on the public ground shall be demolished.

c) Municipality may decide that, for the building occupying public space in areas other than areas of special interest, there may be negotiated form of legalization (legalization for limited period of time and certain fee, or redevelopment according to the planning provisions.)

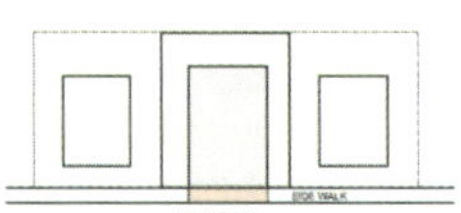

1.3. Infrastructure

With the legalization, the citizens have a right on the improvement or the installation of social infrastructure (public transport, schools, kindergartens) as technical infrastructure (street lighting, electricity, water supply, sewage). This is part of a process of negotiation between the Municipality and the neighborhood.

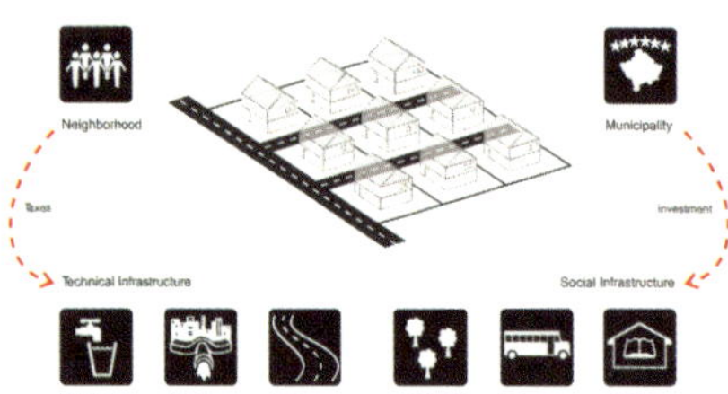

1.3. Infrastructure

A / Technical Infrastructure
(streets, water, sewage, etc.)

B / Social Infrastructure
(education and health facilities, open spaces,

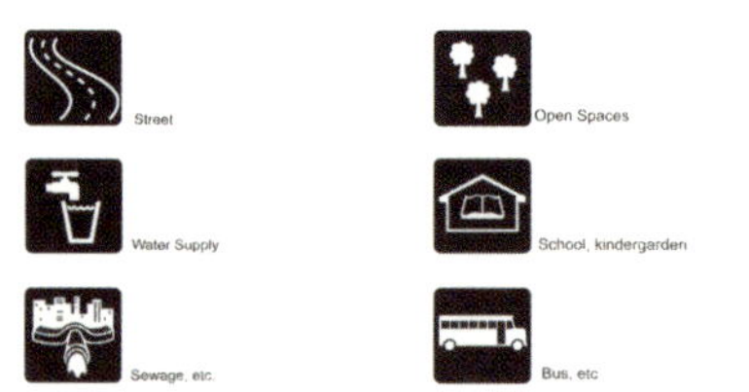

Recommendations:

a) Municipality shall update the inventory of actual existing situation

b) Municipality shall provide better services for legalized buildings

The Process of Legalization in Prishtina

March 2009:
Workshop to create a "Manual for Legalization of Structures Built without a Construction Permit"
Archis Interventions, in cooperation with the Municipality of Prishtina and Co-PLAN, Tirana

July 2009:
City Council resolution to start the process of legalization on the basis of the manual after the mayoral elections in late 2009

October 2010:
Announcement of legalization process. Every owner had four months to submit applications. Start of the legalization process

November 2010:
Workshop on evaluation of the legalization process
Archis Interventions, with the Municipality of Prishtina

June 2011:
Start of issuing legalization permits

October 2011:
Public debate on the topic of recurrent problems in the legalization process Archis Interventions, with architects from Prishtina and city representatives Workshop on concrete examples for providing different strategies for legalization

Achievements up to June 2012

Almost a year passed since the officials had begun reviewing applications for legalization of illegally constructed buildings in Prishtina. Up to now, out of 6158 applications received at the office for legalization at the department of urbanism, about 2500 cases have been reviewed. Out of these, 70 buildings have been legalized; another 250 applications are under review and could potentially be legalized once the technical documentation has been submitted by the applicants. The rest of the approximately 2180 applicants, who submitted incomplete applications or lacked valid documentation, have received guidance as to how to properly complete their applications.

Here, we can quote, for example, Hazir Zhitia, an official from the Sector for Legalization (Municipality of Prishtina): "Work on reviewing the applications is continuing based on the foreseen dynamics. This process is not simple, but is quite 'painful' and complex, because the burden falls on us to deal with objects constructed without criteria, in order to incorporate them as far as possible into urban areas; and those that do not meet the minimum requirements according to the manual's minimum technical conditions must be rejected. We appealed to all citizens who applied on time, and whose documentation is in order, and whose property is in their name, etc., to contact the Sector of Legalization, where they will be treated with priority; their documentation will be updated and the procedures concluded. We provided information and raised public awareness about this process four months before the process began. The procedure as a whole does not merely depend on us, the officials; it largely depends on many other factors, such as administrative and judicial procedures, etc., including the completion and delivery of main designs for the existing structure, along with expert opinions and analyses. All of these things are the responsibility of the applicants; here we add the refusal of applications for those who do not meet minimum technical and procedural requirements."

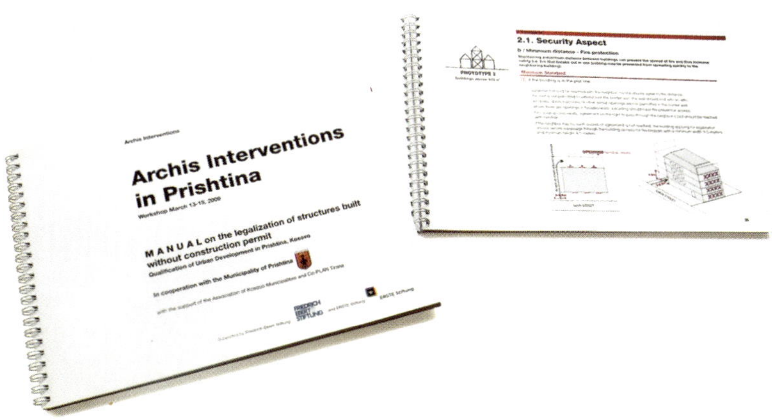

Television show

An eight-part TV series on informal building in Prishtina

A public campaign designed by Archis Interventions/Prishtina accompanied the process of regulating informal construction (including legalization of existing buildings), which started in October 2010. Public presentations and a media campaign are raising public awareness of the most important aspects of this issue (safety regulations, public infrastructure and amenities, impact on the community, etc.). Besides public presentations and reports in different media, an eight-part TV series has been produced in collaboration with Pixels Productions, Prishtina. Visar Geci, co-founder of Archis Interventions/Prishtina and a renowned TV star in Kosovo, produced the TV show in cooperation with Florina Jerliu and Kai Vöckler. Each of the series' eight episodes addresses a different aspect of informal building. Recorded on selected sites in Prishtina from August to December 2009, the TV series gave local citizens and officials a chance to express their opinions on the state of informal building in the city, in dialogue with Visar Geci. It was broadcast daily between July 9 and 16, 2011, by the cable channel KUJTESA. After each episode a guest panel discussed the problems and possible solutions with Visar Geci. A summary of the series was broadcast on July 16 by the KTV channel.

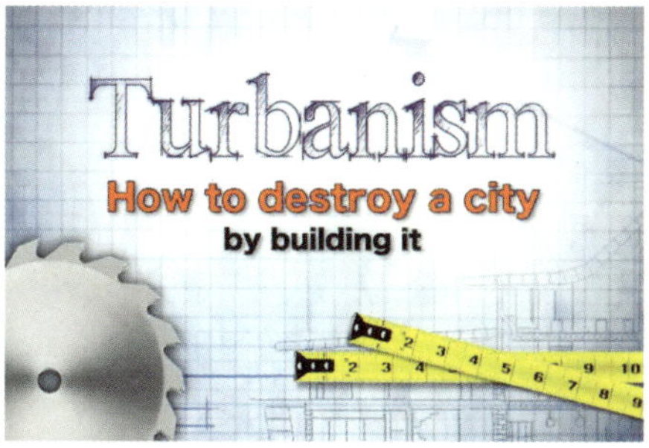

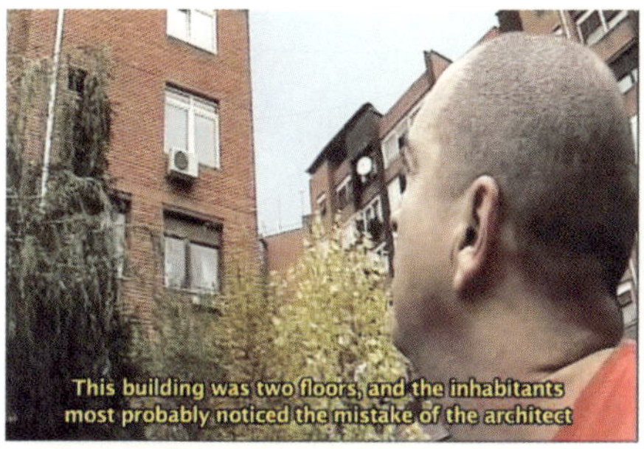

This building was two floors, and the inhabitants most probably noticed the mistake of the architect. . .

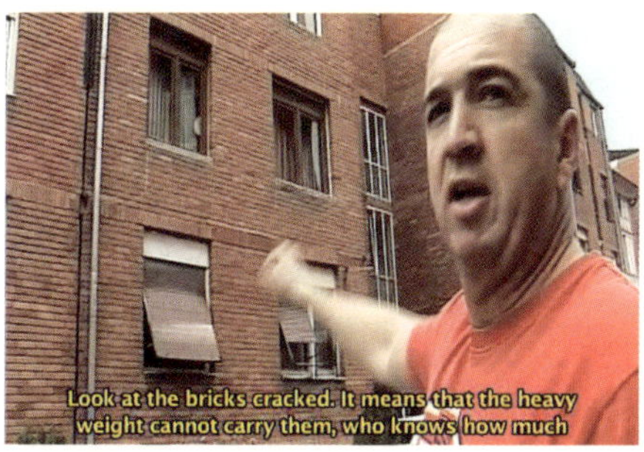

Look at the bricks cracked. It means that the heavy weight cannot carry them, who knows how much. . .

This way of living is like Russian roulette, I hope there is not going to be an earthquake. I don't think. . .

Have you ever thought where do you live? What are you doing? Why it is good or why is bad to live there?

. . . and added a couple of other parts.

. . . concrete the guy added there. Also look at the other side, the bricks cracked too because the building. . .

Ehhhh, we'll survive it because we're Albanians, we'll eat bread and peppers.

View of the university campus with media tower – Radio Kosova and the National Library

Mother Theresa Boulevard

Skanderbeg monument with a Kosovo government building on the right

Agim Ramadani Street with the Parliament of Kosovo on the left and the Bazaar Mosque on the right

"Dynamic City": An urban study

Prishtina's future prospects and how planning might best support them were the focus of an urban study developed in 2009. It is necessary to offer future prospects to citizens by developing a realistic strategy, which takes the current situation into account, but also establishes the principles of viable future development. This strategic plan is based on both a vision and reliable information, and can therefore offer a solid foundation for consensus and negotiations. The study develops a key concept, by analyzing Prishtina's potential as the capital of Kosovo, and identifying knowledge and education as the key factors for future development. The study focused on the latter's implications for urban space and formulated the major principles of future urban development.

Youth is the future

The young nation with its highly significant symbolic spaces and buildings in the inner city is the backbone of future development. Youth is the future: any investment made by the nation and the city in developing knowledge among its young citizens will be returned by the development of a knowledge-based economy.

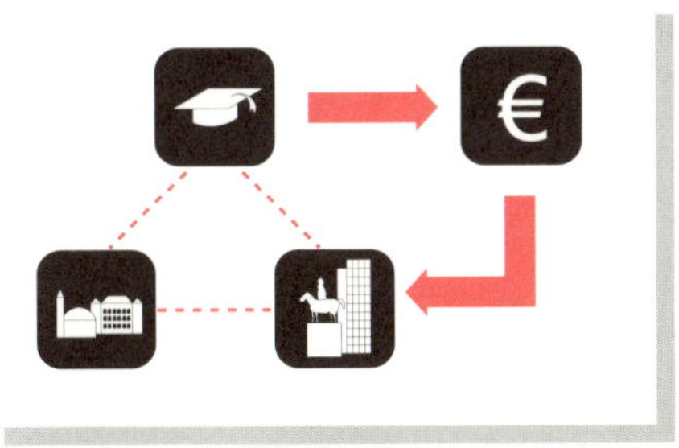

Catalysts

For students, lecturers, professors, and for future knowledge-based economies, a good environment and close spatial connections are necessary. They should be clustered and well-connected. For that, specific catalysts will be required in order to improve the situation.

Student Housing

There is a lack of a specific type of student housing. Investment in this type of housing, which would include public and commercial functions on the ground level, could be implemented strategically in the core zones of an education-related development.

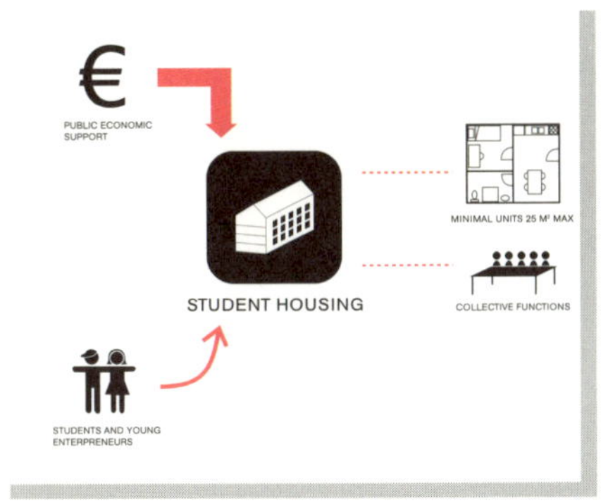

Business Incubator

The city can support new start up-enterprises in the knowledge economy with specific "space incubators," containing a concentration of office and information centers. Specific economic programs could support young entrepreneurs.

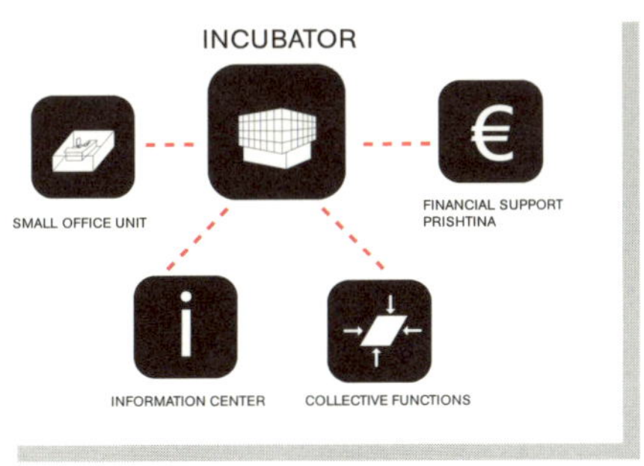

Public Community Center

Public community centers, either constructed in abandoned public buildings or else in new buildings, should combine different functions that will be attractive to students and other citizens interested in information and cultural activities

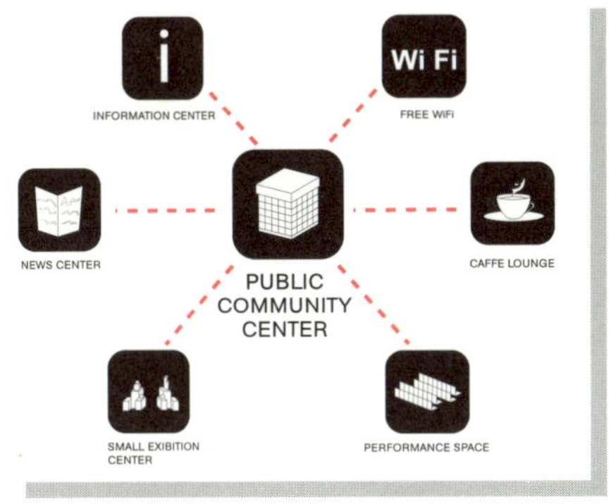

New attraction points

Introducing new types of buildings (incubators, public community centers, student housing) into the city center will strengthen the symbolic links between the nation and its history, economy, and youth. These new buildings should be erected mainly in abandoned areas, or should be accommodated in existing buildings suited to such types.

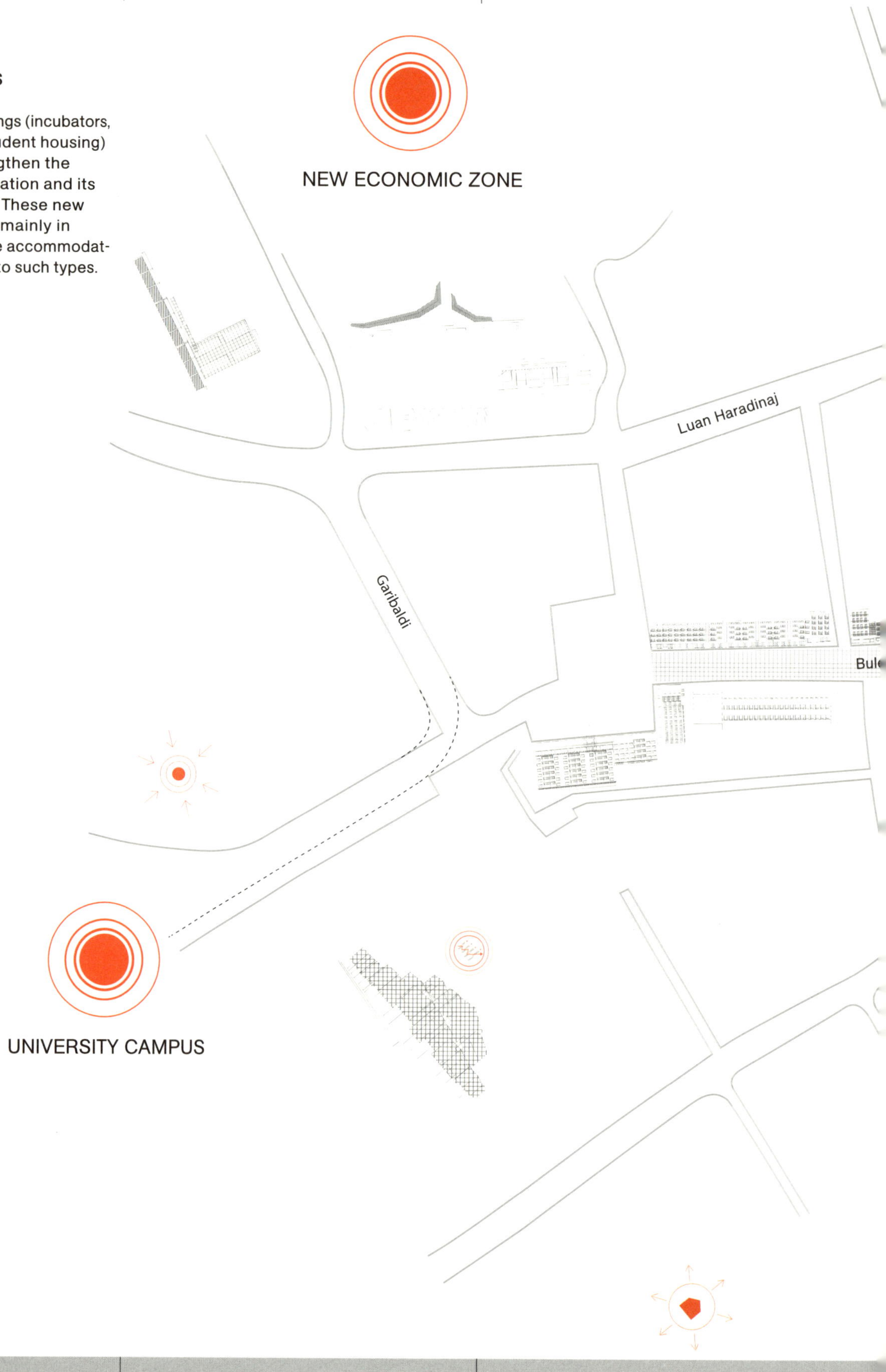

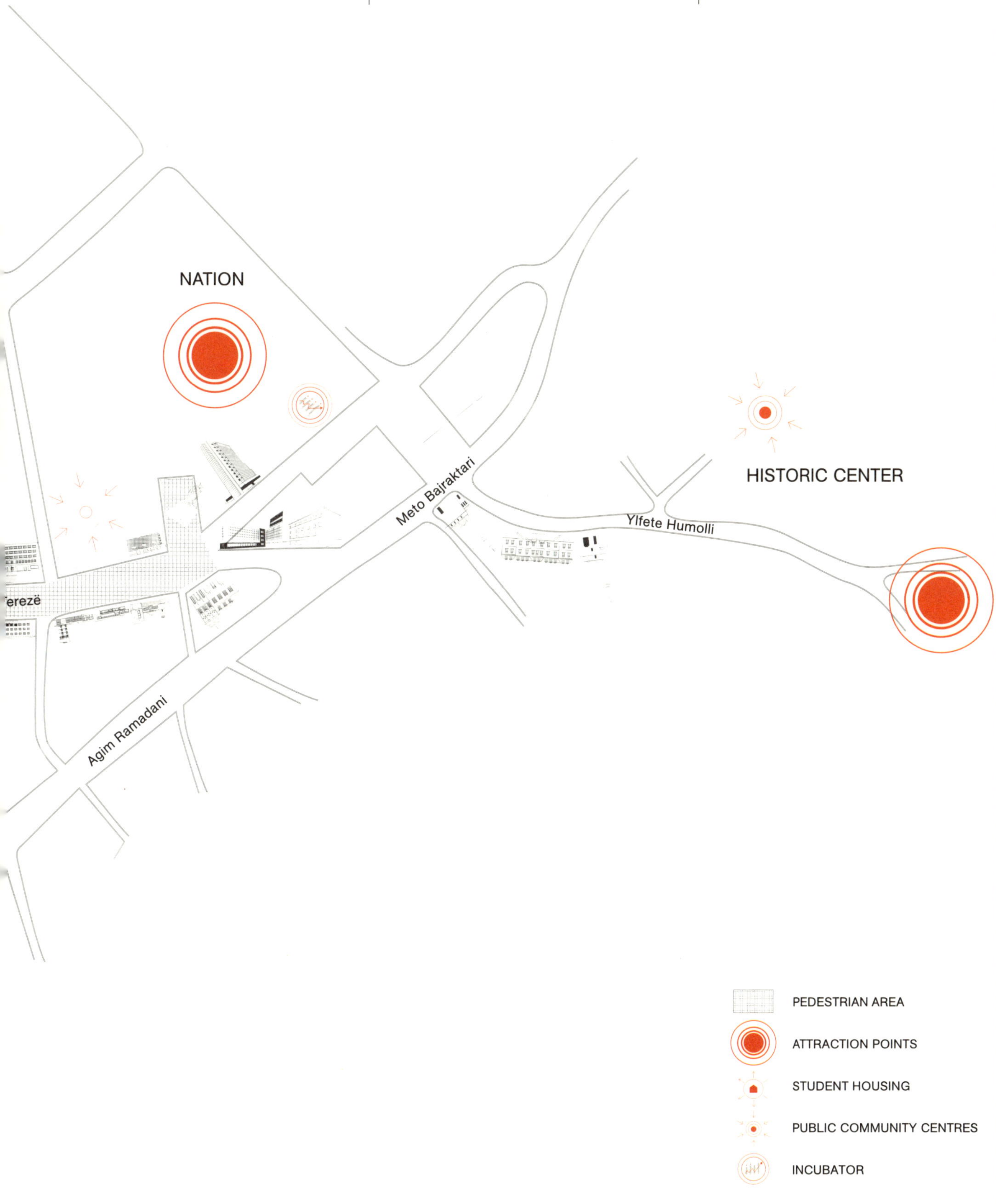
NATION
HISTORIC CENTER
Meto Bajraktari
Ylfete Humolli
Agim Ramadani
ereze
PEDESTRIAN AREA
ATTRACTION POINTS
STUDENT HOUSING
PUBLIC COMMUNITY CENTRES
INCUBATOR

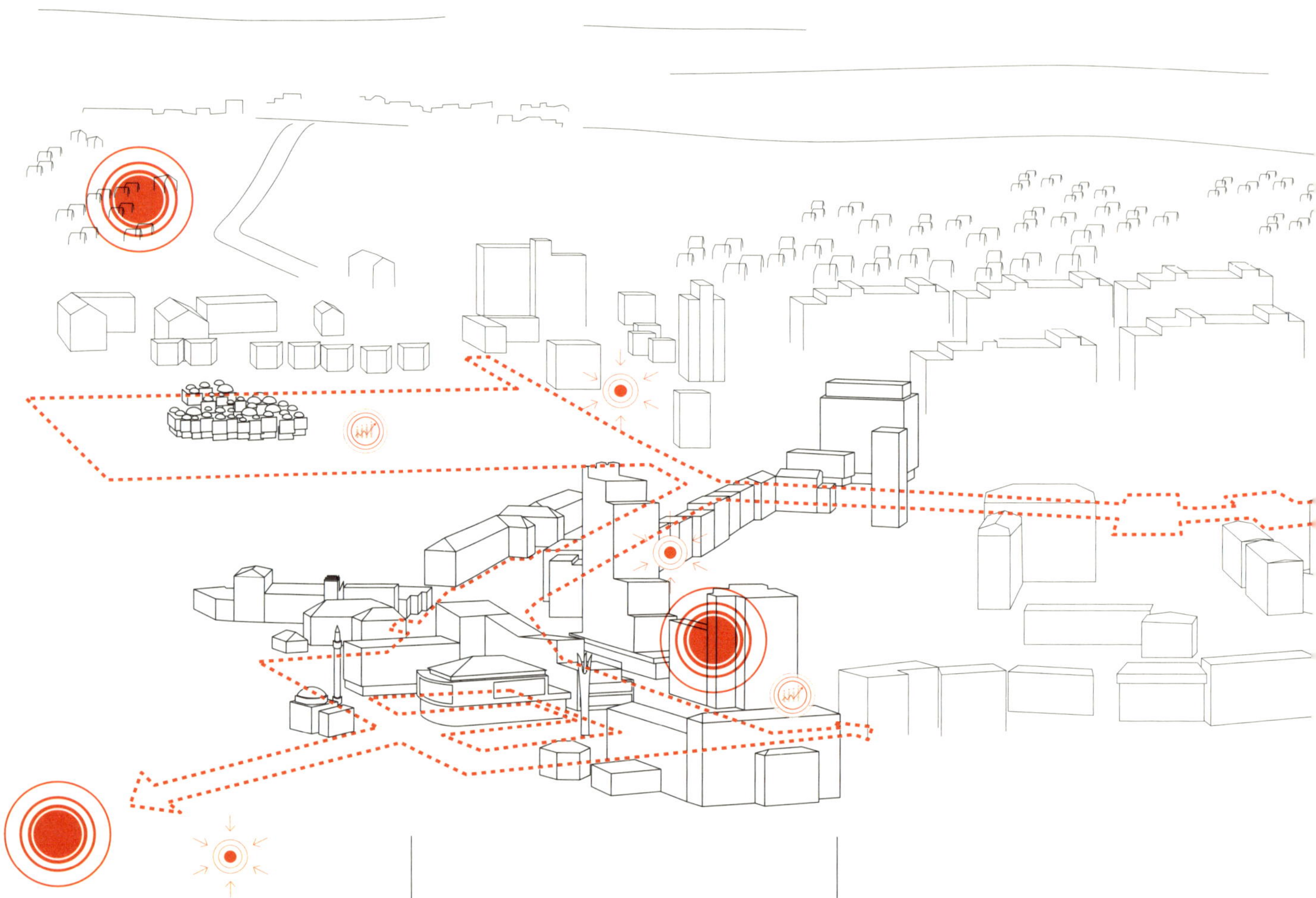

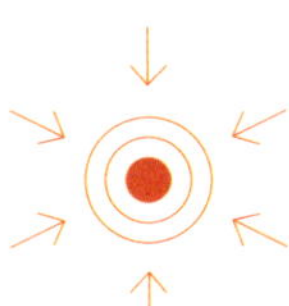

New community center behind the Skanderbeg monument

A public community center should combine different functions that are attractive to students, as well as other citizens interested in information and culture.

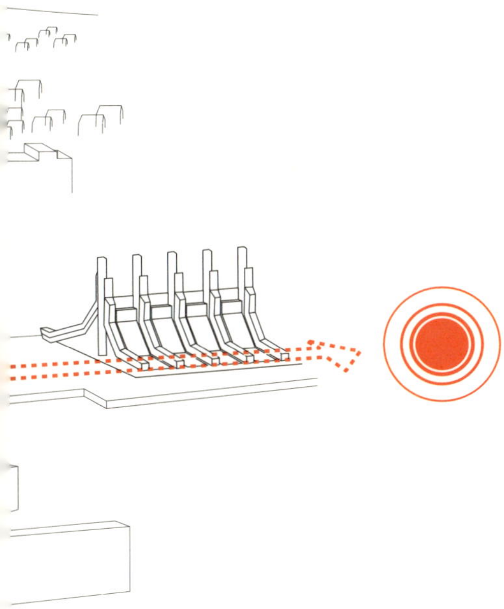

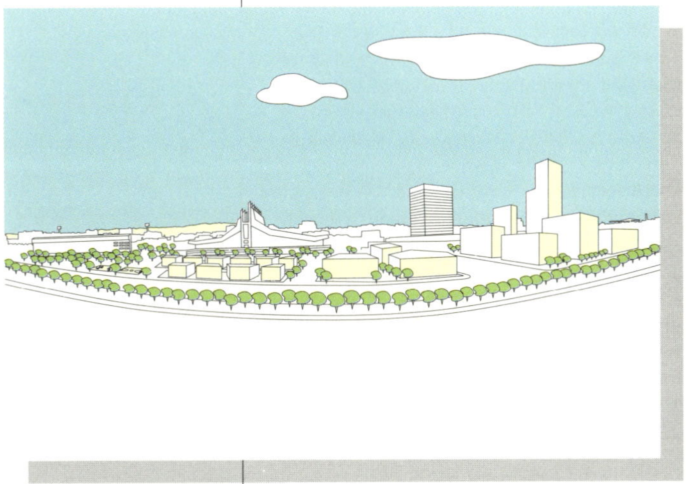

District behind Youth and Sport Center

New recreational opportunities can trigger small and mid-size business development. Space incubators are designed to attract young professionals, offering business space with low-cost overheads, bringing together different forms of new, knowledge-based businesses to form a creative atmosphere, and combining this with public functions to enable interaction with other citizens. Through this combination, incubators provide a lot of stimulus to urban development and become the nucleus of urban regeneration and future economic prosperity.

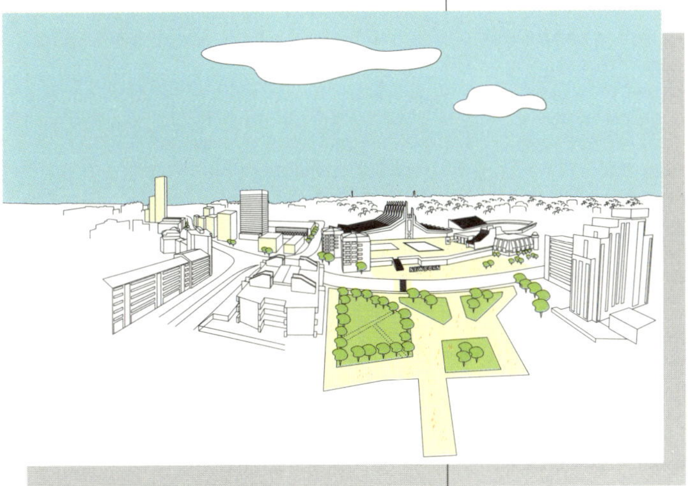

Remodeled public square and business district behind Youth and Sport Center

Remodeled public square and business district behind Youth and Sports Center. A remodeled public square can lead to urban regeneration and small and mid-size business development.

Divided Cities and Building Dialogue

Esra Can Akbil, Demet Mutman,
Giorgos Psaltis, Kai Völckler

When we talk about a city, we usually see it as a solid thing with an identity and unique qualities, the relatively unchanging "essence" of a city. This is inseparable from the specific histories of every city. A city's history can be read in the ways it has developed and been laid out over the years; it is present in its significant historical buildings. Churches, mosques, palaces, and city halls occupy a special position in the latter category. Yet cities change, and they contain strata of very diverse time periods. Thus, it is not clear which layer of time actually establishes the essential identity of a city, since identity is made up of very different layers of history, and hence, tends to remain diffuse. Also, the symbolism of architecture is not really as lasting as it seems: over the course of decades, the same buildings and structures are always re-evaluated according to changing standards. It is important to a city's history, and thus to the identity of an urban community, to have structures that always have to be renegotiated and redefined. The notion of an "unchanging identity" is a fiction, even if it is in the nature of urban identity to give the appearance of constant, eternal immutability.

However, it is not just the cities themselves that change; their populations do, too. There is immigration and emigration. Cities are also marked by ethnic conflicts and social tensions, by battles over space and its symbolic importance. This becomes particularly apparent in cities after a conflict or war. Cities that find themselves in a state of disarray after a conflict always have recurring, similar problems: populations are exchanged, because many residents flee during armed conflicts. For a variety of reasons, many never return to their home town. Some find better opportunities elsewhere, or else political conditions have altered so much at home that a return is not in their best interests. Often, the conflicts are not solved, but have simply become imbedded in the city spaces—the numerous divided cities, from Belfast to Nicosia, Mostar to Beirut, are evidence of this. In addition, migrants stream into cities. The result is that existing communities are dissolved and new ones are formed out of a hodge-podge of strangers who have not known each other previously, and who have little to do with the city and its history. And it is not only the reconstruction of a city, the rebuilding of ruins, which influences the city and its identity in post-conflict situations, but also, to a great extent, the erection of new urban structures. When it comes to rebuilding, international aid strategies usually tend to neglect the fact that it is the new buildings that create the framework for future development and help to shape the city's identity. This is where newly invented community centers begin to play a crucial role in a contested space.

Community Centers in Mostar, Mitrovica and Nicosia

Ethnic composition in 1998

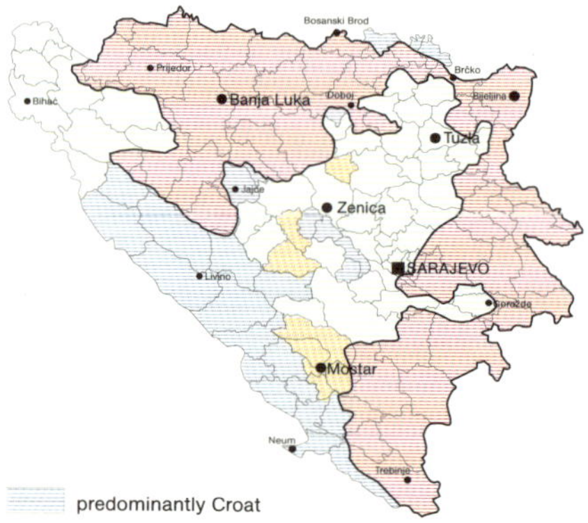

predominantly Croat
predominantly Bosniac
Bosniak-Croat mixed
predominantly Serb
IEBL

Federation of Bosnia-Herzegovina

Croat Canton
Bosniak Canton
Bosniak-Croat Canton
Federation
Republika Srpska
Number of the Canton
IEBL

1- Una Sana (Bosniak)
2- Posavina (Croat)
3- Tuzla Podrinje (Bosniak)
4- Zenica Doboj (Bosniak)
5- Bosna Podrinje (Bosniak)
6- Central Bosnia (Mixed)
7- Herzegovina Neretva (Mixed)
8- West Herzegovina (Croat)
9- Sarajevo (Bosniak)
10- Herceg Bosna (Croat)

Bosnia-Herzegovina: The ethnic composition after the war in 1998 and the Federation of Bosnia and Herzegovina (Source: Office of the High Representative http://www.ohr.int/ohr-info/maps, re-elaborated).

Mostar, Bosnia-Herzegovina

As an example of how problematic the concept of identity can be, we can look at the city of Mostar, in Bosnia-Herzegovina. To refresh our memories: when Yugoslavia disintegrated, armed conflicts began among different populations who were aiming to create ethnically homogenous nations—although the term "ethnic" itself is questionable. All of this occurred in Mostar. Slavs, who shared a common language and traditions, lived in Mostar. Only their religious practices were different, but that was not of great importance in a secular society. Additionally, there was a great deal of "mixing" among the different populations. In 1992 the city was occupied by the Serbian-controlled Yugoslav People's Army (JNA) and by the Bosnian-Serb paramilitary. Fighting bands of Bosnian-Croats and Bosniacs (also known as the Bosnian Muslims) opposed them successfully and eventually drove out the Serbian military, along with the Serbian population of Mostar. Then, in 1993, more armed conflict ensued, this time between the Bosnian-Croats and the Bosniacs, over who would rule the city; this was not ended until the United States' military intervention in 1994. The city was completely destroyed, and large portions of the population left the city. Of the original twenty thousand Bosnian Serbs, only a thousand still live in Mostar today. The city was and still is divided into two halves, with the Bosnian-Croats on one side and the Bosniacs on the other.

During the Balkan wars, both sides focused their military efforts on forcibly displacing the ethnic group each side defined as the "other." However, they also aimed to destroy their adversaries' sacred architecture, as well as the buildings that symbolize a multi-ethnic society, such as the library in Sarajevo. To be sure, after peace was concluded in Bosnia-Herzegovina, the sacred architecture was rebuilt, with the support of the international community, but this project also gave rise to the question of how it would be carried out—a question that was frequently politicized. In particular, the influence of the Arabian states on the design of the new mosques is highly controversial, as Azra Aksamija has shown in her discussion of the mosques in Bosnia-Herzegovina.[1]

Contrary to the goals of the international community, Mostar has not become a "multicultural" city again, but is virtually split into two halves: on one side, there are the Bosniacs (the Bosnian Muslims) and on the

1 See the article by Aksamija in this publication.

other side are the Bosnian-Croats, who are Roman Catholics. The Bosnian-Serbs, who are Orthodox, make up only a small portion of the population and therefore do not exercise significant political power in the city of Mostar. The international community's strategy is based on the notion that rebuilding the secular buildings and other edifices important to the city's history could restore the conditions that existed in the city before the war. Of course, reconstruction would be accompanied by the appropriate policies, which would supposedly create an overridingly "neutral" administration that would be able to guide the city's development. The hope of organizing the various interest groups, or stakeholders, into an equally balanced administrative group, which would then create a binding mission statement for the city's development, foundered on emotional barriers, which were still very strong. Even though a minority of the population was quite willing to overcome the division of the city, most inhabitants of Mostar were still influenced by the trauma they had undergone, such as forced displacement, murder of family members, rape, and loss of social status and property. The United Nations' multicultural, ideological aim of achieving mutual respect through the acceptance of (supposed) differences was not successful. For example, after the local elections in 2009, it took the two population groups eighteen months to agree upon a mayor.

The reconstruction of historically significant structures, such as the Stari Most, or Old Bridge—an outstanding piece of architecture from the Ottoman period—was supposed to link the present day to the city's multicultural past. This turned out to be a problematic strategy, since Bosnia-Herzegovina's checkered history led different groups to perceive the same edifices in different ways. The rebuilt, Ottoman-era section of the city, with the famous bridge, "belonged" to the Bosniac side. Also, the battle lines were not drawn along the Neretva River, as is often erroneously assumed, but along the boulevard further west—in no way did the bridge connect two adversarial parties. Internationally, the bridge in Mostar was frequently confused with the bridge across the Drina River in Višegrad, which was described by Ivo Andric, a winner of the Nobel Prize for Literature. But as a symbol, the bridge as such is practically predestined to represent international reconstruction policy, since the structure itself expresses the idea of unity.

However, the Bosnian-Croats perceived the Stari Most as part of Muslim heritage, not as part of their own history. Even the project of reconstructing secular buildings on their original sites, which were scattered across the whole city, did not result in the hoped-for tolerance. Thus, the section of the peace treaty that required the reconstruction of sacred edifices was interpreted quite arbitrarily. While most of the mosques—especially those in the Ottoman-era section of the city, which UNESCO declared a World Heritage Site—limited themselves to exact reconstruction, the Catholic church interpreted the reconstruction of the Franciscan church very freely by adding an oversized bell tower that would symbolically tower over the minarets. Furthermore, a cross over thirty meters high was erected in the year 2000 on the neighboring Hum Hill, which is visible from all directions of the city; it is clearly a strong attempt to stake a valid claim. Turkey, on the other hand, only signaled its role as a donor by flying the Turkish flag from the minaret of the Mehmed Pasha Mosque, while Saudi Arabia decided to have its name subtly woven in golden letters into the carpets laid out in the mosques it financed.

Even though the reconstruction of the Stari Most was effective on the international political level, as a symbol of reconciliation, international cooperation, and the coexistence of different cultural, ethnic, and religious communities, local conflicts on the east and west sides of the Neretva remained unaffected. The notion that a common identity for the city could be restored by reconstructing historically significant buildings (as is ordained for all post-conflict cities) turned out to be doubled-edged in Mostar. The new Stari Most belonged more to the international community than to the city it was meant to reunite. The idea of reconstructing the city to reflect pre-war conditions was already a questionable one, given the massive exchange of populations that had occurred. Surely, however, the economic impact should not be underestimated, since the rebuilt Stari Most also draws more tourists to Mostar. Still, as far as the reconstruction of the city is concerned, it would have made more sense to look for ways to develop the city that would not only benefit all of its inhabitants, but would also not have been burdened by history. For, as we can see from the example of Mostar, "identity" can be a controversial concept and should not be considered self-evident. In this context the question arose as to how Mostar residents could deal with the space in order to overcome the invisible division of their city. It would have to be a way of dealing with space that would appropriate urban space, yet avoid being assigned to one or the other conflicting party. And it would have to be a grass-roots concept, one developed by local people rather than one imposed from the top down by the international community and manifested in political procedures and administrative policy. This is why the OKC Abrašević is so important in its role as a youth cultural center in Mostar: as an open network of non-governmental organizations, informal groups, and individuals based in Mostar, it represents not only a part of the population that is more than willing to put an end to the division of the city, but it is also a space that doesn't "belong" to either side. It was opened in 2003, thanks to a network of local non-governmental youth associations, which were initially organized around the Mostar Intercultural Festival. With a program that includes concerts, theater performances, art exhibitions, workshops, movie screenings, its own radio station, and actions in the public space, Abrašević pursues a bottom-up strategy, which creates a new, physically embedded space for dialogue about the future of the city. The center plays a part in developing a sustainable civil society and it constitutes an open space for society in the city of Mostar.

Mitrovica, Kosovo

People around the world can well remember the time when NATO-led, international KFOR troops marched into Kosovo. Along with the troops, about 900,000 Kosovo-Albanian refugees, who had been driven out by the Serbian military and irregular militias, returned to their homeland. At the same time, immediately after the troops arrived, up to one hundred thousand Serbs left Kosovo. Some left due to acts of revenge taken by the Albanians, and some because they did not see a future for themselves in Kosovo. Although these numbers are disputed and can be astonishingly disparate, they are symptomatic for Kosovo's history of mutual oppression and persecution, which was essentially influenced by every change in the international political situation. In order to understand the situation in Kosovo (and hence in Mitrovica) after 1999, it is necessary to know something about the historical background that led two groups of people not just into a bitter clash

Serbian enclaves in Kosovo and Albanian population in neighboring countries (Source: Frankfurter Allgemeine Zeitung, re-elaborated).

marked by violence on both sides, but into a war over the region they shared in Southeastern Europe. Both Serbs and Albanians regard Kosovo as the birthplace of their national identity. Both sides base their claims on certain historical events and contexts. With the rise of nationalism in the nineteenth century, these events and contexts became elements of the nationalist myths of each group, which are used to claim the territory. For instance, Albanians trace their ancestry back to the Illyrians of old, who lived in the area now known as Kosovo. Even though the Albanian language is somewhat similar to the Illyrian, Albanians were first mentioned as a group in the twelfth century, and their exact place of origin remains disputed. Serbs, for their part, regard Kosovo as the true birthplace of the medieval Serbian state and deny that Albanian tribes were settled there at that time. Adding to the dispute is the fateful defeat of the Serbs in the battle against the Turks in 1389, which took place on the Kosovo Polje, or "Blackbird field," and left a profound mark on the collective memory of the Serbs. When the KFOR troops marched into Kosovo in 1999 to end the war that had been going on since 1997 between the Serbian military and the Kosovo-Albanian Liberation Army (UCK), the majority of the population, Kosovo-Albanians, welcomed them. Tens of thousands of Serbs, fearing retaliation, fled as the Yugoslavian troops withdrew. As it turned out, their fear was justified, since there were many attacks on Kosovo-Serbs, as well as on other minorities suspected of collaborating with the Serbs, mostly the Roma population. Also the riots in March 2004, where Albanian looters burnt down several hundred Serbian houses and some Orthodox monasteries, confirmed a negative view of future prospects. Over the ensuing years, most of the Kosovo-Serbs retreated to enclaves or left the country, since there were hardly any economic opportunities for them. Disregarding the ideas and intentions of the international community, the wheel of history turned in favor of Kosovo-Albanians.

In the north of Kosovo, directly on the border to Serbia, live 40,000 to 60,000 Kosovo-Serbs in an enclave that is formally part of the Republic of Kosovo, which declared its independence in February 2008. Kosovo's declaration of independence has not been recognized by Serbia, and it still treats Kosovo as part of its national territory, when in fact, control is in the hands of Kosovo-Albanians, except in the north of Kosovo. Here, the Serbian military had to leave the area, and it is still under the control of KFOR forces, but the Serbian state built its own governmental structures, intermixed with local organizations, to create a diffuse political space, which is partially controlled by the Serbian state, and completely out of the control of Kosovar authorities—as the riots in 2011 along the Serbian border demonstrated—while the new Kosovar state tried setting up a border control (the conflict was halted by the intervention of KFOR troops). Actually, this situation in North Kosovo produced a space free of law and order; it is now used in smuggling operations (a functioning, "multiethnic" cooperation between Kosovo-Albanian and Kosovo-Serbian criminals), and that provokes the question of who is actually interested enough to change the situation, since it is profitable for many locals. Interestingly, the situation is different in other parts of Kosovo. The Serbian enclaves in the south, more isolated than in the north, are accepting the opportunities offered them by the so-called Ahtisaari Plan in 2007 (named after the former Finnish president Martti Ahtisaari, who headed the negotiations between Serbia and Kosovo). While the plan was accepted by the government in Kosovo, but not by Serbia, it still gave the Serbian minorities a lot of rights, and the Kosovo-Serbs living in the southern enclaves are taking increasing advantage of them.

The city of Mitrovica is directly involved in the ongoing conflict, as it is divided into a northern section, located north of the Ibar River, where approximately 20,000 Kosovo-Serbs live, and a southern section that is home to about 60,000 Kosovo-Albanians. The two parts are connected by two bridges and a pedestrian walkway. Although in the Yugoslavian era, the population was mixed, it is now clearly separated. Even though a few people ignore the division and live in the "wrong" neighborhood the division is obvious. Besides the KFOR troops' control over the bridges, both Albanians and Serbs live inside a gated city. Trans-border commuters have developed daily routines, such as changing car plates or carrying multiple cell phones, as they go back and forth between the Serbian and Albanian parts of the city. Even though the city is controlled by KFOR troops, riots have occurred which has produced an atmosphere of uncertainty. And a buyout is going on: the Serbian Ministry for Kosovo is buying apartments and houses from Kosovo-Albanians living in the north, offering them a higher price than they could get on the market—which makes it very attractive for sellers in this precarious situation. Actually, this practice is mirrored, since Kosovo-Albanians are buying out Kosovo-Serbian houses in Serbian enclaves, such as Caglavica, near Prishtina, and also offering higher payments.

The situation in Mitrovica remains unclear, as it is a direct result of the larger conflict over the status of Kosovo. Even the Ahtisaari Plan had foreseen two local administrations in Mitrovica, which were supposed to be controlled by an internationally led committee (looking at Mostar, this does not sound very promising), yet the question of how to overcome the division of the city remains. The Center for Civil Society Development (CCSD) of North Mitrovica and the Community Building Mitrovica (CBM), from the south, joined together in 2009 to form the Mitrovica Forum out of politicians and civil society representatives, as elected members from the business, media, and youth sectors. So far, the intention of community-led projects has more to do with sponsoring dialogues between Kosovo Albanians and Kosovo Serbs, focusing on youth in order to encourage multi-cultural, anti-violent interactions, as well as a forum for a dialogue on policy development. In 2011 the Center for Resources, Youth and Media (CRYM) was developed as an umbrella organization for community groups in the city; it formed a youth center in North Mitrovica, where the younger generation performs, and recieves and gives training.

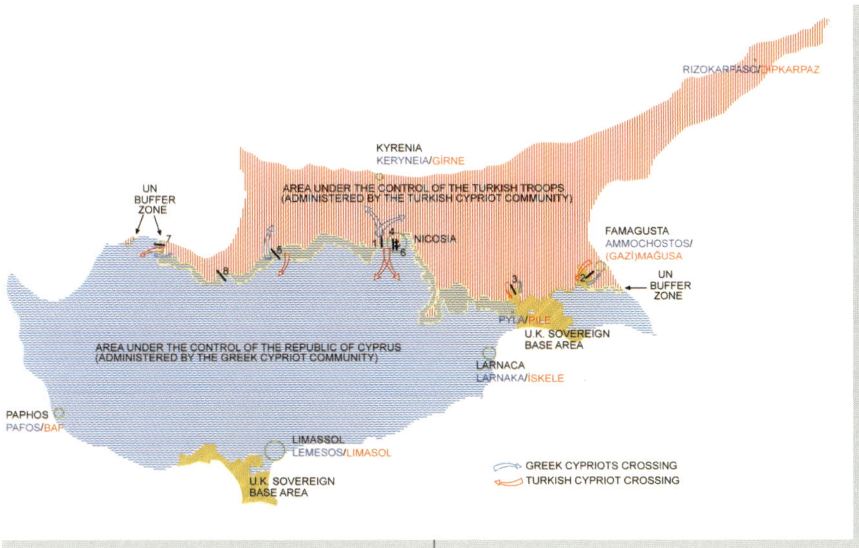

Current situation in Cyprus after the opening of several gates in 2003 (Source: http://www.cyprus-maps.com, re-elaborated).

The center aims to empower and activate Mitrovica's teens and young adults, while hosting a rock school, a radio station, a media center, and offices for other civil organizations, as well as a center for developing civil initiatives.

The Situation in Cyprus

Conflicts between the two main Cypriot communities - Turkish Cypriots and Greek Cypriots - date back to the 1950s, the last decade of the British rule,[1] when the terms "Turkish Cypriots" and "Greek Cypriots" were not yet well conceived, as ethnicity was determined by religious beliefs.

Located at a strategic point in the Middle East, Cyprus has been occupied by several major powers over time. The British colonial administration took de-facto control of the island in 1878 from the Ottomans and formally annexed the island in 1914.[2] At the beginning of the twentieth century Cyprus had already been declared a British Crown Colony, thus entering the wider political game involving the entire Balkan region and often being influenced by the spill-over effects from the on-going conflict between Greece and Turkey.[3] During British rule, the population of the island was composed of roughly seventy-eight percent Greeks, eighteen percent Turks, and four percent other ethnic and religious minorities (mainly Armenian, Roman Catholics, and Maronites). As Greece gained territories[4] from the declining Ottoman Empire and nationalism was on the rise, the desire for *Enosis* (union) with Greece soon spread throughout the Greek population of the island. During the 1930s, the desire for Enosis among the Greek population led to riots, which were suppressed by the colonial authorities, yet increased continuously, without taking into consideration the Turkish population of Cyprus. This resulted in a rising tension between the two main ethnic groups, which was in many ways enhanced by Britain and supported by the motherlands. The British rulers, as one of the main stakeholders in the region, controlled and manipulated the main ethnic groups by applying the well-known adage of "divide and conquer." In the early 1950s the Greek community started organizing in more concrete ways with the help of the Church,[5] which had always been a firm proponent of the idea of Enosis. Five years later, EOKA[6] was founded in order to carry out an anti-colonial struggle that would lead to the island's adhesion to Greece. Britain encouraged Turkey to interfere in the island[7] as a tactic to suppress the Greek riots, by creating a counter argument. In 1957, *Taksim* (division) became the aim of the Turkish population, which was supported by Turkey, with the final goal of dividing the island in two, and unifying the northern half of the island with Turkey, while the southern section would unite with Greece. TMT[8] founded in the same year, opposed EOKA and Enosis by promoting Taksim and defending the Turkish population's interests. The anti-colonial struggle of EOKA, lasting almost five years from 1955-1959, ended with the independence of the island and the birth of the Republic of Cyprus (RoC) in 1960 as a "compromise" solution between the actors involved.[9] According to the treaty guaranteeing the new constitution, Turkey, Greece, and Great Britain became the three guarantor forces behind the Republic of Cyprus. The complex and fragile constitution of the newly formed republic was soon to fail, also due to the persisting feeling of the Greek community that the new state of affairs was an unfair solution and left their aspirations as an unsettled issue. Three years later President Makarios proposed a set of constitutional amendments that resulted in the withdrawal of the Turkish community from the government. During the Christmas of 1963 inter-communal fights began between local, nationalistic paramilitary groups armed by the motherlands. In March 1964 the United Nations peace keeping forces arrived on the island in order to "prevent further fighting between the Greek Cypriot and Turkish Cypriot communities on the island and bring about a return to normal conditions."[10] Due to the inter-communal strife, a substantial percentage of the Turkish Cypriot community withdrew to numerous isolated enclaves within the island territory. Tension continued and inter-communal conflicts broke out again in 1967. In the same year, a military junta overthrew the legitimate government in Greece, paving the way for a consolidated involvement of the British and the Americans. Seven years later, on July 15, 1974, the Greek junta, together with local, nationalist Greek Cypriot groups,[11] organized a coup against President Makarios, who had given up the idea of Enosis several years prior. Five days later,

1 British colonial rule in Cyprus: 1878–1959.
2 See *Library of Congress Country Studies*, "Cyprus"
3 See Greco-Turkish Wars 1821–1922
4 See Treaty of Serves, Treaty of Lausanne, adhesion to Greece of Crete, 1913 and of the Dodecanese Islands, 1947.
5 Makarios, the first president of the Republic of Cyprus was Archbishop of Cyprus.
6 See EOKA, National Organization of Cypriot Fighters
7 With the Treaty of Lausanne in 1923, Turkey gave up all claims to the remainder of the Ottoman Empire including Cyprus.
8 See TMT, Turkish Resistance Organization
9 For more, see Zürich-London Agreement, Constitution of the Republic of Cyprus and attached treaties.
10 See http://www.unficyp.org
11 See EOKA B'

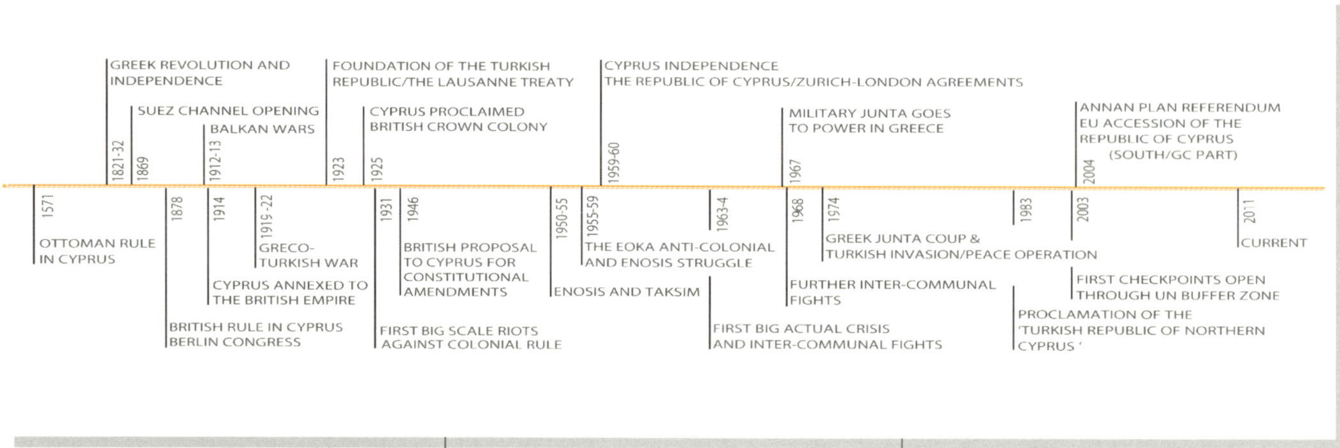

Timeline of the main historical events related to the Cyprus problem.

No contact was possible between the two communities until April 2003. In only a few places along the UNBZ could curiosity about what was behind the wall be satisfied. Nicosia Walled Town 2003.

Turkey reacted with military action[12] assuming effective control of the northern part of the island. Since then, Cyprus has been divided into two geographical areas, with thirty-six percent of the territory under the control of the Turkish army (north), while two hundred thousand refugees have fled, the Greek Cypriot refugees to the south and the Turkish Cypriot refugees to the north. To this day, the UN buffer zone, with its varying width, crosses the island from east to west, dividing the capital of the island, Nicosia, into two sectors.

Despite the creation of two mainly homogenous ethnic areas, some Greeks still live in the northern part of the island, in the Karpaz region. Rizokarpaso/Dipkarpaz and AyiaTriada/Sipahi are the two major villages. Similarly, over a thousand Turkish Cypriots reside in the south. Since 1975 Turkey has been continuously changing the demographic character of the island by transferring thousands of nationals from southeast and northern regions of Turkey, the majority of which settled in abandoned Greek houses after 1974, adding thus another parameter to be taken into consideration in case of a solution.

After 1974 a new page in the island's history began, with repeated negotiations on local and international levels and numerous UN resolutions, all aimed at finding a "fair and sustainable solution" to the saga of the Cyprus problem. In 1983 the north of Cyprus declared itself an independent state, the Turkish Republic of Northern Cyprus (TRNC), recognized only by Turkey, while the international community deplored this proclamation.[13]

Throughout these years, absolute division has eliminated all kinds of contact between the two communities, while national identity has been strengthened on both sides through political propaganda, demagogy, education, as well as—mainly in the south—religion. As a result, sentiments of suspicion and hatred between the two groups increased. Motivated by the chance of becoming EU citizens, Turkish Cypriots organized a series of demonstrations in the north in 2003. The demonstrations emphasized "Cypriot" identity and called for a reunification of the island, resulting in the opening of a number of entry points[14] across the divide and establishing contact between the inhabitants of the island again after almost thirty years. Even though reuniting occurred smoothly enough, nothing was the way it had been previously. A year later, in April 2004, the UN-sponsored Annan Plan for a comprehensive solution was proposed, in order to separate referenda. Sixty-five percent of the Turkish Cypriot community voted in favor, while seventy-six percent of the Greek Cypriot community, led by the President of the RoC (south), Tassos Papadopoulos †[15] rejected the plan. On May 1, 2004, the RoC became a member of the European Union, so that the EU constitution applies only to the south, while the Turkish Cypriots have the right to become EU citizens.[16] Since then, the Cyprus problem has entered a new turning point. After rejection of the Annan Plan, which was criticized for not being locally initiated mainly by the Greek Cypriots, the leaders of two communities have been firmly committed in repeated negotiation meetings to finding solution of the 'Cyprus Problem' under UN supervision.
During the course of time a few more crossing points opened across the divide. As contact increases slowly, more and more people

12 As one of the guarantors of RoC, in accordance with Article IV of the Treaty of Guarantee. Turkey's military operation in 1974 is extensively disputed as it is regarded as a 'Turkish invasion of the island' by the international community while it is known as the "Cyprus Peace Operation" in Turkey.

13 UN Security Council Resolutions 541 (1983) [available at: http://www.un.int/cyprus/scr541.htm] and 550 (1984)[available at: http://www.unhcr.org/refworld/country,"RESOLUTION, CYP,"3b00f15b24,0.html]

14 An ID card or passport is required to cross the border. Turkish nationals are not allowed to enter the RoC. See also: Green Line Regulation (http://eur-lex.europa.eu/LexUriServ/LexUriServ.do?uri=CONSLEG:2004R0866:20080627:EN:PDF).

15 Nationalist politician, strongly involved in the nationalist paramilitary activities of the 1960s.

16 Although the whole island is considered to have access to the EU, the application of EU law (*acquis communautaire)* has been suspended for the areas that are not under the effective control of the Cypriot government (http://ec.europa.eu/enlargement/turkish_cypriot_community/index_en.htm).

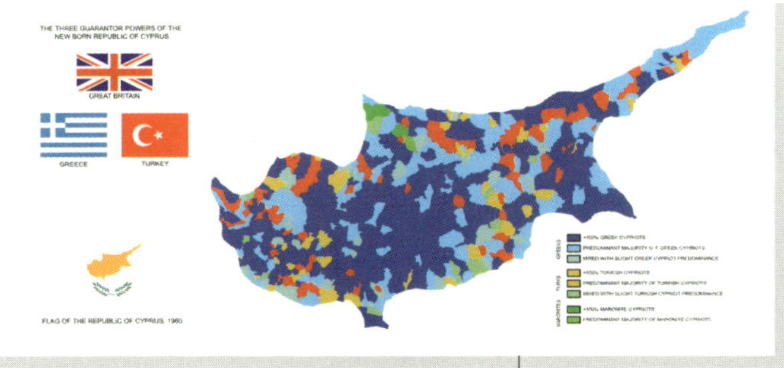

Ethnographic distribution at the birth of the Republic of Cyprus, 1960 (Source: http://en.wikipedia.org/wiki/File: Ethnographic-1.jpg, Author: Alexander-Michael Hadjilyra, re-elaborated).

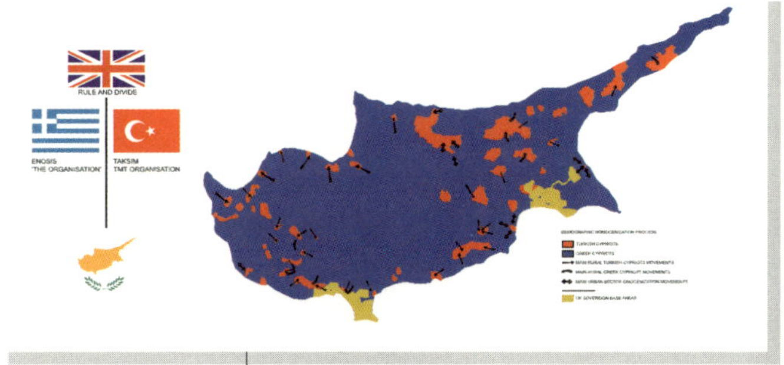

Main ethnographic changes after the 1963-64 conflict, creation of Turkish Cypriot enclaves (Source: http://www.kypros-cyprus.com/maps/ethnic_1973.jpg, re-elaborated).

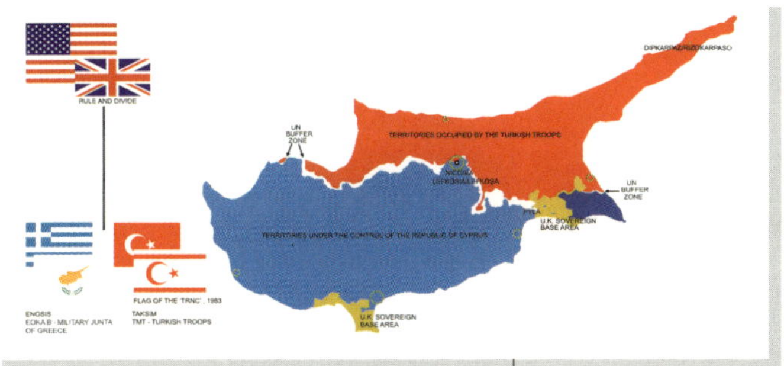

Strengthening of the division, 1974 (Source: http://www.cyprus-maps.com, re-elaborated).

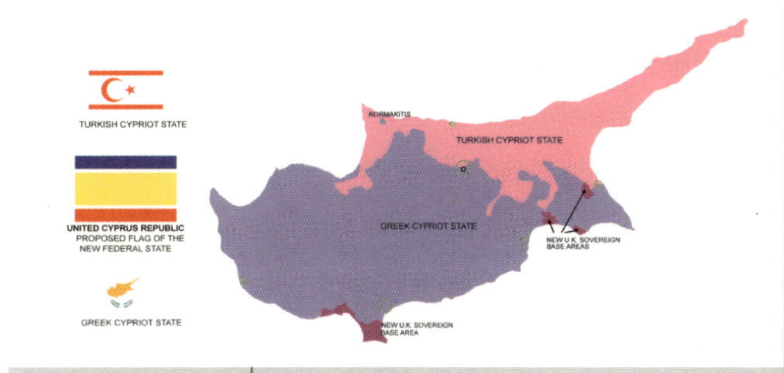

Territorial adjustments of the Annan Plan, 2004 (Source: The Annan Plan for Cyprus, Annex 1, Attachment 2a, re-elaborated).

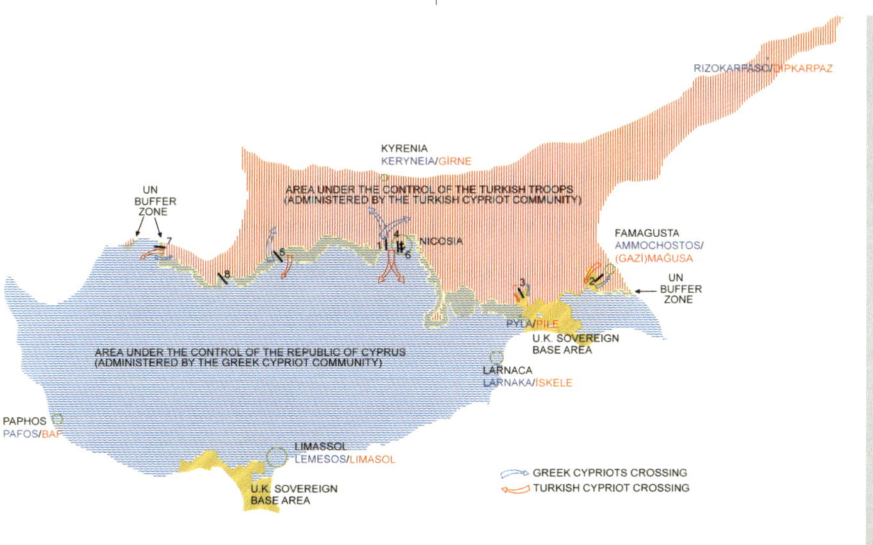

Current situation in the divided core of Nicosia and its walled part: buffer zone and accessing gates (1. Ledra Palace opened in 2003, 2. Ledra/Lokmaci opened in 2008) (Source: G. Psaltis graduate thesis: "Nicosia's No-man's land: Rehabilitating Traces of Laceration"; contribution to map completed by F. Gatta, 2005, re-elaborated).

in the two communities seem to realize the true nature of the problem and oppose the propaganda they have been loaded with in order to prevent what is perceived by many people on both sides to be worse: the permanence of the division. On the other hand, on a political level, harsh negotiations do not give hope towards a union in a new federal state[17] as in a considerable part of the G/Cs the feeling of an 'unfair solution' is still diffused while Turkey does not seem ready to abandon its interest in the island.

Nicosia, Cyprus

Nicosia[18], the capital city, with an old town defined by fortifications built during the Venetian era, is situated in the center of the island and has been divided by the UN buffer zone (UNBZ) since 1964, when UN peacekeeping forces arrived in Cyprus. A previous form of the UNBZ, the UN Green Line,[19] was drawn on the map defining the partition, which follows the abandoned bed of the Pedieos River which used to cross the old town, until it was covered over by the colonial authorities. Initially, the various ethnic groups of Nicosia all lived in the walled part of the town, gathered around their religious centers. Greeks and Turks lived scattered within the walls, but a prevalent presence of Turks in the north sector and of Greeks in the south sector was obvious. During the troubled 1950s the feeling of fear and uncertainty drove the inhabitants of the town to move closer together, forming a more compact ethnic nucleus. Another step that strengthened division occurred in 1958, when the abandoned riverbed, which was an important urban axis, became the border of the newly formed Nicosia Turkish Municipality, recognized by colonial legislation.

In 1964 the buffer zone became the UN Green Line and in 1974 it was expanded to the south, forming the present-day UNBZ. Throughout the years, the town has seen its structure develop, as its urban fabric has changed. Due to the consequences of the division, development moved north-south, replacing the original east-west expansion and demographic changes on the island. The tension between the two communities and the military presence along the "boundary" has led to socio-economic decline and the deterioration of the adjacent urban fabric.

The first collaboration between the two municipalities was established at the end of the 1970s, in an attempt to create a common sewer system. In 1978 a bi-communal committee, comprising representatives from the two communities, was established for the creation of a common sewer system. Even though the project started "underground," a year later, it came to the surface, expanding collaboration to the physical development of the town and the establishment of the NMP. In the beginning of the 1980s, the team focused specifically on the town's sprawl, and, in a second phase, on the cultural and socio-economic aspects of the divided and neglected walled section of town. The funds— mainly from the UNDP Bi-Communal Development Program/ UNOPS, but also from USAID (through the UNDP, the predecessor to Action for Cooperation and Trust, ACT), and the EU—are equally distributed to similar projects on both sides. The NMP has been a unique example of productive co-operation for over thirty years. Its continuous efforts to reverse the socio-economic decline of the walled town through restoration projects put an end to the physical decay of the buffer zone that divides Nicosia to this day and built up bridges. For this, the NMP received the Aga Khan Architectural Award in 2007. Despite its remarkable results and its thirty-three years of existence, the NMP has not evolved into an exportable model able to

17 The first agreement on a federation was signed back in 1977.

18 Lefkosia in Greek, Lefkoşa in Turkish.

19 See UN Buffer Zone, UN Green Line Cyprus.

Socio-economic decline of areas adjacent to the UNBZ, Nicosia Walled Town 2004.

Restoration of the central square in the Samanbahçe quarter (north Nicosia twin project), 2006.

Old wood craft workshops restored in the Phaneromeni quarter (south Nicosia twin project), 2006.

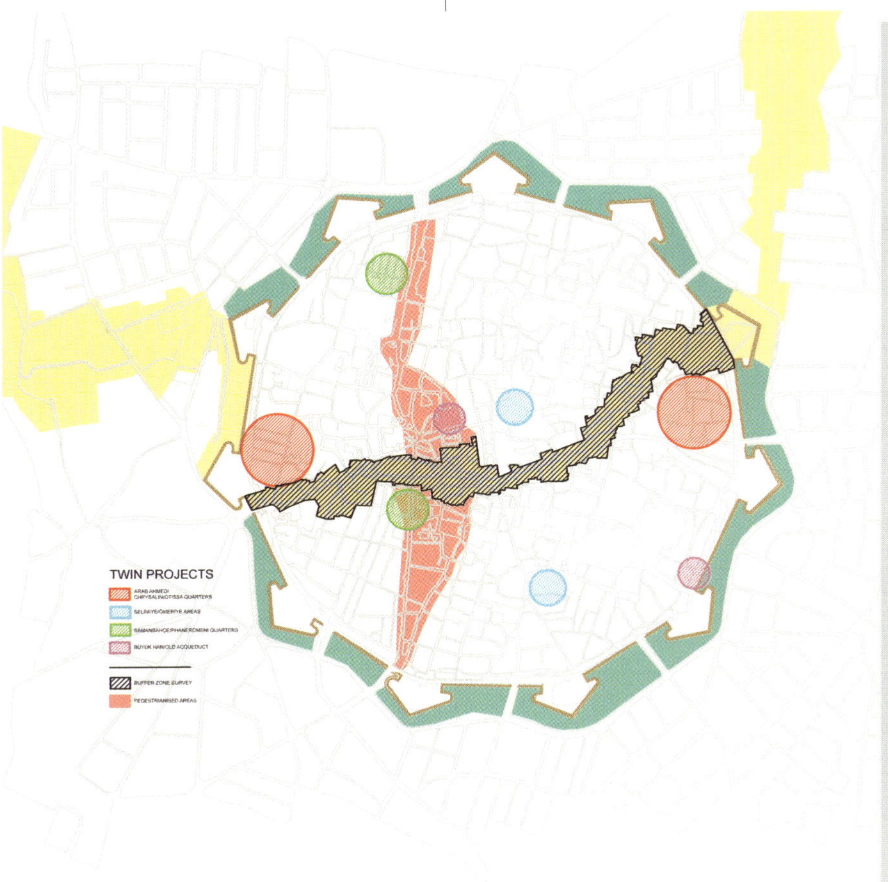

Nicosia Master Plan: Old Nicosia Rehabilitation Program, Bi-communal Priority Investment Projects (Source: Nicosia Master Plan, 2010, re-elaborated).

promote concrete common development elsewhere on the island.

In 2003 one of the first crossing points through the UNBZ was opened in the Ledra Palace area (only for pedestrians), just outside the walls. A second crossing point (for vehicles) followed soon, at Ayios Dometios/Metehan. Another pedestrian crossing point opened in 2008 on Ledra Street/Lokmaci.

Even though Nicosia is still divided, the opening of the crossing points provided an opportunity for the developing civil society to spring into action. A series of projects aiming to overcome the division have been seeking to implement bottom-up strategies, in order to spread a new message of possible co-operation and co-existence. The Association of Historical Dialogue and Research (AHDR), a multi-communal, non-governmental organization—which was set up in 2003 when the crossing points started to open one by one—initiated the project *Revitalizing the Dead Zone: An Educational Center and Home for Cooperation* in 2006, with the aim of creating a meeting point for communication and collaboration in the UNBZ. Located on the street where the first crossing points opened on either side, and positioned opposite the historical Ledra Palace Hotel—which accommodates UN forces and has become a symbolic building where community representatives and civil groups meet—this abandoned post-World War II building has been restored and transformed into a place that has not only become a center for dialogue, but also has a civil touch, being a resource for, and a representative of, a social community in this symbolic location.

The Home for Cooperation, completed in April 2011, is so far the only example of how the Cypriot civil society can overcome financial, legal, and mainly political obstacles; it also shows that it is possible to share a common building, a common space, and a common country.

What can we learn? Being in dialogue

If we look to the three examples, it becomes obvious that the "installation" of a space for communication plays a fundamental role in enhancing the dialectic medium that in fact provides the basis for a dialogue. In this

Bringing down walls and restoring contact through building rehabilitation process (October 2006, October 2011)

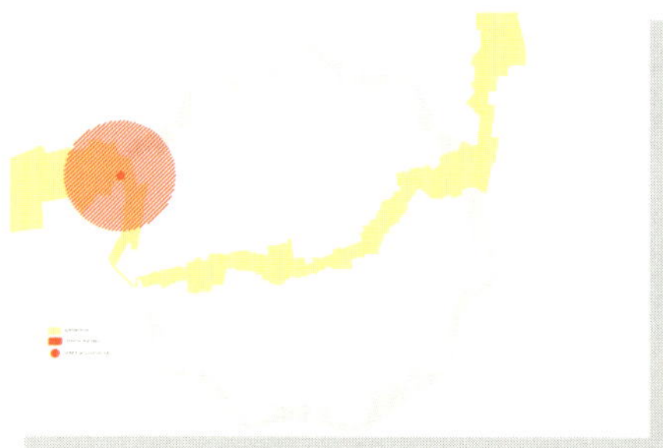

Home for Cooperation and the Ledra Palace area in relation to Old Nicosia and the UNBZ.

Home for Cooperation in relation to its surroundings.

sense, a dialogue needs to be set up and it needs a framework wherein it can happen; this framework should find a way to exist within the coded layers of the contested spaces. The placement of a building for dialogue becomes a sensitive issue, since the location and the building itself should be free of connotations belonging to one or the other side. So it should stay as neutral as possible, and not be categorized within the collective memory gathered throughout the island's history.

International organizations such as the UN can provide this kind of space for talks and meetings, as the organization itself tries to be "neutral" in a conflict (although it is not always seen this way; the role of the UN is highly disputed). But this approach—that an international organization functions as an umbrella to create a neutral space—has its limits, even if it can enable successful projects such as the Nicosia Master Plan. The project, which implies close co-operation between the two sides of Nicosia, was initiated by representatives of Turkish Cypriot and Greek Cypriot communities in the city in 1979. It operates under the umbrella of the United Nations Development Program (UNDP), which still supports the NMP projects. Quotations from the two mayors representing the two communities give clues about their motivations during the period in which the Nicosia Master Plan was initiated:

"We are not going to solve the Cyprus problem, but we are building bridges. They are always useful. I wish more were being built by others."[20]
Lellos Demetriades, representative of the Greek Cypriot Community of Nicosia

20 Lellos Demetriades, representative of the Greek Cypriot Community of Nicosia and former Mayor of South Nicosia. In: *UNHCR. The Nicosia Sewerage Project: A Plan for Nicosia. A Strategy for the World*, 1996.

Ceremony for the opening of Ledra Street/Lokmaci checkpoint, the main commercial axis of Old Nicosia, April 2008.

"We know certain parts of the Master Plan can only be realized when an overall solution to the Cyprus problem is achieved. But for a realistic, viable, and lasting solution, it is necessary to establish areas of co-operation between the two sides. The Nicosia Master Plan is one of the very rare instances of such co-operation. It is for this reason that we look forward to the implementation stage of this unique exercise. Let us begin. . . Who knows? The beginning may prove to take us halfway along the path."[21]
Mustafa Akinci, representative of the Turkish Cypriot Community of Nicosia

This is an example of a typical, top-down approach toward bringing two communities together. And very often it fails, as the example of UN-Habitat in Mostar shows. UN Habitat tried to instill the notion of building institutions from the bottom up as an example of good governance, by establishing participatory planning at different levels to develop a master plan for the city. In the cases of Mostar, Mitrovica and Nicosia exemplified here, the bodies that come up with the idea of building a communication space or transforming an existing building and its collective memories into a neutral zone for communications are not governments, but local organizations. Activities initiated by local civil society organizations gain great importance, since they are rooted in local society and have the capacity to start a dialogue by realizing a project. Developing community centers as meeting points and spaces for communication seems to be a very important way to begin overcoming the division. But as the examples show, this is not enough. Strategies should be developed in order to turn communications sites into more than just meeting places, by creating activities that, in the long run, have the potential to become part of everyday life in the entire city—activities which are themselves creating a new experience of space.

21 Mustafa Akinci, representative of the Turkish Cypriot Community of Nicosia and former Mayor of North Nicosia. (UNHCR, 1996) In: *UNHCR. The Nicosia Sewerage Project: A Plan for Nicosia. A Strategy for the World,* 1996

Divided Cities – Mapping Cultural and Educational Institutions

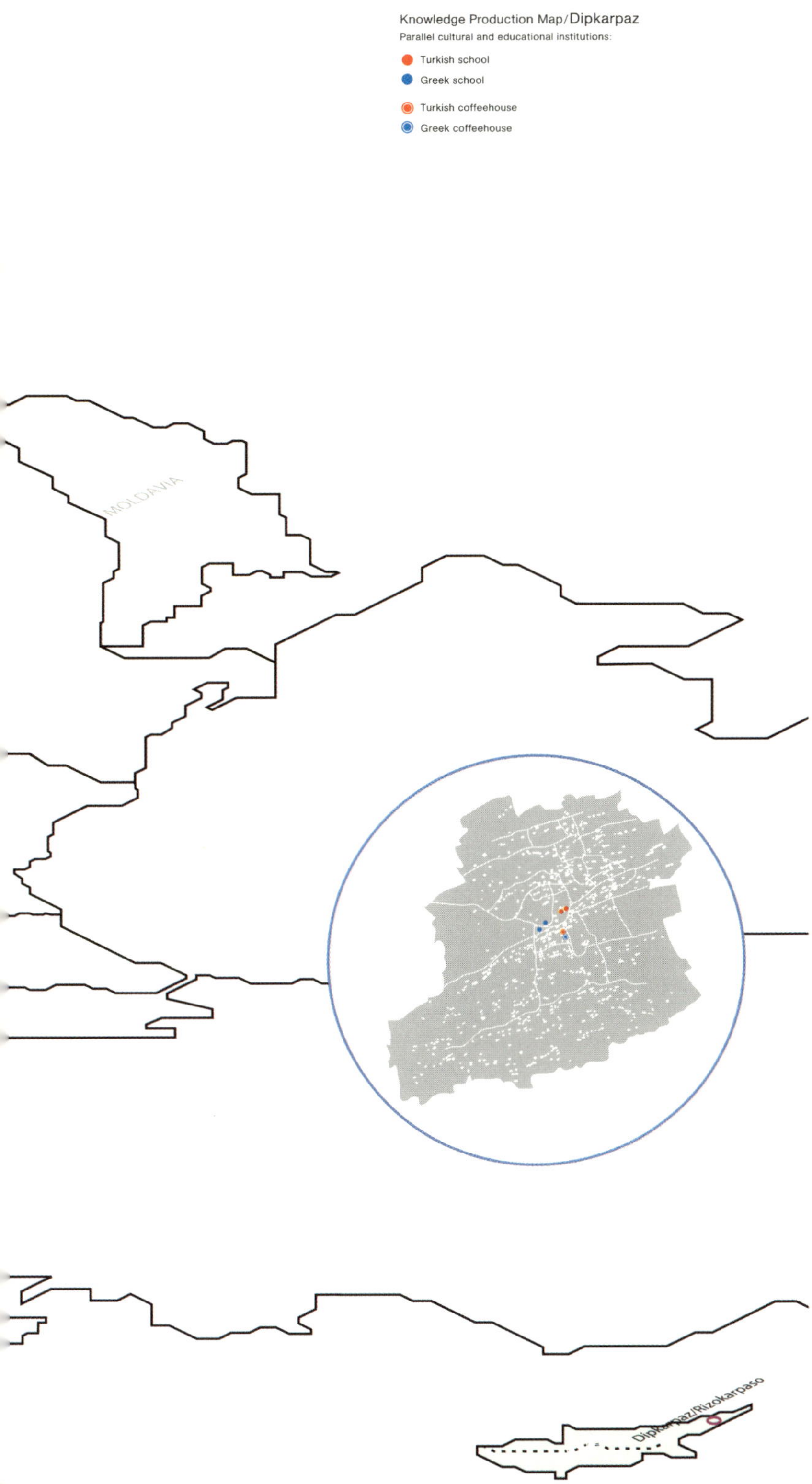

Cities are shaped by ethnic conflicts and social tensions, by struggles to occupy space and to invest it with symbolic significance. They are menaced by social divisions and xenophobia; by a lack of prospects on the one hand, and a lack of mutual respect and consideration on the other, as well as by inner-city rivalries that exacerbate the problems of communal life and erupt easily and violently. Cities are vulnerable.
This is especially evident in cities recently emerged from a period of war or violent conflicts, in which communities continue to defend their interests by physically appropriating parts of the city or fighting for political control. Occupying urban spaces or erecting monuments and buildings that symbolize and edify a particular community are actions intended to strengthen its members' sense of belonging and identity; simultaneously, they lay an exclusive claim to the city on behalf of the community. A mapping of cultural and educational institutions in Mostar, Mitrovica, and Dip Karpaz/Rizokarpaso shows the invisble border dividing the communities—all institutions exist parallel to one another. Even if they are close to each other, the division is manifested in one of the most essential parts of society: the education of young people. Battles rage over the city and architecture. Can the codes governing such spaces be re-written? Can other spaces be created? Can a new spatial practice be established—one that caters for and responds to all the city's inhabitants? To answer such questions requires a careful examination of the particular conditions in each locality, for these vary from city to city. And the cities are influenced in turn by the overall political situation. However many parallels there may be in structural terms—the trend toward segregated educational institutions is a particularly striking example—spatial strategies developed for one city cannot be simply transferred to another. The de facto failure of international organizations (in particular of the UN) in Mostar and on Cyprus demands acknowledgement of the fact that local independent initiatives are better situated to develop spatial strategies for their own contexts. Supporting the initiatives' expanding regional networks, their exchange of know-how, and their development of concepts is therefore of crucial importance.

The Pyla Master Plan Project

Interview with Münevver Özgür and Socrates Stratis

Interviewed by Esra Can Akbil, Giorgos Psaltis and Kai Vöckler

Pyla has always been a mixed village inhabited by Greek and Turkish Cypriots (1973: 586 Greek Cypriots and 488 Turkish Cypriots). This small community, located in the United Nations buffer zone in the Larnaca District (Cyprus), remains one of the very few places on the island where space is still shared somehow on a daily basis by inhabitants of the two communities. Today, around 1500 people live in the village; of these, two-thirds are Greek Cypriots and one-third Turkish Cypriots. The village's contested identity is layered with many controversial legends, while its inhabitants avoid public spaces, as if they were obligated to continue maintaining a balance that was established long ago, but remains fragile. Architects Münevver Özgür and Socrates Stratis have been collaborating with others since 2007 on a common project: the Pyla Master Plan, with the aim of engaging both parts of the community in a participatory procedure, from which a series of urban development projects will arise in order to overcome stagnation and to foster a common future perspective for the citizens.

How and when was the Pyla Masterplan project initiated and how did you become involved?

Socrates Stratis: The Pyla Master Plan is part of a general policy of the Cyprus government and encouraged by the European Union, aimed at establishing coherent community development plans. Such plans could become a roadmap for European funding sources, avoiding any fragmented approaches. We were assigned the Pyla Master Plan after winning a competition. The winning team consisted of architects, planners, and environmentalists.[1]
I personally chose to get involved with the Pyla Master Plan because of the existing specific conditions of the community: Pyla is located in the United Nations Buffer Zone, a result of the Turkish invasion of Cyprus in 1974. It is one of the very few communities with an ethnically mixed population, where Turkish and Greek Cypriots live together, ever since the bi-communal conflicts in the 1960s instigated ethnic segregation, which peaked during the 1974 war. Greek Cypriots were forced to move to the southern part of the island, while Turkish Cypriots went north.
In our proposed methodology, we emphasized the fact that our study team would consist of architects and planners from both communities, in order to address questions of how to share common space, rather than the prevailing practice of dividing space. Such mixed teams are not common in Cyprus. Some of them exist under the auspices of the United Nations.

Münevver Özgür: It was Socrates's idea to create a bi- or multi-communal team. I think it's been a very wise idea/vision, and I do remember how natural it was to be a part of the Pyla Master Plan Project. I guess we started to collaborate at the beginning of spring in 2007. When we made the final presentation to the villagers at the main square, it was already summer 2008.

What are the particularities of Pyla, and what was the socio-political situation in Cyprus and specifically in Pyla when you started the project?

SS: The particularities of Pyla, as I started mentioning before, are first, its location in the United Nations' demilitarized zone,[2] and second, the coexistence of Greek and Turkish Cypriots, even if relations are very bad. The village's location within the UN demilitarized zone is rather unique for the UN administration. When Münevver and I asked them if they knew of any similar situation anywhere else in the world, they admitted that there were not really any—meaning, a community living inside such a zone. The difficulty of this kind of condition is that it is usually rather unclear who is in charge, who administrates the community. The Republic of Cyprus and the UN attempt to operate in this territory through the Larnaca District Office. The local community council is linked to the Larnaca District Office and unfortunately consists only of Greek Cypriots. The Turkish Cypriot local authority is assigned by the Turkish Republic of Northern Cyprus, which is recognized only by Turkey. This poses all sorts of problems that are impossible to resolve. There is no official contact between the representatives of the two ethnic groups. Pyla has become, in fact, a macro-political arena. Residents of the village from both ethnic groups know very well that any local conflict could ignite a crisis on the island, and possibly even a regional one. And vice-versa. Whenever there is an increase in the existing tension between Turkey and Cyprus, Pyla gets its share. I remember when we were working on the master plan, there was local tension when Turkish Cypriot residents of Pyla illegally accessed the community's electrical network, and some employees went to resolve the issue. The whole thing ratcheted up with the help of the media, of course, and community leaders from communities all over the island went to visit Pyla in order to calm things down. Greek Cypriots refer to Pyla quite often as an example of peaceful coexistence, as a model for possible coexistence for the whole island. In contrast, Turkish Cypriots refer to Pyla as a model of how Greek Cypriots suppress Turkish Cypriots. Through our experience with the Pyla Master Plan, we realized that none of this was really true.
Therefore, it was a sort of a paradox to attempt to provide a master plan for such an ambiguous territory. But such ambiguity was very intriguing for us, indeed. In fact, all of the UN's attempts to launch projects, especially for the main square of the village, had failed, because of the unwillingness of the inhabitants to adopt them.
Another particularity of Pyla is the ethnic segregation of common space. Strangely enough, the homes of Turkish and Greek Cypriots are not segregated. There are no separate neighborhoods, even though there are more Turkish Cypriots closer to the northern edge of the village. However, coffee shops, schools, and athletic facilities are separate, even if they are sometimes located next to each other.
The village's main square represents an example of this kind of segregated proximity. The space is used as a parking lot. The Turkish Cypriot coffee shop is located at the western side of the square, next to a mosque. The nationalists' Greek Cypriot coffee shop is located on the north edge of the square; it was built as a symbol after the 1974 war, on the property of a church, which is situated a few meters further north. (In fact, one of our proposals was to move that coffee shop to a new, adjacent building in order to open up the view of the very old church, and provide easier access to it, as well). The leftist Greek Cypriot coffee shop is located further north, beyond the square. In fact, all Cypriot villages and towns unfortunately maintain this kind of right- and left-wing political segregation. On the eastern side of Pyla's main square, you can see the UN observatory, built on top of an existing building. The UN manager's office is at the southwestern edge. What struck us during our first visits was that people were sitting in or just outside their coffee shops, with the UN soldiers in their observation booth, and they were all watching the parking lot in the square, without any contact to each other. You could feel the immobility of things;

1 AA&U For Architecture, Art and Urbanism, (S. Stratis, M. Ozgur, R. Urbano, F. Ozersay), ALA Planning Partnership and Atlantis Environmental Advisors.

2 UN Buffer Zone.

you might even imagine that they have been sitting like that for the last 37 years. Not really . . . during the 1990s, if I remember correctly, the Greek Cypriot inhabitants of Pyla erected an oversized community house just south of the mosque. They used the size of the architecture to show who is in control of the area. (In our proposals, we thought of a tactical move to alter this kind of symbolic gesture: placing a public observation platform and a cafeteria on the top of the building, with external access. It didn't really go through as a proposal . . .)

Did the opening of the gates affect the village in any way?

SS: Yes, decisively. Before 2003, when the checkpoints between the north and south opened, Pyla was economically prosperous, since it was a sort of informal gate between the two sides, where the black market and smuggling could thrive. After 2003 a lot of shops closed and Pyla no longer had this exclusive status. The actual situation in Pyla is that Turkish Cypriot inhabitants are quite poor and some of them seek to move to the north part of the island, as they told our Turkish Cypriot colleagues. Some Greek Cypriot inhabitants are rather rich, since they own land of high value in the tourist areas on the seashore, which is also part of Pyla's territory.

MÖ: Ever since my childhood (I was born in 1967; I was 7 years old in 1974) Pyla has been a special place in my perception. It was a dreamland and a land of fear at the same time. It was a segregated village (Turkish Cypriots could not get in without special permission) and a village of togetherness (Turkish and Greek Cypriots living side-by-side). It was a hilly site and at the same time was not so high. It was neither on a mountain, nor on the shore. However it had close relationships to both. It was both forbidden and accessible. Families secretly met there at restaurants. The fear and joy of meeting together in this heaven on earth was there, served with a traditional side of baked potatoes. Who were friends? Who were Greek Cypriots? Who were Turkish Cypriots? Who was from another nation? Who were members of the secret police? What was so criminal about eating potatoes and yogurt with friends? I cannot tell if the opening of the gates affected the project in any way. But I can summarize the whole socio-political situation in Pyla as artificial and/or synthetic; much more than the one on the island in general. The perception of reality is a trick, as in *The Truman Show.* The villagers are like the hero in *The Truman Show*—unaware of what exactly is going on, living according to beliefs passed down from earlier generations, yet none of these beliefs are related to absolute truths. Only the protagonists (governments on both sides, embassies, the UN, the EU . . .) take part in the generation and modification of knowledge. They construct reality so slowly that it can hardly move, in my opinion.

It is known that, in recent years, the village has undergone huge development and seen its tourism units multiply. How did this affect the community?

Urban development has been occurring mainly outside of the village center, and extending all the way to the seashore. This area is outside the UN buffer zone. We don't have specific information on how such development takes place, who buys the land, etc. The land is mostly owned by Greek Cypriot inhabitants of Pyla, who either develop or sell it. What we do know is what is happening all over Cyprus: all land close to the sea is being overbuilt, in order to house large numbers of tourists for a few weeks during the summer, or else it is sold to foreigners who are attracted by the sunny Cyprus climate. Land owned by Turkish Cypriots in southern Cyprus is managed by a state authority and usually remains underdeveloped and in an uncertain state. Such parcels, close to the sea, are usually under pressure. Because land development is done in a super-private way, no community authority profits directly from it, except for service taxes. Therefore, the new foreign community is becoming part of this tourist development south of the area we have studied. It will be interesting to go back and see how they influence each other.

What was the main idea behind the proposal you developed, and what did you try to achieve with it?

SS: The main ideas behind the proposal unfold on three levels: first, that of the process of making the proposal, to which we gave great value; second, that of the final projects of the master plan; and third, that of what we call "ignition projects," a sort of 'To-Do-Tomorrow' kind of list, which could persuade inhabitants that change is indeed possible, thus preparing for the final projects to be implemented.

We began work knowing beforehand that any attempt at a common project in Pyla involving Turkish and Greek Cypriots would be rather difficult. We decided to make maximum use of the process itself, turning that into a project—a project that could mobilize people, could engage at least some of them, could bypass or divert existing spatial practices. Together with Münevver and Fevzi, we established a sort of a project within the project of Pyla Master Plan. I have faith in the notion of activating public space through people's engagement. Resistance toward physical space, as some authors say, could increase the level of engagement. I could add that resistance toward the process itself could enrich such engagement. It forces people to get out of their private bubbles or normal practices and start creating a common denominator through the physical and social space. It is that common denominator that could allow the slightest communication to start between people. In order to realize a goal like this, a series of "friction genes," as I called them, were developed and inserted into different stages of the project development process. Some of them were very simple. The first of them was to include Münevver and her collaborators in the study team. Reactions of the Greek Cypriot local council gradually calmed, especially when they realized the usefulness of such a team. The second one was to bypass local authorities and establish direct contact with the inhabitants, developed through a workshop we had organized, activating the void of the main square, so far used only as a parking lot. We established informal talks with the local Turkish Cypriot authorities and EVKAF.[3] Unfortunately, they were both excluded from the official references in the Pyla Master Plan due to the non-recognition of the Turkish Republic of Northern Cyprus. No effort was made, in fact, to develop any alternative modes of planning, such as a "Nicosia Master Plan," where professionals from both communities join in the project without any form of representation. They represent themselves and not any kind of state body, and in this way, they bypass any difficulties surrounding the recognition of the state in the northern half of the island.

Another "friction gene" we developed was to make public presentations in both Turkish and Greek, using a translator. It sounds, in fact, like a very common-sense practice, but,

3 The foundation in charge of managing the Muslim religious land on the island.

believe me, it is not. Our aim was to create the best conditions through which a practice of active coexistence between Turkish and Greek Cypriots could take place. Listening to a public presentation in Turkish and Greek is one of the rarest things one could do here in Cyprus, even if it sounds obvious to others. It was in fact, a sort of indirect critique of the given terms of reference, which did not address such issues. Well, you can't imagine the difficulties that confronted us. Even choosing a space for the presentation was impossible. How to choose an equally inviting place for both Turkish and Greek Cypriots? That is why we chose the main square for the final presentation, thinking that it was neutral enough to give us the chance to get a message across. It turned out to be a disaster . . . Not very many people showed up. The atmosphere between the local authorities and the study team was not very nice, because I think we tried a little bit too hard to get our point across; maybe we became very defensive, seeing all our efforts come to nothing. Münevver and I were accused of not being patriotic enough for our ethnic groups, and of not considering their ideas enough during the preparation of the master plan.

Going back to the importance of the process itself: a positive result of the project is that the study team came out much stronger than it was at the beginning. In fact, members of the team had met through the project. All this experience created a nice bond between the team members, hopefully useful in the future. This is a quite important aspect, since the study team could be considered as a sort of a temporary community, with around fifteen to twenty people involved, especially during the workshop and the preparation of the drawings: students of architecture from both sides, plus younger people like Jasmine, Münevver's daughter, and her friend, were involved. Being part of intense discussions with the president and secretary of the local Turkish Cypriot authority at the Turkish Cypriot coffee shop, together with Münevver and Fevzi, was worth all the effort, indeed. A strong bond was created among the three of us during that discussion. In fact, Münevver and Fevzi mentioned after the discussion that it was probably one of those rare times that a creative discussion had taken place, seeking the point of view of the Turkish Cypriots. Just to provide a glimpse of the context of such discussion, I'll mention an 'informal' interrogation we had to go through at the coffee shop, conducted by an officer of the Turkish Cypriot secret police, who was trying to understand what the hell we were about.

Regarding the actual content of the final proposal of Pyla Master Plan: the aim was to emphasize projects that might collectively engage Pyla inhabitants of any origin, both on a very small scale and a very big one. Yiannis Papadakis, an anthropologist who worked on Pyla, suggested we emphasize aspects of everyday life, such as health care and exercise, for example. We were aware of the limits of architecture in such a context, and so we therefore aimed to encourage things to happen, rather than to patronize residents or force them.

Ten projects were proposed, relating to the specific context of the community. Some of them were about activating voids in the community: either strategically placed empty plots, programmed for ephemeral uses, such as open-air cinema, for example. Other cases had to do with residual space gained by new traffic management of private cars, which increased space for pedestrians. For example, a network of playgrounds was proposed, profiting from the ethnic mix of neighborhoods, and encouraging kids to come out of their houses and play. We named it the K.A.A. project (The Kids Are Alright). A negative reaction from a member of the local Greek Cypriot council was that people don't allow their kids to play in the streets, because of safety issues. It sounded to me like a sort of middle-class, suburban logic of "all inclusive residences," where people go from house to house, bypassing any public space.

For the main square we proposed an open-air market, since Pyla had been rather notorious for all sorts of markets, plus it could become a real space of exchange based on commerce, which could hopefully add to productive transactions between the two ethnic groups. A series of links were proposed to re-establish physical connections to the adjacent mosque, church, and the Venetian tower. Such links were proposed with minimum means attempting to get maximum results: Discreetly connecting the beautiful mosque garden with the square, replacing a building of rundown shops located at the edge of the same garden in front of the local Greek Cypriot council building. Plus, as I mentioned already, moving the Greek Cypriot nationalists' coffee shop, allowing space for the very old Byzantine church.

Another project proposed was a Memory Museum: the creation of a people's archive of personal experiences, giving an alternative discourse to the official ones. This museum will be located in the former police station, which would symbolically show the shift from police control to people's self-determination, which will hopefully be possible sometime.

At the other extreme, a very large-scale project was proposed, an "elephant project," as Münevver called it. This proposal was a joint venture, involving the entire community, for the development and protection of state land located on a higher plateau north of the community center, where the Turkish army is strategically located. Creating an environmental park with all sorts of uses and with trans-local importance could provide a common vision for the inhabitants, shifting their interest from emphasizing issues that divide to dealing with challenges that could unite them.

How to start change in such a context is usually a tough thing to deal with. When almost nothing has happened in the village in this direction during the last thirty-eight years, such a goal becomes rather impossible. For a team of architects and planners to reassure the inhabitants that they could make the difference sounds rather naïve, at least. For these reasons, we developed a sort of an "engine" in each project, which

could work as a catalyst for creating the right dynamics for the final project to be implemented. We called it the "ignition project," even if the notion of ignition in Pyla has rather negative connotations; you never know when and what could be used as ignition for a new micro-conflict in the community. In our case, we wanted to give a creative value to such a notion. The ignition project is based, in fact, on a 'To-Do-Tomorrow' project with little means and budget, and a collective initiative. Each final project had an ignition project imbedded in it, which could, in fact, determine the final form of the project to implement, depending on all of the issues one knows nothing about when one designs a project, especially of urban scale.

Unfortunately the idea of the "ignition project" and the main square was very badly received by the local authorities. But that made us think of another kind of use for such a project. I will explain what I mean. The final presentation of the Pyla Master Plan, as I mentioned before, took place in the main square. We presented most of the projects, without any significant reaction from the audience. When we arrived at the presentation of the ignition project involving the main square, which was to draw over existing asphalt lines to create playing fields for different sports, so that young people could play there, the president of the local Greek Cypriot council reacted rather badly, rejecting this kind of idea, being scared, as he said, of quarrels between Turkish and Greek Cypriot youngsters playing against each other, and possibly turning the square into a violent zone. My interpretation of that reaction, which might be wrong, is that the immediacy of such a project forced people to show their real position vis-à-vis this kind of common project. It becomes much easier to put long-term projects away in a drawer, using excuses such as budget issues, acceptance from the inhabitants, etc. In the case of the ignition project, all such excuses were waived, leaving no other way to confront it, except with a sincere reaction, such as the one from the president of the local Greek Cypriot council.

What is interesting is that all our proposals have been approved by the central government and the local Greek Cypriot authority. Our proposals include the EVKAF ideas about developing their property close to the mosque. It remains to re-engage Pyla's inhabitants of any origin in a different manner, trying always to avoid the consequences of the large-scale politics hovering over the community.

So how did the story with the asphalt lines end up? Did they accept it at the end? Or better: has anything—even a small ignition project—been implemented?

MÖ: No, not yet. After the project was submitted, we did not hear from them. I vaguely remember that one day I read some news in the newspaper that the local Turkish authorities in Pyla received some money from the Turkish Embassy in the north for some other projects. I was so upset that I did not continue to read the article in full.

SS: As I mentioned already, our proposals were officially accepted both by the local Greek Cypriot authorities and the Planning Department. But . . . everything is on the shelf, labeled as old attempts. We didn't have the courage to go back with Münevver and try to push any of the ignition projects forward. Maybe we will get the courage soon, hopefully. But, as Münevver mentioned some time just after we had submitted the project—and she was right—we were not able to create some allies within the community who could encourage us to go on, who could also push the things. Of course, it was evidently very difficult. Maybe that is how we should start over.

With whom did you work after the project was initiated; who supported it, and in what way?

MÖ: As Socrates mentioned before, we tried to cooperate with as many parties as possible: e.g., the village community, local authorities, EVKAF, the UN, etc. EVKAF was the most neutral of all the parties involved. They, too, were technical people who concentrated more on the qualities of life and space, rather than on national, economic, and power relations. The thorniest path of communication was the one leading to the local authorities. Even though they were polite, they were very suspicious of us, our moves, motives, ideas, and, most of all, they were both surprised and scared by the human bonds we had among us as a team. We somehow did not fit into their perceptions of scenarios of life.

A very critical incident was the telephone call I received from the Ministry of Foreign Affairs in the north. I was cross-examined, with questions like: What are you doing there? Why are you involved? How did you get involved? Did you get any permission? Who is supporting the project, economically? Very annoying. Very unpleasant. I kept cool and answered politely. They were satisfied. Misunderstandings were cleared up . . . Obviously there was no threat . . . Just a pointless suspicion.

SS: Yes, I guess . . . that was confirmed by the UNDP team, even though they stood somewhere in the middle. They liked us and our ideas, but not the idea of being involved in any way with Pyla. Too hard a project; too impossible to attain positive, constructive, creative, or applicable results . . . that was the personal impression I had from their facial expressions. Too many parties were involved; it felt too crowded, but it still felt too alone. We did not mind! We kept our optimism!

What have been the results and the biggest obstacles during the procedure?

MÖ: Regarding the results . . . we definitely learned a lot about Pyla, from the village people, from nature, from each other. We enjoyed working together, doing interdisciplinary work. Anna was great. Her team was very supportive. Socrates was a luxury to have around. So was Riccardo. Maria and her input with her short film, and the Siamese twins' live demonstration was like a magical touch of art in our process. Fevzi was very helpful. During the interviews, his presence was irreplaceable. His wise and human approach calmed down even the most aggressive party during our coffee shop conversations.

We brought a colorful discourse to the people of Pyla. Against all odds, we were interesting role models, as a team. I am not sure if they fully realized this, but, at least, I am sure we opened a decent crack in their firmly molded perceptions. Good ideas! If they will be used or not, I do not know. But definitely, we as a team produced very good project ideas.

SS: It will be interesting to go back, if we have the courage, and ask the people involved what they remember of this expedition of ours. It has become clear to our team that one has to understand how the architecture of the procedure itself is crucial for the partial success of a project, but maybe it is not clear to the other parties involved. Our team itself, with all of the people involved—architects, planners, students—has become a creative space of exchange and of creation of trust and respect. We sort of created our own micro-environment, which was then harshly tested in Pyla, but, on the other hand, it was thanks to the Pyla project that such an experience was created at all.

Our proposals were approved and they incorporate ideas from some parties that were, unfortunately, not involved in the process like EVKAF. Our productive cooperation, as Münevver mentioned, resulted in ideas worth remembering, worth using and in conjunction with another base of cooperation.

And the obstacles?

MÖ: People. People themselves! Bureaucracy. Mediocracy. "Too many cooks spoil the broth": the UN, the police, local authorities, church, mosque, coffee shops . . . The villagers had almost no voice! Even if they had any, it was hardly audible! And the local authorities . . . the tension between them . . . inequalities, both social and economic . . .

SS: At the moment you realize that you are in a "Truman Show," and that everybody is watching your every single move—which is the case involving Pyla and the rest of Cyprus—then bizarre things begin to happen. First of all, you continuously test to see if people are watching you, by creating small crises that intensify and contaminate the "people watching you." As I mentioned before, a lot of such instances of micro-conflicts start large-scale political crises and vice-versa. That was one of the main obstacles.

Then, the terms of reference of Pyla Master Plan did not take into account the particular condition of the community, and therefore encouraged a lot of misunderstanding and mistrust. Of course, any other plans—like the Jacob plan initiated by the UN, which was sort of a joint venture with the community—also failed. Or even a medieval tower, a very important community landmark, which was renovated through the UN initiative, is now completely abandoned. I think there are various layers of obstacles related to the presence of a long-term conflict and the absence of any sort of civil society.

What kind of impact could the project have on the village in a social, political, economic, and cultural sense?

MÖ: I could say that; socially, the project might function as a "secure communication milieu"—in a metaphorical way—where open space could be created to bring in villagers' voices and choices. For example, the swimming pool project or the kindergarten project ideas were based on very basic human needs, such as getting refreshed in hot summer days or taking care of your children. Different stages of the design process for such projects mean that one has to discuss very human details. Or the environmental research center! Why not focus on environmental global problems, rather than being stuck with local problems, which cannot be solved momentarily.

In a political sense . . . what a great political stand, and what a luxury it is, being able to say, "Look, these are our projects. We, as the people of Pyla, want to go forward with them." It is political strategy originating from the people on the inside toward those on the outside. Just the opposite of what has been happening to Pyla so far.

The other political mission the master plan might have carried out could have been the formation of a pilot project, or proof that things can be done together. In other words, instead of concentrating on the demographic differences, the people of Pyla could be evidence of the fact that, by concentrating on our human similarities, a lot can be done. Maybe it is a dream, but it's a nice dream: Cypriots bringing their own projects into life. What a huge positive step toward the solution of the Cyprus problem! What a nice and colorful source of hope!

In an economic sense? I do not know. I was never very good with money issues! In my opinion, most of the projects we have proposed are like seeds: a new source of life; richness; energy, and work opportunities. The happier the environments are, the happier the people feel—and hence, they are gradually transformed into empowered human resources for a more mature, independent, critical, and stronger country, island, world.

When the dimension of the cultural impact of the Pyla Master Plan Project is considered, the only thing that comes to my mind is the creation of a new culture. Two communities have so far developed a culture of silence and invisibility in Pyla. If women from two different nations get along very well, they experience their friendship behind doors, during coffee breaks, at home, informally. It could be a minor step from a hidden, tense, and rigid culture toward a more transparent, dialectic, and transformative culture.

Are you connected to other projects similar to yours? If so, please specify the project, the partner, and the country/location.

MÖ: Ever since its initiation, I have been a member of the team of consultants for a project called Revitalizing the Dead Zone:

An Educational Center and Home for Cooperation. Fevzi and I have been involved in the Kontea Cultural Heritage Project and also took part in the preparation of anti-discrimination and anti-racism policy documents for the English School of Nicosia.

SS: I have not been involved with similar planning projects concerning bi-communal issues. On the other hand, I have been involved with projects that considered Cyprus as a conflict zone and investigated possibilities of contributing to the activation of public space, of common references, etc.—for example, the Anatomy of Coffee Trips in Spaces of Borders,[4] Leaps of Faith,[5] the Public Private Synergy Convoy,[6] which was a mobile workshop and exhibition space used later on for Pyla, and finally, the KillingFreeTime@Cyprus[7] project, which was a critical stance on the coexistence of military and leisure infrastructures on the island of Cyprus.

What can possible future initiatives learn from your experience? What is your advice?

MÖ: I definitely would try harder to get into the homes of local people and conduct interviews with women and children. I think we unconsciously left out these two very important sources of knowledge and an important sector of our participants during the process.

SS: Keep trying, even if you know you will fail. Failure has become a means of learning, especially for us as a study team. I like Münevver's metaphor of *The Truman Show,* with all the inhabitants being in *The Truman Show,* while the diverse authorities survey and control them, instead of representing them. Where were we situated throughout our project? We tried to step into the "Truman Show" city in several ways, but maybe it was too hard to sustain our efforts. People might not be used to being asked for their points of views about their environment. A lot of work needs to be done there.

4 A research project looking at common means of representation in a divided city, such as Nicosia, mapping the everyday trips taken by coffee-shop owners in both parts of Nicosia and generating new common maps. Contribution to the Venice Biennale of Architecture 2004.
5 International exhibition of Art with the "Call # 192" project, 2005
6 PPS Convoy: a joint project with Maria Loizidou, under the auspices of the AA&U platform and created by its members: an architecture for escorting people back to their homes (Greek Cypriots and Turkish Cypriots) and documenting their experiences. Contribution to the Venice Biennale of Architecture 2006.
7 Contribution to the Venice Biennale of Architecture 2008

H4C – Home for Cooperation, Cyprus

Interview with Chara Makriyianni

Interviewed by Esra Can Akbil, Giorgos Psaltis and Kai Vöckler

In 2006, the project Revitalizing the Dead Zone: An Educational Center and Home for Cooperation was initiated to create a common space, a center for community and culture in the heart of the capital, Nicosia. Located just outside the old center of the town inside the United Nations buffer zone (which divides the town into two sectors separating the Greek and Turkish Cypriots), a two-story post-World War II building has been restored and transformed into a place where, for the very first time, the two sides of the capital's society can come together and work in a productive environment under a common roof. Moreover, this example shows how regaining use of abandoned structures can enhance the increasingly energetic, yet currently blocked dynamics of socio-economic rehabilitation of urban areas adjacent to the buffer zone. This community center is being inaugurated at a time when rapprochement between the two communities can be discerned. Chara Makriyianni, founding member and board president (2005 to 2011) of the multi-communal Association for Historical Dialogue and Research (AHDR) explains the development of the project. (Esra Can Akbil, Demet Mutman, Giorgos Psaltis, Kai Vöckler)

What was the political and social situation in your country and, specifically, in your city, when you started the initiative?

Our journey with the non-governmental organization Association for Historical Dialogue and Research started with the birth of the association, which almost coincided with a historic change that took place back in April 2003, when the restrictions that had long prevented communication and contact across the buffer zone were partially lifted by the Turkish army, and, for the first time in nearly thirty years, ordinary Greek and Turkish Cypriots had their first chance since 1974 to cross the divide.
At that time, Tassos Papadopoulos was the fifth president of the Republic of Cyprus. He had campaigned in the 2003 presidential election on a platform that he would be able to secure a better deal for the Cyprus problem than the previous president. He was backed by his own party, DIKO (Democratic Party), AKEL (Progressive Party of Working People), and KISOS (Social Democrats).
In the north, months later, Mehmet Ali Talat, leader of the left-wing Turkish Cypriot party, CTP (Republican Turkish Party), won the presidential elections in December 2003 by claiming that he was in favor of inter-communal contacts, reunification, and close ties with the European Union.

After a year of negotiations among the communities of the island, and upon acceptance by voters in both communities, the United-Nations-sponsored Annan Plan was supposed to take effect on May 1, 2004, the day that Cyprus was scheduled to become a full member state of the European Union (EU). This would allow Cyprus to enter the EU as a unified state. While the majority of Turkish Cypriots voted in favor of the Annan Plan, the Greek Cypriots overwhelmingly rejected the plan, thus preventing it from taking effect. Prior to the 2004 Annan Plan Referendum, the Greek-Cypriot leader, Papadopoulos, had urged Greek Cypriots to vote "no," declaring, "I received a state. I will not deliver a community."

In the absence of a reached agreement, ever since then the international community continues to recognize only the Republic of Cyprus and its government for all legal and political purposes, even though the government cannot currently exercise its authority in areas in the north of Cyprus, which is currently under military occupation by Turkish troops.

Our project was conceived and started to develop in that post-referendum period. As it advanced through various stages, an inversion occurred on a political level, when Demetris Christofias, Secretary General of the left-wing Greek Cypriot party AKEL won the presidential elections in the south in February 2008, bringing to power a party with a long history of rapprochement. Throughout the election campaign, Christofias pledged to restart talks with Turkish Cypriots in order to find a solution to the Cyprus dispute and reunify the island.

Two years later, in April 2010, Talat and his party lost the elections, with Turkish Cypriots electing Derviş Eroğlu as their new leader. He is a veteran nationalist who favors independence for the north of Cyprus, and the leader of the right-wing, conservative, Turkish Cypriot political party UBP, National Unity Party.

Today, Christofias and Eroğlu, both still in power, continue the talks, moving toward a solution. We remain convinced that cooperation and dialogue are vital elements to any kind of solution.

What is the main idea behind the project? What are your target groups and what are you trying to achieve with this project?

The idea underlying the Home for Cooperation project (H4C) stems from identifying two of the major obstacles that civil society in Cyprus currently faces: first, the limited infrastructure for multi-communal activities, and second, the lack of skills necessary for locating and obtaining institutional support. Right now, public opinion in Cyprus needs examples of successful cooperation based on mutual respect, especially as regards the sensitive issue of education and teaching history.

In our view, the Home for Cooperation, located in the UN Buffer Zone, aims to challenge the current, widely held perception of the "dead zone" (as it is commonly called) as a symbol of separation, and to turn it into a symbol of cooperation by giving it a new meaning and role. Our project combines a substantial proposal to conserve cultural heritage with well-thought-out, concrete suggestions on human resources development through the promotion of education and training, the advancement of research and dialogue, and our empowerment as critical thinkers and citizens of Cyprus, Europe, and of the world.[1] The project will have positive, significant spill-over, standing as a successful example and case study for local, regional, European, and international comparisons.

The target groups embrace a large spectrum of social groups and disciplines on a local, European, and international level; for example, NGOs (with an interest in history, archaeology, cultural heritage, architecture, urbanism, information technology, museum and heritage studies, youth, education, human rights, peace, and democracy); also young people and youth organizations, researchers, educators, historians, sociologists, psychologists, anthropologists, architects, urban and landscape planners, teacher trade unions across the divide, media people, tourists, and visitors (adults and children), UNFICYP personnel, technical committees, the people of Cyprus across the divide, activists, and agents of change who

1 Project objective (as stated in the grant agreement with the EEA and the Norwegian Financial Mechanisms, 2004–2009): to restore a building of significant historical architectural importance and to establish its functionality as an intercultural educational and research center, with the overall objective of conserving European cultural heritage, with a view to initiate sustainable livelihoods in the buffer zone.

View of the building during first project steps, June 2006.

United Nations soldiers removing barbed wire from the building, November 2007.

Workers cutting through dense vegetation surrounding the building, February 2010.

dwell on issues of identity, contact, cooperation, trust, mutual respect, and the promotion of multi-perceptivity and critical thinking.

The Home for Cooperation aims to become the home for NGOs; it will provide opportunities not only to NGOs, but also to individuals who are designing and implementing innovative projects, which will help build the foundations for an empowered civil society and lasting relationships island-wide. It also aims to encourage Cypriots to demonstrate the benefits of cooperation across the existing divide, with collaborations at local, European, and international levels. Furthermore, it will enable young people, educators, historians, researchers, activists, and other agents of change to acquire knowledge and develop critical thinking through educational, training, and research programs. Last, but not least, it will enhance awareness of the complexity and diversity of history as it aims to empower individuals to respond to present and future demands based on understanding and mutual respect.

What are the main activities hosted, and how do they relate to the way that space is distributed on the premises?

The Home for Cooperation is a two-story structure. On the ground floor, the left wing houses a conference room with a capacity of eight to one hundred; it is available for NGOs and other groups to use for their events. At the back of the conference room there is a second room that can be used for film screenings and musical events in the evenings, or as a meeting space, or in support of conferences/seminars when simultaneous translations are needed.

The cafeteria on the right wing ground floor serves light snacks, such as sandwiches and coffee, to those using the offices and building services, attending the conferences, or just dropping in. It will be open from 10 a.m. to 6 p.m., seven days a week, and it is anticipated that it will be run by an experienced café/cafeteria operator, who will be able to serve multilingual customers.

The first floor holds six offices that can be used as office space for NGOs from both the Turkish Cypriot community and the Greek Cypriot community. A total of fifteen to twenty individuals use the H4C as their daily office space. There are also a library and archive on Cyprus history and historical education, a digital archiving room, classrooms, and workshop spaces. The room on the roof of the building will also be used as office space for interested NGOs.

In terms of other facilities and services (other than the obvious), the building offers free wireless Internet access or fixed computer stations. It is fully friendly to people with disabilities, thanks to various provisions, such as the elevator that will be installed during this summer, along with ramps, services for the disabled, etc. At the rear of the building there is a small, landscaped garden with view of the Venetian moat where people can have a break and enjoy some Cypriot coffee under the blue Mediterranean skies.

With whom have you worked since the project was initiated? Who supported it, and in what way?

We had to work with various agents and partners at different levels for different reasons and in different stages. Our vision for a shared space in the buffer zone was very soon shared by a number of individuals, organizations, and authorities within Cyprus and abroad, whose support made the project possible.

On a financial level the project costs[2] were mainly covered by the major donors: Norway, Iceland, and Liechtenstein through the EEA and Norway Grants; Sweden and Switzerland, and the United Nations Development Program – Action for Cooperation and Trust,[3] which supplied us with funding from the United States Agency for International Development through the Multi-perspectivity and Intercultural Dialogue in Education project (MIDE). Norway in particular supported our project by providing ample support in terms of expertise, advice, and ideas on sustainability that have evolved since the AHDR's successful application. It was thanks to this grant that AHDR was able to purchase the building from its former owners—the Mangoian family—for approximately 450,000 euros.

Together with our team of consultants and advisors, we first of all had to collaborate very closely throughout the procedure, with the United Nations (UNFICYP), which has strongly supported the project since the beginning and provided us with all the necessary personnel to escort us through our activities and guarantee our security during the very first visits to the abandoned building. The Technical Chambers and the city of Nicosia actively supported the project, as it was perfectly in line with the main objectives of the Nicosia master plan. They donated the same amount of money

2 Project cost: The originally approved cost of the project amounted to € 1,022,804. (The total eligible costs of the project include € 427,153 for the purchase of the building). However, the total cost of the project has exceeded € 1,243,558, the difference being wholly covered by the Association for Historical Dialogue and Research.
Sponsorship: grant of € 749,920 from the EEA and the Norwegian Financial Mechanisms, 2004–2009. Co-financing: Cooperation program between Switzerland and the Republic of Cyprus, € 118,000; Republic of Cyprus, € 54,560; Swedish Ministry of Foreign Affairs, € 100,000; Association for Historical Dialogue and Research, € 300,000; UNDP-ACT (through the MIDE project) € 100,000; Government of the Netherlands, € 25,000; mayors of Nicosia, € 2,000 each; donations from groups and individuals.

3 UNDP-ACT has been in partnership with AHDR since 2004, when it supported AHDR's first project.

Workers cleaning and preparing the building site, February 2010.

Partial demolition of the roof, April 2010.

Works in progress six months before inauguration, October 2010.

towards the renovation costs and assisted with cleaning and overall support of the renovation scheme.
On a more technical level, we also had to contact the appropriate bodies in order to secure provision of services (electricity, water, sewer system, etc.), investigate the procedure of buying and selling property in the UN Buffer Zone, and securing the consent of the neighborhood. All of the above were required in order to obtain the UN authorization and municipality permits.

We also had to interfere with a series of other governmental bodies, such as the Conservation Sector of the Town Planning and Housing Department, and, above all, with the ones that had been monitoring the procedure since the beginning, such as the Treasury and the Planning Bureau of the Republic of Cyprus. The latter acted as the focal point for the major donors and the project promoter.

Before closing, I would like to mention that we also received a series of supportive and encouraging letters from various individuals and NGOs in Cyprus and abroad, as well as many organizations and foundations, like the Council of Europe and the United Nations Development Program.

Last, but not least, it is important to mention that leaders of the major communities of Cyprus gave addresses at the opening ceremony on May 6, 2011. The events were also widely supported by civil society groups,[4] which participated in the H4C Inauguration Festivities and, of course, all our families.

What were the biggest obstacles?

Bureaucracy certainly has not been of any help, given the deadlines resulting from the agreement with the donors and the complexity and pioneering spirit of the project. We had to recruit a consultancy team, a project manager, and advisors in order to implement the project, and we often had to deal with bureaucratic issues that had never before been faced, until that moment, with regard to the different status of the UN Buffer Zone. We had to revise our constitution in order to allow the association to own real estate, and comply with the long procedures required by the Land Registry Department.

Then there was a long bureaucratic procedure in order to obtain both the planning and construction permits from the city of Nicosia. The whole procedure lasted twelve months, also due to the fact that there was a change in proposed uses that neither the municipality nor the donors would approve. Then we moved on to complete the delicate procedure that highlighted two major issues that needed resolving. The first one was that the initial project had to be extended by six-months, up to April 2011, due to the above-mentioned delays. The second one was the increase of the total project budget, due to the fact that construction costs increased by approximately €230,000 compared to the amount budgeted. Along with the bureaucratic hindrances, securing additional funds was one of the biggest obstacles. The increased cost had to come from AHDR's own resources, according to the agreements signed by the parties. In this connection, AHDR exercised all efforts to secure additional funds from the Ministry of the Interior of the Republic of Cyprus through various financial incentives, which are available according to the regulations regarding buildings on the Cultural Heritage List.

The fact that AHDR did not have the necessary additional funds at that particular time, and that it had to cover the remaining costs of the project by obtaining funds the above-mentioned sources created liquidity problems, since the procedures required to secure such funds were time-consuming and were supposed to be finalized at a later stage of the project. As members of the AHDR board, we had to expedite our efforts for securing additional funding as quickly as possible from various organizations and embassies, so that the cash flow problem could be effectively dealt with and construction would not be negatively affected.

Now, regarding politics and division in its various forms: I would continue by saying that a project titled Revitalizing the Dead Zone: An Educational Center and Home for Cooperation, led by an inter-communal association that enlists members from across the divide, majors in history and historical education, and promotes, among other things, multiple perspectives and critical thinking was (and, to a rather large extent, still is) considered an obstacle in itself to the plans of those who wish to suppress polyphony, smother cooperation and sustain mistrust among the Cypriot communities.

What kind of impact is the project having on the city in a social, political, economic, and cultural sense?

With its emphasis on dialogue and research in history and historical education, our association has made great strides when it comes to the most critical issues facing Cyprus. As the leading example of sustained, island-wide cooperation within Cyprus, AHDR combines a well-grounded, disciplined approach to history and education with practical, accessible interventions at the grassroots level, which empower Cypriots,

4 Hands Across the Divide, EMAA, EKATE, POST, United Platform, CCMC, Youth Activism, ENGAGE, Rooftop Theatre, House of Literature Oslo, Peace Players, Future World Center, Youth for Exchange and Understanding, International Children's Film Festival of Cyprus, the team of the AHDR-MIDE, and all the Council of Europe, Gruntvig and PRIO.

The building at works completion, May 2011.

Ribbon cutting on the official inauguration day, May 2011.

open minds, and enhance understanding. Its contribution to intercultural dialogue in a highly sensitive, post-conflict environment serves as a model of how civil society can best play an effective role in promoting active citizens with critical thinking skills.

In this context, the Home for Cooperation is AHDR's most important achievement to date: an ambitious and innovative project that led to a derelict building in the UN Buffer Zone being transformed into a center for cultural and educational exchange.

Its positive impact has been evident since the very beginning: during the Home for Cooperation inauguration celebrations from May 6 to 9, and particularly at the opening ceremony, held on May 6, 2011. On that day, leaders of the Greek and Turkish Cypriot communities of Cyprus, Demetris Christofias and Derviş Eroğlu, were on hand to address the ceremony; they stood together in a powerful display of solidarity and support with other representatives of the civil society and dignitaries from around Europe, including the Council of Europe, Norway, Sweden, Switzerland and the Netherlands, to celebrate what was described by all speakers and the media that widely covered the event as "a major new initiative that promises to deepen and expand cooperation and dialogue in Cyprus."

Currently, the Home functions as a meeting space and incubator for new ideas and projects and has become a site for non-governmental organizations that share our views, a kind of NGO center. H4C is becoming a symbol of the process and the outcome of dialogue and cooperation; it is an example of how theory-driven practice can result in great achievements, even in places where conflict and barbed wire cut the land in two. The whole operation has acted as the opening, tangible outcome of a civil-society led initiative that brought together, from the inception of the idea, individuals and organizations, foundations, authorities, volunteers, workers, teachers, and researchers to reflect upon and re-address the meaning of the buffer zone; like a kind of driving force behind the creation of a lasting legacy for the buffer zone rehabilitation process, ready to be used as a prototype for inter-communal education and research in Cyprus. Furthermore, H4C symbolizes both the outcome, as well as the start of more questioning, examination, and reflection—skills and dispositions that we all need so much today in Cyprus and beyond.

<u>What were the reasons for choosing the specific building/site in the city? Why was it important to have it physically embedded? What was the meaning of the building/site?</u>

The building chosen has many advantages and much potential, and it is itself a product of cooperative aspirations. The neighborhood hosting it was a living example of multiculturalism: a multi-communal, multi-functional area where commerce and residential life were tightly interwoven. It contained the homes and enterprises of Armenian, Greek, and Turkish Cypriots. From 1949 onward it was also home to the leading hotel on Cyprus, the Ledra Palace

Neighborly cohabitation across this main artery of the city was fundamentally reshaped, as political developments began to unfold from the late 1950s onward, leading to a barren landscape where human interaction was replaced by checkpoints, security forces, abandoned buildings, and overgrown gardens—all forming the so-called UN Green Line, which later became known as the UN Buffer Zone. In this historical context, the AHDR understands that the buffer zone does more than separate communities: it is also the point where they meet.

When the barricades in this road were removed and access to this part of the buffer zone was allowed in April 2003, these venues became passageways for individuals to move from one area to the other. And this movement of people, this interaction, also gave rise to new ideas and new aspirations, like the Home for Cooperation; a formerly multi-functional space where people used to meet and work together would be brought back to life, with elements of change and continuity present in its physical structure and everyday activities. The purchase and renovation of an old building located in a buffer zone crossway was of unique symbolical and practical value. At the time of the conception of the project, the Ledra Palace barricade was the only pedestrian crossing point on a divided Cyprus, making it easily accessible to all people on the island. Our building, located opposite the historical meeting point of the Ledra Palace Hotel (where negotiation processes between community leaders often took place), bears a significant symbolical meaning that justifies its selection as an intervention site.

Now, beyond historic, political, and symbolical values, the building is located in a fascinating area of the town, opposite the Arab Ahmed district, which was recently renovated as part of the Nicosia master plan. Furthermore, it borders on the walled city of Nicosia. The street in which the building is located is surrounded by historic monuments, such as religious Islamic monuments, an Armenian monastery and cemetery, and the Venetian Walls. Local agencies have always been very interested in the potential use and development of the moat beside the building. Recognizing the social, historical, architectural, urban, and environmental importance of the area, the Department of Town Planning and Housing of the Republic of Cyprus declared the Ledra Palace area and its environs an "Area of Special Character." Actually, numerous structures in this area have already been given cultural heritage status by the same department, in accordance with the Nicosia master plan's proposal. Our building stayed out of this procedure, due to lack of access to the buffer zone at the time of the evaluation (which was before the opening of the Ledra Palace barricade). So part of the project was to get this building listed, too, since it was the only one not listed, for the reason I just explained.

In addition to the charming location, it is near many parking areas and there are panoramic views from the roof, but I repeat, what remains very important to us is the fact that it can be easily accessed by pedestrians from across the divide, because it stands in the middle of two barricades in the UN Buffer Zone.

Are you connected to other projects similar to yours? If so, please specify the project, the partner, and the country/location.

AHDR works closely with a number of international and local organizations, including the Council of Europe, teacher trade unions across the divide, EUROCLIO, The Elders, Oxford University, UNDP-ACT, the European Commission, and community groups from all over the island. We are also of course connected to all the projects operated by the NGOs resident in the Home for Cooperation, as well as to the Cyprus Community Media Center, the Goethe Institute, and the JFK Fulbright Center.

Which NGOs have already taken a place in the center and what are their activities? Would you be interested in being part of a network of centers involved in similar activities on an international level?

1. PRIO Cyprus Centre
2. Interpeace
3. The Union of the Chambers of Cyprus Turkish Engineers and Architects (KTMMOB)
4. The Cyprus Scientific and Technical Chamber's (ETEK)
5. Peace Players – Cyprus

We are definitely interested in being part of a network of centers involved in similar activities on an international level—this is what H4C stands for: cooperation at all levels, including beyond the local.

What can possible future initiatives learn from your experience? What is your advice?

Well, first of all, these projects need full-time commitment and dedication from the promoters, and an experienced management team comprising an experienced project manager, project coordinator, and a team of consultants from a range of disciplines, who are ready whenever necessary to contribute actively and effectively throughout the project to issues regarding organization, planning, implementation, monitoring, sustainability, evaluation, reflection, action, etc.

Our advice for future initiatives could be summarized in a statement produced by members of the association in relation to H4C:

It is, of course, too early to determine the magnitude and quality of the influence that the H4C might have. Yet, it is evident that by its very existence H4C proves that perceived impossibilities can become realities. Facts have been created that prove cooperation across a particular divide to be possible. In their way, these facts build on and memorialize positive inter-communal relations that existed at various points in the past. These facts are also points of "departure" for possible futures. History does not compel us to forever relive cycles of conflict and uneasy co-existence written into the past. This notwithstanding, a peaceful and prosperous future for Cyprus is not guaranteed and will not be given just because we wish for it. But such a future is possible if, through the actions of people in Cyprus and the rest of the world, we choose and strive to make it so.[5]

5 D. Shemilt, M. Epaminondas, M. Koumantari, E. Michail, M. Pittaou. & D. Urfali, Home for Cooperation, Nicosia: K & L Lithofit Ltd., 2011, p. 35.

The Mitrovica Forum

Interview with Momcilo Arlov and Valdete Idrizi

Interviewed by Kai Vöckler

What was the political and social situation in your country and, specifically, in your city, when you started the project?

Kosovo and the Mitrovica Region

Kosovo is one of the poorest regions in Europe and was one of the least developed provinces within the former Yugoslavia. The Kosovo conflict in 1998/99 led to the displacement of a majority of the population, and while most Kosovo-Albanians (K-Albanians) returned immediately after the conflict, more than 200,000 members of minority communities (including the Kosovo Serb [K-Serb] population and more than 8000 extremely vulnerable Roma, Ashkali, and Egyptian [RAE] communities) remain displaced.

The interruption of health, social, and education services, and the continuing high rates of unemployment and illiteracy, combined with long standing ethnic tensions, have resulted in a worsening situation for all Kosovars, with a disproportionately negative impact upon women and minority populations. Additional social and political pressure derives from the challenges of inter-ethnic accommodation in Kosovo, and the acute need for the social inclusion of all minority groups, including RAE communities.

On February 17, 2008, the Kosovo Assembly declared independence and a clear commitment to implement the Comprehensive Status Settlement proposed by UN Special Envoy Martti Ahtisaari, following two years of intensive negotiations that failed to reach a final agreement between Kosovo and Serbia on Kosovo's future status. Despite the fact that guidance from the Security Council is still pending, the UN in Kosovo will continue to consider UN SC Resolution 1244 (1999) as the legal framework for the implementation of its mandate, in light of evolving circumstances.

The decision on the final status of Kosovo, as well as on the far-reaching decentralization plan, was designed to transfer responsibility for minority-related policies and activities to Kosovo authorities at both the central and local levels. The lack of capacity, experience, and previous active involvement of local authorities in development and reintegration projects has to be addressed in order to improve the ownership of local structures and enable future municipalities to adopt an all-inclusive approach to minority integration in Kosovo.

In particular, the municipalities of North/South Mitrovica and the neighboring municipality of Zvecan face numerous challenges. Once a single-company (Trepca Mining) area, they are now de-industrialized and divided. The area has very high levels of unemployment, pollution, rural under-development, a small and inexperienced private sector, a young and relatively unskilled population, severely inadequate infrastructure, and a complicated, divided structure of administration.

The municipalities of North/South Mitrovica and Zvecan are situated approximately 40 kilometers north of Pristine/a and cover an area of 454 square kilometers. Up-to-date, accurate population figures are unfortunately unavailable for North/South Mitrovica, and Zvecan, because a census has not been conducted since 1981; however, it is estimated that over thirty percent of the population in the north of the town was Kosovo-Albanian before the conflict, while today less than a quarter of them remain.

The division of the town has complicated and politicized the provision of public services, and led to the creation of separate facilities for the north and south. These "parallel structures" have differing management and accountability structures, which has inhibited efforts to develop coordinated capacity and strategic planning for the town as a whole. The international community has undertaken measures to improve the situation, but the town and its social, health, and economic infrastructure remain divided.

Tensions between the K-Serb and K-Albanian communities remain high, making it one of the most difficult locations in Kosovo to carry out concrete development activities on either side of the Ibar River. Numerous activities have been undertaken by both the local and international communities as they seek to address a situation that has escalated since the March 2004 riot that started in North/South Mitrovica and spilled over to the rest of Kosovo. Resulting in nineteen deaths and a subsequent increasing lack of security and freedom of movement, the effects of the riot are still a major obstacle to the establishment of normal life in the Mitrovica area. On top of these and numerous other challenges, Mitrovica is also home to one of the largest displaced populations in Kosovo, including many that have been displaced within their own town, so that it is now a target area for one of the largest minority return efforts in the whole of Kosovo.

Available statistics for the North/South Mitrovica and Zvecan municipalities indicate unemployment rates in the range of fifty to eighty percent—way above the Kosovo average, predominantly among segments of the population at low educational attainment levels and with work-based skills that are no longer relevant to the labor market. The economic situation of ethnic communities and minorities in both parts of Mitrovica is extremely challenging; NGOs active in these communities estimate that unemployment levels in the multi-ethnic communities of Boshnjacka Mahala/Mahalle and Boshnjakeve top the seventy percent level.

The same applies to K-RAE communities in the North and K-Ashkali communities in the South, while unemployment among RAE communities in Roma Mahala is practically one hundred percent. Little is documented on the level of domestic violence and the exploitation of women and children but—evidence—for now mainly anecdotal—suggests fearsome figures, accompanied and reinforced by all of the problems related to the prevailing practice of very early marriage in RAE communities.

The central challenge for the Mitrovica region municipalities, therefore, lies in finding a new orientation for the region; eliminating divisions and social exclusion, while improving the security situation and facilitating the re-integration-based development of a local economy and a social fabric in tatters.

The City of Mitrovica – a brief history

The Mitrovica region is ethnically diverse, containing approximately eighty percent Albanians, ten percent Serbs, and ten percent other minorities. The following demographical statistics were drawn from estimates in a recent OSCE report, as no official numbers on the exact ethnic composition are currently available.

Population	Kosovo Albanian Number	%	Kosovo Serb Number	%	Slav Muslims Number	%	Roma-Ashkali Number	%	Turks Number	%
Unreliable 1991-census	82,837	78	10,698	10.02	5,205	4.96	4,851	4,63	431	0,41
1998	95,231	81,74	10,447	8,96						
Current estimate figures	N/A		N/A		2,000	1,76	545	0,48	600	

After 1999 the town was divided along the Ibar River. The municipality of Mitrovica administrates one town and forty-nine villages, including Zvecan, Zubin Potok, Vushtrri, Skenderaj, and Leposaviq. The northern part of the region is mainly populated by Serbs, whereas the south is mostly Albanian. The region was hit hard during the war, with massive Albanian displacement and human losses, followed by similar suffering on the part of the Serbs during and after the NATO intervention.

The human losses and suffering were further aggravated by massive material losses on both sides, primarily of real estate and goods, which have proved hard to regain in an environment ruled by a punishing unemployment rate of approximately seventy-seven percent on both sides.[1]

Despite these enormous challenges, however, inspiring reconciliation efforts—seeking to create a peaceful environment in this troubled region—have been made on both sides. According to UN, OSCE, UNHCR, and NGO databases, approximately two hundred local and around eighteen international NGOs are operative in the Mitrovica municipality and are officially registered with UNMIK. The number of NGOs present, however, is declining, with many operating at significantly reduced capacity, when compared to some years ago.

Taking into consideration statements made by key national and international stakeholders (the Kosovo government, EULEX, ECLOK, ICO, OSCE, UNKT) that describe the local civil society organizations as their main partners and a driving force in the overall democratization process, this reduction significantly jeopardizes the overall capacities of the society to undertake much-needed change with respect to interethnic dialogue, peace building, and reconciliation. It is acknowledged that of the 213 registered local NGOs in Mitrovica, only 26 remain active—and a majority of the active ones are still without basic institutional support, offices, and the elementary technology needed to perform services in an adequate and qualitative manner, and in the best interests of the communities they spring from.

In line with the Ahtisaari plan, the "division" of the Mitrovica municipality became more prominent after the declaration of independence last year, with the municipality of Mitrovica being split into the new municipalities of North Mitrovica and South Mitrovica inside the current municipal boundaries. Since cooperation and dialogue between these new municipalities—as well civil initiatives and local administrations—is vastly underdeveloped to non-existent, bridging this divide is essential if there is to be a peaceful, multi-ethnic, and prosperous future for this severely tested region and people, and, accordingly, the whole of Kosovo and its wider region.

<u>What is the main idea behind the project? What are you trying to achieve with it?</u>

Despite the fact that, following the end of Kosovo conflict in 1999, significant funds were invested by international stakeholders in the development of Kosovo civil society in general and civil society organizations (CSOs) in particular, it is only fair to say that the North Mitrovica civil society sector still lacks the organizational capacities needed to significantly contribute to the development of a healthy, participatory society. This is all the more poignant when one considers the extremely youthful makeup of Mitrovica's communities. Thousands of young people are growing up in a cynical environment with few opportunities for personal development or active citizenship.

Particularly in view of the de facto political vacuum in Northern Kosovo, CSOs could, and should, be the driving force behind the development of a pluralistic, participatory society. CSOs could contribute significantly to this process by serving as watchdogs against the corrupt and/or non-functional governmental institutions at municipal, regional, and national levels, by providing policy guidelines for administrative, social, and judicial institutions and developing projects based on genuine community priorities, rather than on inconsistent donor priorities.

A significant number of CSOs are currently undergoing transformation processes with regard to their internal technological and human resource capacities. These processes, however, are still challenged by a number of constraints: unresolved legal status, internal tensions born out of the competition for foreign funding, ethnic divisions that have only partially healed, public mistrust, and a lack of focus that has left too many organizations willing to reshape themselves to accommodate donor priorities.[2]

Out of an estimated 4900 legally registered Non-Governmental Organizations (NGOs) in Kosovo,[3] only approximately 600 are currently operational to any extent.[4] Out of the 213 legally registered NGOs in Mitrovica (North and South),[5] only 26 were operational as of June 2009.[6]

In Mitrovica, the situation is additionally complicated by the existence of parallel institutional structures (managed respectively by Pristina and Belgrade), a lack of rule of law, an extremely hostile environment when it comes to the inter-ethnic initiatives, the devastated socio-economic situation, and a low level of accountability for CSOs.

If pro-active, accountable, and grass-roots CSOs are to be the main engine in promoting democratization processes, in order to render Kosovo a genuinely multiethnic society, it should be acknowledged that something is wrong with the engine. Ten years after the end of the armed conflict, we do not have the luxury of time.

1 Attached as appendix 16.

2 Civil Society and Development – UNDP Kosovo Human Development Report, 2008.
3 Office for NGO Registration and Liaison, Ministry of Public Affairs.
4 According to field assessments conducted by the Advocacy Training and Resource Center (ATRC) and the Center for Civil Society Development (CCSD) among NGOs of all ethnic background Kosovo-wide.
5 Office for NGO Registration and Liaison, Ministry of Public Affairs.
6 According to a rapid survey conducted by the CCSD, CBM, Me Dore Ne Zemer (MDNZ), and the Center for Migration Studies (CMS).

CRYM Member: Association for Peace Kosovo (AFPK)

To address the problems described above, the CSO community needs to move from competition and fragmentation to cooperation and synergy. The CSO community seeks to achieve this by establishing a coalition of complementary CSOs and CSIs (i.e., civil society initiatives). Working together in the same building under the same name, coalition members will be able to rely on each other's expertise and network, identify opportunities for joint activities, and cut costs by sharing their facilities—a first step toward sustainability. Perhaps most importantly, the coalition members can draw inspiration and support from each other in developing genuine grass-roots initiatives and raising the funds to carry them out, rather than waiting for donors to issue calls for proposals and basing their priorities on the available funding.

By bundling the strengths of a number of successful, established CSO/Is on the one hand and a number of young, talented CSO/Is on the other, the CRYM Coalition will provide for peer training and internal capacity building. In addition, the coalition form will offer a significant level of protection from outside pressure. Jointly, the CRYM Coalition has extensive media reach and a large network of political and social activists, as well as a proven track record of avoiding political cooptation. Finally, as a group of largely young civil activists, the CRYM Coalition has a far better grasp on new media than traditional political stakeholders

CRYM Member: Contact Plus Radio (CPR)

do. It will thus be able to act as a quicker, smarter communicator and reach a broad audience without inviting any immediate reaction from those currently in power, who largely rely on old (or no) media.

CRYM Member: Association for Peace Kosovo (AFPK)

Despite the fact that AFPK has its present premises in a more-than- inadequate office facility (a container), they are still able to reach out to a considerable number of the RAE population on a daily basis. Unfortunately, even these inadequate office premises will soon become unavailable for them, because the landlord is not keen to extend the usage agreement.

CRYM Member: Contact Plus Radio (CPR)

Contact Plus Radio is the most widely heard Serbian language radio station in northern Kosovo and a leading partner in the Association of Serbian Language Media in Kosovo. Despite their status as the most professional K-Serbian radio station in Kosovo, they work in inadequate circumstances that do not allow them to further expand their services, such as establish a media center. Moreover, due to budgetary constraints, they will be forced to vacate the existing office space in the near future. Establishing the CRYM Center remains their best available opportunity for survival.

CRYM Member: Mitrovica Rock School (MRS)

CRYM Member: Mitrovica Rock School (MRS)

Mitrovica Rock School succeeded in developing more than a fruitful relationship with the youth of Mitrovica South and Mitrovica North, generating unexpected interest in enthusiastic teens interested in music and cultural events. However, this interest should be matched with adequate facilities, since the current space does not meet the criteria of quality needed.

CRYM Member: Youth of JAZAS Kosovo (OJAZAS)

OJAZAS is the only K-Serbian organization in Kosovo dealing with issues concerning the prevention of HIV/AIDS and the promotion of healthy lifestyles among the youth of minority communities. Despite their wide base of peer-to-peer educators and volunteers, when it comes to office space, they are sharing one with the CCSD and ISU, as part of the efforts to reduce their operational costs.

CRYM Member: ZDRAVLJE (ZDRAVLJE)

ZDRAVLJE is one of the most credible local NGOs dealing with women and health prevention issues. Despite the fact that they

CRYM Member: Youth of JAZAS Kosovo (OJAZAS)

CRYM Member: ZDRAVLJE (ZDRAVLJE)

CRYM Member: Center for Civil Society Development (CCSD)

operate from more than inadequate offices, they are succeeding in maintaining social communication while reaching out to a wide range of community members in need. It goes without saying that adequate CRYM Center premises and the group's membership in the CRYM Coalition would further increase the quality of its services.

CRYM Member: Center for Civil Society Development (CCSD)

CCSD remains one of the leading CSOs in the area of northern Kosovo sincerely devoted to partnership and networking among civil society, media, and community representatives. Due to the fact that existing office space is shared with OJAZAS and ISU, it is easy to imagine that, besides the programmatic benefits achieved as a member of the CRYM Coalition, an additional benefit of an adequate CRYM Center facility will directly improve the quality of future activities, and allow the expansion necessary to serve the best interests of a wider scope of CSOs and concerned community members.

When you started the project, with whom did you work, who supported it? And what have been the biggest obstacles?

The beginnings of the two-year program described above, BRIDGING THE DIVIDE (the Center for Resources, Youth and Media (CRYM) is an elaborate sub-component of the program) can be traced back to August 2009, when Professor Padraig O'Malley, from Boston University in Massachusetts, initiated a gathering of four divided cities, namely: Mitrovica (Kosovo), Derry/Londonderry (Northern Ireland), Kirkuk (Iraq) and Nicosia (Cyprus). This gathering required representatives of these cities to form city-based FORUMS, which would include representatives of political parties and civil society. To that end, the MITROVICA FORUM was formed in August 2009, and its representatives participated at the orientation session in August 2009 in Boston, Massachusetts. During this initial session it was decided to provide the body with a more pro-positive name, so it became FORUM OF CITIES IN TRANSITION instead of DIVIDED CITIES, while the decision was also made to invite other cities to join the FORUM OF CITIES IN TRANSITION at the first Annual Conference of the Forum of Cities in Transition. Mitrovica, Kosovo, has been named the conference host.

In order to prepare adequately, the already existing Mitrovica Forum, which initially included only politicians and civil society representatives, was further expanded with newly elected members from the Mitrovica business sector, the Mitrovica media sector, and the Mitrovica youth sector.

The First Annual Conference of Forum of Cities in Transition took place in Mitrovica, Kosovo, in May 2010 and was widely supported by key international donors within Kosovo (as can be seen in the Conference Report attachment).

What kind of impact did the project have on the city, in a social, political, or cultural sense?

Following the successful implementation of the Annual Conference of the Forum of Cities in Transition in Mitrovica, Kosovo, during May 2010, CBM and CCSD, two leading NGOs from Mitrovica South and Mitrovica North respectively, initiated a two-year program called BRIDGING THE DIVIDE. It has three main components: (1) establishment of the Center for Resources, Youth, and Media (2) establishment of a bilingual magazine, M@Mag, focused on youth and Mitrovica, and (3) support the improvement of municipal infrastructure in Mitrovica North and Mitrovica South.

Having said this, the project had more than a significant impact on the overall city and community life, as it started to improve the quality of everyday life of citizens in a number of areas, i.e., through renovation of playgrounds, renovation of apartment building façades, repairing damaged city roads, supporting local media and civil society organizations, providing grants to youth for cultural and sport projects, etc.

Why did you choose this place in the city for the project? Why was it important to have it physically embedded? What was the meaning of the building/place?

Mitrovica remains the symbol of physical and psychological division between the K-Albanian and K-Serbian community in Kosovo. It is the place in Kosovo that still has the highest potential for violence in Kosovo; however, due to this particular reason, the CBM and CCSD (with adequate acknowledgement and support from the Dutch Ministry of Foreign Affairs) decided to address the issues of concern to citizens in this environment of frozen conflict, acting in line with the rationale that if we want to deliver change, we need to start at the place where that change is most needed, despite the fact that there are constant constraints in such a complex political and insecure environment.

Are you connected to other projects like yours, and if so, where, and who is it?

Through the Forum of Cities in Transition, MITROVICA FORUM is connected to participating city forums.

What can we learn for the future from your experience? What is your advice?

If change is needed, it has to be initiated. Often, in an environment that is not open to a culture of tolerance and ethnic reconciliation, this change has to be initiated by a handful of, not necessarily skillful, but definitely devoted people.

Abrašević Center, Mostar

Interview with Tina Ćorić

Interviewed by Kai Vöckler

<u>What was the political and social situation in your country, and specifically in your city, when you started the project?</u>

When we started the campaign to reclaim the youth center in 2003, the overall situation in Bosnia Herzegovina was pretty much as it is today: a divided society, segregated education, lack of public places, weak institutions and media in the hands of political and ethnic interests, corruption, a lack of public funding, no transparent funding criteria, no effort to face the past, no political will to go forward, the manipulation of the electorate, etc.

Specifically, in our city, Mostar, all of the above was reflected on the local level, with one extra dimension, and that is the division of the city into two de facto cities. Each side had its own government/administration, media, institutions, schools, other educational facilities, water and electricity companies, etc.

The city was in that position in 2003, and today the only difference is that the city administration has been united by the 2004 statute of the city of Mostar, which was imposed by the Office of the High Representative, since the two sides could not agree.

<u>What is the main idea behind the project? What are you trying to achieve with it?</u>

The main idea(s) behind the project specifically responds to the local context. Providing a public place in a divided city, in an interesting geographical location in Abrasevic—the central zone, where it is impossible to determine to which side it belongs. Here, young people in particular have an opportunity to meet, reflect, exchange, participate, as there are no such other places in the city. For us this was a direct response to the growing, omnipresent nationalism that is tearing our local society apart. Our aim was to position ourselves actively in the socio-political and cultural life of the city, mainly, as well the country.

<u>When you started the project, with whom did you work, who supported it? And what have been the biggest obstacles?</u>

We started the campaign in March 2003. We worked as a network of local youth and cultural NGOs, artists, collectives, civic activists, etc. We also had our architect from France, since the space was a ruin and needed to be reconstructed. The biggest

obstacle was exactly that, getting the space permanently and obtaining all of the necessary permits and funds to reconstruct. Politically, we would have had obstacles had we not prepared and organized the campaign well. After three months of hard campaigning, we managed to get our request on the agenda of City Council meeting, when they unanimously voted to lease us the space for one year on a renewable contract. We had the significant help of the city's urban planning department, which aided us in elaborating our original reconstruction plan. We sought and got the support of international organizations, governments, networks, our partners from abroad, different youth and cultural centers, UNESCO, etc.

<u>What kind of impact did the project have on the city, in a social, political, or cultural sense?</u>

It had and still has a significant, irreplaceable impact on the city. It is still the only common, public, youth center; it is the most active center of all in Mostar, with the biggest number of diverse events per year. We are the only place in the city that does cinema screenings, because Mostar has not had a cinema since before the war. We were the first to have festivals (from 1998 on, before Abrasevic came into existence) and bring culture and arts to the city, in public places. We are the only center that systematically works with youth and schools (here, we still face political obstacles, i.e. we still have not received written authorization from the canton minister to approach the schools). On a political level, we are considered left-wing activists. We often advocate for different changes (public spaces, laws affecting non-profit radio stations, cultural policy in Bosnia-Herzegovina, demilitarization in the region, conscientious objection campaign until the army was no longer mandatory), we are one of the most vocal local groups when it comes to city-level decisions (annual budget, urban planning, grants, youth council, and so on), and we

support local civic initiatives, while also voicing our own concerns.

<u>Why did you choose this place in the city for the project? Why was it important to have it physically embedded? What is the significance of the building/place?</u>

The significance of Abrasevic and its current location is a crucial part of the project, and an element in its identity. Namely, Abrasevic was founded in 1926 by workers, as a left-wing workers' cultural association. One of Abrasevic's traditions has always been to maintain the values of equality, justice, humanity, solidarity, and personal growth. Until the war, Abrasevic was a central place for culture and socializing in Mostar, where it raised many generations of Mostarians through its amateur theater and choir, guitar, accordion, and folklore instruction, afternoon dances, different social activities, quizzes and competitions, and cooperation with other, similar centers throughout Yugoslavia. With the arrival of the 1980s there was a slight modernization, with rock concerts and similar activities.

So our wish was to continue this mission and uphold the significance of Abrasevic in Mostar. Obviously, the best place to do it was the old Abrasevic. We carry on the name and the tradition; we became the legal heirs to the previous association and won the property case in court. In today's situation—being in a divided city—the second, physical meaning of the place was the fact that it is situated on the former demarcation line and as such is again the symbol of the "bridge on dry land." Since the building has two entrances (the only one now open active until the second Austro-Hungarian building has been remodeled), one on Santiceva Street (a former front line) and the second on the Boulevard (the demarcation line dividing the city), it is in a perfect position for a common public space. It denotes a zone where we invite people from both sides to meet and join. Keeping in mind that—

especially as far as young people are concerned—this problem is present (they do not go to the "other" side), it seems to be in a good position for a youth center and helps them overcome the fear of going to the "other side."

Are you connected to other projects like yours, and if so, where and what are they?

We are connected to similar projects, but we do not know of any case like ours. For example, in France, we were and are connected to various places that were once squats, but have now been legalized, or else the squatters have been evicted—Mix-Art Myris in Toulouse, for example. We know of different "housing of associations" in France, Italy, Serbia, Croatia, and Ireland, but they do not operate in the same way, although the idea is similar (joining forces, ideas, capacities, resources). In Bosnia-Herzegovina there is no project exactly like ours, but we do cooperate with similar, individual organizations, some of which some have space (like Banja Luka and Travnik).

What can we learn for the future from your experience? What is your advice?

There are many lessons to be drawn from our experience. The best advice I can give is to not give up and to believe that it is possible! There will be many obstacles and setbacks, but one should never give up. When our colleagues from France suggested the possibility of doing something like this—before our campaign, in the years 2000 and 2001—we said "forget it, it will never be possible in this city." And look at what we have today! We thought we would never get the space, never raise enough money for reconstruction, never achieve a stable structure, never have success in the community, and, finally, after all that we went through in the last eight years, after all sorts of obstacles and problems, it showed us that it is possible, it is important, so "where there is a will, there is a way." The second most important piece of advice I can give is never to lose continuity, never close the doors of your center. We worked continuously and proposed different programs and activities, even during the worst periods, when we were working without Internet or telephone, with roofs leaking, with equipment falling apart, with the reconstruction not being finished, in the middle of construction . . . this is very important when you need to establish your position in the community and when you have this task, as we did, of attracting and educating the audience/public. Third: always be present as much as you can, in the media, in debates, in street activities, in support of other fellow initiatives, in support of everything that is progressive and positive in your community. Do not "sit on the fence"; have an opinion! Also, be cautious about "professionalization." Once money comes in and standards rise, it is easy for people to start quarreling. We saw this in many other organizations and centers. We managed to avoid this by being transparent and respecting the principle of solidarity. Value your volunteers, because without them, it is hardly possible. When you can support something free of charge, do it; when you can do it as well by volunteering human resources, do it. You and your center will gain gratification and a reputation by it, and in the future, probably some other favor when you need it. Finally, be honest with your partners, donors, and media; be true to your own principles and values. Nothing will get you farther than being regarded as a credible actor with a genuine identity. Oh, and one more, do it yourself, all that you can (we remodeled the performance hall entirely by ourselves, so it saved us a lot of money, which permitted us to do much more than if we had paid a professional firm), recycle, do everything low-cost.

(Re)collecting Mostar

Mapping Public Space to Generate Memory Collections

Giulia Carabelli and Mela Žuljević
ABART Group

The project[1] (Re)collecting Mostar started in November 2010 when the Abart group began—under the auspices of OKC Abrašević (Abrašević Youth Cultural Center)—developing a collaborative project with students from the two universities in Mostar. On the one hand, the project aims to critically analyze the situation of public space in Mostar and, on the other hand, to collect and creatively assemble public memories. The process will lead to the establishment of a depot/ museum, where the contested pasts and presents of the city can be displayed, discussed, and re-worked. Here, the process of collecting memories is understood to be crucial in the creation of an archive, where the often conflicting histories of Mostar could be gathered and rendered to re-position them in contemporary urban narratives. Further, assembling and creating objects capable of materializing the intangible space of memory might possibly support the process of putting together divergent and convergent stories, in order to create an appropriate space that could contain them all, while symbolically reattaching them to the city. Thus, this contribution aims at critically reflecting on the process of collecting memories in the particular case of a contested city. In specific, the extent to which objects could become tools for active collaboration and a sharing of authority will be taken into account in relation to the political context of the city.

Abart's Activities in Context

Mostar was one of the many cosmopolitan cities in the former Yugoslavia, home to a very mixed, unsegregated population. The city, once celebrated for its vibrant urban life, is now mostly acknowledged as "problematic," "abnormal," "contested," and "divided." The division was brought about by the war that led to the dismantling of Yugoslavia. Since then, a street in the center of the city (the Bulevar) has functioned as an internal border between the dominant Bosnian-Croat and Bosniak (Muslim) communities.

Despite the absence of a physical barrier and the fact that the city was declared reunified in 2004,[2] the process of recreating social cohesion is far from successful. Consensus has so far been reached only in matters regarding the strengthening of urban polarization, discarding any possibility of rehabilitating shared spaces. The political and institutional vacuums left on the city, regional, and state levels certainly do not facilitate any progressive movement toward a real unification, but rather support the divisive status quo.

For this main reason, the NGO sector is the leading vehicle of reconciliation, promoting and implementing peace-building initiatives, thanks to extensive, international financial support. Among the NGOs active in the city of Mostar, the Abrašević Youth Cultural Center is the one with the longest and most successful history of engaging with the polarization of the city. The center functions as an umbrella organization for several independent groups active in the fields of art, environment, education, and media. Abart was funded three years ago, with the intent of promoting and supporting art projects and it relies on the collaboration of Mela Žuljević (designer), Anja Bogojević and Amila Puzić (curators), Husein Oručević (political scientist), and Giulia Carabelli (sociologist).

Over the last two years in particular, Abart benefitted from two large grants to carry out cultural projects directly targeting the division of the city. Activities so far implemented have been successful in attracting the attention of the media and in engaging the population of Mostar. Abart has also been working on the establishment of international networks with other organizations working in divided cities, in order to exchange experiences and offer comparative material. Here, it is important to mention that Mostar suffers from a general lack of cultural activities and initiatives. The majority of the existing cultural institutions are obsolete or support nationalist discourses. Therefore, Abart aims to promote and sustain initiatives that could fill this gap and employ art as a tool to critically reflect on the contemporary urban situation.

Given the context, the main goal of Abart is to use art and artistic interventions as strategies to create a contact vocabulary capable of reconnecting the citizens of Mostar for both the long and short terms. In 2009/10 Abart initiated a collaborative project with artists from Beirut, Berlin, and Mitrovica, in Kosovo, which culminated in a three-day festival in Mostar (April 2010). During the festival, the city became an open-air stage for performers, storytellers, and visual artists aiming to explore art's potential as a critical tool for reflecting upon the city's current situation. The success of the initiative and the enthusiasm of the Abart team led to a proposal for a new project for 2010/11: (Re) collecting Mostar.

This is not my piece, installation, artist Gordana Andjelic Galic (Sarajevo)

The project targets two main issues: (1) the neglect of public space and the consequent loss of public memory and (2) the absence of a space where post-war debates can be negotiated, and discussions of city's future (rather than versions of its past) can take place. Whereas the previously implemented project had an ephemeral nature and basically aimed at animating the city, the ambitious goal of this new project is to create a space where the material produced and accumulated could be stored and archived.

This ideal space, which would be part of the existing infrastructure of the Youth Cultural Center, is imagined as a space where works of art can be displayed and archives will make research material available and initiate new projects. This depot/museum space functions as a sort of horizon, toward which all of the various project activities work.
In fact, it hasn't been designed or conceived yet, in any concrete form. This museum, without any provisional name or shape, embodies a potential. This is not only the project's potential , but also the potential that the city has to create its own future by working out its contested past. In a city without political cohesiveness, in a state still contested and monitored by international political bodies, the relationship between conflicting parties could be perhaps re-negotiated outside the political arena, in the everyday.

1 The project has been sponsored by MDG-F (Millennium Development Goals Fund) and ERSTE Stiftung.

2 The new statute for the city of Mostar (as a single city) was imposed by the Office of the High Representative (OHR) in January 2004, even though the city council refused to adopt it. The statute became operative in April 2004, and it has never been changed. In fact, to amend the statute, the city council has to formally adopt it. For an extensive discussion on the topic, see the International Crisis Group Policy briefing number 54 (July 2009).

Intervention in public space, March 2011: OpSjene ver 1.0, artist Božidar Katić (Zagreb)

Washing, performance, artist Gordana Andjelic Galic (Sarajevo)

Urban cut1: Map, exhibition of maps, March 2011

(Re)collecting Mostar – Rationale

The rationale of the project is well summarized by its main research question: *In a city where history has not yet been written, but is contested and advocated to reinforce division, could the re-collection of public and personal memories proactively engage the process of making sense of the past by critically offering a perspective other than a nationalist one?*
This is the main question that (Re) collecting Mostar aims to answer. The purpose is not to replace the writing of history, but rather to gather thoughts about the process per se. In fact, it is a possibility that, due to the difficulties faced by those in charge of outlining the recent history of Mostar—namely the impossibility of agreeing on a common plot able to satisfy and acknowledge various versions of what happened in the 1990s—the storytelling comes to the fore as a potential place to sustain and support antagonistic factions and feed irresolvable debates, transcending the capacity of history to systematize the past in order to move on toward the future.

Both history and memories could be read as part of the continuous process of becoming; in fact they are subjects of transformations and revisions made according to social and political contingencies, emotional drifts, or (self) deception. But, even though it is advocated that history is unified and makes sense, memories themselves are actually fluid, multiple, and diverse. Memories connect to historical events in a particular way, acknowledging the banality of the quotidian. History needs to be supported by personal memories, just as much as personal memories require history as a framework. The recollection of personal memories is therefore instrumental in the validation of history, but it could also provoke counter-discourses willing to criticize and problematize official narratives. Yet, given the hierarchical structure of power, different groups will gain visibility according to their position in the political realm, and therefore official memories and counter-memories will play divergent roles, often antagonistic ones.

Places are part of the infrastructure crucial to the collection of memories: places trigger and locate memory. This is the reason why the process of talking about memories and history has to deal with space. Cities could therefore be acknowledged as archives that are continuously re-shaped by the re-drafting of history. On the one hand, we could consider new monuments as the material manifestation of a new course of history and, on the other hand, the neglect of certain areas as an example of how it is felt that certain events must be forgotten or erased.

The strategy chosen by (Re)collecting Mostar to unravel the complex crafting of histories is spatial and focuses on public spaces. In particular, the project focuses on the development, usage and the roles played by public spaces. Public spaces are gathering spaces, key locations for the erection of monuments, playgrounds for children, as well as deserted areas, empty lots, highly secured and controlled zones. Whether used or not, what public spaces have in common is the fact that they are repositories of memories. We all walk through the cities where we live, facing outbursts of the past that not only inform, but sometimes re-direct our paths.

(Re)collecting Mostar began with acknowledging that public places in contemporary Mostar have been definitely neglected, treated with uncomfortable indifference, and underused. In particular, the project is interested in understanding the extent to which the present political and social fragmentation is reproduced in public spaces, so that they are left empty.

(Re)collecting Mostar feels that it is an urgent necessity to gather memories of the recent history of the city, not only to keep them alive, but, more importantly, to critically engage with the shared history of the city, in order to produce spaces where the ongoing process of authorizing and neglecting memories can be discussed. In the city of Mostar, where history is not yet unified, remembrance could create an appropriate space to re-collect all that has been lost in the process of transferring material from imagined pre- and post-war urban archives, and to critically engage with the information as it unfolds. (Re)collecting Mostar wonders whether the process of intervening in the urban space by attaching and/or re-attaching memories to a specific place might create the potential for confronting memories and deciding whether what has been lost is lost forever, or simply dormant; whether it is necessary or not to remember forgotten places or events, or whether partial and/or momentary amnesia is necessary, in order to start afresh.

If, on the one hand, the goal of (Re)collecting Mostar is to collect information, another goal is to proactively intervene in the public arena by employing art as a tool for intervention. Urban performances will temporarily occupy the urban space and engage with citizens in reflecting on the city's potential, sparking the imagination, and rehabilitating the role of public space as a place for productive discussions.

(Re)collecting Mostar – Phases I and II

The project is articulated in four main phases. The first two phases concentrated on public space: first, the mapping of public spaces in Mostar (by Abart) and, second, the artistic/creative mapping of public spaces (by students and invited artists). The last two phases deal with public memory and account for collecting data on public memory in Mostar (Abart and students) and assembling, archiving, and displaying the materials in a depot/museum (Abart and students).

Phases I and II involved various mapping exercises conducted both by the team members of Abart and university students. Particular attention was given to detecting shifts that occurred in the understanding of public space. In fact, according to the historical context, not only the location, but the very meaning of public space has changed. For example, in the 1980s and beginning of the 1990s, the main spaces for mingling and meeting were certain areas and streets, but today, the very same spots are abandoned or treated with increasing suspicion. Maps were drawn by combining archival research with interviews conducted across a wide range of participants according to age, gender, and place of residence (citizens living outside Bosnia-Herzegovina were also part of the sample).

As a way to structure the work, the students were asked to focus on a section that cuts across the city from west to east, crossing major leisure, retail, and historical areas: the Musala-Rondo section. In fact, according to the research results, this area has always been popular and highly used in the everyday life of the city, both for the location of retail spaces and for the presence of many popular cafes and gathering points. At the present, despite the busy look of this section, its usage is complicated by the fact that the unofficial border, the Bulevar, crosses the area right in its middle. Supervised by architect Dubravka Sekulić, the students worked from March to June 2011 and were able to produce an interesting set of "emotional" maps, site-specific interventions, and collages, adding a very personal perspective to the project as a whole. The results were presented in the exhibition *And They Lived Happily Ever After,* hosted by the Abrašević Youth Cultural Center in June 2011.

As the research and mapping processes were going on, two artists were invited to take up a residence in Mostar for a week. In March 2011 the first artist, Božidar Katić, selected a deserted area along the Bulevar to work on his multi-media performance, *Where People Should be Walking Upside Down with Their Legs Lifted Up in the Air,* which questioned the abandonment of this area by reanimating it through a multi-sensorial intervention. After drawing on the ground shadows of imaginary people using the space, the artist added voices recorded in a park, and scents of flowers to the scene, recreating the negative of what an inhabited public place could look like. In June 2011 the second artist invited, Gordana Anđelić-Galić, intervened in the area under the famous Old Bridge. Her highly provocative performance, *Washing,* saw the artist washing the many flags that signify the history of Bosnia Herzegovina in the Neretva River. As she was washing them, the water of the river turned a deep shade of red, a clear reminder of the many wars and deaths that accompany political changes.

The exhibition was enriched by an audio-photo lecture prepared by Husein Oručević and Ronald Panza, entitled *The Dormitories of Mostar – From Ideology to the Subculture of Habitation,* which expanded on the role played by socialist architecture in the urban fabric of Mostar, particularly focusing on social housing and dormitories and the ways in which they affected the everyday life of communities living in them. The lecture attempted to confront the transition from socialist urbanism, through war and post-war reconstruction, to the city's contemporary assets, highlighting the different uses of these spaces. The concluding remarks were the words of the famous architect and writer Bogdan Bogdanović. A selection of texts from *Grad i Budućnost* (The City and the Future, 2001), *Gradoslovar* (Urban Dictionary, 1982) and *Urbs & logos: ogledi iz simbologije grada* (Urbs and Logos: Essays on the Symbolism of the City, 1976) guided the audience through a more theoretical reflection on the concept of the urban and the nature of cities.

(Re)collecting Mostar – Phases III and IV

The project is now entering its third phase. The students are about to start collecting memories by conducting interviews and research in conjunction with the members of Abart. This new collection process will gather memories of the city by navigating its space, thanks to the new knowledge acquired during the mapping of its urban expansion/changes and its public spaces.

Since this part of the process is still ongoing and there is no material to be presented and discussed, we hope that the depot/museum will be able to display written and visual material, in order to create a space where memories could not only be at the disposal of visitors, but could also become a way through which the past is made present and is discussed in order to produce an inclusive future.

Mostar, 2005

Photos: Kai Vöckler

Mostar, 2005

...gdje ima
mjesta
za sve
Hrvatska
je dom
svih njenih
građana.

PROJEKAT 2000

6 M

DISKONT
BAŠTA

Toward a Third Space: Dipkarpaz/Rizokarpaso

Şebnem Hoşkara, Esra Can Akbil,
Giorgos Psaltis

The conflict between the two main communities of Cyprus, which dates back to the early 1950s, reached its peak in 1974 with the division of the island into two geographical areas, causing hundreds of thousands of Greek and Turkish Cypriots to leave their houses and move to those areas where their respective communities exercise control. Turkish Cypriots now live in the north, with thirty-six percent of the territory having declared itself an independent state in 1983; the Turkish Republic of Northern Cyprus (TRNC) is unrecognized by the international community exept Turkey.[1] Greek Cypriots populate the south, under the rule of the Republic of Cyprus.[2] To this day the UN Buffer Zone (UNBZ), with its varying width, crosses the island from east to west, also dividing the capital of the island, Nicosia, into two sectors. From 1974 until 2003, when the first checkpoints were opened, people were unable to cross the UNBZ and go to the other side of the island. While reunification negotiations have gone on over the last thirty-five years, the division of Cyprus has had a direct impact on the development of urban and social structures. Collaborations have rarely been possible; most have failed although there are a few exceptions, such as the Nicosia Master Plan.

Archis Interventions_Cyprus is an informal initiative established through the collaboration of architects and academics across the divide, with the aim of increasing the quality of urban and social space by promoting sustainable development, enhancing social interaction in urban spaces, and creating urban awareness through strategies that extend beyond the social and physical borders of the island. As a first step—before focusing on implementation—the Archis Interventions_Cyprus initiative undertook an analytical investigation of the various projects developed from 1978 onward, which critically investigated the spatial implications of the division, with the aim of defining guidelines for successful project management and the effective resolution of problems. Through this research, the group aims to define the obstacles to project sustainability, in order to develop various methods and strategies to overcome them. The majority of the projects analyzed had an urban perspective or were related in some way to the urban fabric (including UNBZ). Most of the local projects initiated failed, whereas projects implemented with international support (UNDP, USAID, EU) achieved partial success. Research has also established that long-winded and/or ineffective bureaucratic procedures tend to diminish the communities' (or project initiators') confidence in project implementation and in potential benefits. This situation also brings with it a lack of systematic management for a sustained project.

Throughout the ongoing research several main factors that hinder the implementation of a sustainable project were defined. These research findings are derived from one-on-one interviews with project leaders, initiators and partners, community leaders, local inhabitants, academics, and local politicians. According to the findings, general support for and belief in sustainable and beneficial multicultural projects seems to be largely lacking. Combined with the low efficiency of systematic project management and community organizations, engaging donors in a project when bureaucratic procedures take ages to be resolved, appears to be the major obstacle, in general. The most common obstacles faced in the different stages of the projects can be summed up as:

- lack of an expert system in project management and community organization
- extensive bureaucratic procedures and authorizations
- limited effect of governmental policies on the rights of local administrations to make decisions
- limited support of/belief in local administrations when it comes to supervising bi-communal/multicultural projects
- slow and insufficient development of a civil society, which results in perpetuation of mental barriers, prejudices, or discrimination based on ethnic background/external appearance
- lack of sustainability in project investment
- lack of service provisions for the community and infrastructural master plans
- failure to achieve systematic, strategic, sustainable planning for regional development and a lack of investment
- conflicted ownership issues and difficulty in engaging donors, due to unsettled ownership situation

After this in-depth study of failing projects and investigations on a local scale, Archis Interventions_Cyprus team developed a set of strategies to be implemented in Dipkarpaz/Rizokarpaso, a village in the north of Cyprus where the Greek Cypriots who stayed in the village after the 1974 division are sharing this space with the Turkish population that moved from north and southeast Turkey.

Learning from the Shared Space: Dipkarpaz/Rizokarpaso Project

Despite the creation of two mainly ethnically homogenous areas on two sides of the divide, some Greek Cypriots still live in the north part of the island, in the Karpaz Region. Rizokarpaso/Dipkarpaz and AyiaTriada/Sipahi are the two major villages. Similarly, over a thousand Turkish Cypriots reside in the south. Since 1975 thousands of migrants from southeast and northern regions of Turkey have moved to the region, creating a new demographical pattern. Uncertainty regarding the region's future administration, unclear ownership issues, and strict legislation on environmental protection, combined with the dramatic demographic shift creates a fragile social and urban case to work on. The demographic composition before 1974 (1891 census: 1,810 GC/4TC; 1946 census: 4,053 GC/11TC; and 1960 census: 3,152 GC/2TC) indicates that no shared life between the Greek Cypriot and the Turkish Cypriot communities had been previously experienced in Dipkarpaz/Rizokarpaso. Today, according to the municipality office, the village population is about 3,000 and nearly one-tenth of the whole population are Greek Cypriots (the 2006 census states 1935 people live in the village,[3] but the number of Greek Cypriots is not mentioned). Due to its isolation from the rest of the island, Dipkarpaz/Rizokarpaso experienced a decline in the 1960s, with decreasing population and little investment. There is very little support for local production and the economy is therefore very weak. Given the limited opportunities available to its traditional residents, as well as the more recent immigrants whose status is ambiguous, it is extremely difficult to foster a sense of belonging and social commitment in the village, or to promote positive social interaction, a sustainable development policy, and support for the settlement's future.

1 UN Security Council Resolutions 541 (1983) [available at: http://www.un.int/cyprus/scr541.htm] and 550 (1984)[available at: http://www.unhcr.org/refworld/country,,,RESOLUTION,CYP,,3b00f15b24,0.html].

2 The Republic of Cyprus (RoC) was established in 1960 as a compromise solution between Greek and Turkish Cypriots. For more, see the Zürich-London Agreement, Constitution of the Republic of Cyprus, and attached treaties.

3 DPO, "Devlet Planlama Orgutu Genel Nufus ve Konut Sayimi Kesin Sonuclari" (Government Planning Organization, 2006 census results, http://nufussayimi.devplan.org/, 2006.

Since services and space are limited, there is youth drain in both Greek Cypriot and Turkish communities, as young people leave the village for bigger towns in northern and southern Cyprus.

The interest of the Archis Interventions team in Dipkarpaz/Rizokarpaso dates back to the Revitalization of Dipkarpaz Project, which was handled by a group of researchers and academics from the faculty of architecture at Eastern Mediterranean University in 2008.[4] During this project, one of the main challenges was reaching local people and integrating their feedback into the project while at the same time having the project embraced by the local people and authorities. Although the methodologies and strategies introduced resulted in a project conceptualizing an Agro-cultural Tourism Area in the village, the project could never be implemented and remained on paper. At that point, a new project, supported by Archis Interventions, was developed with the aim of digging deep into the shared space in the village, using social and spatial analysis in order to explore possible bottom-up interventions to enhance the perception and usage of urban space in the village.

The research has been undertaken with an awareness of the peculiarities of situation, in which relations among the various groups are fragile, and the Turkish Cypriot community is absent in the village. Dipkarpaz/Rizokarpaso is the only actual place on the island where Greek Cypriots share a common space and common daily practice with the mainland Turkish population in Cyprus. The houses of Greek Cypriots and Turkish people are not segregated; as a result there are no physical borders in the village. Population that migrated from Turkey in a number of streams since 1975 settled in the empty houses left by Greek Cypriots, which resulted in coexistence. Since then, the political instability in Cyprus on the macro level has resulted in ambiguity in the daily lives and built environment of the village, causing physical and social transformation. The eccentric situation of "otherness" is visible in the everyday life of the village. A specially defined status has been given to the Greek Cypriots, who are accepted as "citizens" of the TRNC with restrictions: for instance, they cannot be elected, nor can they vote for representatives. A Greek inhabitant is paid a stipend of sorts every month, and receives provisions from the RoC every week, brought by UN forces to meetings at the old market building. Apart from the aid from the south, Greek Cypriots participate in local production, by fishing, animal herding, and agriculture. Although the Greek Cypriot villagers claim that they have difficulties in getting licenses to run shops, they run a coffee shop and a few restaurants in the region. A Greek primary school and a Greek high school are active in the region, with teachers from the south, although the number of students is very small. Religious practices are allowed as demanded, and the main church in the village center is active. There is a priest, who is an active member of the informal commission dealing with the Greek Cypriot community issues. Greek Cypriot villagers have to deal with the fact that their daily activities are eyed suspiciously, as they have been watched at all gatherings and meetings, and this was eventually reflected in every step of this project. Being representatives of the Greek Cypriot community on the most sacred Orthodox Christian land of Cyprus, their activities are also under observation by the authorities of the RoC and the diaspora in the south, limiting their interactions with migrants from Turkey. Turkish nationals—who moved into the houses abandoned by Greek Cypriots, in the hopes of a new life—have not been able to achieve a sense of stability, because their new homes are always on the negotiation table when community leaders meet. When negotiations returned the Karpaz peninsula to Greek Cypriot owners on some of the optional maps of the UN-sponsored Annan Plan for Cyprus,[5] no investment was made in the maintenance of the buildings in the village until 2004, when the Greek Cypriots rejected the plan with a seventy-six percent majority, while the Turkish Cypriots voted in favor with a majority of sixty-five percent in a separate referendum. This result transformed Turkish nationals' fragile relationship with the physical environment, as they developed a belief in their continuous existence in the village. Since then, supported by representatives of the Turkish authorities in north, many houses and public buildings in the village have been remodeled, while investment in the region brought new roads, hotels, a new marina, and several guesthouses.

The various parties involved tend to deal with the situation in accordance with popular political policy, rather than by responding to the communities' present-day need for interaction in the social and physical environments. A fomented nationalism, as well as strong religious belief, encouraged by funding religion classes for youngsters in the village, is reflected in the over-usage of symbols in the area. The resulting situation in the village constitutes a *contested space*. In contested spaces, competing cultural groups, like nationalists and loyalists, strengthen and legitimize themselves and their efforts through the development of adaptive spatial practices.[6] This can be observed in the ways that communities in the village use space. In DipKarpaz/Rizokarpaso however, one of the groups is almost absent from public space: the village center, for instance, is used by the Turkish population, while, except for the Greek coffee shop, the gatherings of Greek Cypriots are usually at houses, where they will be least seen. Yet, digging deep into peoples' lives during several meetings and gatherings in the village reveals various modes of interactions describing the way they have produced new codes of communication as a result of living together for more than thirty-five years.

"One morning we woke up seeing some foreigners on the streets. Women, wearing scarves, were walking around hiding from us, looking shy rather than afraid. But we were afraid!" a Greek Cypriot woman says, describing the first days of the meeting of two communities. She adds, "In time, we learned how to communicate, we live together you know. They changed a lot as well, they adapted to us, to Cyprus. You can rarely see women wearing [the] *mandyla*[7] anymore." When we were having coffee together, a young Turkish woman brought a wedding invitation; she sighed and said, "Every week there are marriages in the village!"

A young policeman in his twenties, chatting in the Greek coffee shop with an old Greek man, comments on the situation, "This man is a father to me. My mother came pregnant to this village, giving birth soon after. We both survived from the hard labor only because he used his car, one of the few vehicles in the village that time, to bring my mother to the hospital in Famagusta. He saved our lives."

4 N. Doratli et al, , Kırsal Yerleşimlerde Yerel Dokunun Korunması ve Sosyo-Ekonomik Canlandırma: Dipkarpaz Köyü Canlandırma Projesi (Conservation of Local Pattern and Socio-economic Revitalization in Rural Settlements: Revitalization Of Dipkarpaz Project), research project report, ongoing publication, 2010.

5 UN Annan Plan for Cyprus: The Comprehensive Settlement of the Cyprus Problem, 31 March 2004. http://www.unficyp.org/nqcontent.cfm?a_id=1637.

6 E. McCann, "Race, Protest, and Public Space: Contextualizing Lefebvre in the US City," Antipode 31:2, 1999, pp. 163-184.

7 A head scarf.

The main vehicular axis dividing the village into two—an upper and lower village, topographically speaking—does not imply any ethnic division, but a regional separation that affects the actions of people's daily lives. As there are no means of public transportation in the village, people rarely cross the main axis, and they usually meet in the village center, where most services are found. Schools, religious buildings, and gathering places, such as coffee shops, coexist almost side by side, or facing each other in the public space, although they rarely share them. Beyond the watchful eyes, everyday informal relationships among villagers are defined through their relationships with neighbors. Neighbors, mostly women and children, socialize daily, learning each other's language. One son of a family that moved to the village from southeast Turkey after 1974 has been working since his childhood at a Greek restaurant and speaks fluent Cypriot-accented Greek; he introduces himself as a "Cypriot Kurd," a new identity that has emerged in the village.

On-site research into the physical environment, quality of urban space, socio-cultural interaction, and community involvement laid out specific problems, such as the lack of public spaces, the low quality of infrastructural services, the lack of empowerment strategies for the young population, including failure to provide adequate incentives for youngsters to stay in the village, or to promote the broader participation of women in the socio-economic life of the settlement. This also exacerbates the already limited interaction between both communities, and precludes improvements. The team observed that one of the main obstacles to fostering new initiatives and improvements throughout the village is an exaggerated sense of their "otherness" and the emphasis on political obstacles. As a result, residents of all communities in the village are in a passive state, not willing to speak up, mobilize, or attend to activities in order to change the current dynamics.

Visualization of the village in children's drawings.

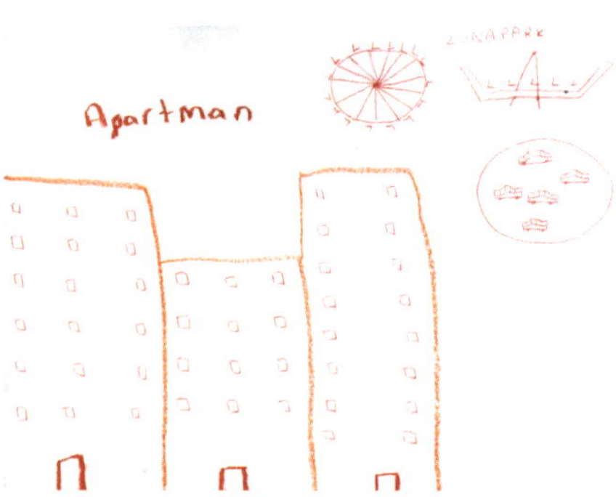

Visualization of a future image for the village in children's drawings.

Experience-based Methodology and Strategies

Given the circumstances of the case, where the social and physical space is contested at local levels, and the coexisting communities represent politics on the macro level in a small-scale environment, the timing of the project and its methodologies went beyond known theoretical methodologies. An experience-based methodology, comprising alternative directions, has been developed. Here, predictions are constantly tested in order to adapt to reactions, and processes and short-term results become definitive for future steps. With the aim of empowering the communities in order to achieve creation of shared social space, the focus in such an environment is on short-term steps and outcomes, i.e. the process, rather than a pre-defined, final outcome.

The Archis Interventions_Cyprus team espoused a bottom-up approach for intervening in socio-cultural relations, in order to reveal the potential for a mature, interactive platform at the physical level. Thus, the Dipkarpaz/Rizokarpaso project has been developed through a series of participatory projects on various scales, involving meetings, events, and workshops organized in collaboration with local residents, unions, and Dipkarpaz/Rizokarpaso village authorities, with the purpose of reading, learning from, and contributing to their understanding and usage of space.

Two major gatherings with local residents—a hands-on workshop and one called Gathering Children's Perspectives Workshop—are specifically worth mentioning, due to their outcomes. On May 2011, a so-called Hands-On Workshop[8] took place at Dipkarpaz/Rizokarpaso village. The goal was to discuss the needs of the village, its potential, the spatial environment, and the inhabitants. This participatory workshop aimed to bring all the communities of the village together to evaluate the potential of their living environment. Signage at the workshop site was in two languages, Turkish and Greek. This first participatory gathering in the village was supported by the municipality of Dipkarpaz, as well as the local communities. However, due to ongoing social and political tensions that have endured to this day, it was not possible to gather all of the communities at first. Therefore, the hands-on workshop took off first for the Turkish nationals of Dipkarpaz. Small meetings with the Greek population of the village were arranged afterward, in order to include their contributions to the project, as well. Besides being a first attempt at bringing all the communities of the village together for the purpose of achieving a higher quality of life in the settlement, the hands-on workshop was a good tool for bringing out the potential of the area.

8 "Archis SEE Network Divided Cities Project. Hands On Workshop, 21 May, 2011, Dipkarpaz/Rizokarpaso, Cyprus," Newsletter 22, 14 June 2011.

Map of interaction zones.

interaction densities in Dipkarpaz/Rizokarpaso
according to uses of spaces

- low interaction zones, local production areas
- 4th level interaction zones, houses and neighbourhoods
- 3rd level interaction zones, pensions, market places
- 2nd level interaction zones, schools, wedding hall, fair area and sports facilites
- high interaction zones, village center and main social facilities

Map of transporatation of schemes.

transportation map

- voids of transportation in the village
- most common community movements
- most common touristic movements

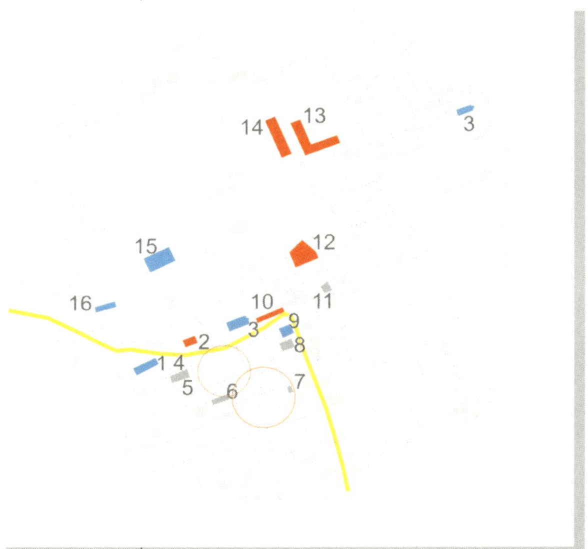

Map of the proposed interventions.

interventions map

- info point location in village square
- proposed location for the repetitive event
- most dense community and tourist axis

1. greek cooperative
2. turkish cooperative
3. church
4. bakery
5. former cinema
6. former closed market-place
7. open air wedding hall
8. health center
9. greek cofeehouse
10. turkish cofeehouse
11. town hall
12. mosque
13. turkish primary school
14. turkish secondary school
15. greek primary school
16. greek secondary school

General photo of the village center, with coffee shops facing each other.

The two religious symbols in the village center, the mosque and the church together, a touristic photo.

Village square, recently built monument in front of the church.

'Hands-on Workshop' and 'Gathering Children's Perspectives Workshop', bringing the local input into the project.

Photos side by side representing the dress code of old ladies from the communities in the village.

The workshop tried to define the needs of the women, men, youth, and children living in the area. In the discussions, several important socio-cultural and spatial needs and necessities were highlighted. Since the area is already a natural tourist attraction, the villagers said that a major obstacle is the invisibility of the village. The village is a "by-pass" for many of tourists, instead of an attraction itself. The features of the village were further explored in the common discussions, including the possibility of coexisting buildings and signs representing communities. As a result, a number of possible interventions were identified with the contribution of people:

- development of a village map showing the main routes and highlighting a brief history of each significant site,
- creation of a tourism information unit would help to make the entire village accessible and visible
- a community center, to be occupied by several educational, cultural, and social facilities (a temporary structure or provisional use of space, due to the problematic ownership status of land)
- a recurring event, i.e. a local, public bazaar, which could eventually help to nurture a festival at Dipkarpaz, in order to bring public attention to the village and to create a vibrant economic and social cycle, while transforming an open space into a public place. The proposal suggests that this event could take place during the high season, when the tourism sector could positively contribute to the event. The possible location of the event was also discussed and further elaborated by a physical analysis of the village.

The aim of these events will not be to reinforce the construction of existing identities, but to enhance multi-perspectivity, by focusing on characteristic advantages of multicultural realities and interaction. Promoting an event as a place of social interaction, in combination with several sub-projects on various scales, is expected to upgrade the village's spatial and socio-economic features and environmental conditions, and thereby overcome the divisions there—not by addressing differences, but by promoting social interaction.

A workshop called Gathering Children's Perspectives was then organized and took place on August 5, 2011. In order to select the attendees, permission was personally requested from families, instead of trying to reach the children through schools, which was not possible, since this would have given a formal status to the workshop. During this workshop—which aimed at bringing together children from both communities to discuss existing characteristics of the village from their point of view and envision a future image for the village—children not only produced their own reading of the village to contribute to the village map, but also explained their use of space through their movements. Throughout the process the children had the chance to discuss the physical features and social environment of the village, including cultural interaction among groups of people, with the research team, among themselves, and with their families, providing them the chance to re-think and re-evaluate their environment and social dynamics in the village. By investigating the ways that children use space, potential intervention spaces were identified; these are places that all members of the society, children especially, will eventually pass by at some time during their everyday routine. This strategy aims to discover neutral space in the routes of the youngest societal group in the village. Photographs of the village taken by the children, as well as drawings they have produced in order to explain their village, are included in a village map.

Contacts developed in the village during several visits played an important role when it came to getting local people to participate in the workshop. The Women's Union and the local NGO contributed to attendance, providing support by announcing the events in both communities. The municipality of Dipkarpaz officially supported events and provided space with the aim of collecting ideas for a future with better socio-economics in the village.

Toward a Third Space: Opportunities in Multiplicity

The ongoing project in Dipkarpaz/Rizokarpaso inspired a new understanding of sustainable public space for the multi-communal residents of the village. Qualities for sustainable, socio-economic development in the village are being identified, together with potential human resources and support. Local organizations and local production are supported within the scope of empowering residents to mobilize to organize an event. This temporary, recurring event would eventually become a shared cultural reference. Through mappings and social input, a neutral space in the village is being defined, based on the movements of people—younger generations specifically. This neutral space can be used for temporary interventions, which eventually will form memories of common references in the space. With local input, a village map is being produced, to identify the historical and touristic sites of the village for visitors and tourists. Several alternative info point and signage systems to supplement the map of the village are being designed with the support of EMU, by Industrial Design Department students, and will be evaluated by the locals. Recent developments in the village include the Greek Cypriot's desire to renovate the village church; which is supported by the municipality, in order to improve the village square. The newly emerging women's association, supported by the Archis Interventions_Cyprus team, is adopting a multi-communal image, representing the village through their handiwork and demonstrating that this is an asset to the village. Their handicrafts are examples of local production, which will be exhibited during the Dipkarpaz Festival envisioned. Altogether, the dynamics in the village lead toward the creation of a third space in Cyprus, inhabited by Greek Cypriots and Turkish settlers who are adapting newly emerging cross-identities. Thus, the celebration of their coexisting differences has the potential to enhance the physical environment and provide the opportunity for socio-economic development by generating tourist attractions.

Post-Socialist Urban Transformation

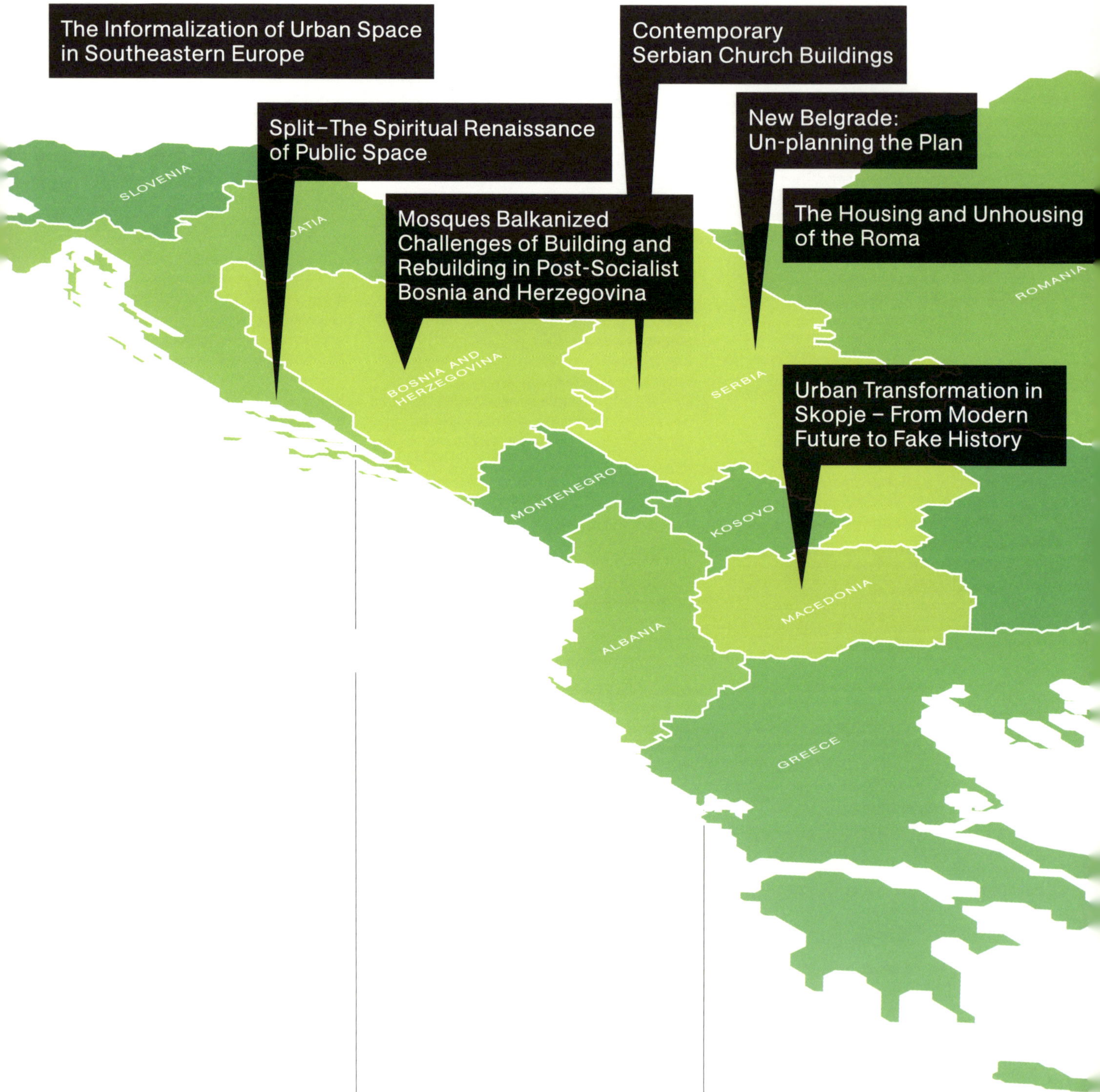

Project in collaboration with Archis Interventions

ıUStávE]© | musthave©
ɔject Proposal for Social Integration
Bulgaria via Consumerism
MOLDOVA
Magic Blocks: Strategies and Projects
for the Socialist-era Neighborhoods
in Bucharest and Romania
Fakulteta, the Invisible City
BULGARIA
TURKEY
CYPRUS

The Informalization of Urban Space in Southeastern Europe

Srdjan Jovanović Weiss and Marko Sančanin, in discussion with Kai Vöckler.

Kai Vöckler: Informal construction activity is a typical development in transforming and post-conflict states, where the lack or weak presence of institutional structures makes regulating building activity problematic. The erratic sprawl of makeshift buildings is a product of the urban crisis that has shaped the region since its post-socialist transformations and wars. At the same time these urban changes highlight a new typology that differs significantly from the kind of informal settlements known up to now outside of Europe. They are, in fact, an expression of the developments taking place across wide sections of society, developments, which, to a large extent, tie up investments. In this sense, "Turbo Urbanism" is not so much a phenomenon of accelerated and excessive urban development owing to its somewhat questionable self-regulation and the lack of state control, but rather the result of a certain economic situation—in those cities heavily destroyed or burdened by a high migrant population, the construction sector was able to offer high profits. A lack of engagement on the part of responsible government agencies led to obvious difficulties: unsafe conditions, deficient social institutions (schools, kindergartens) and public spaces, (green spaces, parks), and little or no technical infrastructure. Ultimately, these examples demonstrate that self-regulation in a society reaches its limits if it does not take into consideration all aspects of society as a whole. It does not take the entire city into consideration, and thus results in physical as well as social problems.

Srdjan Jovanović Weiss: This is a beautifully acute reading of the situation, which also recognizes the difference between the post-socialist informality of urban space and non-European informal cities in, for example, Latin America, not to mention Africa. The link that is challenged here is not so much an urban, but a political one, meaning, that we are not confronting the history of urban typology per se, but that we see—in the reality of the dispersion of the political realm—culture unfolding in the cracks of the post-socialist landscape.
The post-socialist landscape would not be identified as such if it were not for its systematic opposition to socialist architecture and urbanism. As in "Turbo Architecture," which burgeoned as a vehement reaction against clean, modernist forms, "Turbo Urbanism" may be rising against the clarity of urban versus rural territory. Thus it may be that the rise of radical forces will be seen primarily in the expression of ambiguity in any form of uncharted course, any kind of intervention.
We "love" these examples, because they are ugly-beautiful, self-made, optimistic, and full of energy. We respect them because they are a funny alternative to the systematic nationalist zeal of post-socialist countries that project ethnic or religious identity as the national state identity, as well as a cultural one. This zeal includes Orthodox and Catholic Christianity, as well as Islam. These humorous alternatives are embedded in the political systems rushing to solidify national identity, and so are head and shoulders above them in adding the latest touches to the post-socialist landscape.

Marko Sančanin: It is plausible, if not only for the sake of argument, to state that deregulated state sovereignty or transition creates deregulated urban phenomena—this was also the case in the former Yugoslavia. However, the history of modern urban development is full of peripheral conditions that, while reconfiguring notions of modern order, appeared to be de-regulated, but also presented another kind of modernity. In that sense, it is also important to understand that illegal building happened quite often during socialism. In that sense, what you refer to as "turbo architecture" is not a totally new phenomenon.
Frankly, I was always uncomfortable with the "turbo" nicknames, although I fully understand the need to invent suitable urban terminology. To me, the term was never more than one of the numerous free translations of the cultural landscapes that grew in the cracks of the unfolding, post-socialist landscape, as Srdjan nicely put it.
The new architecture of the 1990's never used existing architectural typology as a reference, because it was ignorant of all aspects of the social, common, and political. For Platforma 9,81 it was necessary to be able to examine the "super private" condition of these phenomena. We never would agree that the process was a funny alternative to the systematic nationalist zeal, but definitely an announcement of the process of neo-liberalization and the erosion of the public political sphere. The way we research and produce discourse on the new urban landscapes (that you refer to as "turbo") primarily occupies me, because of the cultural aspects of our role.
Boris Buden says that the only social experience available to us today is the one contained in different forms of its cultural articulation or rather its cultural translations."... [T]here is no original experience of society as society, except the one that is made in its cultural translations." He primarily talks about past political struggles and the present-day inability of cultural workers to articulate new social experience. For an architect, as a cultural worker, the only way to understand the new urbanity is primarily to look at it through its implicit political struggles, not simply through architectural phenomena. Most of our activities—the way new discourses are produced and displayed—are clear examples of cultural translations.
On the other hand, as Buden lucidly points out, the process of culturalization has a dangerous ideological consequence: de-politicization. This is our primary task: how to operate within a culture that reproduces itself at the expense of politics, while urban policies and the development of cities are, by definition, dependent on political imagination.

KV: I agree with Marko, that we have to ask ourselves which role we play as experts dealing with these phenomena. I would like to point out different aspects from my point of view, being, on one hand, a stranger in the region, and, on the other hand, part of an international, urban discourse. One of the most important reasons that brought Ole Bouman and me together with *Archis* to start the Archis Interventions project was that Ole realized that *Volume* magazine (where he was, at that time, in 2005, editor-in-chief, while I was editorial consultant), as an international magazine, "produces" an urban discourse and has subscribers everywhere in the world—but we actually don't know what they are doing. For that reason Ole started the Archis Events, a tour of discussions to get closer to the readers, who are mostly architects, planners, and activists. And we realized that everywhere in these cities people are actively intervening in the development of their city. Out of this experience, we got this request for support from a group of architects in Beirut and, at the same time, from Prishtina, too—which brought us to start Archis Interventions.
I am explaining this because it is fundamental that we only work with Archis Interventions if local, independent (so, obviously, non-governmental), but also non-commercial initiatives ask for collaboration and support. And we certainly want to link this to an urban discourse and begin an exchange of knowledge; on the other hand, we try to

support our local collaborators in their projects as much as possible (and so far, this is much needed). This goes far beyond the kind of academic projects we all know of, where a group of students and their professors sometimes produce an interesting analysis and strategic concepts, but without any real perspective. During the past ten years it has become very fashionable to produce and publish these investigations. But we also have to acknowledge the good part of it: it made a lot of people, especially in the so-called Western countries, pay attention to what is going on in other parts in the world. The most problematic thing—and here, I agree with Marko—is that, in most of this research and investigation, there is no analysis of the driving social and economic forces behind the phenomena and the political framework that are structuring these processes. Just to give one example, when we presented the *Balkanology* exhibition, about southeastern European architecture and urban phenomena in Basel and Vienna, the visitors were highly interested in the research on migrants from the region who work in Switzerland, Germany, and Austria, and the money they send back to their families—a big portion of this money is invested in housing. That there is high interdependency within these states and the region was, for most of the visitors, a completely new idea, and they had never before associated migration, remittances, and housing with each other.

But back to the question of how to cope with the political framework: the so-called post-socialist transformation has been going on now for twenty years, and is now being overlapped by the global financial crisis. And what I can state is that governmental institutions are no longer the center of planning, they no longer regulate the process. They are extremely dependent on supra-national governmental institutions, such as the EU, and their financial support, and, on the other hand, on private investments. They now do more moderating than structuring. But it is still the national state and its institutions that regulate, so nothing is possible without them. And here, it becomes tricky—how far you can go with cooperation, and how much do you have to oppose local governmental bodies, if you want to intervene in a development and improve it? I don't think that you can just do a good design or plan; you have to think about all of the implications of its implementation.

SJW: What both of you seem to be proposing—and so rightly backed up by Buden's statement that the transformational forces are actually being solidified as society, not the original forces per se—is that future research needs to work on the split between politics and knowledge. In a Nietzschean construction, we can just assume that architects and planners have no power, other than to attempt to encroach upon both politics and knowledge, as separate forces, and not go insane with managing the complexity of this separation. So the split in politics and knowledge runs even deeper, vis-a-vis traditional architecture and urban planning practiced in southeast Europe. Why? Because designers who become politicians or get involved in the political demarcations of contemporary party structures are doomed to be lost on the design table, where transformation is actually drawn, most likely by an unpaid intern. So then the real challenge here is whether or not expert knowledge is viable on the political market of exchange. Eyal Weizman just recently reminded me of Slobodan Milosevic's telling testimony in front of the International Tribunal at The Hague. He was confronted by an art historian, who delivered a study of the cultural and historical relevance of Kosovo, as one of the places where both Christian monasteries and mosques could be built and tolerate each other—something that Milosevic violated. According to Eyal, the horrible truth was that Milosevic dismissed the study as "traditional" and "old fashioned." He said that the engineering of territorial management is the only force that can move culture to transform itself. In this case, even though Milosevic is evil, we cannot be stunned enough at how right this monster may have been, not in terms of politics, but in terms of protected knowledge.

When I was engaged in preserving the grounds of the handball stadium in Novi Sad, turning it into an institution for youth, the split between daily politics and professional practice proved for the silent local consensus to keep this space untouched. The existing authorities of the city were not politically interested in this project. However, they allowed the urban planning regulations to be changed, so that this property could be turned into a site for combined culture and recreation use. Together with kuda.org-center for new media in Novi Sad, NAO found this handball stadium hidden in plain sight in the central park of the city and then started a political campaign to recognize it, and then preserve it as public space. We were successful at first in recognizing that former socialist planning law created a window for citizen participation in the process, and we made a formal request. This incentive was not only to preserve the stadium from erasure, or from being transformed into a shopping mall—a project that was in the works—but also to lawfully re-cast its designation, which is beyond its primary function as a place for recreation. And so we got the approval for this, and the new master plan preserved the stadium and allowed it to be adapted for cultural programs. My point is that this was not thanks to the new democratic politics—it was thanks to our knowledge of socialist planning law. Today the European Union requires the city to form and fund an organization for youth, in order to begin any talks of Serbia joining the EU. We have been informed that the necessary organization will be located on the grounds of the handball stadium. However, the separation between politics and knowledge is the main local reason that this project has been continually postponed, and will be postponed until knowledge and politics eventually connect. Simply put, the expert knowledge that we provide at all times has been tagged as "old fashioned."

For now, whatever the crisis is, I believe that the main urban challenge is the knowledge about the timelines of political development in the western Balkans and their political capacities as distinct entities after the fall of Yugoslavia. It is irresistible not to succumb to the cliché that Slovenia, part of the EU, is ten years ahead of Croatia, twenty years ahead of Serbia, and a number of years ahead of other new countries in the western Balkans, not to mention the cultural or minority enclaves in Balkan countries. This is a real, but dangerous way of thinking—that a large scheme should drive particular and distinct knowledge of what is possible to change in separate cities. Plus, doesn't democracy provide real change to anyone who is supposedly behind, in order to be the next? The forty thousand Slovenian tourists coming to Belgrade to party for the New Year holiday are met with organized and informal entertainment infrastructure. The 400,000 visitors to the Exit festival held over four days at the iconic Petrovaradin castle in Novi Sad every July are also met with both organized and informal infrastructure. But it is exactly this ad-hoc service industry that delays the projects that set social standards, like the handball stadium, which has scope for surviving long-term.

Any government occupied with large infrastructure projects that are sometimes purposely delayed simply does not have time to work with smaller agents of change. Yet, there is also the complex relationship between Belgrade and the rest of the country, such as the autonomous province of Vojvodina. Belgrade is still collecting and centralizing all the money and dispensing it according to unknown criteria. According to the news, Vojvodina alone contributes sixty percent to the budget and sees a return of seven percent to its budget. Whatever the case is, there will be no sustaining projects in this part of the western Balkans until decentralization takes a meaningful turn. On the other hand, if the lack of decentralization inspires individuals to take action, we may see some interesting developments in the private realm, shared under various conditions with the public. We shall see where dissent from any of these two trajectories—the decentralization desired by the autonomous government of Vojvodina, or the way Belgrade would like to control decentralization as marginal development—may lead.

The knowledge possessed by architects, individual planners, and activist groups like Archis Interventions, the Erste Foundation, and other initiatives that may be more internal may start to matter, but will be in a precarious exchange with rampant, daily politics. If you take the small, but critical project orchestrated by Vladimir Macura, who is building his own small museum in Novi Banovci, just outside of Belgrade, one might think that more idiosyncratic projects could occur in the region. Macura even had the courage to hire an architect, Ivan Kucina, to come up with a proposal, but then just went out on his own and built whatever he felt was important. The result attests to the limits of an individual initiative. Idiosyncratic projects, like Macura's contemporary art collection on Vojvodina territory, attract the public mostly from Belgrade, but not from the autonomous province itself.

Another distinct story is the compound in Novi Sad called the Black House 13 (Crna Kuca 13), a youth center largely administered by the kuda.org, with absolute zero help from the local government. What is phenomenal about this place—giving a house (and a garden) to urban minority communities, such as LGBT organizations, social workshops, and international art residences—is, at the same time, activist, idiosyncratic and dissident in nature, in comparison to mainstream politics. The point is that each project like this, even though it is absolutely necessary and key for the transition toward democracy, draws the resistance and resentment of both the government and the new ultranationalist complex. At the same time, the Orthodox Church is reserving more and more urban territory for building new churches and is imbedding itself in legal documents, such as master plans. The conundrum of common architects and planners is that they are unsure about where to align themselves, and furthermore, whether they should align with either the law that involves the new clerical complex supported by the government, or with idiosyncratic projects like CK13. Back to the handball stadium project, which kind of balances the government and the idiosyncrasy of the local youth under oppression: one of the conditions for joining the EU is that cities must provide institutions for youth, so we now have the stadium on the list as one such institution. We have great interest from the Lafarge cement corporation, the French company that purchased one of the largest cement factories in the region, which would support the project. But the government itself has constantly delayed the project. And, in my opinion, this is not due to meanspiritedness or a lack of interest. It is simply that they are active elsewhere, most visibly in engineering; they are presenting it as beneficial to the common good and using it as political capital for the next elections.

MS: Judging from my experiences in the region, and the contacts that I have with people from ex-Yugoslavian capitals (Novi Sad included), it is pretty obvious that—alongside religious and ethnic fundamentalism and a lack of political culture (present from the beginning of nineties) during the past ten years (especially after relative normalization, political stability and EU accession processes), it is possible to observe clear shifts in governing policies, cultural development, and social stratification, which were not visible during the first half of the 1990s. These shifts, which may lead to interesting developments, are also highly problematic.

For example, when Srdjan refers to the EXIT festival and its negative influence, he probably refers (if I am correct) to the cultural hegemony that cultural (or so-called "creative") industries are building up around what used to be known as the new and innovative cultural landscape of Serbia. The traditional culture that blocked cultural development in the nineties is now coupled with the cultural industry, which is just as trivial, although contemporary and pro-European. Belgrade Design Week is another such event, although it is very popular among designers and architects.
Secondly, when he explains the lack of cultural policy and decisiveness to do something about the stadium in Novi Sad, it greatly echoes the crisis of government that is occurring in most of the big cities in the region. EU standards have also contributed to this, because responsibilities and competencies overlap, while the administration is still run according to the old socialist routine. Macura Museum is an example of private enterprise that co-exists parallel to the official and institutional realm. This is also the case all over the place. In Zagreb there are all sorts of enterprises like these. I do not think we can fully engage in these processes, but we have to be aware of them and, if possible, investigate their architectural or urban implications. I do not think that judgment should be postponed, because it can't be avoided in order to understand relations and antagonisms among different social actors. However, judgments shouldn't interfere with our will to produce architectural effects. When it comes to the architectural medium in which to produce those effects, I am pretty open.

SJW: I fully agree with you, Marko, on this. Cultural architecture and urbanism does not have the upper hand, compared to the cultural industry. In Serbia this is evident in the proliferation of festivals as the means of representation; production is rare. Although that is not just to taint all festivals in one stroke. Perhaps, again, quantity produces quality, according to the traditional Marxist mantra. And, indeed, it may be true that cultural production in the form of a festival may be a model that anyone can imitate on any small scale. That is fine. The question is, what sort of permanent mark on space or urbanist practice will any of these efforts make? I do believe that any project, any activity that is pragmatic will generate knowledge on its own, simply through the process of accomplishing it. We need to help find a way to share this knowledge generated through practice with everyone.

Magic Blocks

Strategies and Projects for the Socialist-era Neighborhoods in Bucharest and Romania

Ştefan Ghenciulescu, Constantin Goagea, Cosmina Goagea, Justin Baroncea, Wilfried Hackenbroich, Kai Vöckler

INTRODUCTION

Although seventy percent of the inhabitants of Bucharest (and surely, at least half of the population of the whole country) live in socialist-era apartment blocks, these structures have been almost totally absent from the public discourse. Meanwhile, their physical state is degrading continuously, their prices are falling, and future social and economic problems seem inescapable. Rehabilitation programs have finally started, but they still concentrate on partial and uncoordinated solutions.

The Magic Blocks project is based on an essential idea: the rehabilitation of these neighborhoods should not limit itself to technical problems; instead, it should be conceived as a complex regeneration program, taking into account all aspects—including spatial, social, and economic ones. Moreover, we think that these neighborhoods have more than just big problems. They also have remarkable urban potential: social integration, millions of densely built square meters, and a reserve of open space for urban equipment and public use.

Magic Blocks started in 2009 as an initiative by a group of Romanian and foreign organizations.[1] We decided to dedicate the first year to general research and a discussion of the situation, defining principles and case studies for intervention strategies. The results were presented and discussed with inhabitants from the selected study areas, and afterward published in a book and brochure, and then presented in an exhibition in Berlin and Bucharest.

In 2010 we concentrated on one of the three case studies: activating the areas behind the socialist boulevards in the center of Bucharest. Calea Mosilor Boulevard was chosen as a prototypical example, and an urban strategy was developed for it, which integrates a community project and interventions in public space.

In the mid- and long-term, one of the main aims of the project is the realization of pilot projects and institution of regulations. We worked through 2011 on the construction of partnerships, in order to start several of these pilot projects and build up a community-based urban strategy. We also intend to intensify our urban interventions.

1 An Archis Interventions, Zeppelin and Point 4 initiative, in cooperation with Hackenbroich Architekten (Berlin). An initial workshop was presented in 2009, in collaboration with ATU, Space Syntax Romania, and Platforma 9,81 (Zagreb). A public intervention was made in collaboration with studioBASAR.

Calea Moşilor. On the boulevard and behind it

Magic Blocks 2009 – Scenarios for Socialist-era Collective Housing in Bucharest

Despite sharing certain similarities with big social housing developments in Western Europe, the origins and character of socialist-era estates differ radically. Firstly, they were not meant for economically disadvantaged people. They represented quite simply the only type of new housing. Urban planning and architectural developments were part of a general planning system, one that addressed the economy, as much as the creation of a new society. Hence, such blocks were inhabited by everybody (except the establishment).

And yet, living conditions during the socialist era were far from uniform. Superimposing the differences results in features that vary greatly, according to locale, age, the period when they were put into practice, urban and architectural typologies, height regulations, building systems, and density.

Socialist blocks of flats in Bucharest may be Stalinist interventions, immense functionalist neighborhoods that can count as many as 300,000 inhabitants (Balta Albă, Drumul Taberei, etc.), or the delirious centralized projects of the Ceauşescu-era city extensions (the Militari; Ferentari, Aviatiei neighborhoods, etc.).

The reality of major urban and architectural differences implies different needs and priorities, which range from bridging fractures in the historical old center to developing urban policies for the city's biggest neighborhoods. Every single intervention strategy should define the main categories it addresses, by superimposing urban planning, architectural, technical, and social and economic criteria, while setting up action plans for all of these categories.

Who (continues to) live in apartment blocks, and where? An unsettling social evolution

Following the collapse of the regime in 1989, apartments in Romania (like everywhere else in former communist European countries, except East Germany) were sold to the tenants for a symbolic amount. Economic growth, great demand, and belated new investment in housing developments caused a steep increase in prices. The present economic crisis forced a reverse trend, with prices of old flats dropping even more than those of new ones.

There is a marked tendency toward segregation between rich and increasingly poorer neighborhoods. Present statistics do not collect data on various categories by location, and therefore a proper analysis is impossible. However, information on prices by area, location, and accessibility is readily available, thus giving us a pretty clear picture of the phenomenon.

It is interesting to analyze a map that reflects the degree of accessibility of the city's various "socialist" neighborhoods and a map from 2007, comparing prices by areas (rendered through intensifying shades of color). Overlayering the two maps yields an almost perfect match. Accessibility results in greater appeal, hence higher prices, and, from a long-term perspective, great social differences. An existing mix slowly turns into a pattern of segregation: blocks in the center are occupied by increasingly wealthier people, while those in the suburbs or more isolated areas start to decay. A map from 2009–that is, at the peak of the crisis–shows that this tendency continues.

4 MILITARI
6 AVIAÞIEI
2 STEFAN CEL MARE
2 MOSILOR
5 FERENT
1 BALTA ALBĂ
3 UNIRII

Mapping the accessibility of socialist neighborhoods in Bucharest. The color intensity corresponds to the degree of physical accessibility. (Map: Space Syntax Romania)

We are still a long way from the problem-generating suburbs of major European cities, which are strictly defined socially and perhaps even ethnically; however, should the present tendency continue, we will not be able to prevent large chunks of the city from becoming "privately owned ghettos." Up until now, all programs, regardless of whether they address thermo rehabilitation or the remodeling of open spaces, etc., have failed to take this reality into account.

Steep increases in housing prices in certain areas, coupled with sharp depreciation in other areas, should force the administration to take action, rather than hope that self-regulating market mechanisms will do the job. First and foremost, the current situation requires a differentiated strategic approach with regard to rehabilitation. The economic crisis and a dramatic drop in available resources make action more necessary than ever.

Public space as communal space: Why we need an urban project

If we accept that a dwelling also includes the space around buildings, then we cannot fail to see the schizoid nature of the present state of these ensembles: all buildings are privatized, even though the open space around them remains public property. The growth in individualization has been taken to the extreme. A natural reaction to the imposed collective spirit of yesteryear has

Price comparison by area, 2007 (darker means more expensive). The map overlaps perfectly with the accessibility map, showing that central and very accessible areas are getting more expensive, and therefore tend to be acquired by a wealthier population. (Map: Space Syntax Romania)

led people to withdraw into their privately owned shells, while taking no interest whatsoever in what has evolved into no-man's land.

Public space became a hunting ground, the domain of isolated retrocession, incoherent temporary or permanent construction, abusively framed parking lots, plots turned into individual gardens, ground for isolated administrative actions taken by the municipality or public domain department that involve green areas, traffic- and public-works maintenance. All of this is conducive to the creation of a disjointed puzzle of territories and wastelands.

This entire collection of non-places occupies a vast territory and has huge potential, not only with respect to large-scale operations that might benefit a district or the entire city, but also as a space for living.

We believe that all strategies aimed at the rehabilitation of socialist dwellings should make public space integral to all operations and that interventions on any such territory should be based on urban projects, rather than disparate actions.

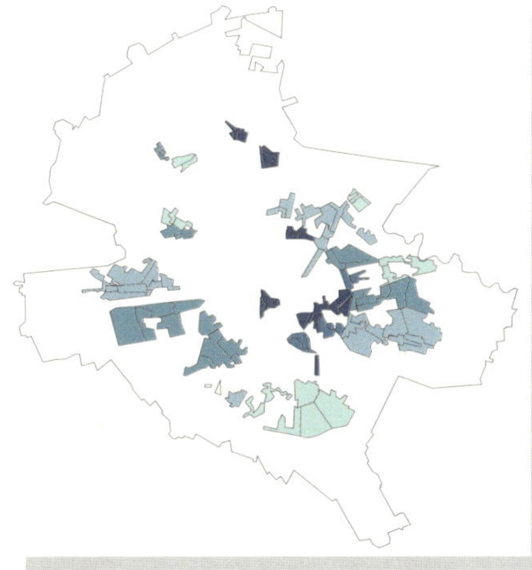

Price comparison by area, 2009, after the first results of the crisis (estimation after a preliminary survey). Differences continue to increase. Although all prices fell sharply, neighborhoods in the center retain most of their market value. (Map: Space Syntax Romania)

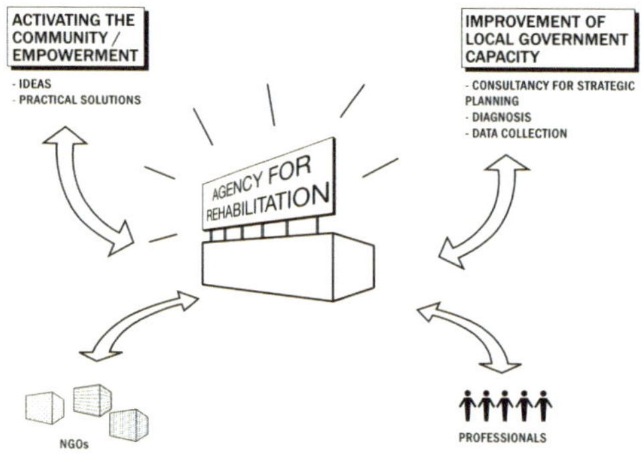

The project combines different strategies:

A governance strategy: by supporting the Municipality with concepts and ideas for improving the situation, to support the home owner associations and to empower residents to articulate their needs

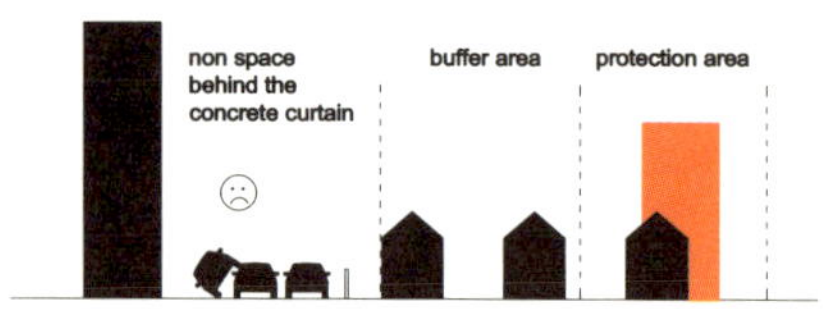

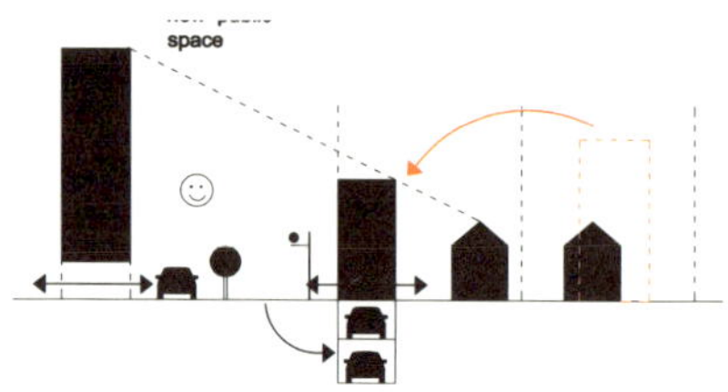

An urbanistic strategy: by defining different zones, an »intervention zone« (the non-space behind the blocks), which should be activated and improved and a »buffer zone« behind, where new building projects can be developed and which will have a positive impact on the existing situation by taking the pressure out of the »protection zone« behind

TOP DOWN-STRATEGIES

Governance Strategy
Urbanistic Strategy

BOTTOM UP-STRATEGIES

Intervention Strategy
Architectural Strategy

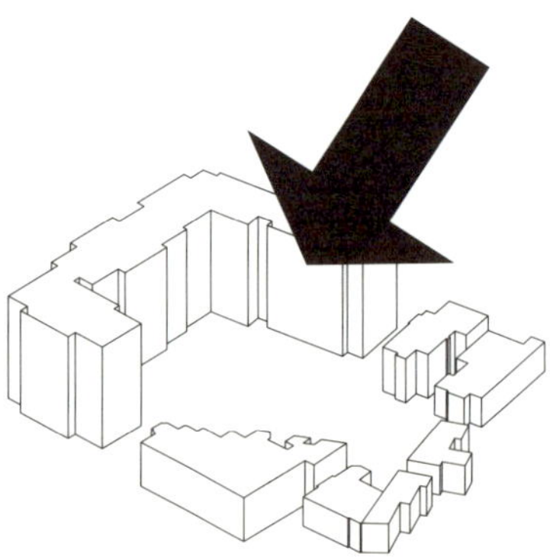

An intervention strategy: by defining »chill ponts« to activate through peformative actions which will attract residents to interact

An architectural strategy: developing new concepts of financing the complex rehabilitation of buildings is an important part of an architectural strategy. A possibility is to create new roof apartments to accommodate the residents currently living on the ground floor. The space that becomes available on the ground floor could then be leased as commercial space. That revenue could, in turn, be used to cover the cost of maintenance and enhancement of the building and the outdoor space. To this end, coordinated finance and refurbishment concepts are necessary.

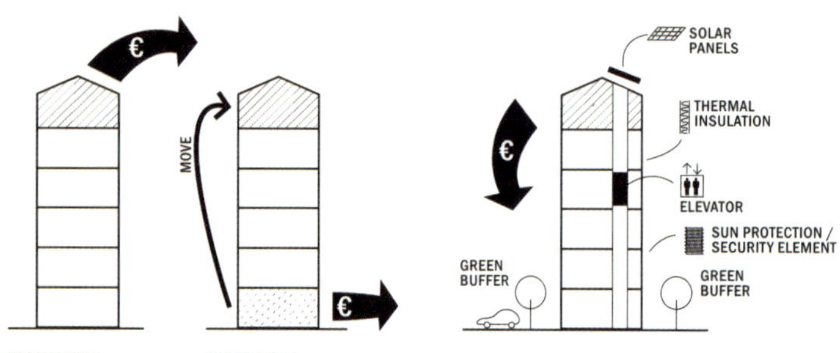

Rehabilitation as a community project

Extreme individualism and the refusal of any collective responsibility become evident in the evolution of buildings proper. Lack of urban values, coupled with an exclusive focus on private space on the part of a large percentage of the population, transformed former uniform ensembles into vertical villages. Today every block has become a collection of private spaces on which all improvement efforts are focused. There is almost no understanding of the need to maintain the building as a piece of property shared by all owners, in order to avoid damage and safety issues and to maintain the value of the building as a whole and with that, the value of each single apartment. Society as a whole needs to relearn how to coalesce, to figure out how their communal spaces can function—and the process is a lengthy one. However, any overall rehabilitation project requires some form of common action if it is to be successfully completed.

Such activation can only be achieved if an organization is set up to bring the various partners together for counseling and communication. Partners can be homeowners' associations, local and central administrations, lending institutions, project designers, construction companies, etc. Legal provisions currently stipulate that nearly all rehabilitation-related operational costs will be state-subsidized, but, given the size of the problem, this solution can hardly be efficient.

A realistic strategy would comprise a participatory mechanism. Problems would be identified in conjunction with the inhabitants; terms of reference would be established and accepted through a process of negotiation; the project outline would comprise both clearly identified costs and technical solutions; project implementation would be based on coordinated actions.

FINANCING REHABILITATION – STRATEGIC CONCEPT

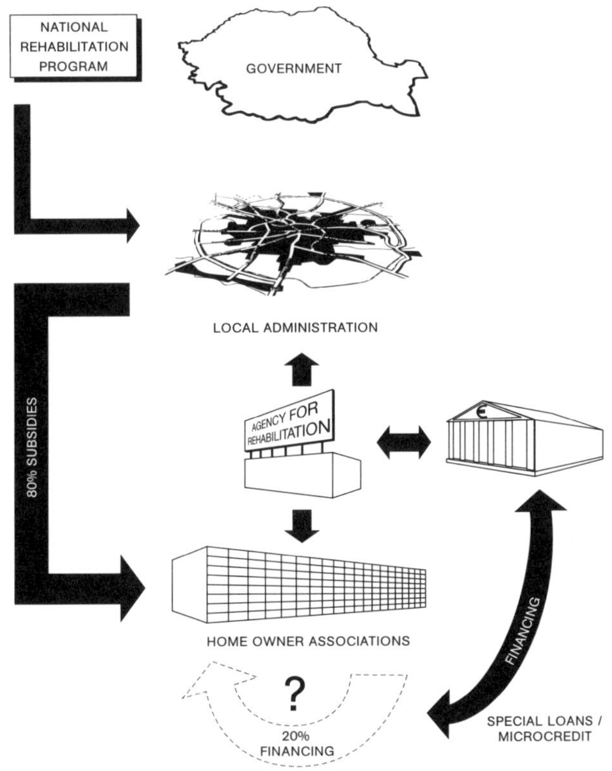

Three case studies

Following the general analysis, we looked closer into three specific categories of issues and briefly outlined principles for action (legal, economic, social, and professional). Three study cases based on real, very different city contexts enabled us to create a model of possible ways to put these principles into practice.

The first scenario (Activating the downtown) concentrated on the open space behind the huge totalitarian-era axis that cut through the city in the 1980s. The project was developed in 2010 and in chapter C contains an extensive presentation of it.

The second scenario (Negotiation) is also mainly about public space and examined the frequently occurring type of ensemble that features continuous fronts and interior courtyards, and was built in the 1970s and '80s. Despite their overwhelmingly bad architectural and construction quality, these buildings, which were radically different from the functionalist ones of the 1960s, created areas that enjoyed different degrees of intimacy and protection, in comparison to others. We felt that minimal intervention would be required to align this type of ensemble with the classic models of the urban block. A strategy for these kinds of places would essentially define an alternative approach to open space, one that would enable conversion into some sort of communal space—in other words, a semi-public area, a buffer between the overall public space and the private worlds inside the buildings.

Financing rehabilitation. The present National Rehabilitation Program defines legal subsidies for insulation projects: individual HOAs have to apply for it and eighty percent of the sum required will be provided by the national government and the local administration. Private owners have to pay the remaining twenty percent. This conflicts with the ability of the individual owners to acquire their part of the financing. Socially disadvantaged owners will need special loans depending on the value of their apartments (and to increase the value of their own property).
In return, through this financing and rehabilitation operation, they will be able to increase the value of their own property. In order to achieve this, a specific economic strategy is mandatory.
A "Rehabilitation Agency"—an NGO or an agency collaborating with and supported by the municipality—could help to improve the communication process between HOAs and local administration by bringing in professional expertise.

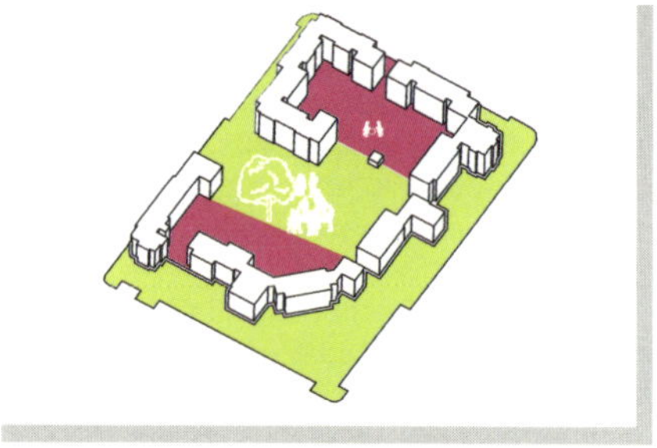

Simulation of an urban and landscaping solution: necessary parking is assured (and at the same time provide a source of income for the administration); semi-private areas are clearly defined; a public passage will activate the ground floors and serve as a dynamic recreation space.
1. Public passage
2. Public space for sports and play – basketball, running, gymnastics, etc.
3. Interior semi-private courts (used and landscaped according to owners)
4. Benches that separate the different areas
5. Parking space outside the block, for inhabitants and visitors
6. Parking inside the block (controlled access)

This supposes not just a re-planning of those areas, but also a participatory process, the construction of a partnership between the inhabitants and local government. To bring the latter together and coordinate the entire operation, a dedicated body becomes necessary. Whether this should be an NGO, an agency, or a central or municipal department is less important than the team's multi-disciplinary membership: it should comprise architects, planners, sociologists, community activists, and economists. For instance, how to administrate these semi-public spaces is crucial: they should remain public ground, but they could be taken care of by an association of homeowner associations.

An ensemble in the Aviatiei district was chosen as a case study. A rough simulation of rearranged areas showed that it would be possible to conduct a negotiation while balancing every interest. The courtyard could become an intermediary place between the public and the private; it could accommodate parking, but also be a pedestrian area, contain neighborhood gardens, and a space for sports, meetings, and relaxation. All of this could occur without additional building or demolitions.

The third scenario (Upside down) develops a case study and a pilot proposal for an apartment block in a functionalist neighborhood called Balta Albă. The huge group of long slabs immersed in green is marked by wear and tear. There are no sports, cultural, or social centers, but there is potential in the existing entrepreneurship, a certain degree of social and communal cooperation, an open attitude toward urban values reinforced by a balanced social mix, and also the reserve of open space.

Our proposal mainly targets the big apartment blocks located on the neighborhood's main streets. Their ground floor apartments are still inhabited—a situation that is uncomfortable for the owners and rather impractical when it comes to using the spaces in front of these blocks. "Upside down" envisages the building of more spacious and comfortable new apartments above the top floor. Residents of ground floor apartments will be able to move there, thereby freeing up the ground floor space, which can then be rented out by the municipality, so as to help develop various services.

Then each respective homeowners association could negotiate to lower its contribution to the block's maintenance costs, as well as to those covering communal spaces, such as gardens, alleys, and parking lots. Rental income could contribute to a more sustainable long-term approach to rehabilitation-passive elements, such as shutters and sun shades, or even solar panels.

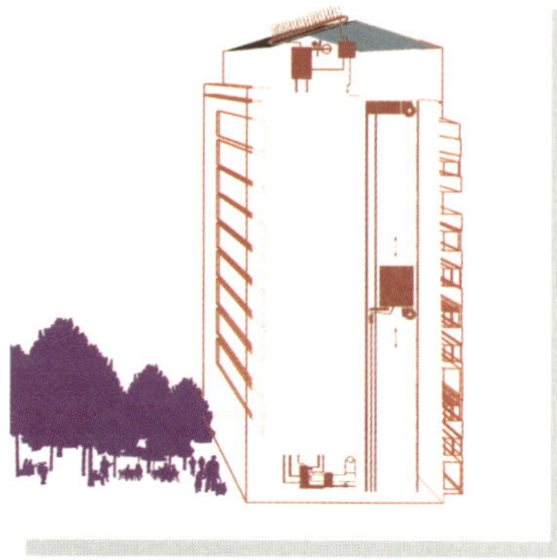

Constructing and activating a financial mechanism
1. Founding an agency (independent or integrated into a city hall office)
2. Building up a project with the homeowners association
3. Fundraising from a private partner
4. Launching the project
Building top-floor apartments, moving inhabitants of the ground floor to the top floor, activation of the ground floor, integrated rehabilitation

Such a pilot program could generate integrated, multi-functional ensembles, where living and services coexist; this could enhance the neighborhood's quality of life standards, lower transportation costs, and lead to less vehicular traffic. The project might also generate greater social cohesion, and a new urban identity for the area.

Regarding other types of buildings, like the five-story apartment blocks situated behind the big slabs: it would not be really sustainable to insert commercial functions in their proximity, because of poor accessibility and the probable destruction of the strong domestic atmosphere. Hence, our proposition for a simplified version: invest in building a new top floor and an absolutely necessary elevator, sell apartments there, and use the profits for renovation projects and a semi-private, protected area in the proximity of the ground floor.

Obviously, the project requires a broader framework that could integrate individual operations with functional rehabilitation on a wider scale, covering more zones, and addressing the area's recreational, commercial, and community needs. To make this possible, an agency should ensure transparent communication of the project to homeowners associations; the agency would also be able help them formulate their requests and negotiate on their behalf with local authorities. This could be a department run by a district or municipal authority, a self-contained institution, with branches in Bucharest's districts, or even an NGO that specializes in such services.

Magic Blocks 2010 – Behind the Concrete Curtain: Activating the Areas behind the Socialist era Boulevards in the Center of Bucharest

The entire central area of Bucharest is strewn with concrete curtains, dozens of kilometers of boulevards featuring uninterrupted rows of apartment blocks built in the 1970s and '80s. Behind them lies the old city, with its narrow streets and houses, churches and trees.

This unique situation is due to the abrupt stoppage of work on Ceausescu's great project, caused by the December 1989 Revolution. The dictator aimed to completely raze the historical city and replace it with a new, socialist one; the concrete curtains were intended as the first step in this process.

Today, the back walls of the blocks meet the blind walls of the old houses, and people can hardly make their way through the maze of cars that eat up every available space, the enclosed plots of vacant land and facility areas. Lately, villas and even office buildings and new blocks of flats have been rising chaotically for a couple of years on retroceded plots, or by replacing some of the surviving old houses. And yet . . . if you take a closer look, all these forlorn or badly used areas represent acres of vacant land in the very heart of the city. Perhaps we should start regarding them as not just a serious problem, but also as a resource, with huge potential for becoming vibrant public spaces, a new front for the historic city. A hidden and forgotten area could become an attractive spot for the community and a point of attraction for investors.

The Magic Blocks 2010 Project suggests an urban strategy for this type of Bucharest area, and Calea Mosilor was chosen as a case study in point—a prototype for deeper analysis and urban interventions. An exhibition and two publications present the results of the 2009 project.

Not just improvements, but a global urban vision: Structure, methodology, and principles

1. Strategy on an urban scale: we chose to broaden the perspective, from the refurbishment of public space to a bigger urban context. These places could activate the urban regeneration of the historical areas behind them and should not be considered separately.

2. Prototypical solutions: we decided not to try to cover the whole central area, but work on a case study that would be capable of becoming a prototype. Calea Mosilor is significant to the city's history and very representative of projects from the 1970s and '80s. Therefore, principles applied here can become models for the whole central area.

3. From the big scale of the city to of the scale of immediate intervention: Integrating two levels of action
The first level would involve planning, regulation, and actions that could only be applied gradually over a relatively long period. The second one refers to a strategy involving intervention in public spaces: very small, inexpensive actions that would accompany actual planning and be developed in collaboration with local communities. We are considering a form of bottom-up urbanism that would link the large-scale strategies and urban operations to the small one of community actions.

Strategy on an urban scale

As shown in the prototypical example of Calea Moşilor, zoning of the territory defined or influenced by the totalitarian axes comprises three categories:

An intervention area, covering the remaining empty space behind the rows of blocks. It is essentially public property now and can be transformed into a system of public spaces through refurbishment conducted by the administration.
A protected area, more or less coinciding with the one defined by heritage regulations.

In between, there is a buffer area, made up of old streets and private plots and buildings, which should develop according to urban regulations. By attracting investment in commerce, housing, and public services here, present-day pressure on the protected area would decrease, thus preserving its identity. The buffer area and the intervention area reinforce each other: on the one hand, a well-furbished public space raises the standard of a place and activates general urban development. On the other hand, new investments will make this public space work properly, solve problems that cannot be covered by the existing free space (like parking), and improve the living conditions of the inhabitants in general.

Prototypical solutions: A toolkit for urban regeneration

Beyond the general framework—the curtain, the open spaces, the old city—the real situations are actually very different and require adapted answers. Therefore, we built up the strategy in terms of methodology, not a global project. We searched for prototypical situations that would describe the essential relations among the boulevards, the blocks of flats along it, the open space behind them, and the historical fabric. Ultimately, the whole of Calea Moşilor is composed of variations and combinations of these fundamental typologies.

On the other hand, these prototypical situations are not only specific to Calea Moşilor, but show up all over in areas along the socialist-era arteries in Bucharest. Thus, the solutions can become a model for the rest of the city.

According to their characteristics, we called the five prototypical areas Direct Collision, Diffuse Border, Hybrid Backspace, Enclosure, and Compact Socialist Area.

The actual proposal does not mimic detailed solutions, but tries instead to model principles and a clear framework for a process. The first step is to build up a toolkit for urban regeneration: activities that could take place in the intervention area or reorganize the public space in it, as well as institute regulations and new functions in the buffer area.

The solutions have been organized according to function types: recreation, sport, entertainment, meeting space, and commercial or cultural equipment, as well as social and technical infrastructure.

Apart from functional schemes, the intervention also relies on the key instrument of creating clear and richer spaces. Instead of the present chaotic condition, we can define space by the simple means of three categories. A gradual passage is thus created, according to the degree of accessibility, protection, and intimacy: areas open to cars and pedestrians alike, as well as purely pedestrian areas composed of public and semi-public spaces.

For the buffer area there is a series of recommendations for urban regulations regarding density, the reorganization of lots, and the reorientation of the new buildings so that they face the public space. In the second step, this toolkit has been applied to the prototypical areas described above, and then to the whole of Calea Mosilor. We show here an example: the area between the boulevard and Marcel Iancu, Episcopul Radu and Ardeleni streets. The now fenced-in green space facing Calea Mosilor would become a true urban square; the now continuous alley behind it would be divided into two cul-de-sacs, that would integrate parking spaces, and the areas behind the blocks of flats and houses could become community gardens for residents.

From the big scale of the city to the scale of immediate intervention: Integrating two levels of action

We introduce "urban acupunctures" that test how the strategic principles work, and may also activate the community, advertise the general project, and, most importantly, build up trust by achieving immediate, visible results.

Actions in public space are by now quite a common alternative instrument. The originality of this concept relies on integrating this level with the level of urban studies, regulations, and projects.
Programmatically, the interventions are:

- an answer, however limited and symbolic, to a real problem and therefore are of interest to the inhabitants
- inexpensive and easy to carry out immediately
- coherent, in terms of the general proposal for the area in question, therefore activating space in line with possible future refurbishment
- a way to involve the local community
- focused on quite derelict and therefore forgotten and non-controversial places

Intervention 1:
"A passage between two worlds"
A passage becomes a gate to the historical fabric. Partial paint leaves portions of the old graffiti free and thus suggests a transformation into an urban art gallery.

Intervention 2:
"A place for the community"
Minimal paint and a new mesh transform a platform between two technical buildings, turning it into a playground. A bench created by Studio Basar is reused by the inhabitants for chatting or watching games.

This was the intervention that got the best reaction from the inhabitants. They (especially the children) helped and supported us, and the space started being intensively used even before it had been completed. It is an embryo of public space located among cars and technical buildings; and maybe it is start of an action that will transform the area.

Intervention 3:
"Please step on the grass"
A stairway/bench allows people to cross the fence that surrounds a dead "green" space, making it accessible to the public—and symbolizing the future creation of a real urban square.

Intervention 4:
"An urban living-room"
A neglected space in between old houses and the back of a block of flats turns into an urban living-room, by placing recovered furniture on an existing concrete slab and creating a gravel area.

Magic Blocks 2010. Behind the concrete curtain. Activating the areas behind the socialist boulevards in the centre of Bucharest.

The entire central area of Bucharest is strewn with concrete curtains, dozens of kilometres of boulevards displaying uninterrupted rows of blocks built in the '70s and the '80s. Behind them, the old city with narrow streets and houses, churches and trees.
This unique situation is due to the abrupt stop that the December 1989 Revolution brought to the great project of dicator Ceausescu, who aimed the complete razure of the historical city and its replacement by the new socialist one; the concrete curtains were only meant as a first step in this process.
Today, the back of the blocks meets the old house blind walls and people can hardly thrust their way through cars that eat up every space available, enclosed plots of vacant land and technical areas. Lately, on retro-cessed plots or by replacing some of the surviving old houses, villas and even office buildings and new blocks of flats have been rising chaotically for a couple of years. And yet...
If you take a closer look, all these forlorn or badly used areas represent acres of vacant land in the very heart of the city. Perhaps we should start regarding them not just as a serious problem, but also as a resource with a huge potential for becoming vibrant public spaces, a new front for the historic city. A hidden and forgotten area could become an attractive spot for the community and a point of attraction for investors.

The two types: tall concrete slabs on the boulevard, and smaller buildings behind them

Non-places behind the socialist-era boulevards: abandoned or poorly used areas, but also an unacknowledged reserve in the heart of the city

NOW: The concrete curtain, a derelict area behind it, dense, unregulated parking, unrelated bits of green space, and the edges of the central historical area. The latter has been further destroyed, not by a big project, but through individual speculative projects.

VISION: An intervention area (a new public space), opening the curtain via public functions, and a regulation system in the buffer area. The latter can become denser in a planned way, thus injecting money into the area, required housing functions (parking, tertiary, cultural, and community spaces) and also relieving some of the investment pressure in the protected area.

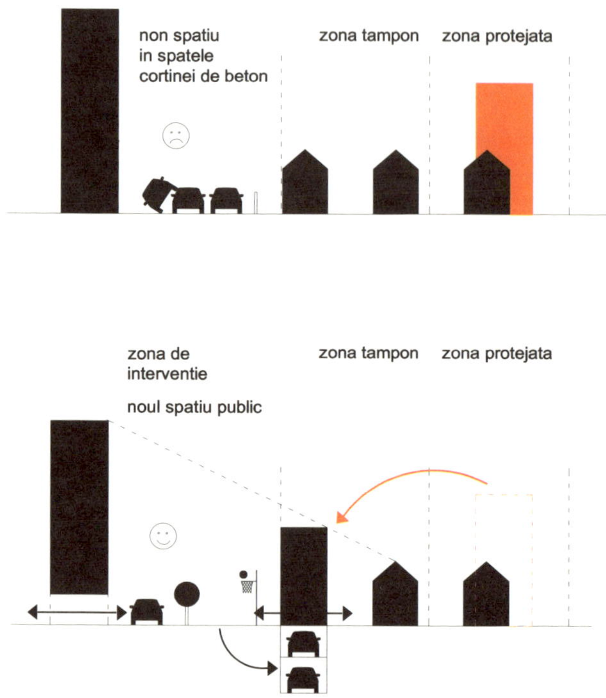

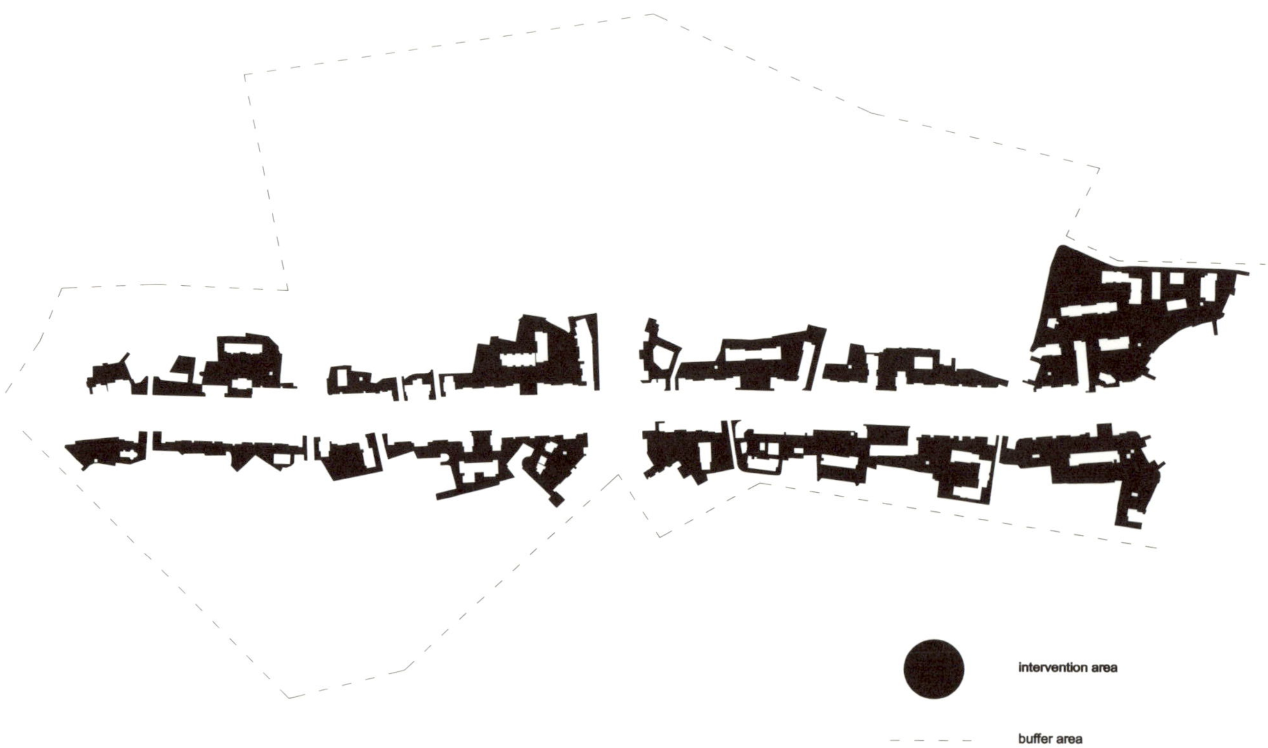

Beyond the general frame—the curtain, the free spaces, the old city—real situations are actually very different and ask for adapted answers. Therefore, we built up the strategy in terms of methodology and not of a global project. We searched for prototypical situations that would describe the essential relations between the boulevards, the blocks of flats along it, the free space in the back and the historical fabric. The whole of Calea Moşilor is finally composed from variations and combinations of these fundamental typologies.
On the other hand, these prototypical situations are not only specific to Calea Moşilor, showing up all over the socialist axes in Bucharest. Thus, the solutions can become a model for the rest of the city. According to their characteristics, we called the 5 prototypical areas Direct Collision, Diffuse Border, Hybrid Backspace, Enclosure and Compact Socialist Area.

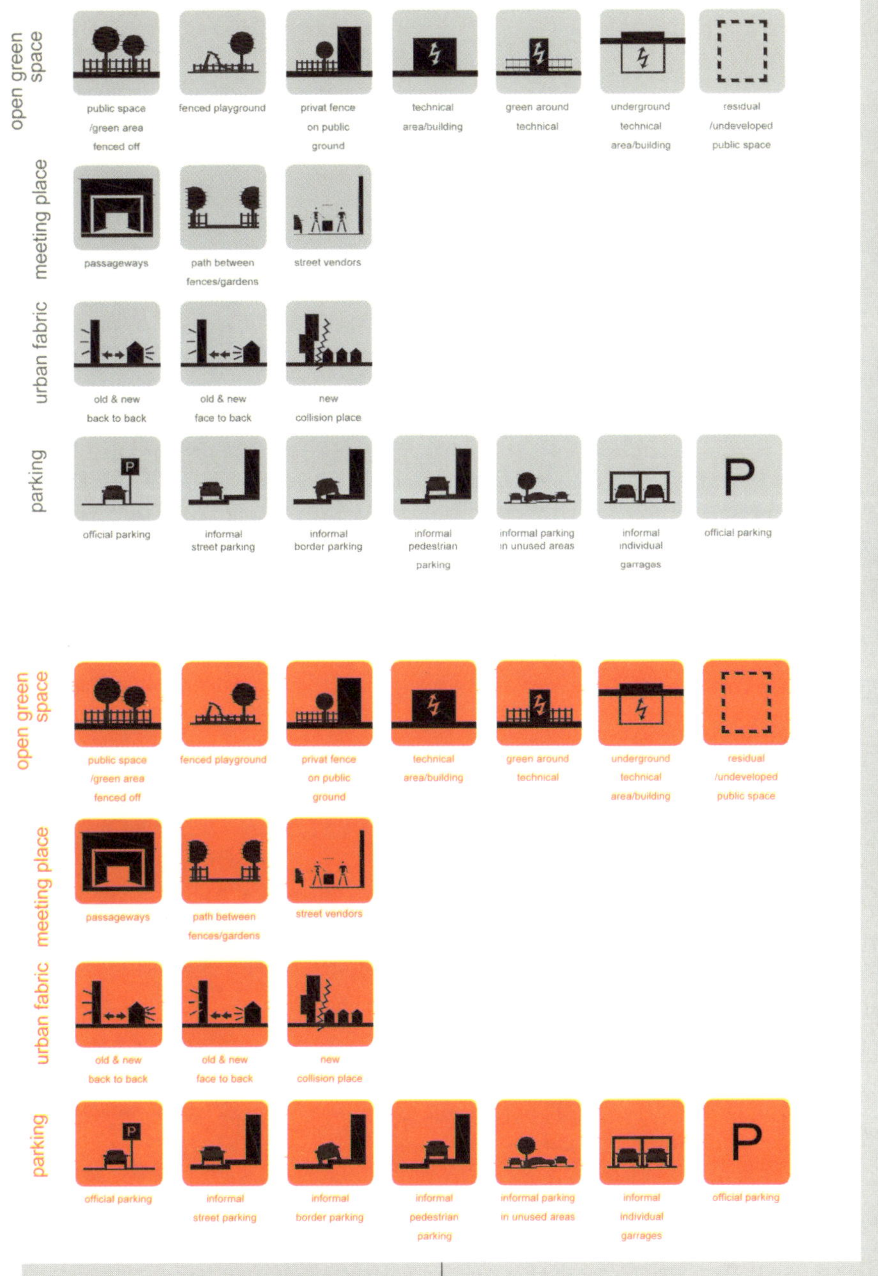

Series of analytical icons are representing the general condition as problems identified in regard to parking, the green space, open space and the urban fabric.

Calea Moşilor Analysis

Five selected areas

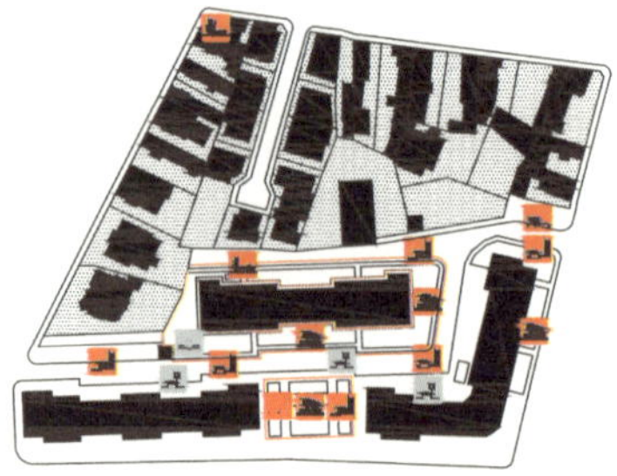

Sometimes, setbacks from the general alignment of the boulevard, interruptions in the fronts and individual apartment blocks built behind the boulevard create a situation in which the old fabric and the socialist developments are intertwined, rather than clearly separated. A new fabric, with a strong connection to the boulevard can be created.

Enclosure

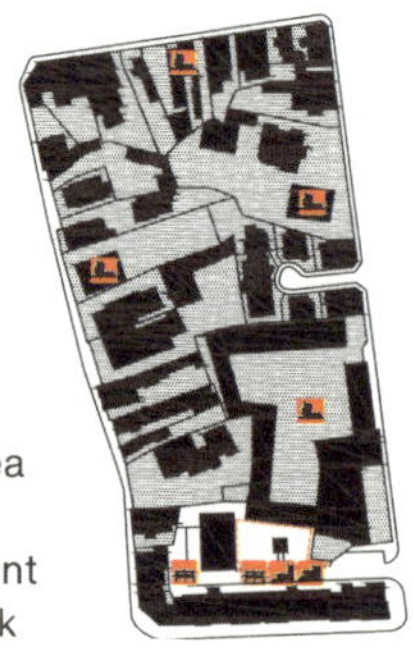

When the concrete front and the limit of the surviving historical area come extremely close together, an active public space behind the apartment blocks would be impossible to achieve. But reinforcement of the semi-public character and the reconstitution of an urban block is possible and would improve the environmental condition.

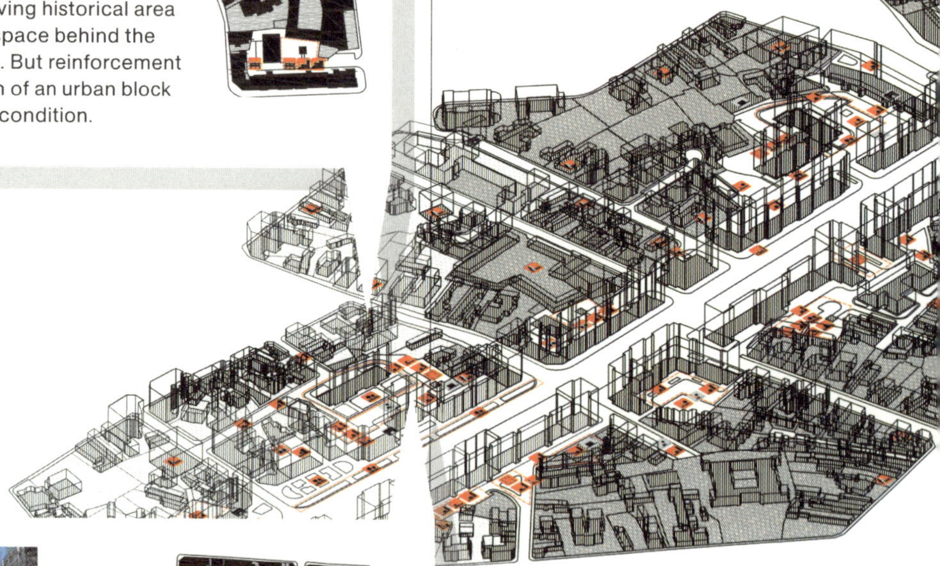

Hybrid Backspace

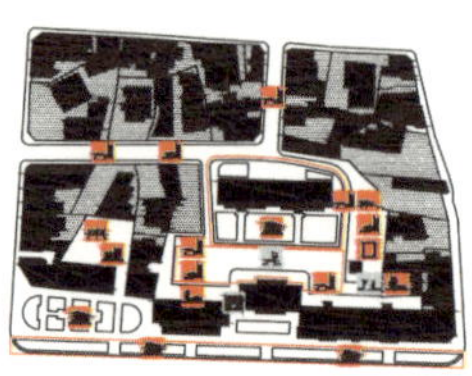

This prototype refers to areas where all conditions mix: intact historical blocks, semi-destroyed ones, almost uninterrupted border, apartment buildings behind the first line of the boulevard. This situation doesn't need radical actions but rather a "cleaning-up" and improvement of the existing situation

Compact Socialist Area

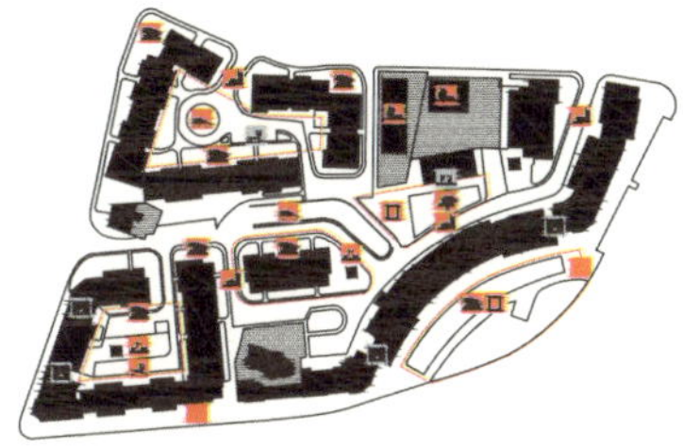

The totalitarian axes are an interrupted project, one that aimed at the complete remaking of the central area. In certain areas, the operation was pushed into the depth of the fabric, creating a homogenous structure of apartment buildings and empty spaces. Still, the more or less defined interior courtyards have the potential to be turned into more defined neighborhood units.

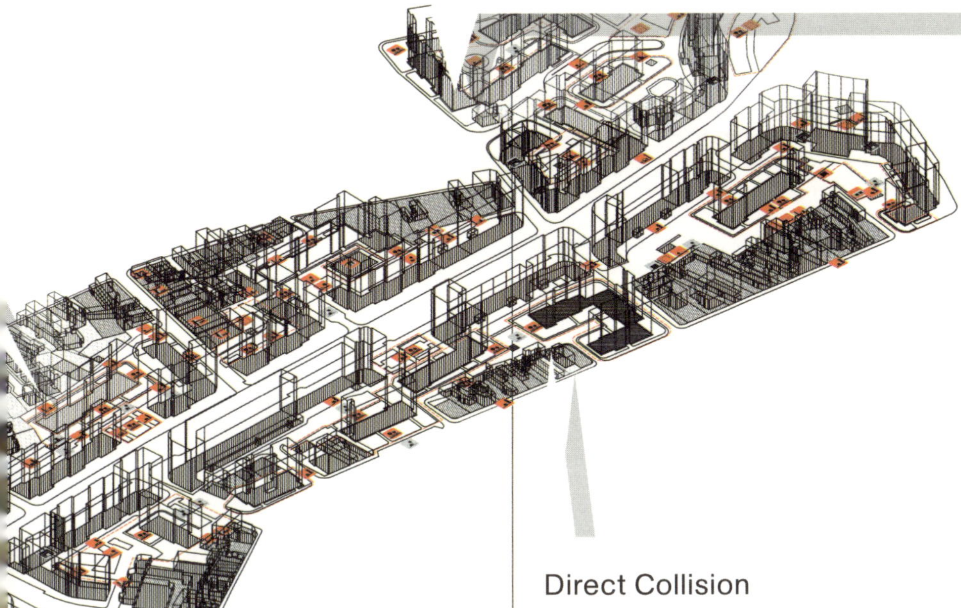

Direct Collision

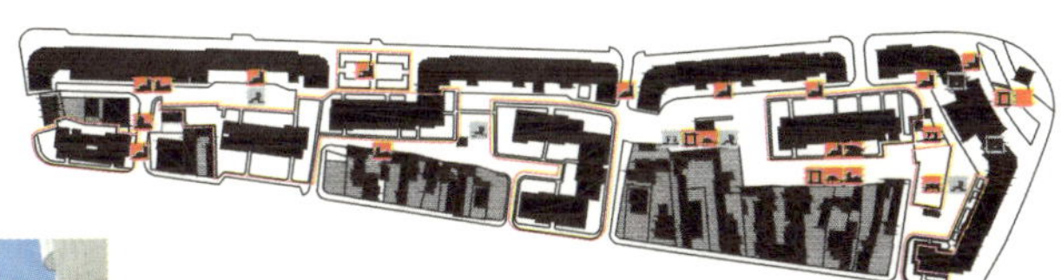

This prototype defines the areas where the almost uninterrupted rows of apartment buildings meet the amputated historical blocks. Undefined and sometimes considerable areas lie between these two worlds. The situation calls and has the potential for a new urban order.

Prototypical solutions. A toolkit for urban regeneration

The actual proposal does not mimic detailed solutions, trying instead to model principles and a clear framework for a process. The first step is to build-up a toolkit for urban regeneration: activities that could take place in the intervention area or the reorganization of public space within it, as well as regulations and new functions in the buffer area. The solutions have been organized according to function types—recreation, sport, entertainment, meeting space and commercial or cultural equipment, as well as insertions of social and technical infrastructure.

Apart from function schemes, the intervention also relies on the key-instrument of creating clear and richer spaces. Instead of the present chaotic condition, we can define three categories by simple means. A gradual passage is thus created, according to the degree of accesibility, protection and intimacy: areas open to both cars and pedestrians, as well as purely pedestrian areas composed of public and semi-public spaces.

For the buffer area a series of recommendations for urban regulations regarding densification, reorganization of plots and the re-orientation of the new buildings towards the public space.

In the second step, this toolkit has been applied to the prototypical areas described above, and then to the whole of Calea Mosilor. We show here an example—the area between the boulevard and the streets Marcel Iancu, Episcopul Radu and Ardeleni. The now fenced green space towards Calea Mosilor would become a true urban square, the now continuous alley behind would be divided into two dead-ends integrating parking space, and the areas behind the blocks of flats and the houses could become community gardens for the inhabitants.

An overview of icons representing different solutions to improve the environmental condition. The solutions have been categorized into different functions such as recreation, sport, entertainment, meeting space and commercial or cultural, together with social and technical infrastructure.

The Intervention Area has been differentiated into public, semi-public and private space. For the Buffer Area recommendations for an urban regulation have been made with regard to densification, the reorgansiation of plots and the reorgansiation of the direction of buildings. The programmation of the Intervention Area and the Buffer Area shows the possible direction to improve the environment by keeping it flexible to the needs and to possibilities. It allows the interaction with the residents in the planning process and supports the local authorities by developing a set of possible actions.
It also gives a clear outline of what should be achieved and what should be changed in the future.

A tool for urban regeneration. From top to bottom: commerce, events, technical buildings, meeting places, recreation, parking, social functions, culture, sport, urban regulation strategies for the buffer area, space types (public, semi-public, private)

Diffuse Border - Integration into new fabric

The programmation of the Intervention Area and the Buffer Area leads to a more clear differentaition into public and semi-private spaces by a clear distinction between car-related and pedestrian space.

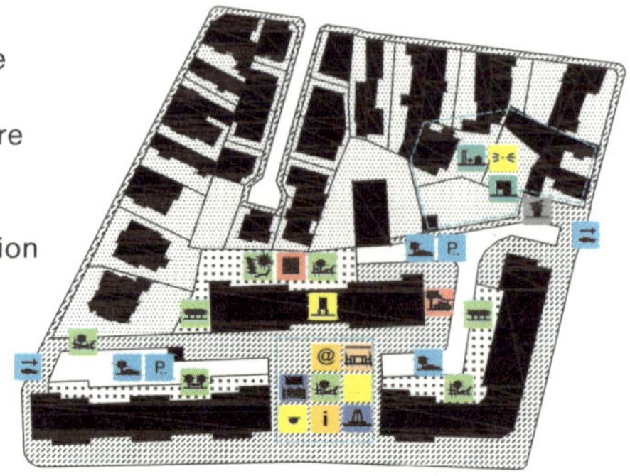

Enclosure - Urban block

The area behind the block of flats remains public, but achieves the quality of a green and quiet "backyard", turned towards the interior of the ensemble and adjacent to the courtyards of the old buildings.

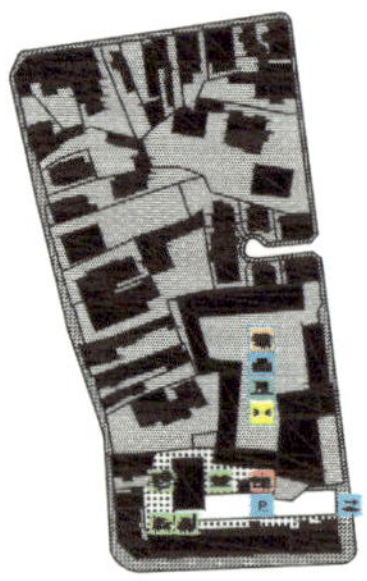

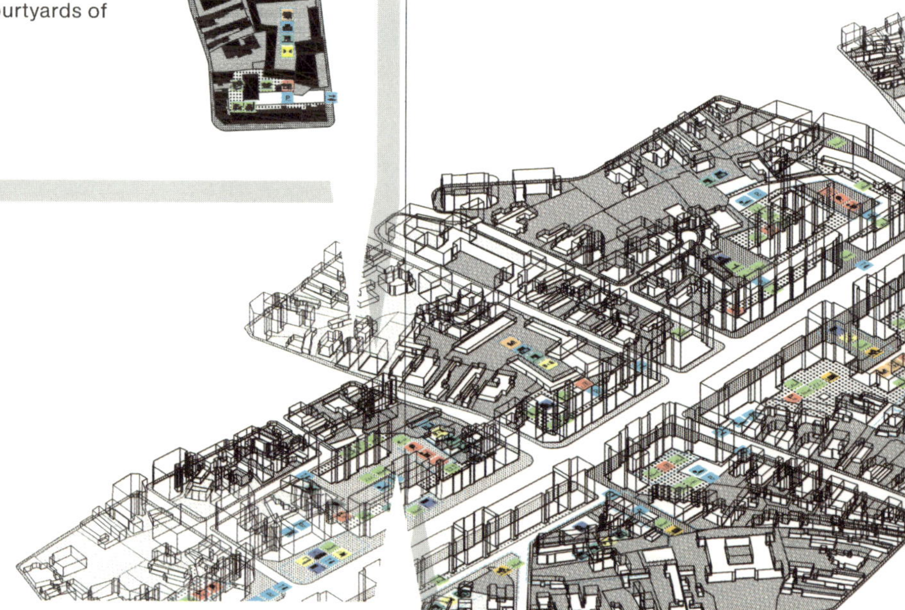

Hybrid Backspace - Cleaning-up

The strategy departs from the mixed situations and relative seclusion that define the character of the hybrid backspace. Through the project, automobile circulation becomes limited and discontinuous, the quiet atmosphere is reinforced by the introduction of functions that meet the dwellers' needs.

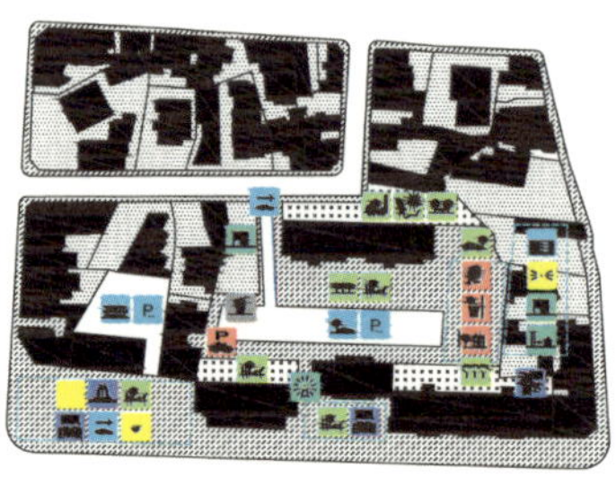

Compact Socialist Area—Neighborhood courtyards

The basic strategy consists of restructuring the empty spaces in order to transform the apartment buildings and the existing amorphous and semi-open courtyards into functioning neighborhood units, a reinterpretation of the classical "Hof (courtyard)" concept.

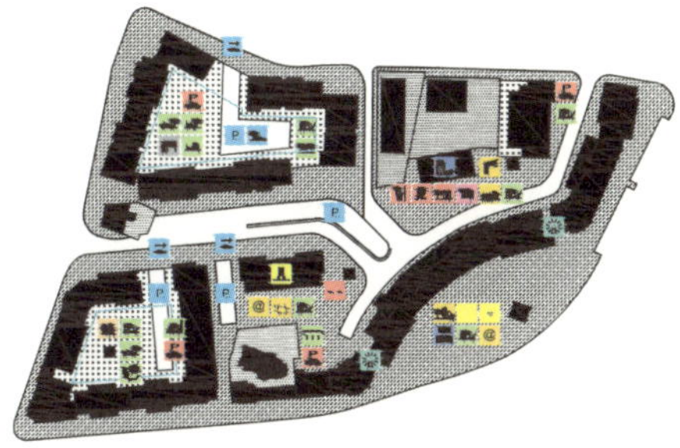

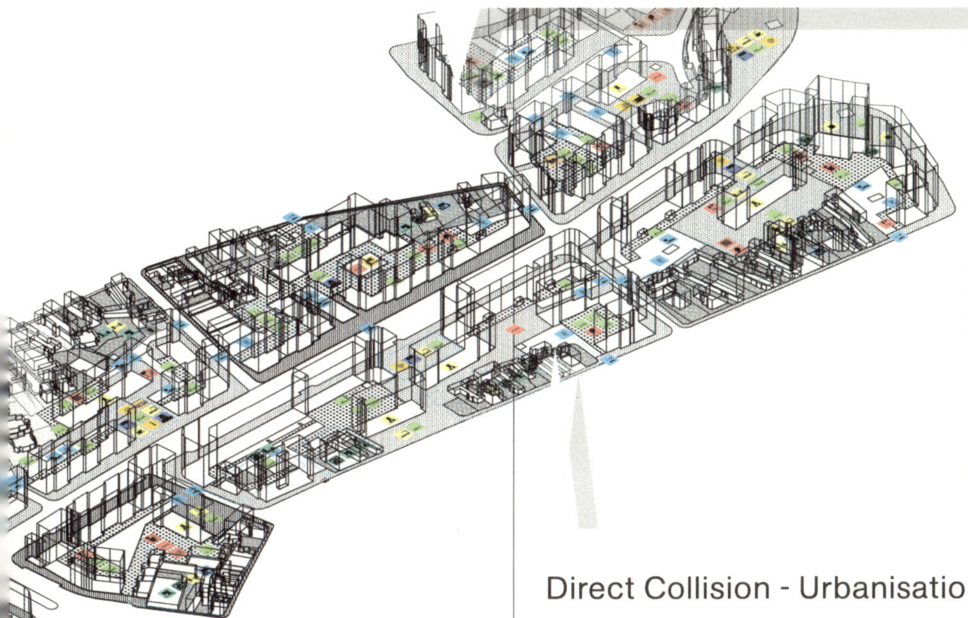

Direct Collision - Urbanisation

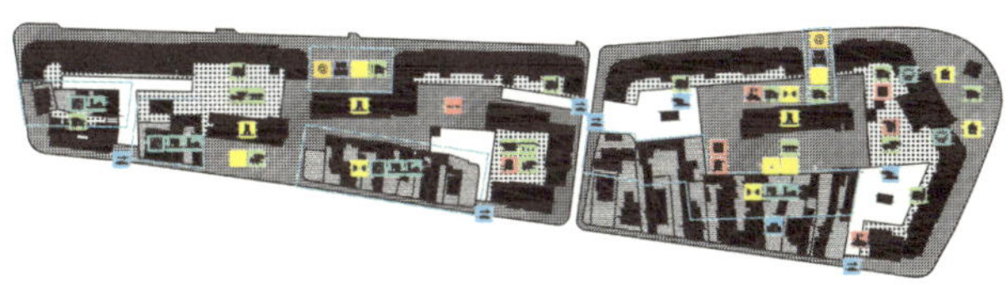

The direct collision of the old urban fabric with the new left a space over, which can be improved by differentiating it more clearly into public and semi-public zones, and car-related areas. The program in the Intervention Area focuses on an urbanisation of the area.

From the big scale of the city to the one of immediate interventions. An integration of two levels of action

We introduce "urban acupunctures" that test how the strategic principles work, and may also activate the community, advertise the general project, and, most importantly, build-up trust by achieving immediate and visible results.

Actions in public space are by now a quite common alternative instrument. The originality of this concept relies on the integration of this level with the one of urban studies, regulations and projects.

Programmatically, the interventions are:

- an answer, however limited and symbolic, to a real problem and therefore interesting for the inhabitants;

- cheap and possible to be carried out immediately

- coherent with the general proposal for the respective area, therefore activating space in line with future refurbishment

- a way to involve the local community

- focused on quite derelict and therefore forgotten and non-conflictual places

Diffuse Border—Integration—Extension of Public Space/Usage

How to make a dead "green" space accessible to the public? How can the improvement of an abandoned area become a symbol for a future development?

Hybrid Backspace—Cleaning-up—Activation of Non-Space

How can a neglected space be activated and become a place for neighbors to meet?

Direct Collision—Urbanisation—Urban Connection

How can a passage become more then a devastated way through a building and signify the connection between new and old urban fabric?

Direct Collision - Urbanisation - Community Action

How can an almost unusable concrete platform between two technical buildings become a useful and active area?

Urban Connection

Intervention 1: A passage between two worlds"

A passage becomes a gate to the historical fabric. The partial painting leaves portions of the old graffiti free and thus suggests a transformation into an urban art gallery.

Community Action

Intervention 2: "A place for the community"

Minimal painting and a new mesh transform a platform between two technical buildings into a playground. A bench created by Studio Basar is reused by the inhabitants for chatting or watching the games.
This was the intervention that received the best reaction from the inhabitants. They helped and supported us (especially the children) and the space started being intensively used even before it had been completed.
An embryo of public space lying between cars and technical buildings and maybe, the start of an action to transform the area.

Extension of Public Space/ Usage

Intervention 3: “Please step on the grass”

A stairway / bench allows to cross the fence that around a dead “green” space, making it accessible for public use – a symbol for the future creation of a real urban square.

Activation of Non-Space

Intervention 4: “An urban living-room”

A neglected space in-between old houses and the back of a block of flats turns into an urban living-room, by placing recovered furniture on an existing concrete slab and creating a gravel area.

Photos: Dragoş Lumpan

SHARP

New Belgrade: Un-planning the Plan

Dubravka Sekulić and Branko Belaćević

At first glance, when looked at from the air, New Belgrade resembles any other new, modernist city, planned in one breath and built in the next. But upon closer inspection, both from the ground and the air, the expected rigor starts to disappear. That is because New Belgrade was never built, nor was it, to put it boldly, conceived as a whole. Neither was it immune to the turbulent changes happening every day in Yugoslavia, which had an immense influence on its core concepts. Although the idea of extending Belgrade to the other bank of the Sava River (historically considered a no-man's-land) existed before socialist Yugoslavia came into being during World War II (the first manifestation being the construction of an international fairground in 1937), the need to build a new capital city for a newly formed country gave a definite push to this idea. The push was so great that de facto construction of New Belgrade started in 1948, before the first general plan for New Belgrade was approved in 1960. Initial construction, however, already marked a departure from the original concept of an administrative city. Besides the federal government buildings and the international hotel, both of which fitted in with the intention of making New Belgrade a strictly governmental city, the other buildings constructed were residential. The shift in policies that slowly occurred after 1948 turned Yugoslavia from a highly centralized socialist country into a decentralized, self-managed nation. Policy shifts first left their mark on the actual situation, and then in the plans. In reality, a number of plans attempted to regulate New Belgrade as a whole, or in part, and they were all partially implemented, sometimes overlapping and sometimes leaving unregulated gaps of space (to be regulated in future). The top-down, centralized plan stemming from the 1950s would soon be confronted with—and adapt to—the new, decentralized, self-managed society of the 1960s and 1970s. Following the changes in 1974, every block of New Belgrade became an entity unto itself, whose future would be ultimately decided by the investors developing it. Following the economic crisis in the second half of 1970s and then a second crisis in the 1980s, it became increasingly difficult for society to continue building the much-needed social infrastructure that was lacking in areas dominated by housing blocks. Nevertheless, construction companies, most of which derived their economic power from the projects they were developing in non-aligned countries, were political because of the profit these projects were bringing the country. They became increasingly influential, not only on the level of single block development, but on the level of overall development in New Belgrade. In 1986, when the decision was made to start creating regulations just for locations that already had existing investors, planning officials slowly started handing over power to the developers. And then, in 1991, with the breakup of Yugoslavia, everything came to a halt. At least, when seen from above. Almost no large construction sites, almost no activity at all. But the situation on the ground was again totally different, with a lot of construction taking place on the micro-scale of apartments or communal spaces inside buildings. Following the privatization of housing, individuals started adapting their space to accommodate their everyday needs, adding provisions they were desperately lacking (e.g., small shops). Besides having an impact on space, these small-scale interventions also affected policies and laws. Confronted with the fact that the majority of the population was now engaged in transformations that were, to put it mildly, loosely legal, laws and regulations were changed to deal with this, and some new procedures, such as legalization, were added. However, although the activity of large construction companies was minimal during this period, it cannot be said that they were at a standstill, as they were closely observing the processes happening on the ground and preparing to utilize new legislation, once the economy took off.

Therefore, it cannot be said that, in the wake of the political changes dating to the year 2000, the strategies practiced in the 1990s were abandoned, but it can be suggested that they were further refined. The only thing that really changed was the scale of intervention, as the attitude toward planning stayed the same, but this time it was practiced by developers involved in larger projects. When the processes of legalization were introduced into law, initially to deal with "untamed construction," developers were assured that their "overbuilding" would be legalized and the plans amended. The original plan was subsequently relegated to serving as the starting point for negotiations between the developer and the city. Typically, a developer would first present its own plan; then the city would revise the official zoning plan to please the developer. What came about as a legitimate survival strategy in the 1990s became the standard procedure by the year 2000, creating a new, legitimate, urban relationship between facilitator and facilitated, and establishing the perception of space as a commodity.

New developments (after 2000) in New Belgrade: although all have a seemingly different relationship to the existing structure, the common thread is the need to negate the original modernist plan, or what is left of it, or any plan whatsoever. In all case studies, the zoning plan was changed to accommodate the developer's project, and the plan was revised again when the developer's plans changed. Case studies show different approaches, but with the same result: the city is governed according to developers' needs. In that process, institutions "planned globally and un-planned locally," thus creating a new gap large enough to accommodate them all. Sequential "planning" and "un-planning" reaches its final stage, when all plans have been obliterated, and all that remains is un-planning, sugar-coated in the discourse of growth and prosperity.

Map of New Belgrade

Photos: Marija Strajnić, Petar Stelkić

#1 BLOCK 21: Superimposing "traditional" on a modernist (super) block

Block 21 was the first block built in the central zone of New Belgrade, defining how all other blocks would be developed, and was one of the few to be completed according to the established plan in 1960s. Block 21 was continually built throughout the 1960s (housing) and 1970s (school and other amenities), and by 1990, approximately eighty percent of it was finished according to the initial plan. From 1990 onward, the density of the block was increased when specific lots were introduced, defined, and handed over to powerful construction companies (Energoprojekt, Napred, Imel group) to develop in collaboration with foreign investors. The lots, defined in what had been a super block open plan, are lined up along the two main boulevards and disregard the existing structure. The size of each lot is smaller, to ensure the amount of investment needed to develop is not great, although it was possible to merge some lots, which was done. Ultimately, the result was that the outline of a „traditional" street grid from the old part of Belgrade was superimposed on top of the modernist block in a much more radical and brutal way than postmodernists critiquing New Belgrade in the 1980s could have ever hoped for.

#2 BLOCK 67: Delta city shopping mall and Belville residential complex

Until the building boom in New Belgrade—which began in 2001, with the construction of Mercator in block 31 (see case study #4)—block 67 was one of the blocks left completely undeveloped. In 2004, as part of Belgrade's bid to become host of the 25th University Games in 2009, block 67 was chosen as the building site for University Village. When, in 2005, Belgrade officially became the host of competition, the site entered the planning process. One corner of the block had been previously marked off as an independent lot, where a private developer (Delta) started to build a shopping mall. The regulation plan for the rest of the block was done by the Belgrade Land Development Public Agency. It was promoted as a „baroque concept for New Belgrade" and did not follow the parameters of density and size set by the master plan for that area. The initial plan to develop the site as a social housing block, included subsidies for a private developer, but it had to be abandoned, due to the lack of city funding. Therefore, although the construction site was acquired under favorable terms, the private investor continued to develop the project as any other, putting apartments on the market even before construction had begun and the University Games had taken place.

#3 BLOCK 65: Airport City—a plan within a plan

June 13, 2009
Airport City organizes an open house, opening its gates to the public, advertising the event as City within the City.

A large office complex is inserted into the block, and New Belgrade, as a gated community, a city unto itself, follows its own logic of growth, density, and development. While the block itself remains within the framework of "traditional" New Belgrade regulation, the interior of the gated complex is governed by owner of the complex, which defines its own regulations. In this way, the open block structure of New Belgrade, built under the system of a classless society, is most obviously confronted with the establishment of a capitalist class power and its power over space.

#4 BLOCK 31: Mercator shopping mall—Developer as urban planner

Following the political changes in the year 2000, the first developer to invest in New Belgrade was Mercator, the largest Slovenian retail chain, which had already had a presence in Belgrade before 1990. The Mercator shopping mall was the first piece of major construction in New Belgrade in ten years and was presented as a symbol of the new economic prosperity. The project benefited a lot from the emotional connection the local population had with the Mercator brand, which was present in Belgrade until 1990, and now presented itself as a sign of the return of the "good old days." With that name, the only issues surrounding the highly anticipated project were where it would be situated and how large it would be, and it turned out that the developer was entirely free to choose. The only thing urban planners had to do was to note the change in the master plan. City officials, pleased with the size of the investment, were open to negotiations of this kind, and this precedent actually became the rule. The government and the municipality became the facilitators of the developers' needs.

#5 BLOCK 26: The orthodox church as developer

Block 26 is considered the prime location in New Belgrade, part of a central zone (together with Blocks 24 and 25) in which all of the public buildings were to be located, at least according to the plans from the 1960s—but they never came into existence. When the crisis of the 1990s started, the central zone was split between the two largest construction companies, Napred and Energoprojekt, to be developed in collaboration foreign investors, without any obligation to conform to any urban plan. In 1992 Napred donated one part of its block to the church, without foreseeing the implications of that act. From that point on, the block had to be developed as a collection of lots, and not as an entity unto itself. After the year 2000 efforts were made to relocate the church's lot, but to no avail; the church quickly started construction and the change had to be accommodated in the master plan. The lot became the only one that is not leased to New Belgrade for 99 years. The church behaves like any other large-scale corporation/developer, acting as a state within a state.

#6 BLOCK 16: Ušće shopping mall—Amending the plan after construction

The former headquarters of the Central Committee of the Yugoslavian Communist Party, which occupies the smaller of two parts on Block 16, was partially destroyed in 1999 by NATO bombing. It was acquired by a developer (MPC properties) after 2000. The larger part is a park, but the building's underground garage extends beneath it. This is used as a reason to make a new regulating plan for this block, in which the two parts are merged, with ownership given to the developer, without any public tender or additional payment. On the pretext of erecting a "building of special significance to the members of the public," part of the park was rezoned for construction. A competition was held for a design for this lot, and construction of a shopping mall soon followed, following a completely different design. As the construction was progressing, the shopping mall grew larger than allowed in the permit, at the expense of the park. Since the park was already destroyed, there was pressure to amend the changes in the official plan. In the public dispute over the legality of such an action, the Belgrade city council held a special session to address the warranted accusation, only to grant approval to the shopping mall—merited by its "special significance."

#3 BLOCK 65: AIRPORT CITY - A PLAN WITHIN A PLAN

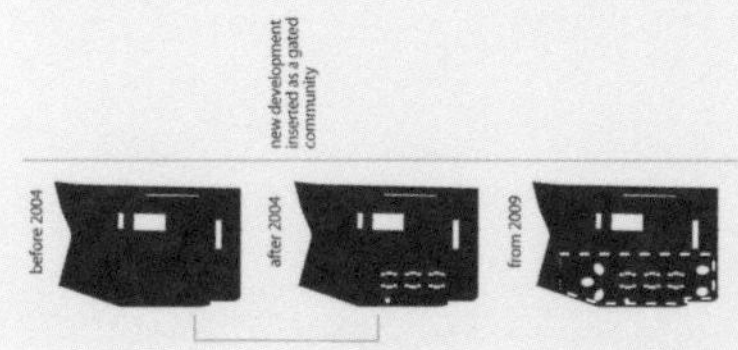

#2 BLOCK 67: DELTA CITY SHOPPING MALL AND BELVILLE RESIDENTIAL COMPLEX

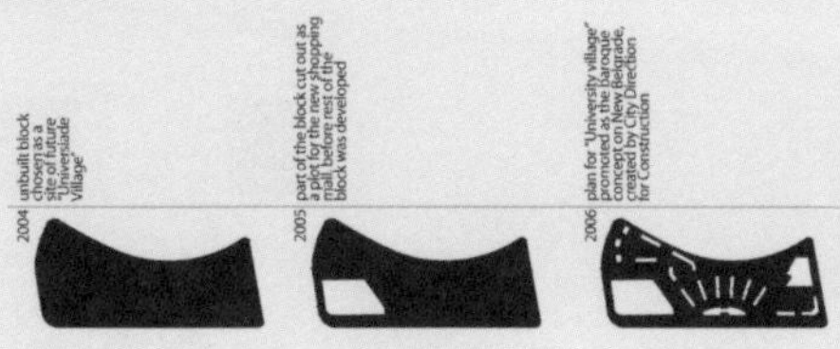

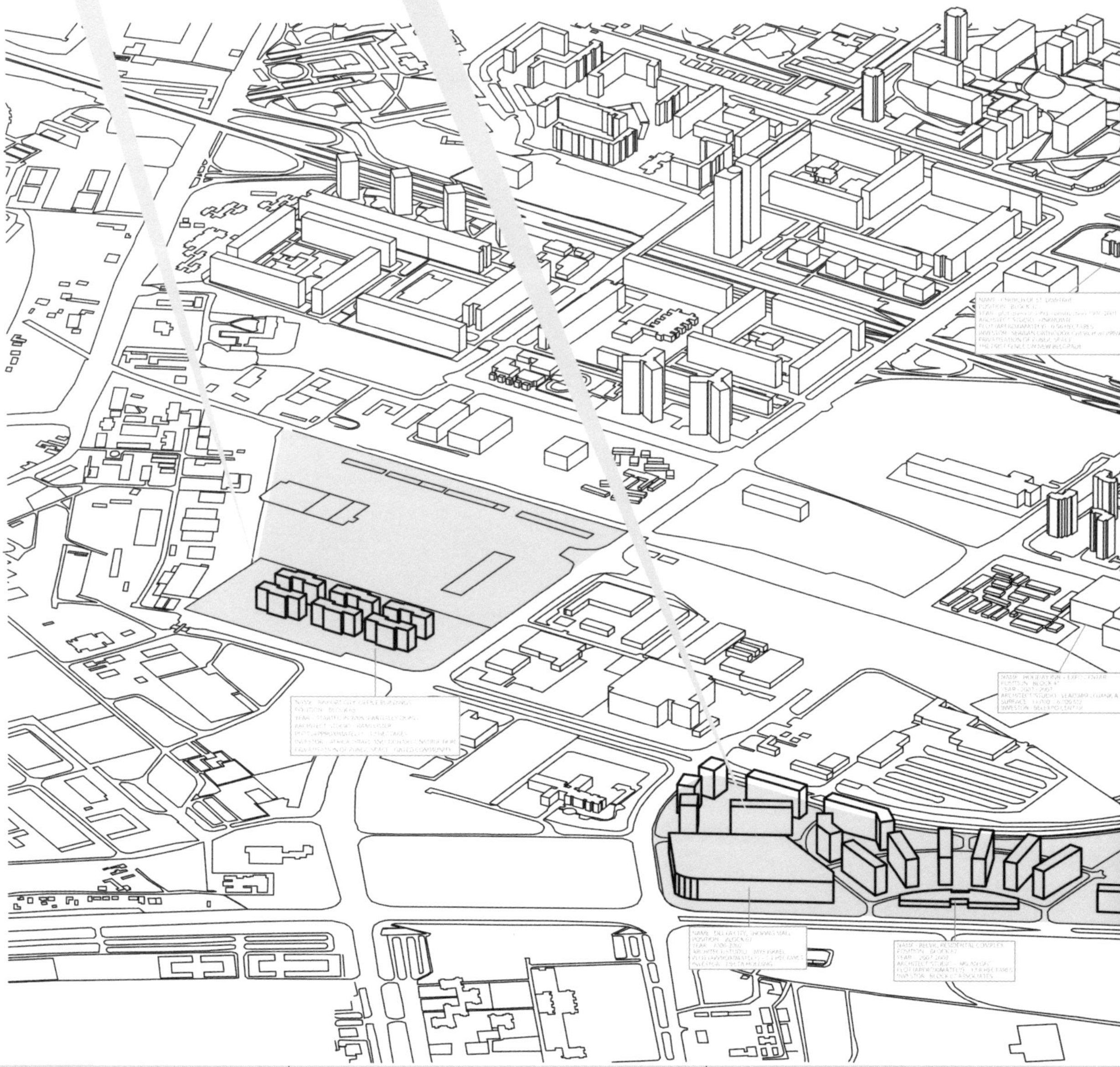

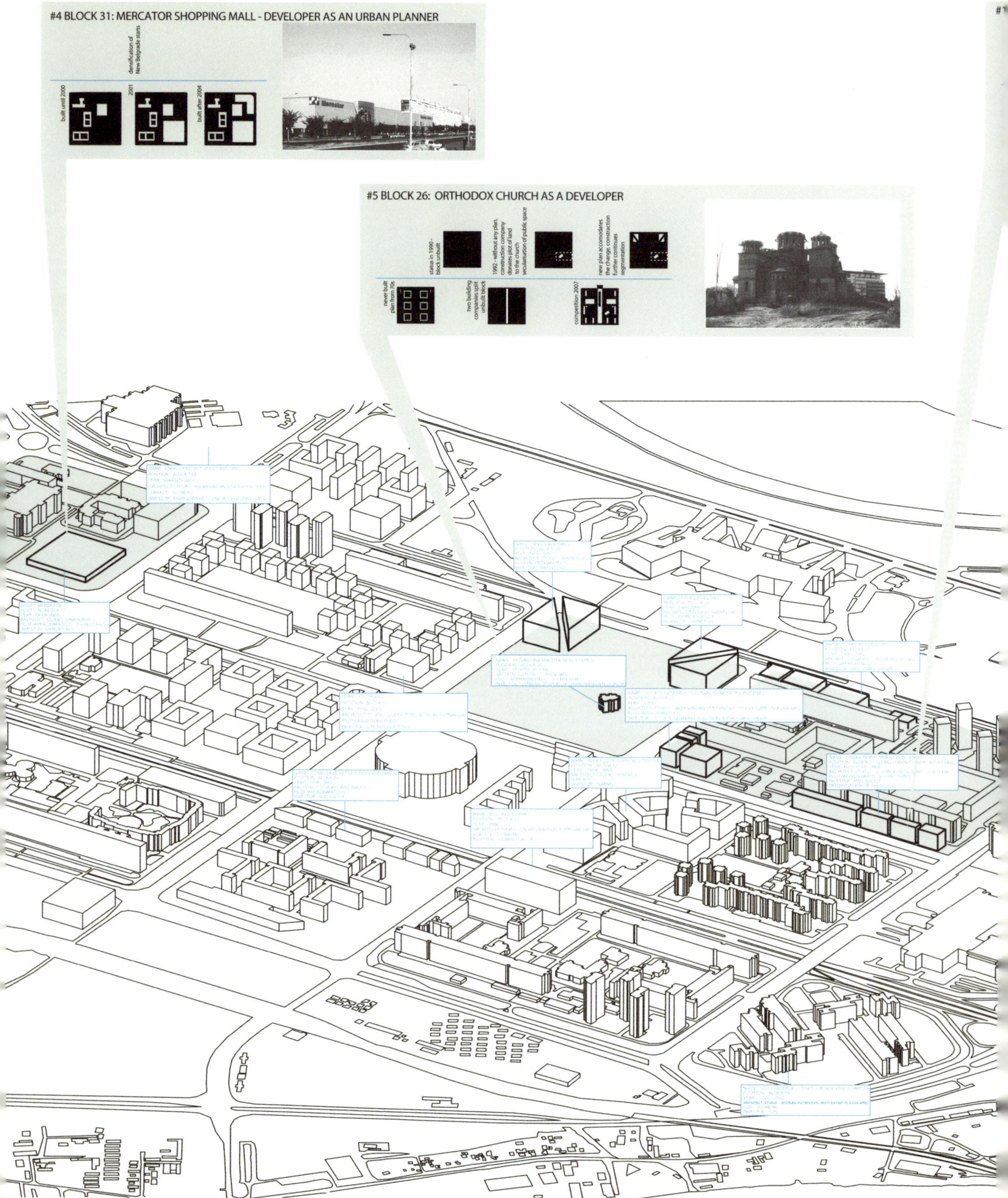
#4 BLOCK 31: MERCATOR SHOPPING MALL - DEVELOPER AS AN URBAN PLANNER
built until 2000
2001
densification of New Belgrade starts
built after 2004
Mercator
#5 BLOCK 26: ORTHODOX CHURCH AS A DEVELOPER
status in 1990 - block unbuilt
1992 - without any plan, construction company donates plot of land to the church secularisation of public space
new plan accomodates the change, constraction further continues segmentation
never built plan from 70s
two building companies split unbuilt block
competition 2007

RIMPOSING 'TRADITIONAL' ON A MODERNIST SUPERBLOCK

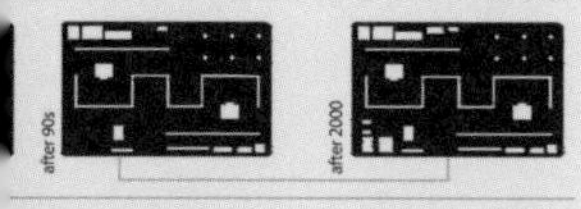

#6 BLOCK 16: UŠĆE SHOPPING MALL - AMENDING THE PLAN AFTER CONSTRUCTION

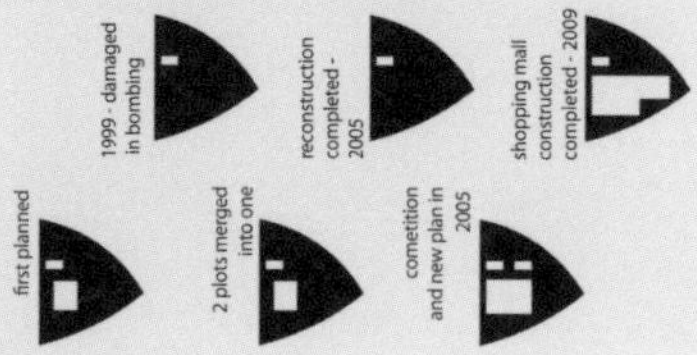

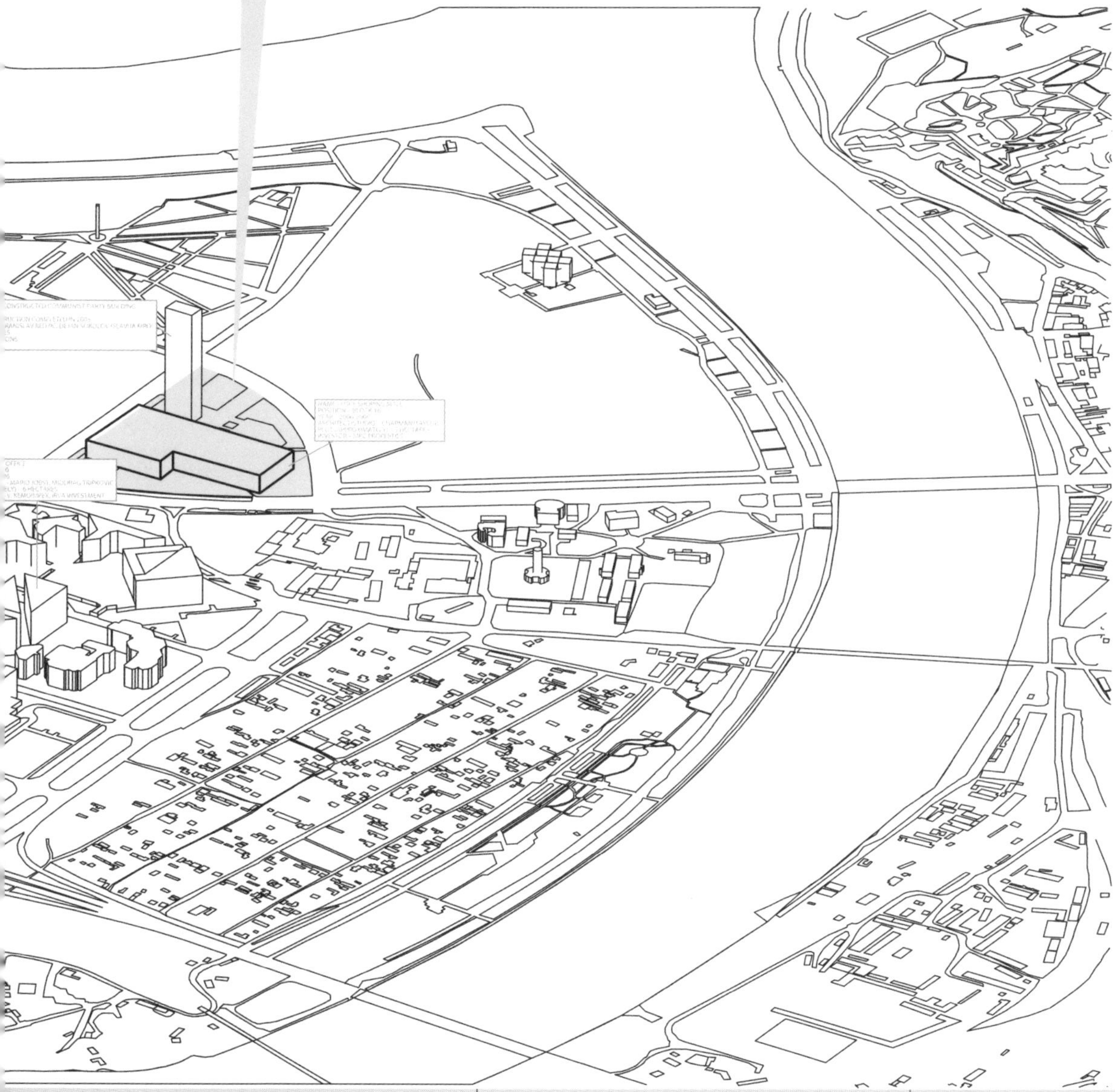

New Belgrade

Photos: Wolfgang Thaler

BANCA INTESA
BANCA INTESA

GRAWE

Urban Transformation in Skopje – From Modern Future to Fake History

First Archi Brigade

Snezana Domazetovska, Aneta Spaseska, and Slavica Chavdarovska

Skopje, the capital of Macedonia, is located in the center of the Balkans, approximately halfway between Belgrade and Athens. Its geographic position brought Skopje great importance in the past, making it a trading, cultural, and political center in the region. At the same time, it has passed through quite a turbulent history, marked by many cases of battles, invasion, and occupation. Furthermore, Skopje has suffered several seriously destructive natural disasters and each time has gotten back on its feet. The last catastrophic earthquake happened on July 26, 1963. Almost eighty-five percent of the houses were demolished or damaged, over one thousand people died, many more were injured, and most of the population was left homeless. For a brief time, this tragedy attracted huge international attention. Back then, Macedonia was part of Yugoslavia, and due to its well-established foreign policies, seventy-seven countries from all around the world helped Skopje to be rebuilt. With enormous speed a small and not very well-known city became an international symbol of brotherhood at the peak of the Cold War, and became known as the "City of Solidarity."

Besides receiving a huge amount of help in meeting the urgent demand for housing units, another important event was the United Nations contribution to the planning process of rebuilding what was left of Skopje. In 1965 the UN announced an international competition for a new master plan for Skopje, which was won by one of the most important architects of the twentieth century, Japanese architect Kenzo Tange. His futuristic vision rests on the concepts of structure, function, and symbol.

Comments about his plan went from one to the other extreme. While some focused on the great, revolutionary dimension of his project, others pointed out how impractical, unrealistic, and out of proportion it was. The original concept underwent some adaptation, but still, the realization faced a lot of problems, mostly of a financial character. In the end, Tange's plan was far from fully realized. The only recognizable element from the original plan is the City Wall, a strip of buildings around the city center, representing a contemporary interpretation of the medieval Skopje fortress. The way he incorporated traditional elements into his futuristic vision is unexpected and therefore quite impressive, especially when one takes into account current happenings in the city planning of Skopje's center. Now we are witnessing a government attempt to aggressively display national identity, but instead, due to the corrupt roots of this idea, we get a visual overload of fake history. This might be depressing, given the fact that real architectural heritage is falling apart due to neglect. But let's go back to the post-earthquake period.

This period meant intensive construction activities for Skopje and a chance to realize a contemporary, socially active city that would offer a better life to its citizens. The new residential buildings contributed to the image of Skopje as a city of Modernism. This tendency was evident because of the focus on raising the living standards of its citizens.

Also, with the mass use of prefabricated building elements, modernist housing units were among the most affordable projects of that era. Their quick construction allowed Skopje to react rapidly to the increased demand for housing. In this period many outstanding public buildings were built. That is how a small city like Skopje ended up with great examples of representative buildings that reflect the global principles of Modernism, such as: the Macedonian Opera and Ballet, the Museum of Contemporary Art, the Skopje City Archive, the City Trade Center, the Hydro-Metrological Center, the Post Office and Telecommunications Center, the Macedonian Academy of Sciences and Arts, etc.

After the breakup of Yugoslavia (in 1991) and the passage into capitalism, there was a change in the city's established architectural and urbanist values. During the social transition, the dominance of the private over the public interest began to emerge. The city suffered irreversible damage caused by newly constructed buildings that violate architectural and urbanist rules and do not meet basic standards of design. In this situation, nobody took functionality and aesthetics into account, so the city was oppressed by buildings that looked like decorated cakes. Construction principles were often neglected, as well as the fact that Skopje lies on ground with high seismic risk. The infrastructure remained almost unchanged, although it was overburdened by a flow several times higher than originally planned. Political "games" did not allow a long-term strategy for the city to be created. In their everyday life citizens witnessed the work of the so-called "urban mafia," but, except for some cases of individual revolt, they did not show any organized collective reaction. The profoundly corrupt privatization agenda left the functionality and image of the entire city deeply scarred. Then another distinctive period for city planning occurred in Skopje, when governmental institutions started acting like private owners of the city.

In 2007 a citizens' association, "Mother Theresa of Skopje," presented to the Ministry of Culture an initiative and a complete architectural project for a memorial house dedicated to Mother Theresa. The ministry accepted the initiative and suggested the architectural project be chosen through a public competition. The winner of the international competition was Portuguese architect Jorge Marum, who proposed a minimalist cube as an answer. Explaining that none of the proposed projects complied fully with all the criteria, the Ministry held a new competition. This time, first prize went to the proposal by Vangel Bozhinovski, which had been in the previous competition, but was considered "problematic" by the jury. It is a building with an overemphasized shape and decoration, thus suggesting an image opposite to that associated with the world's most famous humanitarian, who comes from Skopje. This provoked a strong reaction from architects and other cultural professionals, who raised their voice against the final decision, which unfortunately stayed unchanged.

In 2008, on the initiative of the prime minister, the government decided that a church was going to be built on Macedonia Square, even though such a building code was not evident in the Detailed Urbanist Plan (DUP). Soon after, without any expert opinion, a building permit for a church appeared in the DUP. It was decided that the building should stand on the spot adjoining the entrance to the City Mall and the street leading to the National Assembly. This area, shaped like a small square (piazzetta), is the most frequented and liveliest part of the square, and building on it will create an obstacle for pedestrians. The main argument in favor was the fact that another church, St. Constantine and Elena, which was demolished after the earthquake in 1963 to make room for the commercial district, once existed near the area. It is ironic, however, that three churches are already located near the square. The Islamic Religious Community also protested, asking for reciprocity and demanding the reconstruction of the Burmali Mosque, demolished to make room for the Army Hall in the 1930s. (The Army Hall was badly damaged in 1963 and then later demolished, but there are also plans to reconstruct it, as well.) In addition, it was decided that the "rebuilding" of St. Constantine and Elena would be financed by the government, even though Macedonia is a secular state and around one-quarter of its population is made up of Albanians, most of whom are Muslim. There was yet another public dispute and subsequently the government decided not to finance the project with state money; instead, it will sell this highly attractive central land to the Macedonian Orthodox Church for less than thirty euros per square meter.

In 2009, without paying attention to the actual needs of the citizens, the detailed urban plan for the city center went through unreasonable multiple changes and additions. The public became aware of this in 2010, after repetitive mass media broadcasting of the controversial video project called "Skopje 2014." In this video, a highly realistic 3D animation of the center of Skopje can be seen; it depicts what the center will look like after the construction of all facilities contained in the detailed plan. It caused a major socio-political debate among the public countrywide. The Ministry of Culture, as initiator, defended the project with arguments related to rising national awareness, attracting tourists, and solving the problem of the lack of offices for several state institutions. Aware citizens opposed the lack of public transparency in the creating of such radical solutions, and objected to irrational spending in a critical economic situation, as well as to the premature and inappropriate planning for what is relatively the most important square in the country. A competition was not announced for the plan, and it was developed and signed by a private company, which never appeared to explain it in public.

The citizens' right to participate in the decision-making process was not respected, and public opinion polls were conducted as a pure formality under some substandard conditions during holidays and vacations. The lack of a viable concept and strategy was obvious. Public spaces were converted into building lots, where conditions were unsuited to such bulky structures.

According to this project, the left bank of the river Vardar will be occupied by buildings containing state institutions, which will create a new city wall and put an end to the idea for a city cultural center on the same location. One of the most controversial objects is the historicist triumphal gate at the entrance of the square. Furthermore, the appearance of the center is to be radically changed, by the classicistic treatment of the old and new buildings' facades. This process of so-called "antiquization" intensified diplomatic conflict with Greece at a moment when state foreign policy is in a serious crisis because of these relations. The biggest dispute was caused by the central element of the plan, a megalomaniac fountain with an equestrian statue of Alexander the Great, about twenty-three meters high, set in the middle of the square. Even if this is interpreted as a small symbol of state dignity and self-esteem, opposing the "stronger and unfair player" (in this case Greece), all of it is undermined by the fact that the government decided not to use the name Alexander the Great for this statue, but instead calls it "Warrior on a Horse."

Models of the post-earthquake master plan for Skopje.

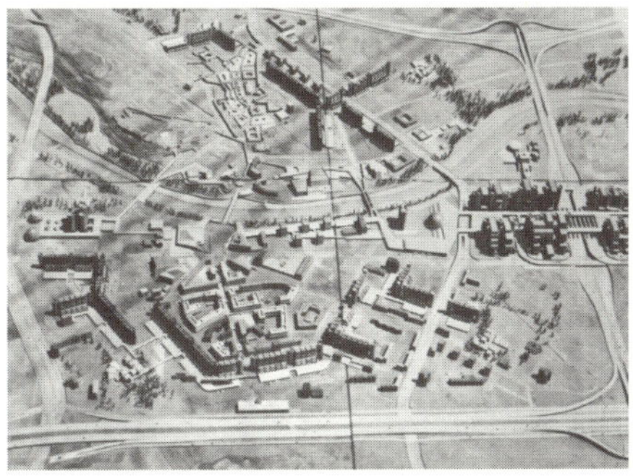

Furthermore, the plan consists of numerous monumental sculptures. The supporters of the project say that this is supposed to bring our country out of the identity crisis. But whose identity are we talking about, if all these sculptures are only powerful male figures from Macedonian national history? Did someone perhaps forget that there is big population of other ethnicities living in this country? Instead of bringing together its citizens, it is easy to say that this project is deepening the gap between them. Even the female population is not regarded in this case. There is not a single monument to a woman in this project. Ironically, some of the statues are placed in the old Memorial Park of the Female Soldier.

The current mayor of Skopje has said that the city is about to enjoy a forthcoming urban renaissance, which would give it the character of a European—instead of a socialist—metropolis. The main agents of this project have not even once used the terms: improving the quality of life, sustainability, solving traffic chaos, improvement of infrastructure, environmental protection, protection of public cultural heritage, or standards and principles in planning.

This is why we formed First Archi Brigade, a spontaneously gathered, informal group of students of architecture and young architects who share the same ideas. We are guided by the inclination to take a proactive role in designing the architectural and urban reality of our city today. Nonetheless, we cannot, and do not want to, close our eyes to the fact that in Skopje, placement and building of (new) structures is done in a completely misguided manner. This leads to successive, irreversible damage of the city center. Instead of having urban solutions that are a result of public and expert debates and ensure the most adequate solutions for public spaces, there is a closed process that will radically transform our city.

New Skopje

Photos: Marta Ilievska

On March 28, 2009, we decided to express our concern in a peaceful gathering on the city square. We wanted to raise citizens' awareness for the problematic location, which was designated a construction area, as a way to take a small step toward solving a deeply complicated problem. Our slogan was "Don't rape Skopje." We stood up for good architecture in Skopje, for a better tomorrow, and in this particular case, to generally prevent the damaging of one of the most important public spaces in our city. But we were attacked by counter-protesters from radical groups, which defended this spot because the building planned was a Christian temple. Hiding behind religious excuses, they did not hear our professional arguments, but attacked us verbally and physically.

We continued our activity by organizing different events, making small attempts to summarize what happened to Skopje in the previous period, to face reality, and to think of new challenges. Our main idea is to show symbolically that, in the process of city planning, debate, choice, different ideas, transparency, free creative thought, and public presentation are inevitable.

We will not give up on our love for the city and architecture. We will continue to be committed to working on what we believe a city should be. Skopje is an exceptional city and deserves that.

Mother Theresa Memorial House
(Vangel Bozhinovski, 2009)

New building that is supposed to host the Constitutional Court, the Archaeological Museum, and the State Archives
(Slobodan Zhivkovski, construction begun 2009)

"Warrior on a Horse" statue
(Valentina Stefanovska, 2011)

Old Skopje

Central post office
(Janko Konstantinov, 1974)

Old railway station
(Vladimir Gavrilovik, 1938)

Archive of the City of Skopje
(Georgi Konstantinovski, 1966)

Telecommunications Center
(Janko Konstantinov, 1974)

Macedonian Opera and Ballet
(Biro 77, 1979)

Fakulteta, the Invisible City

ADAPTations/EU In collaboration with FRONTAL (Bucharest) and Archis Interventions

Nina Ilieva

It was 1987 and my parents finally got an apartment in a prefabricated apartment block complex in Sofia, Bulgaria, after twenty years of waiting. I remember my disappointment at the location of our new home, which was in the Ovcha Kupel district, far from the city center where I grew up and where all my friends lived at that time. The windows of our new apartment overlooked the freeway separating our new complex from the Romani neighborhood of Fakulteta. Every morning, while having breakfast and before going to school, I stared at the other side of the road, which resembled a garbage dump and smelled more like one than any other neighborhood in Sofia, where citizens like us lived. One could see half-naked kids and dogs, playing among piles of trash and mud. The sound of Romani music was drowned by the yells of fighting neighbors and crying children.

I never crossed the road to go into Fakulteta, even just out of curiosity, nor did anybody from my family, or any of our neighbors in the apartment block. Somehow we all had a mutual agreement to ignore what was happening there, and life went on like that.

Twenty years later, in 2007, after spending the last seven years in the United States, I am visiting my sister and her family, who are currently living in our old apartment in Ovcha Kupel. So many things have changed in Sofia and Bulgaria since the last time I was there, but it seems that the Fakulteta neighborhood has stayed the same. As if time has stopped there. Everything looks exactly the same as it did twenty years ago, when I first moved in. But new houses are popping up, like wild mushrooms after a rain, in the most unexpected ways and places, trying to find their right to exist among the piles of trash. Most of the buildings have apparently been constructed without permits or any consideration of building and urban planning regulations. Isolated, forgotten, and trying to function by itself, the neighborhood is not only physically separated, it is the invisible city within the city.

It is almost impossible to find Fakulteta on the official map of Sofia, nor will you find it in the Lonely Planet guide. The physical separation is the manifestation of the social segregation happening currently in Bulgaria. But it is a phenomenon not only in Bulgaria. Currently, according to official statistics, there are almost 9.2 million Romani people in Europe. They have been historically rejected by the majority of the population, persecuted, singled out, and targeted for discrimination for centuries all over Europe. During the Middle Ages, they were expelled from Spain and France. In Romania, the Roma were sold as slaves as late as 1856. During the Second World War, almost 1.5 million Romani were killed by the Nazis. They were called „Gypsies," because the Europeans mistakenly believed that they came from Egypt. Even in the twenty-first century, the Roma remain segregated from mainstream society across Europe. They are still seen as criminals and undesirable. Because this European phenomenon is not restricted to Bulgaria, cross-border collaboration is essential for solving the problem and dealing with it.

I started a discussion about this issue with colleagues from the USA and Bulgaria, people with different professional backgrounds and experiences. They were very happy to offer tremendous support and advice, and suggested better strategies that stemmed from their experience and perspectives. Stela Krasteva, a sociologist[1] working with Romani people in Sliven, fed us with information, photos, contacts, and insights, which was a turning point for our project. David Bergman, an economist and expert on urban development[2], gave us important insight into how similar problems have been dealt with in South and North America, and suggested other public-private strategies, which have been very successful in other parts of the world. Elitza Ranova, an anthropologist from Rice University[3], also joined the team, adding her unique perspective and competence as an anthropologist. Dr. Blagovest Valkov, together with the architect Biser Hantov, shared with us his valuable experience working on Romani projects in Bulgaria with the United Nations Development Program (UNDP); Krasimir Kanev from the Bulgarian Helsinski Committee, as well as Michail Georgiev of Romani Baht and Zornitza Stoichkova from the Hesed Foundation, all joined forces to initiate the project and move it along very fast. We all learned from each other, exchanging diverse professional information, ideas, and visions.

1 Stela Krasteva is doctoral candidate in sociology at the University of California, Los Angeles.
2 David Bergman is a professor at the Southern California Institute of Architecture, as well as the head of the Metropolitan Research and Economics firm in Los Angeles, CA.
3 Elitza Ranova is a lecturer at Rice University, Houston. She received her PhD in 2010, with a dissertation titled "Re-inventing Europe: Postsocialist Change, Culture and Style in Bulgaria."

In the summer of 2010, the collaboration effort was supported by Kai Vöckler from Archis Interventions, and Catalin Berescu from Frontal in Bucharest, which was a great opportunity to share experiences and ideas with experts in urbanism and Romani integration from Europe. They joined several workshops[4] in Fakulteta for a collaboration effort organized with the support of several Romani NGOs. Three main case studies were identified and future strategies were discussed during and after the workshop. We met at the Romani NGOs in Fakulteta, discussed the issues and after that, we strolled around the neighborhood, trying to achieve a better understanding of the experience of what it means to live in Fakulteta.

We walk down the unpaved streets of Fakulteta, guided by Romani leader Naiden Kostadinov, who was born and grew up there. The air is saturated with a heavy smell, forming an invisible bubble around the settlement, as if it were trying to protect it from the rest of the city. The neighborhood looks and smells more like a municipal garbage dump than a residential area in Sofia.

After an intense discussion about the problems in Fakulteta and potential solutions for it at the workshop organized by the Romani foundations, Kostadinov begins showing us around, telling very vivid stories of his friends and family, local people who have been living in the neighborhood for generations: the indigenous history of Fakulteta.

"Almost 40,000 people live on approximately 180 hectares on the outskirts of Sofia. The unemployment rate is almost ninety percent. Most of the people still cannot obtain the deeds to their properties," Kostadinov says. Most of the buildings have severe habitability and sanitation issues. "Having running drinking water and a working sewage system is almost a luxury here," he continued, "it is not accessible to everybody." Then he points at the sewage and water pipes running directly to the street, and adds, "Some of the streets are turning into a sewage system, since a proper one has not been built."

After being discouraged by the responses from the municipality and Sofia Water, the utility company, and convinced that they would never build a proper system, the people from Fakulteta decided to take the initiative to construct their sewage system

4 The workshop and exhibition at Sofia Architecture Week (SAW) was supported by the ERSTE Foundation.

independently. Several families raised money and volunteered labor to collaborate, digging up the ground and installing the pipes. Everybody was really happy after they had finished installing the system, which worked properly, until the unprofessionally installed pipes broke and a fountain of sewage water overflowed in the streets. "It became even worse than it was before," adds Naiden.

As we continue to walk down the street, people start crowding around and everybody wants to tell us his/her own story. People try to pull us into their homes to show us how they live without water, electricity, and basic services. These people thought that we were government officials trying to run a re-election campaign, because they don't see visitors like us every day. "Tell Boyko Borisov[5] to find us work," somebody from the crowd shouted behind us.

On Street 313 in Fakulteta, we stop in front of number 14. We knock on the door and suddenly a middle-aged man with a big smile and a lot of hope in his eyes opens the door and welcomes us into his house. He introduces himself as Nedko. We enter Nedko's house, which is impeccably clean, as opposed to what we imagined the house of a Romani family should look like. We enter his living room and sit over tea and cookies, while listening to his story. "We haven't had water since 2004," Nedko begins, "since 2004 we have been sending letters and requests to Sofia Water, to Sofia Municipality, to all of the institutions, which might eventually help us solve the problem. It still has not been solved, even though we have to pay for the water we don't have." Then he shows us a bag full of letters of complaint, which he has sent to different institutions and has collected over the years. We documented everything and continued our journey into the unknown world of Fakulteta.

We ask questions and look for answers. Three main case studies were identified and future strategies were discussed during and after a workshop. Questions were posed: What if the Romani neighborhood went off the grid? What if Fakulteta were to become a unique Bulgarian-Roma center, where local people and tourists can come to experience and celebrate Romani culture? What if the Fakulteta becomes a place in the alternative travel guide in Bulgaria and the Balkans, something that can be one of the most educational, exciting and inspiring things an adventure traveler might do during his or her lifetime. What if it becomes a place for production, rather than a place for consumption? What if we turn the existing hills of waste into energy? Fuel and garbage into fuel? We discussed sustainable technologies, such as gray water reuse and rainwater harvesting, the "living machine and topics" as integral parts of our future improvement of the neighborhood. A self-help program, where the Romani can participate in each step of the work, and new jobs will open up for them, was an important step in each of our proposed future strategies.

The issues were brought to a public discussion later that year during the Sofia Architecture Week (SAW), where the attempt was made to establish a sustainable way to integrate positive working conditions that do not lead to the destruction of the neighborhood, a solution widely supported also by the Romani residents. The curator of Open House at SAW 2010, Ephgenija Hodkevitch, and Boris Enev from fordewind architects ltd., embraced our ideas and helped us organize the exhibition in the best possible way. They also made tremendous efforts, inviting more experts from Europe, who were working on informal housing, to join the discussion; organizing additional workshops on the topics, and inviting Romani bands to introduce their amazing culture and tradition to the public. In order to provoke discussion, Fordewind ltd also proposed the idea of bringing the Sofia Museum of Modern Arts to Fakulteta, but it has been proposed that the Cultural Center of Romani Minorities will be built on this location. The exhibition was supported by the work and participation of the offices AGENCY from New York, and SUPERPOOL from Istanbul. Both of the firms showed very innovative solutions to similar problems in different parts of the world, such as Rome and Diyarbakir.

All of the proposed strategies aimed to develop alternative ideas for improving living conditions and better integrating the segregated neighborhood, without destroying existing neighborhoods and evicting the people there, a solution strongly supported by the current Fakulteta residents. Until now, the bottom-up approach initiated by the Roma residents and volunteers has not been applied in tandem with the top-down approach of regulated long-term planning by the city administration, backed up by national government policies. So the key questions now focus on the new urban typology that would emerge from the new strategies that incorporate the existing informal conditions while improving city regulations and offering a more humane urban environment for diverse ethnic and cultural groups.

We wonder if we can learn from the experience of places worldwide, which face similar challenges, such as China, India, and Latin America. Could we implement and maybe further develop the good example of sustainable incremental strategies of housing development in the inner-city slum of Yerawada, in Pune, east of Mumbai, a collaboration between Urbanouveau and one of India's largest NGOs? A strategy simple enough to be carried out by the slum dwellers themselves, which works against the widespread top-down planning approach that would destroy the existing slums and relocate the people. Is the market-driven approach for low-income housing improvement, developed by TATA Housing, Inc. in India, and Skidmore, Owings & Merrill in the US, suitable for our economic, political, and cultural environment? Or we should develop a totally unique approach to our conditions, which can be followed by other slum improvement redevelopment projects in Eastern Europe and around the world?

After the meeting with Nedko, Naiden, Zornitsa, and the rest of the Romani—very hardworking, warm, and helpful people—we all strongly believe and agree that a far better future for the Romani people in Bulgaria and across Europe is coming soon.

5 Boyko Metodiev Borisov is a Bulgarian politician who has been the prime minister of Bulgaria since July 2009. Previously, he was the mayor of Sofia.

buildings which are documented by the official city of Sofia maps

buidings which are not documented by the official map of city of Sofia

Map of Fakulteta neighborhood in Sofia, Bulgaria, 2010

It was very difficult to determine the percentage of regulated and unregulated buildings in the Romani neighborhood. Close to impossible to find any official data. In the current map of the city of Sofia, only some of the existing buildings were found. These are all houses shown in gray in fig.1. Even the ones that were mapped were often still not regulated. The rest of the existing buildings and structures were not found on any official maps or documents of the city of Sofia. See all houses in red on fig.1.

Whole areas of the neighborhood, such as Cambodga, were invisible to city officials and the rest of the inhabitants of Sofia.

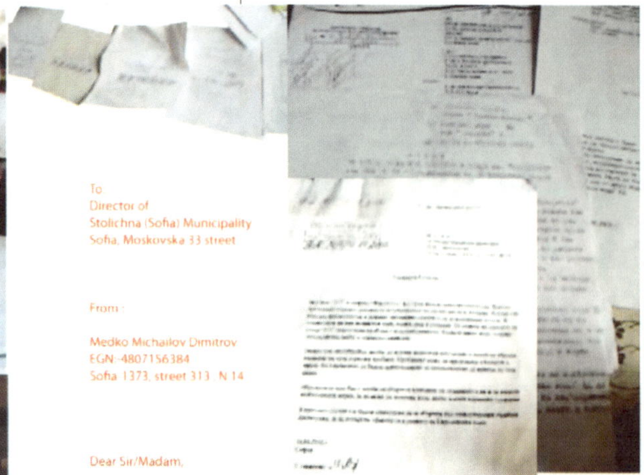

To
Director of
Stolichna (Sofia) Municipality
Sofia, Moskovska 33 street

From :

Medko Michailov Dimitrov
EGN:-4807156384
Sofia 1373, street 313 , N 14

Dear Sir/Madam,

On street "313" in the neighbourhood "Faculteta" in Sofia are living several families. All of them are having proper and legal documents for their land and their houses. We are all paying our taxes regularly too. In our families there are retired people, small kids and schoolkids. From years there is an existing problem with water on street "313". In the houses there is no water because there is a problem with the water pressure.

We already have sent many inquires to all possible institutions and nobody is really paying attention to this really seriuos problem. The problem can bring deseases which can spread quickly too. It is impossible to be forced to live in that way.

We are sending this letter to you and hope that you will take the urgent measurments in order we , as all normal citizens can get water too.

If that does not work agin we will take measurments to get in touch with international lawenforcement institutions , in order to find our rights as citizens of Europeon Union

16.04 2010
Sofia

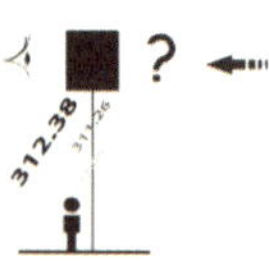

ЗВЕЗДИ ИВАНОВА МЕТОДИЕВА
ZVEZDI IVANOVA METODIEVA
&
КОСТАДИН ЙОРДАНОВ ГЕОРГИЕВ
KOSTADIN JORDANOV GEORGIEV

АНЕЛИЯ улица 307, парцел 60, Факултета
ANELIA street 307, parcel 60, Faculteta

Анелия Траянова Димитрова
Anelia Traijanova Dimitrova

On September 17th, 2003 Anelia and her husband bought parcel 60 on street 307 in Fakulteta. They have built their house without a building permit and without any other documents.

Anelia and her husband have two older daughters at the age of 21 and 22.

1

2

3

Electricity

In Fakulteta all meters are located very high on the electricity post, so that they are not accessible to the Romani residents (see page 168). Only employees of the electric company can see how much electricity is being consumed, and detected by the meter. As a result, there are constant complaints from the Romani residents that they have been severely overcharged. Kostadin Georgiev shows his monthly electricity bill for a single family house in the amount of 312.36 leva, while at the same time the current minimum wage in Bulgaria is 240 leva per month.

Water supply: a constant struggle

Having basic amenities, such as running water, turns out to be a constant struggle for the residents of Fakulteta.
Since 2004 Nedko Mihailov Dimitrov has been living on a property that does not have water. The land and the building he legally owns are regulated. The constant complaints, the endless letters and requests sent to Sofia Water to fix the water problem have not produced any results. The paradox is that Nedko does not have water, but still has to pay Sofia Water for it.

Fakulteta, Sofia

Photos: Kai Vöckler

The Housing and Unhousing of the Roma

Cătălin Berescu

It was not easy to get over the shock of visiting a Roma community living in severe poverty some eleven years ago in Romania. Previously, I thought that this kind of poverty can be encountered only in the slums of Africa or the *favellas* of Latin America, not in our own country, statistically and symbolically placed on a higher level of the poverty ranking. Of course, now I know this was a very naïve assumption, but for the first years I thought that people don't understand much of my concern, mostly because they've never been there to see with their own eyes, and because of the lack of information in the mainstream media. So I produced an exhibition and conferences, tried to show the life stories of those affected by extreme and severe poverty. I still do it occasionally, but I no longer think that the main problem is that people reproduce racism because they are actually uninformed. Instead, it looks to me as if there is an important part of society that is driven by racism and other forms of prejudice and actually creates misinformation as part of more general exclusion policies.

The ethnic division is therefore no longer a part of a general human geography, but a huge symbolic gap beyond an opaque wall of hate, resentment, and fear. In this game of (over)representing otherness, the poverty of the Roma is always ignored by the narrow focus on ethnicity, while general moral judgments on topics like access to decent housing or the right to work are opposed by a variety of discourses about respecting law and order, the lack of obligation toward the poor, and the presupposed, innate lack of responsibility and commitment of the nomads, etc.

These discourses have a specific function; they are delivered precisely when it comes to putting aside the problems of the Roma ghettos, or demolishing them without having a guilty conscience, or promoting the creation of new ones with no fear of future consequences. Blaming the victim is the name of the game we are taught to play by every authoritarian actor, be it a dictator or a small public servant, an impetuous, far-right intellectual, or just our racist neighbor.

The softer versions of these political discourses are embedded in a cultural vision of the society that emphasizes the difference among people and populations, while tending to overlook the similarities. Europeans are interested to an obsessive degree about the difference between the Germans and the French, or between the Romanians and the Hungarians, comparisons being built usually on the supposedly irreducible alterity that creates the array of regional and national identities on our continent. Similarities, which are actually overwhelming and form the basis of coexistence, are not valued in discourse, but fortunately valued in everyday practices. Every time we pass judgment on the poor, every time we visit an impoverished community, we are confronted with *our* values, *our* educated visions about otherness, and *our* prejudices about ethnicity and race than with the way of life present there.

This statement can be tested by any person who decides to live in an impoverished community, or participate in its daily life in one way or another. All of my experiences show that, once they move beyond the emotions of the initial impact, most outsiders (researchers, visitors, social service providers, etc.) tend to adapt very quickly to local conditions, and this is precisely because we are more similar to "them" than we are different. The vast majority of people living there are perfectly normal, regular folks that had the bad luck to be born in the wrong place and then systematically excluded by the surrounding society.

In brief, it's not mainly *their* problem, but *ours*.

In this equation, cultural difference plays an ambiguous part, as always: it is favored by both sides for different reasons. Roma leaders would like to stress their identity in order to build unity and achieve more political power, while politicians from the majority favor the ethnic discourse, because it allows them to individualize very tough issues like unemployment, infant mortality, lack of social housing, etc. "They are Roma, that's why child mortality is six times higher than in the rest of the population, they should modernize…" you can hear in informal discussions. "We are Roma, don't erase our identity, we want to be different, we need special programs!" is one of the common thoughts of Roma leaders. Exclusion may also take a positive appearance: the idea that they are so talented, such good dancers and craftsmen, and that programs that address Roma should develop these natural skills is often just another way of saying that a Roma cannot be a software engineer.

There is a standard discourse on Roma: they came from India as a nomadic population, were enslaved in the East and killed in the West, not allowed to live beside the majority anywhere, then, when slaves were released, they became the victims of social exclusion. They love gold and value endogamy and early marriages. Their language is related to Sanskrit and they are excellent craftsmen. They live in small or medium size groups of extended families that form closed societies, which observe traditions and are reluctant to integrate, have a nomadic way of life and different values from the ones of the majority, etc. There is a fine glissando from historical truth and objective description to common prejudices and then, consequently, to a politically constructed image, be it positive or negative. None of the above statements is false in itself; nevertheless, the overall vision of Roma as an ethnic group that shares an important number of common features is probably the main problem that every Roma group and every Roma individual has to face almost every day. After centuries of mass consumption of the Gypsy mystery and of labelling their culture as exotic and nomadic, we are in a position to design public policies for inclusion that are likely to target mostly the richly traditional, isolated, rural communities and generally miss the horrible, new, urban ghettos, which are mixed, ethnically impure, illegally settled on public or private land, miserable, and, ever since Romania and Bulgaria joined the EU, also boldly growing overnight in Western cities.

BELGRADE, Gazela Bridge (2008)

IDP is the acronym for Internally Displaced People, a euphemistic term used by technocrats to identify war refugees. Under the Gazela Bridge it was hard to distinguish among those who fled because of the war and those who were chased away by rural poverty.

Hard-working activity in the recycling industry supported families, for whom a generous relocation plan was designed using a participatory method. The enthusiasm of the planning team, led by the architect Vladimir Macura, was soon replaced by disappointment when the inhabitants were evicted and transformed again into IDPs in 2010.

BELGRADE, Bellville (2011)

The eviction of the Gazela community led to divisions in several groups. Some relocated to other cities, some within Belgrade, and some others left without any other option but to find the next informal settlement and settle there. The option was not that hard to take, as an estimated six thousand people now live just one-and-a-half kilometers to the north, near the railway, at the edge of a brand new residential area named Bellville. This area of Novi Belgrad has a typical third world image, made up of luxury apartments, glass office buildings, and a huge field covered with shacks, garbage, and debris.

Europe's new ghettos are loosely connected to the older ones, since migration should not be understood as a flight of the destitute, but more as migration of the more intrepid, who are seeking work. Despite the resemblance of the images from informal settlements in the East and West, the same people do not live there. Eastern Europe is home to extreme poverty, destitution, and desperation, while Western camps (campo, platz, campo nomadi) are home to families that adapt quickly, in search of opportunities.

SCAMPIA, Italy (2007)

She came to Naples with her husband, from Călărași, Romania, in search of work. Her children married after a while and moved into their own homes. She and her husband split up when the Romanian group left, and now she lives with a small Serbian man named Maradona, in Scampia, beneath the highway, in an old, illegal settlement that numbers around six hundred inhabitants. The shelter has two "rooms": a bedroom decorated with many portraits of Padre Pio in the caravan, and a living room in the wooden shack, with a nice sofa for the guests and a play area for the child.

The new child has to have better conditions, so Maradona will have to do his best to build the bathroom planned by his wife, who identified a sewer in the vicinity of their shack and is pushing him to connect to it. The piece of land was "bought" from a previous inhabitant for one hundred euros.

The Serbian community is spread out beneath the highway that connects Scampia to the north, and it is divided into several zones with important variations in the quality of the shacks and living conditions, ranging from the picturesque "Casa Rosa," an enclosure with oleanders, running water, and decorated sheds, to the more precarious shelters built by more recent dwellers.

Is this a European problem, as most politicians say, or a national one? Nicolae Gheorghe[1] claims it is not. His argument is based on the observation that the diversity of Roma groups—well acknowledged, not only by researchers, but also presented in the analytical part of any policy document—contradicts the idea of building a single strategy for all of the Roma in Europe. A second observation is that some politicians are attempting to define all Roma as nomads and criminalize the whole Roma population. "This is a Romanian problem, not a European one." "Getting rid of the Gypsies" has been part of the Romanian psyche since the Second World War deportations. The mass Roma migration that has occurred since Romania joined the EU has served a similar purpose: getting the Roma people out of local communities. This approach tolerates the idea of the Roma "becoming European" on the assumption that the Roma will leave, while the westerners will take on the burden and then start to "understand our bitterness." This harsh, highly racist critique aims not only at the national level, but at the local level as well, and deserves extra comment. There has not yet been a mass migration of Roma; it is a phantom perception of the European public, and politicians are merely speculating upon it. The real mass migration is occurring inside the borders of Romania and is related to the lack of secure tenancy, forced evictions, and the lack of land and housing.

In Romania, many Roma neighborhoods have a dual nature that is both historical and transitory. Although the existence of some settlements can be easily traced back at least a century, there are no official documents that register the houses of the inhabitants and, as the existence of a domicile is required in order to have an identity card, for many years even identity papers were not issued. The process of legalizing people did not affect their homes, and the battle for cheap votes leads to sometimes ridiculous situations, like the one in a village where inhabitants live on the territory of one community and have identity papers issued by the authorities from the next town.

1 Nicolae Gheorghe is one of the main Roma international activists and intellectuals. He makes an important critical contribution to the idea of Roma nation, and, as the former head of the contact point for Roma and Sinti in the Office for Democratic Institutions and Human Rights of the OSCE, he had the opportunity to advise on Roma policy at all levels and across Europe. The quotations are taken from his intervention at the conference "Contribution of EU funds to the integration of Roma," held in Bucharest in October 2010, later published in *The Guardian*. See(http://www.guardian.co.uk/commentisfree/2010/nov/03/romania-shirking-roma-responsibilities).

VALEA RECE (Cold Valley), Tirgu Mureș, Romania (2005)

Almost every Romanian city has several impoverished neighborhoods, but usually only one of them draws the attention of authorities, media, and the public. The fame of Cold Valley as a *no-go* area is relatively recent; its poor reputation began spreading when a new wave of rural migrants—some involved in thefts and prostitution—arrived and settled on the upper plateau of the peripheral neighborhood. Before 1989 the place was a typical Transylvanian, multiethnic street inhabited by some eight hundred people, with gardens and trees and old people standing in front of the gates. The area is registered in the urban planning regulations as municipal pasture, and just two properties have property titles, while some others figure as gardening land. The new inhabitants live on the *no man's land* defined as a protected area containing some gas installations and the city water reservoirs (ironically, the entire community shares just one source of water, a public water pump).

Nowadays there are more than 1500[2] people living there, but community leaders, authorities, and public opinion claim that there might around 4000. Numbers play an important political role, not only during an electoral year like 2008, but also when it comes to shaping policies. Through numbers, local leaders try to direct most of the resources to their community, while politicians use it to argue that the problem is too big for the available resources. The same game can be noticed at the national level: there are only 535,000 Roma according to the census, but an estimate of 2.5 million is the figure that is used by almost everybody.

2 The exact number was 1565 according to a census taken by our team in 2008, and it is closer to the 1360 people registered by the former leader in 2004, during our first visit, and to the rough estimate of the newcomers.

The question of the number of Roma in most European countries might be answered by the observation that the real number is usually 3 to 3.5 times higher than the official census. Bulgaria, for example, with its 370,000 self-declared Roma, might expect to have nearly one million. The endless debate on the size of the population has a lot to do with the fears of the majority and probably with an unacknowledged guilt. The forced settlement of the nomads, the slavery episode, and the forced migration culminated in the Holocaust (Samudaripen in Romani), and is now followed by new forms of discrimination. "Anti-Gypsyism" is spread on a scale that starts with a "No Gypsies allowed" poster on the door of the local disco and ends with shootings in Bratislava, marches in Gyöngyöspata, Hungary, and people sleeping in the woods for a month after arson attacks in Sanmartin, Romania. But besides the presence of so many "historical" settlements (i.e. with a long history), we are witnessing the emergence of many new places, built on very different grounds, and of a very different nature: informal work colonies, brand new ghettos built as unofficial prisons, semi-soft incarceration facilities, social housing with an ethnic touch, and charitable compounds.

SOFIA, Fakulteta (2011)

Here is the perfect stereotype: a Mercedes near a shack, puzzling the viewer and urging him to conclude that people living in shacks are actually rich; they just live there "because of their lifestyle and cultural heritage." Actually, the car belongs to an inhabitant living in a good quality house, just near "Cambodgia," as this part of the Fakulteta neighborhood is called. As a result of policies developed during communism, Bulgarian Roma were gathered into large communities, Fakulteta being probably the largest, with a number of inhabitants that is reported to be between 22,000 and 40,000. Again, the imprecision is part of the *no-man's-land* policy and the *no-go area* public image that is promoted for various reasons by local authorities.

GREECE Trikala region, recent Roma settlement in a remote area.

After being condemned by the European Committee for Social Rights "for continued serious and widespread discrimination against Roma in respect of housing rights,"[3] Greece started a number of housing programs, most of them loan-based. Through the program, every family can get sixty thousand euro to build a house, but the money is often used for starting a small business, or buying a car. The actual financial scheme also requires a house design, which, because of lack of information, time, and understanding, ended up being the same for everybody, regardless of the size of the family. The picture above was taken in a place that was built on an empty field, far from any locality, with no access to public services.

Below you can see one of the successfully finished houses that illustrate the main type of "Roma house": a two-level, square structure made of concrete that is rarely completed; sometimes there is just an improvised shack on the concrete slab, in most of the cases with one empty floor. The house below belongs to one of the leaders of the community of Aliveri, a quarter of Volos, and has a shop on the ground level and the apartment of the owner on the first level.

3 See http://cm.greekhelsinki.gr/index.php?sec=194&cid=3646.

GREECE, Volos, Aliveri neighborhood (2008)

Sitting on a chair, surrounded by many flowers carefully planted in larger or smaller plastic or ceramic flowerpots, seems to be one of the favorite activities of the inhabitants of this part of Greece. Otherwise, the whole activity of the Roma in Thessaly would be anything but rational. Their trade consists entirely of selling chairs and, to a smaller extent, flowerpots. Hundreds of large Japanese pick-up vans or even small trucks tour the villages, advertising their merchandise through megaphones. Tens of thousands of plastic chairs populate the yards and the unfinished floors of the Roma houses, sometimes in stacks that reach five meters in height. It is still hard to understand who can buy so many chairs; the trading scheme seems to resemble the one-size-fits-all project for the houses.

Aliveri might be on the outskirts of Volos, but it has its own outskirts, an area in between the city and the highway, in the river flood zone. Here you can find a mixture of situations: poor relatives of the people living in the mainland Roma neighborhood and newcomers, both living in shacks; some bigger houses built according to the design from the loan investment scheme, and a colony of prefab containers previously inhabited by the workers who built the highway.

As elsewhere, the main idea is that Roma should live separately, grouped together on a piece of land of little value, with unclear or transitory legal status. For architects and urban planners, acknowledging the existence of new forms of apartheid should be part of the reflection that accompanies our professional practice. Europe has a large number of established Roma ghettos, a growing and extended phenomenon of informal Roma settlements, and contradictory integration policies that are actually developing new ghettos. We have to look closer at the diversity within the Roma groups and at their potential to support our aging and divided societies. At the same time, we should try to review our planning instruments and tune them to the reality of the world of the poor and excluded.

['mUStávE]© musthave ©

Project Proposal for Social Integration in Bulgaria via Consumerism or How to Set Up a Professional Crafts School and Turn It Into a musthave© Brand

Fordewind architecture, in cooperation with Archis Interventions and C.E.G.A.

Ephgenia Hodkevitch and Boris Enev (fordewind architecture), background, site selection and description by C.E.G.A.

Background

Over 800,000 Roma—ten percent of the population—live in Bulgaria, according to World Bank data. It is estimated that the majority of Roma live in segregated Roma neighborhoods and rural areas, where poverty and social exclusion are established facts of life. Poverty is generated by a vicious cycle involving poor education and professional training, which closes access to the labor market and reliable sources of income. The mainstream approach to combating social exclusion is focused on children at the preschool and elementary school levels. Thus, all other Roma are excluded from mainstream programs, including young people who drop out of school early and those who are between twenty and thirty-five—in other words, future parents or parents. There are no school drop-out prevention programs, or lifelong learning programs for those who have already dropped out. Youth between twenty and thirty-five never have opportunities for professional training and education. At the same time there is a dearth of successful policies aimed at professional training and self-empowerment for adult Roma. Thus, there is a policy gap that abandons young and adult Roma to the cycle of poverty.

Background: zoom

One of the major specifics of the Bulgarian Roma that makes them different from others in the vast majority of European countries is their inner ethno-cultural diversity, hinged on the history of the region. More than twenty subgroups exist in the country, and they vary in self-identification, religion, language (dialects) traditional means of living, origin, and other respects. This diversity may be a possible reason why it has not been possible over the decades to generate a strong Roma community, enforced by broad support that might have promoted a sustainable integration policy.

From the 1950s to the early 1970s the Bulgarian government ran a policy of cleansing the city centers by displacing the Roma communities, pushing them to the outskirts of the cities. These measures created segregated, extremely impoverished Roma neighborhoods. The majority of these neighborhoods remained outside the law, and they were not included in town planning. They have minimal access to public utilities, no infrastructure, no sewage system, no post office, medical care services. Even public transport, drinking water, and electricity are rare. But what does this mean for the inhabitants of these "poverty pockets"? The extra-legal status of the Roma neighborhoods makes the existence of the inhabitants of these ghettos illegal too. With no official place of residence, a person has no chance to obtain proper employment; if children do not legally exist, there are no places in schools for them, and from a political point of view, non-existent people cannot vote.

No integration

For the last twenty years the state policy concerning the integration of Roma has not had any visible impact on the quality of life in Roma neighborhoods. The lack of visible change results in the perception that Roma integration and the state policy are processes doomed to failure. This demotivates both Roma and non-Roma. Additionally, integration fails because the majority fears the minority to be integrated, while the Roma are disappointed and distrust the efforts of the majority, believing there to be an absence of will on the part of the majority. The absence of will for integration on both sides and the existing evidence of failed efforts leads us to the thought that integration has to be a must, you musthave© it.

['mUStávE]© musthave©-Project philosophy

The musthave©-project is based on the idea of a functioning business model. It is also a project about synergies—about the creation of synergies and their benefit to personal development and social inclusion. But how is that to be achieved? Via consumerism. We want to use the biggest weakness of our society as the strength for this project. Since our society seems to be addicted to consumerism, and the longing for goods appears to be a strongly motivating force, this project wants to use exactly these phenomena. The project wants to develop a hybrid association between a school for teaching life skills and crafts, and providing professional training for young people, a small factory/workshop for creating products, and an exquisite boutique for selling them to interested visitors.

In our case, the school will educate pupils in sewing. The social enterprise—coordinating and operating the education line, the production line, and the trade line—will have to develop a strong fashion brand first of all, which could guarantee the success of this undertaking. To create this strong fashion brand, the project initiative is aiming for international cooperation.

Fashion is not social? – Fashion is not social; it is a way to establish a unique identity.
All over Europe fashion schools, colleges, and fashion institutes in universities are working on models, ideas, and collections with educational purposes. We want to acquire leading teachers—famous fashion designers themselves, together with the young future fashion designers—to create a collection for our social venture and to donate this collection to the project, along with permission to confect the samples. The common understanding will be that the fashion thus created will have nothing in common with the so-called Roma look, but will be a modern fashion statement. Samples will have to be easy to produce, given that the project trainees will be producing them, and the collections will have to be made with customary, affordable, or recycled materials.

Fashion is not social? – But it could be
In return for this donation, the classes and colleges acquire credit for playing an active part in European integration, and the students will have the additional advantage of having their fashion sketches and collections put into production and worn. The target is to produce and sell designer clothes "made by Roma" for an appropriate price—products that you musthave©. Yet, the project will try to apply a more responsible model of consumerism, which also has a strong social aspect, while providing both quality goods for consumers and fair educational and work opportunities for the disadvantaged producers.

Hypothesis
If the minority group could offer a range of services or products, then the target group of attracted consumers will be willing to accept the differences and go beyond borders. Desire seems to shift old habits aside and makes people willing to move beyond them. If this happens frequently and over a long period, the switch to familiarization will have been accomplished. Both target groups—Roma participants and customers—will get used to each other and to the otherness. A common interest will create a feeling

of solidarity. The aim is to transform the existing ethnic barrier—which is so difficult to overcome that crossovers only occur rarely—into an integration zone, where communication and integration can increase and be established. This would be the origin of integration: integration can happen then.

Analysis

During a research visit in autumn 2010 to the Fakulteta Mahala in Sofia, the biggest Roma enclave in Bulgaria with an estimated 150,000 to 300,000 inhabitants, it became evident that, contrary to common opinion, business is lively in the Roma district; traders and craftsmen are shaping life there.

The research showed that during the communist period a huge number of Bulgarian Roma were trained and employed in national companies, factories, and corporate groups—mostly in the textile and clothing industry, wooden furniture production, and furniture textiles. The workers were well-trained, educated, and partly integrated. After the political system changed and subventions for national companies were cut, the Roma employees were the first to be laid off. These well-educated, integrated working people have disappeared into the Roma enclave. Local business has developed there, but this local business is based upon limited economic security, technical skills are only common among the generations that are over forty-five, and they are not being passed on to the generations between sixteen and thirty-five.

Three questions arise: how to revive this forgotten potential, how to develop both life and professional skills, and how to transfer trade skills, including modernized technical skills, to younger generations?

Three answers occur: by investing in individual potential and self-empowerment; building professional skills and small enterprise, and through community development and consumerism.

Project priority areas

Setting up a school and motivating young Roma to participate, build up their skills, and become empowered is a process of developing their community, which is, in turn, an integral part of this project's methodology. The school is a community development tool, as long as investing in the personal potential of Roma students and qualifying them to be competitive on the labor market makes them role models and agents of change in their community. The musthave© brand will have a strong ownership, which will add positive synergy and have an impact on the Roma community.

The goal of this project is to look for multiple cooperation opportunities with universities, schools, etc.—not only for design and fashion design, but also for the development of innovative marketing strategies, the project's business plans, business models, economic research, and the creation of the brand.

Fashion-point /design-point/ architecture

Architecture, design, and the art of living are the basic topics of this project, as well as the creation and recreation of synergies in thinking, acting, and processing. The design of the schools and shops should follow these principles. Since energy efficiency, gray energy, and energy balance is a leading theme in today's approach to architecture and urbanism, we think that all architectural and design measures taken for this project should follow these principles. The school, the production workshop, and the shops have to be a design work themselves. They are the visual and philosophical flagships of this project's idea. The buildings should be made out of recycled and other alternative materials. With these standards, this project establishes its unique position on the cutting edge in Bulgaria and in Europe. The material bases aim to become an attraction themselves, since every kind of positive and innovative publicity would be helpful for the success of this project.

Entering the integration zone

The target groups of this project are students, mostly young Roma between the ages of sixteen and thirty-five, teachers, university students, couture producers who contribute design samples, textiles, materials, etc., and customers: fashion victims, trendsetters, hitchhikers, students, globetrotters, mountain climbers, generation X, generation Y, and other open-minded people. The proposed beneficiaries are fifty trainees in the Personal and Professional Development programs, fifty trainees in the social enterprise program, and fifteen trainees employed in social enterprise.

The project duration is divided in two stages; the preparation stage is estimated to last eight months; the implementation stage should be three years. The goal is to reach the break-even point, so that after a certain time the organization should be able to take over financial and administrative control.

Location

The education and production site, along with a small "factory outlet," will be located in a small Roma community in the country. The location of the future flagship shop (fashion boutique in the form of a culture and event club) has to be situated in the town center of the capital city, Sofia.

Three communities have been preselected, based on the following criteria:

- Having a segregated Roma community
- Having a large number of impoverished Roma and Turkish communities in the region as potential beneficiaries as future students of the school
- Potential to have an operating textile and couture industry in the region
- Potential to have entry points to the communities;
- Potential to have a good partnership with the local government;
- Based on needs assessment

The final location will be chosen during the second phase of the project, based on a participatory approach and discussions with the communities. This phase has not begun yet, to avoid raising great expectations.

Blageovgrad

The Blagoevgrad district is situated in southwest Bulgaria and borders Greece, Macedonia, and four other districts. The population is 343,370, or 4.3 percent of the country's whole population. The administrative center is the town of Blagoevgrad with a population of 70,000. Two universities are situated there: the Neofit Rilski Southwest University and the American University in Bulgaria, with 19,000 students. The region is characterized by a diversified economy: food and tobacco processing industries, agriculture, tourism, transport and communications, textile industry, timber and furniture industries, iron processing and machinery industry, construction materials industry, as well as pharmaceuticals, plastics, paper and shoe production. Approximately ten percent of the population is unemployed (close to the national average).

The Blagoevgrad district contains remote communities of Turks and Pomaci (Bulgarian

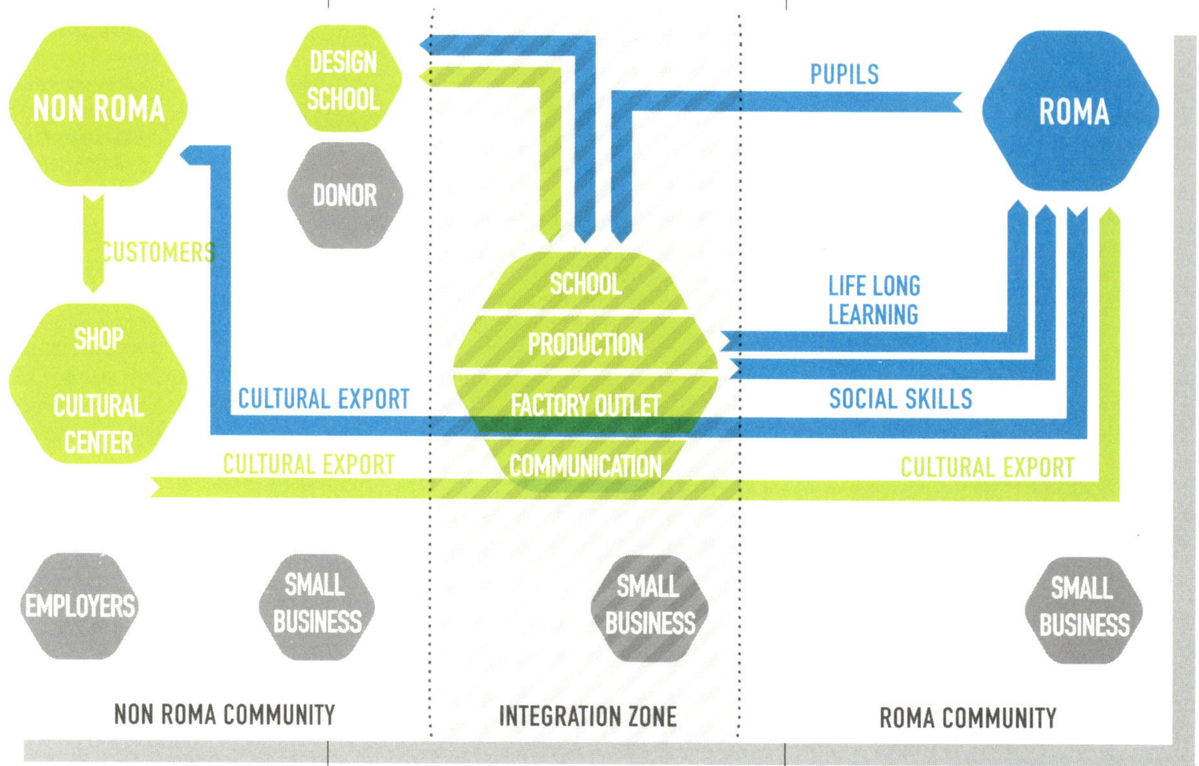
NON ROMA
DESIGN SCHOOL
DONOR
PUPILS
ROMA
CUSTOMERS
SCHOOL
PRODUCTION
FACTORY OUTLET
COMMUNICATION
SHOP
CULTURAL CENTER
LIFE LONG LEARNING
SOCIAL SKILLS
CULTURAL EXPORT
CULTURAL EXPORT
CULTURAL EXPORT
EMPLOYERS
SMALL BUSINESS
SMALL BUSINESS
SMALL BUSINESS
NON ROMA COMMUNITY
INTEGRATION ZONE
ROMA COMMUNITY

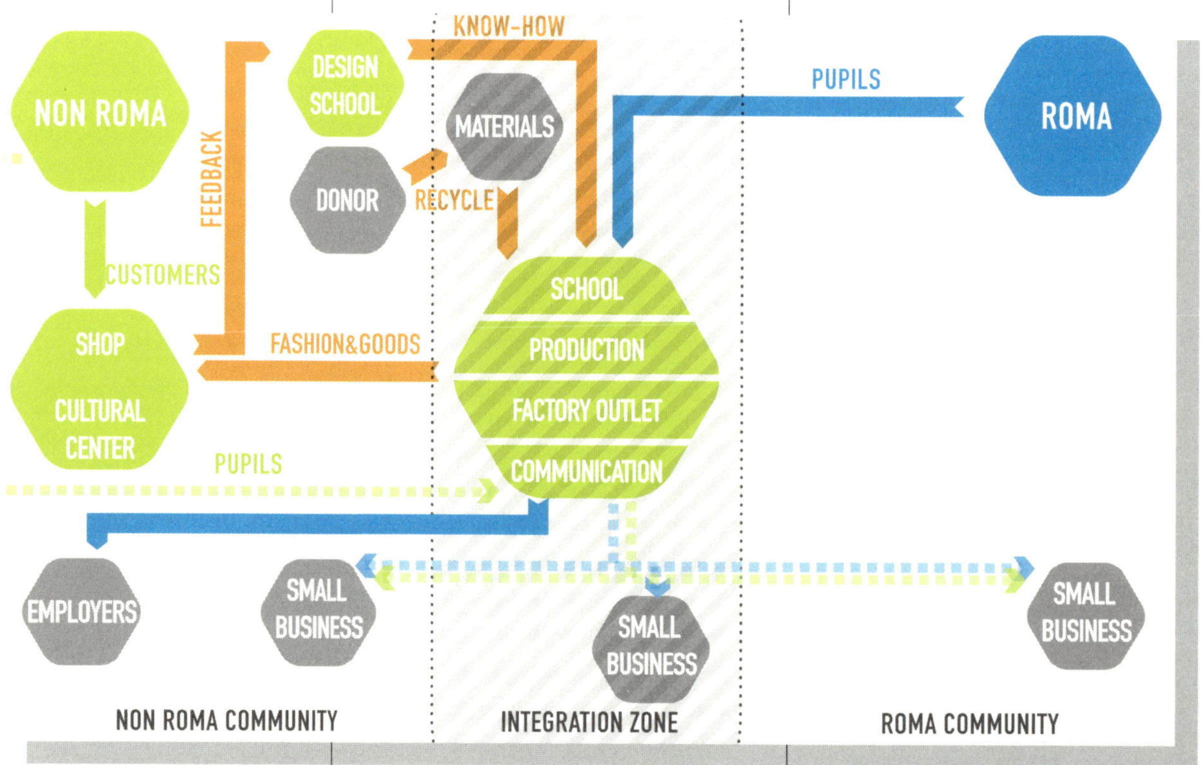
KNOW-HOW
NON ROMA
DESIGN SCHOOL
MATERIALS
PUPILS
ROMA
FEEDBACK
DONOR
RECYCLE
CUSTOMERS
SCHOOL
PRODUCTION
FACTORY OUTLET
COMMUNICATION
SHOP
FASHION&GOODS
CULTURAL CENTER
PUPILS
EMPLOYERS
SMALL BUSINESS
SMALL BUSINESS
SMALL BUSINESS
NON ROMA COMMUNITY
INTEGRATION ZONE
ROMA COMMUNITY

Muslims) who are potential beneficiaries of the project as well. The Roma communities in Blagoevgrad comprise about twelve percent of the population there.
They are part of the Roma subgroup known as the Erlii (settled Romas), whose mother tongue is Romani. The Roma community lives in three major settlements: Nova Mahala (new village), Stara Mahala (old village), and Predel Mahala (situated at the *predel,* the point where the three mountains surrounding Blagoevgrad meet). Only six people from the three Roma communities have a university degree. The percentage of people with a secondary school degree is about 5.8. Forty-six percent have an education on the sixth or seventh-grade level and thirty-seven percent have an education up to the third or fourth grade level. Nevertheless, almost ninety percent of the inhabitants are illiterate. Lately, a strong tendency toward illiteracy among youth has been perceived.

The social situation is the worst in Predel Mahala: ninety percent of the population are illiterate; truancy rates are high; most of the housing is illegal, and infrastructure is almost entirely absent—no running water, no sewer system, no electricity—and the birth rate is rapidly on the rise. The Roma community is segregating itself more and more into three living environments. Stara Mahala has a better standard of living; besides poor people, there are families with stable incomes and jobs, whose children attend school. Nova Mahala has the best reputation among the Roma community: new, big houses and infrastructure, while a large percent of the adults have finished school and have regular jobs and children attending school.

Dupnitsa, district of Kyustendil
Dupnitsa is situated in southwestern Bulgaria, in the Struma River valley at the foot of Rila Mountain. The E 79 international corridor passes close by the village; it is one of the main thoroughfares in the country, leading to Salonika, the Adriatic Sea, Istanbul, Macedonia, Serbia, and Western Europe.

The Roma community is spread all around the outskirts of Dupnitsa. There are five major Roma communities with an overall population of about 6,500 to 7,000. In 1998 only one person had finished high school. A few Roma (five or six) have university degrees. Children drop out of school after the fifth or seventh grade. At both stages the loss of motivation plays a large part in a child's decision to leave school, but after the seventh grade, early marriage plays a huge role. The main source of income is from the building construction sphere; men are ordinary construction workers, but construction decreased dramatically after the financial crises in 2008. Women do seasonal work as cherry-pickers, but most of the time they stay at home and take care of their children. In the past there were some Greek clothing factories, but currently they are out of the market and many women are unemployed. Housing is moderate: cheerful houses with tidy gardens.

Karabunar, district of Pazardjik
Karabunar is a village in the municipality of Septemvri, in the Pazardjik district, situated in southern Bulgaria, one of the most developed agricultural regions in Bulgaria. It is twenty kilometers from transport corridor 8 and sixty-five kilometers from Sofia.

Septemvri is a rural municipality with fifteen villages and 23,957 inhabitants. Sixty-seven percent of the citizens live in villages. In July 2011 the official rate of unemployment was seventeen percent; unofficially, it is over fifty percent. In the villages it is as high as seventy percent. Over ten thousand Roma live in the municipality. About two thousand Roma live in a segregated neighborhood in the city of Septemvri. Large Turkish communities also exist in the villages. The education level is very low: over 3300 residents have a basic education (up to the fourth-grade level). 1500 have not made it even to the fourth grade; most of them are Roma and Turkish. Most of the Roma and Turkish children in the villages around Septemvri barely achieve an elementary education; early marriages are frequent. Karabunar is a village situated in the center of the municipality, on the main road connecting the municipality with TC 8 and the district center. 1388 people live in the village, including about 300 Roma. The main source of income is part time, seasonal employment in agriculture. Most of the youth remain unemployed.

Expect the expected

This report of the ['mUStávE]© project has to detail an alternative idea for an integration project in its developmental stage. Success will depend on several factors: besides financing—that is a clear *conditio sine qua non*—success will depend on the strength of the partners involved in the project, selecting the right community for collaboration, and the broad support of the community selected. Very important is the work of the local NGO, which must communicate with and motivate the target groups. Without strong and honest field work, this project cannot be implemented. Collaboration will be only sought with successful and NGOs that operate transparently—not necessarily with the so-called Roma NGOs, some of which have doubtful reputations, even among Roma communities. Just like a business idea, this idea has to be highly promoted at every stage of development. In our opinion, the right marketing strategy and the development and promotion of the fashion brand are of enormous importance.

In the current project, fordewind architecture ltd. is setting up the project structure and goals. During the research phase of the musthave© project, fordewind architecture ltd. and its partners will analyze the concept's needs, estimated success, process, and possible obstacles.

Project partners: The project ['mUStávE]© musthave© is being developed by the initiative fordewind architecture ltd., in cooperation with Archis Interventions and C.E.G.A., supported by the ERSTE Stiftung. Strategic partner is BALKANTEX Ltd., a Sofia-based fashion enterprise that develops and executes high-quality fashion goods. It has been in operation in Bulgaria for fifteen years now, and maintains a strong position on the European textile and clothing market. The Balkantex enterprise has attached importance to social issues and the pioneering notion that business should be committed to a common social responsibility. See www.balkantex.com.

District of Pazardjik
District of Kiustendil
District of Blagoevgrad

roma population | official | estimated

24 000 50 000

8 300

12 400 25 000

Dupnitza

Karabunar

Blagoevgrad

Contemporary Serbian Church Buildings

From Tradition to Political Correctness

Vladimir Mitrović
Photos: Orfeas Skutelis

There are many reasons, justified or not, for the picture of what our Orthodox architecture looks like today. Church architecture is in the state of the late-romantic and uncritical acceptance of tradition, following a fast but wrong lane. There is the rigid attitude of the Serbian Orthodox Church (SOC) regarding all new forms, due to the well-known conservative views (which is not denied) of clergy circles, especially high-ranked ones; the unchanged liturgy, which requires a suitable space; practical and pragmatic situations regarding construction work, fund raising, and organizing construction processes, which are mainly assigned to the local church communities; and then there is the disinterest of architects, the so-called "mass production" of churches, the lack of educational curricula in this field. These are but a few of the reasons for the situation of the present sacral architecture around us. From time to time, one has the impression that not even the Church and its dignitaries are satisfied with its contemporary sacral production. Having concentrated on renovating the old, historical structures—mainly using state funds, not their own—the SOC has not completely developed an approach regarding the building and designs of their new churches, apart from the fact that they keep pointing out that the new churches should resemble old, monastic structures. This notion is an idealized one thought up by benefactors and local priests, as in the case of the church in Ub (architect Predrag Ristić, 1990–2001), whose investor is a controversial *nouveau riche*. Apart from this general attitude, projects are quite often chosen for various reasons, such as the pure volunteerism of the investors and the assigned priests; or even personal reasons, such as a person's origins, an individual's desire for a memorial, and other, similar reasons. Building a new church in a local environment is seen as a fulfillment of an oath, which, almost as a rule, has to lean on some of the solutions from the rich history of sacral building.

Political parties based in Vojvodina also strongly criticize the construction of new churches in the cities and villages of Vojvodina that follow the Serbian-Byzantine style, demanding the "return" of the authentic baroque concept of building churches. This ultimately political (or everyday political) attitude requires additional explanation. Sacred architecture in Vojvodina does not have such a long tradition as the one in Serbia proper, due to the historical processes in this area.

From the eighteenth century onward— or, to be more precise, its latter decades—churches for all confessions in Vojvodina were built according to a unique scheme, because plans were made and approved at the highest state level. Their unique style—single-nave constructions oriented towards the sides of the world (East-West), according to the confessions they were built for—was inspired by a (political) wish for the temples not to differ too much, so that they would not become a cause for protests on a national level. Apart from this legislation, there were a few more solid, practical reasons for such a way of building: a simple, single-nave temple was much easier to finance and build than a church with a dome, which is considered to be the most complex part of an Orthodox church, both from the points of view of construction and aesthetics. The large capacity that a single-nave construction offers is not to be disregarded easily. Some Vojvodian settlements required the raising of suitable churches that could accommodate a large number of people, and this was assured by choosing a single-nave type of church. One of the other reasons was that there were no professionals, architects, and experienced builders who would be ready to realize certain projects, since most of the professional architects and engineers of the time worked exclusively for the army on behalf of its needs. This kind of construction practice, which can be said to have been "politically correct" under the Austro-Hungarian monarchy, was usual during the first half of the nineteenth century. During the seventh and eighth decades of the nineteenth century, great changes occurred in that field; namely, since then, Roman Catholic churches have been built almost exclusively in a neo-gothic fashion, and very rarely in a neo-Romanesque style, while sacred Orthodox architecture has turned toward the Serbian-Byzantine heritage for its basic inspiration. It is also interesting that this new approach to sacred Orthodox architecture is basically the product of so-called Hansen's Serbian pupils. Teofil Hansen (1813–1891), a Danish architect and long-term professor at the Academy in Vienna, was a famous builder of his time and left his mark on the architecture of Vienna and Athens, where he was a guest architect at one time. Hansen promoted a mixture of Byzantine and European influences and is considered to be one of the first Europeans who pointed out the architecture of Byzantium and its influences, and included some of its influences in his own work. Hansen's Serbian students, originally from Vojvodina—we shall mention Svetozar Ivačković (1844–1924), Vladimir Nikolić (1857–1922), and Jovan Ilkić (1857–1917)—designed a large number of Orthodox churches around the turn of the twentieth century in Serbia and Vojvodina: Paraćin, Trstenik, Jagodina, Pančevo, chapels in Sremski Karlovci, Melenci, etc.—and their manner reflected the return to old Serbian-Byzantine ideals. The buildings were based on the cross, following a neo-Byzantine model, and had a monumental cupola and a (physically) separate bell-tower, instead of one that was adjoined to the church. These architects can be seen as bearers of the idea of the restoration of the national style in the Serbian sacral building, as has been meticulously studied by Miodrag Jovanović, PhD, and Aleksandar Kadijević PhD,[1] both art historians. Unfortunately, the topic of contemporary sacred architecture built during the past two decades in Serbia has practically not yet been touched, neither from theoretical nor from historical and artistic aspects.[2]

The Role of Architects and City Planners

Although the Church speaks reluctantly of authorship of sacral architecture, because they think that a temple represents anything but an individual designer's seal or contribution, historians of art and architecture have managed to note down (and study) a large number of authors, as well as their creative contributions in the field of sacral architecture. Almost every Serbian architect has had the experience of building sacred objects. Even the very modernist architects of the not-so-distant past had an Orthodox church design or two in their portfolios.

1 M. Jovanović, *Srpsko crkveno graditeljstvo i slikarstvo novijeg doba* (Serbian sacral building and painting of recent times), Belgrade-Kragujevac, 1987 (1–255); A. Kadijević, *Jedan vek tra enja nacionalnog stila u srpskoj arhitekturi, sredina XIX—sredina XX veka,* (A century of finding a national style in Serbian architecture, mid-19th to mid-20th centuries), Belgrade: Građevinska knjiga,1997 (1–344).

2 Except for some collected papers (See *Tradition and Contemporary Serbian Sacral Building,* Z. Manević, B Stojkov, eds., Belgrade: Institute for Architecture and City Planning, 1994), as well as a couple of unsuccessful attempts. Not only are there no reviews or artistic-architectural interpretations of contemporary practice in sacral architecture, but there are no published data about the authorship of the Orthodox churches built in recent decades. It is very rarely that one of the churches is presented in current architectural magazines. One of rare papers to deal with this problem is: V. Mitrović, "Svetionik vere na Dunavu–Neimarski duh Predraga Ristića," in: DaNS, no. 47, September 2004 (www.dans.org.yu).

Recently, very contemporary-oriented authors have started to work in this field of architecture. One of the main attitudes that the Church has regarding this is that the construction of churches should be done in such a manner that it does not single out the individual, the builder, but should emphasize the materials used to build the space. So, it is clear from this attitude, what role the Church assigns to architects. The notion that personality should be absent in the process of building new objects resembles the notion underlying tasks given to architects in totalitarian regimes.

With the exception of bright, yet rare public competitions, the roads that lead to the construction of most churches include architects by all means, but they also involve city planners. There is a saying: if a painter is a pig, an architect (and a city planner) is a chicken. The market has created a servant and a yes-man from the frightened chicken. And he is ready to compromise about everything and to please everyone, sometimes even the completely banal wishes of investors. Those with power in Serbia during the Milošević regime in the nineties, as well as in the post-October governments, have realized that cooperation with the Church should be very close and it should be regarded as a national institution of highest importance. After the retrograde introduction of religion into the state education system, the church is expecting a massive reimbursement of their assets in the forthcoming period, in the form of flats, building lots, arable land, forests, etc. What else can be expected after such decisions? The sudden wealth of an already wealthy Church and the subsequent stampede to build new objects is very surpising. The authorities have already given back the Church's social status, among other things, by letting it build hundreds of sacral objects, which was a result of primarily political, not religious reasons. And so the "state within the state" has been given an impressive number of most attractive and important locations in Serbian and Vojvodian towns and cities. Free of charge, of course. The effect of this religious town planning in neighboring Croatia is also catastrophic; the best example here is the so-called "Spiritual Ring" in the city of Split, where the construction of ten new churches is expected. So far, it has not caused any reactions from city planners or their services. Yet, to be honest, they were not expected to react. From the socialist yes-man practice, our town planning has thrown itself into the jaws of new investors, rich people, as it moves through the so-called transitional phase, while, parallel to the processes that are devouring the urban structure of our towns and settlements, not a single word or sentence has been written or said about these phenomena of "the state within the state."

Practice and Pragmatics

In the provinces, all issues and phenomena are slowly radicalized, almost to the point of banality, for more and more reasons, from the insufficient education levels of the people hired to build objects, to their obsequiousness to central authorities. The example of the recently built sacral objects in Novi Sad and its outskirts eloquently speaks of the degree of the builders' practice when speaking of sacral objects. Out of the thirteen Orthodox churches that have already been built, those that are being built, and those that are planned in and around Novi Sad, a vast majority (to be precise—all of them) almost do not deserve any serious architectural or artistic analysis.[3]

The only thing that can be done is to name the facts regarding which of the so-called historical churches they have copied, or identify the origins of the mumbo-jumbo compilations of elements in some of the eclectic combinations of this and that, from the basic spatial scheme to the details copied from the ornamental repertoire. These temples will remain as silent, unoriginal, and hastily erected monuments built by a conservative and uncritical spirit, incapable of facing reality, just as the SOC is, and furthermore, with obvious, preconceived ideas uncritically treating traditionalism in architecture, often with caricature-like forms.

The need to build Orthodox churches arises from the fact that certain narrow territories—parishes, mainly—do not have places of worship. Of course, this fact stands for itself and is true. In the past ten years, parishes without a place of worship have quite easily been able to obtain the most attractive construction sites from their town planning institutions. If the SOC is given the right to build a church in Telep, then the construction is a "poke in the eye" of the local majority in this part of town, namely Hungarians. This is a matter of morality—and not just a religious one, but a common one, a matter of human morality. If this temple has been horribly designed, without a main idea, harmony, and proportions; if its shape is hypertrophied, then it represents an additional problem—if anyone sees it as a problem at all. In my opinion, the number of new Orthodox churches is certainly not the key problem (although it is up to a point), i.e. the quantity is still considered inadequate by the Church's standards, in its position as the institution of authority.

The problem is the architecture itself, the artistic value of the new objects that pop up with incredible speed, and the amounts of money spent on them in a society that can still be considered to be poor. The official answer to the question of why the SOC is not building hospitals, hospices, sanatoriums, old people's homes, orphanages, and similar objects, as it used to do, is that the Church is there to care of spiritual health, not physical health. That is, as the Church sees it, the task of the state. This is a classic example of the religious-hypocritical point of view. Ambitiously and with immense support from the state, the SOC is building a great number of churches, yet, on the other hand, it does not do enough to satisfy the earthly needs of its subjects, something that has long been the major feature of the Church's activities among Serbs. Thanks to their disproportionate care about the heavenly, there is no time for the earthly. Or, is it one of numerous, unsolved relations that the Serbian Orthodox Church is projecting toward its believers? It is a matter of taste not to mention the many examples of the side-effects of building the churches embodied in the ever-present corruption

3 New SOP churches in Novi Sad and its outskirts: Church of Christ's Ascension, Klisa, Novi Sad, 1994, design: Milojko Korać, architect; Church of the Raising the Honorable Cross, Klisa Prison, Novi Sad, 2002–2003, design: Živan Jelić, architect; Church of St. Cyrill and Methodius, Telep, Novi Sad, 2003, design: Bata Božić and Miloje Maraš, architects; Church of the Birth of Mother of God, Šangaj, Novi Sad, 1998–2004, (after the Petkovica Monastery), design: Milorad Milidragović, architect (1938–1999); Church of the Transfer of the Remnants of St. Sava, Novo Naselje, Novi Sad, design: Vlasta Matić, architect; Church of the Birth of St. John, Detelinara, Novi Sad, design: Sava Ristić, architect; Church of St. Simon, Veternik, 1994, design: Milojko Korać, architect; Church of St. George, Temerin, 1994,design: Mile Zec; Church of St. King Lazar, Stepanovićevo, 1990 (the first one in Vojvodina after WWII), design: Branko Pešić (1921–2006), architect; Church of St. Petka, Petrovaradin, design: Ljubica Bošnjak, architect; Church of St. Vasilije Ostroški, Sirig (after the Krušedol Monastery), design: Branko Kosović, architect; Church of the Ascension of the Mother of God, Bački Jarak, 2003, design: Dušan Arbajter, architect; Church of the Gathering of Serbian Saints, Budisava, design: Radoslav Prokić, architect; building of SOC churches is expected (the lots have been allotted) in Adice, Liman, and Grbavica.

of the so-called lower circle of clergy—i.e., the clergy that does not come from monasteries. Meanwhile, clergy from monasteries are the only ones with the right to make decisions within clerical circles. The duality among the clergy, where those with the really difficult experience of living in a monastery are the only ones that are considered higher and more official—as opposed to the ordinary, parochial priests who mainly care about their earthly problems (house, car, easy life, and a suitable job for the wife)—has, of course, never been publicly recognized by the Church, although everybody knows everything about it—both the clergy and interested believers. Besides, the top echelons of the Church, as the official representatives of its political and religious view, only recognize those with a monastic background that is usually decades long. Church circles have long known about the relationship between the two types of "clergy."

Unless construction is about to take place in a bigger town, the decision as to how an Orthodox church is going to look is mainly left up to the lower clergy and Church boards made up of "average" believers. When we know what "average" means in the local context, it is crystal clear who makes the decisions about the look of the new sacral object, and how the decisions are made. Regarding the degree of artistic values, and no less important details, such as the work on the interiors of new churches—lives of saints, iconostasis, wood carving, the entire corpus of work from the wide spectrum of applied art—the main decisions are also made "on the local level." The fact is that such people cannot be up to their noble task—choosing the right values for the work on the interior of a place of worship. Of course, it would be unjust not to mention the efforts of a certain segment of the clergy, which has tried to raise the entire story concerning the design and decoration of churches to a higher level. That was, of course, one of the reasons for initiating the organization of institutions of higher education in this field. Still, these institutions should not be treated as regular educational institutions, financed by the state, if only for just one of numerous reasons: only believers can attend those schools, with the blessing of the Church, and ordinary citizens should not be obliged to finance such projects through the state budget.

Another realistic question is: does the SOC need so many new churches at all? At least in urban environments, where churches already exist? It is a fact that believers deal with their religious rituals not only on the basis of where they currently reside, but on the basis of where their ancestors used to be. Christenings, weddings, and the rest are supposed to be celebrated in the churches of their ancestors, so this is an intentional attempt to traditionalize new believers, which is a very anti-traditionalistic approach. This disrespect of family norms, among other things, leads to the decadence of family values and tradition. The practice so far has shown that new churches become places where new believers come and go; they are not a place for family gatherings, as the Church is trying to present it. Probably, as has happened many times in contemporary history, this will ultimately have a boomerang effect: i.e., the new churches will remain empty, in accordance with common practice, and will eventually come to symbolize an old-fashioned, retrograde attitude toward citizens.

The article was previously published in Serbian and English in: AFANS, Anti-fascists Action Novi Sad, ed., Kritika klerikalizacije Srbije/The Critique of Clericalization in Serbia, 2007 (www.kuda.org), and in German in: Bauwelt, Die Wiederkehr der Gotteshäuser, 43/2009, Kai Vöckler, guest ed.

Svetosavski dom, Kać, 1999–2000.

The Church of "Uspenje Bogorodice", Bački Jarak, 2003. Projektant: arh. Dušan Arbajter

The Church of "Sveta velikomučenica Marija (Ognjena Marija)", Paragovo

The Church of "Sveti Vasilije Ostroški", Sirig, 2004. Projektant: arh. Branko Kosović

The Church of "Sveti Đorđe", Temerin, 1994. Projektant: Mile Zec

The Church of "Roženje Bogorodice", Šangaj - Novi Sad, 1998 - 2004. Projektant: arh. Milorad Milidragović (1938 -1999)

The Church of "Sveta Petka", Petrovaradin, 2004 - Projektant: arh. Ljubica Bošnjak

The Church of "Sveti knez Lazar kosovski", Stepanovićevo, 1990. Projektant: arh. Branko Pešić (1921–2006)

The Church of "Sabor srpskih svetitelja", Budisava, 2004. Projektant: arh. Radoslav Prokić

Split – The Spiritual Renaissance of Public Space

Miranda Veljačić and Dinko Peračić

The city of Split provides a clear example of the causes and effects of a new spatial development strategy exercised by the Croatian Catholic Church. Today, Split has 188,000 inhabitants, of which eighty-eight percent are Roman Catholics. The area of six square kilometers comprises twenty-five parishes, of which sixteen have no adequate sacral space, as a result of state policy in the period between 1945 and 1990. In 1993, the framework for a study entitled "The Spiritual Ring of the City of Split" anticipated the planning of sixteen new church buildings, with the presumption that "spiritual identity is a precondition to vitality and a stimulating impulse to all the social values." During the last eleven years, most of the sacral objects planned as part of the "Spiritual Ring of the City of Split" have been realized. The buildings are at various stages of completion, while the realization of intended additional social services inside the sacral spaces has mainly failed.

The rise of the Catholic Church in Croatia was largely supported by the nationalist movement, which strongly influenced official state ideology during the 1990s. More than anything, Catholicism, as a dominant religion, served to regenerate traditional values and the reconstruction of national identity. This was the main premise behind all of the other aspects of political power given to church authorities—power that was followed by subsidies for religious activities and hence for urban development and buildings that housed religious activities at the core of its program. Since its partnership with the state was legalized in official documents, the Catholic Church in Croatia became a state project and actually the only big cultural development planned through most of the 1990s. It appeared as a kind of déjà-vu of communism: the number and scale of the religious building projects, and the accurate planning resembled the programmatic populism of the socialist era, reminding us of big housing projects from the 1960s, where the state was the only planner and investor.

Urban planning in the communist era relied strongly on zoning principles that excluded the possibility of religious programs. Thus, most of the central sites in areas zoned for housing were built and planned to serve other functions. Under the new political circumstances, opportunities to build new religious centers were few. To avoid the long process of obtaining a building permit, different kinds of professionally immoral or illegal solutions were invented.

Platforma 9,81

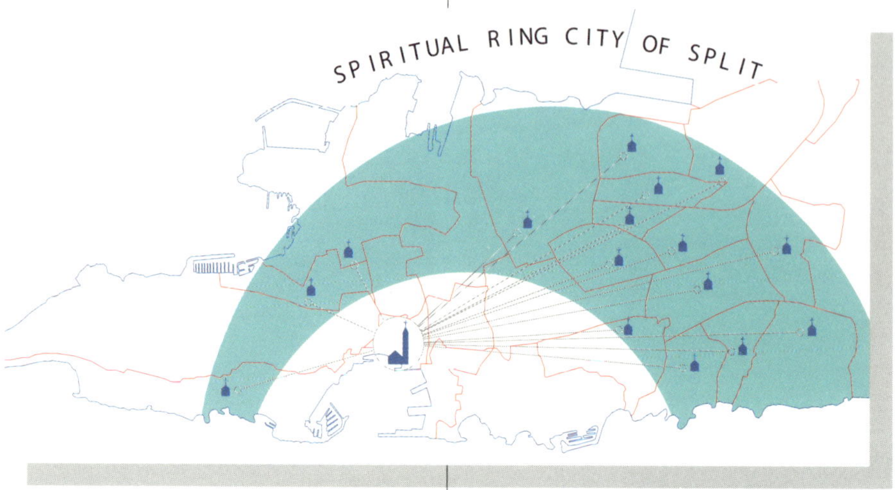

The most radical example is the town of Split, Croatia's biggest coastal center. In 1993 the municipality entered a partnership with the archbishop's district of Split and started "The Spiritual Ring of Split," a project that was to plan and build sixteen religious centers throughout the city. It was named the "Spiritual Ring of Split" and was advocated through mass media. Due to the hasty urban planning that was to follow, the project resulted in buildings in very awkward locations. New religious buildings were built in formerly public spaces or in dense, illegally built areas. An untamed urban landscape emerged as a crossover between pre-modernist cultural practices and postindustrial building techniques. In new housing areas with no communal infrastructure, churches were supposed to make up for the lack of public space.

In spite of intentions to counteract the degradation of traditional values and to practice the spiritual renewal of society, new religious objects generated the same anti-urbanity as the surroundings they were about to change. Unable to make new public space, they were becoming parasites on it instead.

Veiled behind the kitschy combination of traditional forms in reinforced concrete with prefab plastic balustrades was the exclusive religious monoculture these spaces installed: in a time of economic crisis, the only cultural and public facilities that were planned, financed, and built were churches, being the most dominant urban and cultural landmarks. Pretty soon, everybody realized that the actual number of practicing believers was far less than it seemed during the period of national delirium that began in the 1990s.

Thus, many churches were left empty or even unfinished. As this produced no effect on the number and scale of religious developments, church authorities resorted to simple strategies of re-functionalizing and renting spaces to commercial and business activities. A new generation of churches was planned and designed to suit these mixed usages. Ironically enough, the situation could be seen more optimistically than the critics of the Catholic Church are prepared to admit. Although new programs that sprout under the "cross" can be good business, we might expect to see changes in the diversity of users, as well as the accessibility and social openness of these venues.

In order to survive within the production-consumption cycle, every group or organization wants to institute its own particular politics of space. The Catholic Church is one of the actors involved in the process of privatizing urban space. What is problematic about the economic transformation of sacral space opaque is the interaction of mechanisms from socialism and the new, liberal economy. One operational strategy would be to shift our attention from physical space to the spaces of politics and culture, and to comprehend the seemingly opposing forces that inhabit them. This could also be the first step for architects, between the opportunistic belief in the Church as an empowering investor, and the will to take on their cultural mission.

St. Leopold Church, in Barutana, a peripheral quarter.

New churches in the self-organized settlements only represent a sense of community identity. Interwoven into the "wild" fabric, they are treated as points of orientation. In the network of bars and small grocery shops they are the main focus of events.

Parish church at Mejaši, partially finished, half-empty, and with no planned social facilities, such as a kindergarten.

Ravne njive, parish church. Built near the Kaufland shopping center, the church has become known as "Our Lady of Kaufland."

Our Lady of Health Monastery

Property developers tend to introduce shopping or business facilities to the ground floors of monasteries, in the desire to be market-oriented and additionally profitable. Commercialization generates interwoven, hybrid typologies.

Monastery at Dobri Square in the center of Split is an example of how new religious buildings do not create a new public space, but occupy existing public space.

Bishop's Palace in the city center.

By reinstating the Bishop's Palace in the city center, a few colleges, the city library, and the art academy lost work space.

Don Ivan Grubišić
Catholic Priest

In the early 1990s, a new relationship with religious communities emerged not only within Croatia, but in many of the ex-communist countries. Authorities realized they had to cooperate with the Church and restore its onetime social reputation. The causes of this change were not religious, but rather political, providing legitimacy to those in power. Presently, the new rulers collaborate with the Church and issue permits for building churches in areas that have already been defined as urban. It is a political will that turned from opposing the Church to collaborating with it. The same political will permeates urbanism as it does all other spheres of life. This happened in Split. The reason why new Church edifices do not dovetail with urbanism lies with a political will and a change in the ratio of power. On the other hand, as projects are realized in already defined urban areas, there is a desire to meet the wishes of the Church, since it is partnering with the authorities. Political will was exercised at the expense of a profession. Namely, architects were ordered to produce edifices that will stand out, rather than fit in. The same thing happened with historical objects. An example is the Bishop's Palace, the monument entirely devastated due to the political situation. The next step was to bring this relation to the level of a contract with the Vatican. These were international agreements that bypassed the civic society and parliamentary procedure, and were instead arranged by representatives of the state and the Vatican. As such, these agreements are still effective.

Vjekoslav Ivanišević
Architect

I designed the parish church of St. Leopold Mandić at Barutana in 1990. This church was among the first in a series that was developed later on. Construction was delayed because parish priests sued to perform liturgies in illegal houses. By freeing national spirit which had direct ties to the Catholic Church over generations, all of the long-suppressed activity has suddenly expanded, and parish priests started building churches wherever they could, since there were no spatial obstacles any more. Through the "birth" of the Croatian state, I have received a commission for one of the first churches. In the communist era, religious objects were not anticipated by urban plans. At the time, I was still at the urbanist institute. In order to build a particular church, an area allocated for a military object was rezoned for a religious object. That church has not been finished to this day, since it was built in a most primitive manner. Actually, it provides a wonderful example, since encountering such a building procedure in the twenty-first century is simply unbelievable. A concrete slab was built with a twelve-meter-high wooden construction. The technique was determined by two factors: the budget was modest and the parish priest was able to obtain cheap wood from Bosnia. There is an entire forest inside, one wooden pillar for every meter. The parish priest and three laymen, all retired, built a six thousand square meter church without understanding the project, proceeding with many an intervention, modifications, and my benevolent smile. If I had a chance to design a church again, I would never do it in the same manner. At the time I saw it as a symbol of a new time, a new spirit, and newly gained freedom; it was more than a place of worship. Today I would design a softer, more humane church, closer to man, but at the time I saw it as my own victory. There was no space, nor money for building. However, I made it to be seen and known. Have I made a mistake?

Jurica Pavičić
Journalist

Abrupt expansion of the ecclesiastic construction commenced at the onset of the 1990s, when the Church briefly occupied the role of guardian of nationalism, as an official state ideology. This increase in construction has somewhat been justified, since some of our cities (e.g. Split) grew five hundred percent during the fifty years of communism, and parish buildings did not keep up with that growth. The problem is that the Church authorities came to believe the number of believers will always remain the same as it was in the period of Catholic revival after 1990, and so they conceived objects that are too large. New churches proved to be devastating to their environment. Due to the exaggerated intoxication of the 1990s, their designs were overambitious. Their authoritarian and preposterous measures trespassed beyond their parish function, which left lots of the churches unfinished. Instead of symbolizing the dominant spiritual role of the Church, the objects conceived transformed into spatial symbols of the Church's powerlessness to realize this domination within capitalism, which, in its essence, has an atheist attitude. Most of the new church buildings reveal the arrogant delusion of the epoch in which they originated. They also demonstrate the bad taste of the Church elite, which mostly consists of individuals with undeveloped artistic taste. This horrid taste especially comes to the fore in adapting old and often artistically valuable church edifices. Two of the most horrible examples in Split are the renovations of the St. Francis monastery and the Bishop's Palace. Some of the ecclesiastic buildings, such as an unfinished monastery at Dobri in Split, represent the true delirium of the debauchery of form.

Ilvica Škarić
Former mayor of Split

The Republic of Croatia signed a protocol with the Holy See that regulates proprietary and other questions. During the communists' reign, most property was nationalized, and only a few cities allowed churches to be built. During the 1990s the political climate changed, and the Church was given back its property. These are the basic conditions that led to producing a study titled "The Spiritual Ring of the City of Split" which envisaged building sixteen new churches in Split. During this period, studies on religious edifices were made, independent of other plans. Due to the change in the political climate, people accepted the buildings with enthusiasm. We are, first of all, a Catholic milieu. Churches were planned to have youth halls; however, they have not been constructed yet, since the sacral sections of the building had priority. For the visit of the Holy Father in 1998, the city constructed the plateau at Žnjan. When it was confirmed that the Pope would come to Split, the authorities immediately decided to fill and level the Žnjan area, for the aforementioned purpose, and afterward, this move was included in plans. The area was prepared and quite a large part of unused sea was reclaimed. We have more than enough seawater, and this procedure gave us a large chunk of seaside. The building of the plateau was financed by both the city and the state, and the actual construction was carried out by the army.

The text was previously published in „Superprivatno/ Superprivate" (Zagreb 2004) and in German in: *Bauwelt, Die Wiederkehr der Gotteshäuser,* 43/2009 Kai Vöckler, guest ed.

Mosques Balkanized

Challenges of Building and Rebuilding in Post-Socialist Bosnia and Herzegovina

Azra Akšamija

The balkanization of Yugoslavia in the 1990s marked the beginning of a disjointed ideological era in which the diverse and competing nationalist sentiments are still in search of new icons for public representation. With religion now filling the ideological gap left after socialism, the process of defining and asserting ethno-national identities is producing a highly varied religious architectural landscape in the region. This paper examines the visual and cultural contestations of Bosnian Muslims' quest for identity though a discussion of mosques built in the unstable and difficult post-war geopolitical context.

The war in Bosnia-Herzegovina began in March 1992, soon after the international recognition of the country's sovereignty. The territorial lines of separation between the three warring parties—Serbs, Croats, and Bosniaks—were created by means of population displacement and "ethnic cleansing"—that is, the eviction and mass murder of civilians identified as enemies because of their ethnicity and religion—as well as the systematic erasure of their historical traces. Apart from numerous human victims, this process of territorial "decontamination" resulted in a cataclysmic destruction of the country's cultural heritage, including museums, major libraries, archives, and important historic monuments.[1] The record of demolition also includes over 1200 mosques and 200 Catholic and Orthodox churches.[2] The Ottoman historian and expert investigator at the International Criminal Tribunal for the Former Yugoslavia in The Hague, Andras Riedlmayer, contends that religious architecture was particularly targeted in order to render the newly conquered territories "ethnically and religiously pure" and erase any evidence that a peaceful multicultural coexistence had ever been possible.[3]

While this form of cultural warfare was pursued to different degrees by all sides, Bosnian Muslims suffered the greatest human and material losses. In many instances, mosques were destroyed in a way to prevent any future reconstruction. For example, the rubble of the Ferhadija Mosque (1579) in Banja Luka, and the Aladža Mosque (1550/1) in Foča, two of the most prominent monuments blown up by Serb nationalists, was removed to a remote location: the rubble of Aladža was dumped into a nearby river, while the stones of Ferhadija are still being collected from several different garbage dumps around the city.[4] The absence of adequate documentation about what was destroyed adds to the political and economic difficulties of the post-war rebuilding and reconstruction.

A decade after the end of the war, many communities are still struggling to come to terms with their traumatic war experiences. For example, in the Bosniak-Croat village of Ahmići, in which 116 Bosniaks were killed in a single day during a raid of the Croat militia on 16 April 1993, the rebuilding of the two destroyed mosques produced an internal conflict within the local Islamic community. One side urged the preservation of the ruins of the Donji Ahmići mosque as a war memorial, while the other favored a quick reconstruction with less visible reminders of the massacre. Subsequently, two mosques were built on the ruins of the destroyed ones, each serving one side of the divided community. With the recent appointment of a shared imam, however, the two groups managed to settle their differences. Yet, the only visible reminder of those killed in 1993 is a modest marble cenotaph in the courtyard of the Donji Ahmići mosque.

Another type of social conflict has arisen around the question of what comprises the adequate reconstruction of protected heritage monuments; the issue at stake here is the more general clash between pragmatic and professional approaches to renovation. A notable example is the recently renovated minaret of the Truhan Emin-beg Mosque (1446) in Ustikolina, which was destroyed down to its foundations by Serb nationalist extremists in 1992, but now is almost twice its previous height. Because this is considered the country's oldest mosque, the Institute for the Protection of Cultural Monuments in Sarajevo developed a project especially for its reconstruction. Inpatient for its completion and needing a place for worship, the *jamaat* (mosque community) decided upon a do-it-yourself renovation.[5] The result is a minaret sixty meters high,

1 Given the fact that many deaths occurred without being recorded, and that the process of recording was chaotic and uncontrolled during the war, it is very difficult to provide an exact number of victims. According to the research conducted by demographic experts from the International Criminal Tribunal, "the number of war-related deaths in Bosnia and Herzegovina can be estimated as 102,622 individuals, of which 47,360 (46%) are military victims and about 55,261 (54%) are civilian war-related deaths." The same experts contend that "the size of emigration from Bosnia (forced and voluntary) at the end of the Bosnian war has been estimated by UNHCR at approximately 1.2 million persons." See: Ewa Tabeau and Jakub Bijak, "War-related Deaths in the 1992–1995 Armed Conflicts in Bosnia and Herzegovina: A Critique of Previous Estimates and Recent Results," *European Journal of Population* (2005) 21: 207, 210. This data excludes a great number of Muslims who could not become refugees, as they were imprisoned in concentration camps, where they suffered physical and psychological damage through torture, mass rapes, and other violations of human rights.

2 The exact number of mosques and their devastations in BH is still unknown. According to the records of the Center for Islamic Architecture at the Riyasat in Sarajevo, circa 72% of mosques and circa 56% of masjids in BH were entirely destroyed or were severely damaged during the war of 1992–95. The process of rebuilding and reconstruction has progressed greatly, with about 70% of the mosques and masjids renovated and rebuilt. In reviewing the indictments of Karadžić and Mladić, the Trial Chamber of the International Criminal Tribunal for the former Yugoslavia (ICTY) stated that: "Throughout the territory of Bosnia and Herzegovina under their control, Bosnian Serb forces...destroyed, quasi-systematically, the Muslim and Catholic cultural heritage, in particular, sacred sites. According to estimates provided at the hearing by an expert witness, Dr. Kaiser, a total of 1.123 mosques, 504 Catholic churches and five synagogues were destroyed or damaged, for the most part, in the absence of military activity or after the cessation thereof....Aside from churches and mosques, other religious and cultural symbols like cemeteries and monasteries were targets of the attacks." (Karadžić and Mladić, Review of Indictment Pursuant to Rule 61 of the Rules of Procedure and Evidence, 11 July 1996, para. 15) See: ICJ Judgment of 26 February 2007, Destruction of Historical, Religious and Cultural Property. pp. 121–124, para. 336. <http://www.icj-cij.org/cijwww/cdocket/cbhy/cbhyjudgments/cbhy_cjudgment_20070226/ibhy_judgment.pdf> accessed on 10 September 2007.

3 András J. Riedlmayer, "From Ashes: The Past and Future of Bosnia's Cultural heritage." In *Islam and Bosnia: Conflict Resolution and Foreign Policy in Multi-Ethnic States.* Maya Shatzmiller, ed.,pp. 98–135. (Montréal;Ithaca: McGill-Queen's University Press, 2002), 114. For more information on Riedlmayer's quantitative survey of the destruction of Islamic religious buildings in the period between 1992–95, see:András J. Riedlmayer, "Destruction of Cultural Heritage in Bosnia-Herzegovina, 1992–1996: A Post-War Survey Of Selected Municipalities," Expert Report commissioned by the International Criminal Tribunal for the Former Yugoslavia, (2002), 9, 10. Among data about the destruction of Qur'an schools, Dervish lodges, mausolea, and buildings of religious endowments, Riedlmayer's records render the devastation of 255, or 92% of surveyed mosques as heavily damaged or destroyed. "Of these, 119 mosques were heavily damaged while 136 mosques were almost or entirely destroyed." Riedlmayer also notes that there are no complete and exact numbers about mosque devastations and the actual figures might be considerably higher.

4 Source: Andras Riedlmayer's database on mosque devastations, prepared for the International Criminal Tribunal for the Former Yugoslavia.

5 Reportedly, some of the remaining stones from the ruins of the mosque were used by individual *jamat* members as construction material for houses and gardens. Source: Safet Jahić, Interview by Azra Akšamija on 9 April 2009. More recently, another violation of the monument's status proceeded without consequences, when the French SFOR used the mosque's remaining rubble for the construction of a local road and a bridge. Retrieved on 15 April 2009 from: http://www.aneks8komisija.com.ba/main.php?mod=vijesti&extra=saopstenja&action=view&id_vijesti=511&lang=1

which now proudly holds the title of the highest in Bosnia and Herzegovina.

Subsequently, these monumental dimensions have overshadowed the war history of Ustikolina, provoking a larger, politicized debate centered on two issues. First, the public was polarized into those arguing for its "authentic" reconstruction versus those "in need of a place of worship, and not a monument," as some community members had argued. Second, the political instrumentalization of the minaret in mass media has led to its equation with other illegally constructed Croat and Serb religious and ethnic symbols, such as the contentious churches and crosses in Mostar, Stolac, and Konjević Polje.[6] These examples stand for the continuation of ethnic animosities at a time of peace and are part of a country-wide trend of ethno-religious demarcation of territories achieved through visually competing, ethnically distinguishable monuments. The diverging views on how these issues are applicable to the Turhan Emin-beg mosque have contributed to the minaret's ongoing survival and its unresolved future.

The third type of challenge to Bosnia's post-socialist mosque architecture reveals the difficulties of negotiating between religious and secular ideologies in the post-socialist period, and, within this context, the potentially increasing centrality of Islam to the ethnic and national identity of Bosniaks.[7] While the majority of Bosniaks are Sunni Hanafi Muslims, this ethno-national group also includes agnostics, deists, atheists, and Christians—in short, diverse people whose national identity does not necessarily intersect with mosque architecture. The discrepancy between the different visions of Bosniak identity is currently expressed, reinforced, negotiated, and contested though mosques.

That the question of what it actually means to be Bosniak can be answered with diametrically opposed replies is evident from the recent controversy centered around a small and modern-looking mosque currently under construction in Sarajevo's modernist housing quarter of Ciglane. The repudiation of this mosque started in spring 2008, right after the local *jamaat* initiated legal proceedings for its foundation. A wave of arguments that followed in mass media (mainly in "pro-secular" newspapers such as *DANI, Oslobođenje,* and *Nezavisne Novine*) initially included assessments about the choice of location, for the mosque was reported to occupy the only remaining free space in the area. Criticisms ranged from discrediting the *jamaat's* religious devotion, to reproofs of the *adhan* (call for prayer), to the critique of local Muslim politicians and religious leaders. Finally, the very need for a mosque in Sarajevo was put into question, for the city already has ninety-six active mosques, while lacking other social programs. Activated by this aggressive media campaign, some six hundred inhabitants of Sarajevo, of all ethnic backgrounds, signed a petition against the mosque. Their number and identity remains controversial and their efforts without avail; the construction of the Ciglane mosque is already well underway.

The interpretation of the Ciglane mosque and nine other post-socialist mosques in Sarajevo as a sign of the intensifying significance of Islam in post-war Bosnia and Herzegovina, as promoted in the mass-media, needs to be contextualized against a very real need for new houses of worship, since their construction was not possible in the previous regime. This is particularly true for the newest parts of the city such as Ciglane, which was built during the 1980s to house the Yugoslav regime's predominantly secular elites, and therefore never had any religious edifices. The need for new mosques also needs to be considered in relation to Sarajevo's dramatic demographic shift, caused by the war and the great influx of rural Muslim refugees, who are traditionally more religious than the urban population.

The Ciglane mosque debate sheds light on the pressing question of how the Bosniak nation will define itself in the post-socialist period as a part of Europe, or a potential future member of the European Union. What adds further complexity to this matter is the pressure of global Islam, propagated mainly by Saudi Arabia and other Islamic countries, which comes along with donations for the building and rebuilding of mosques.[8] Over the course of the past decade, the King Fahd Mosque and Cultural Center in Sarajevo, for example, has become a symbol for the infiltration of radical interpretations of Islam and Wahhabi Islam into local Islamic religious life. Opening in 2000, this largest mosque complex in the Balkans was built to promote the intercultural exchange between the Kingdom of Saudi Arabia and Bosnia and Herzegovina. Despite the fact that the King Fahd Mosque complex offers a wide range of socially beneficial services that are open to all residents, the ideological phenomena associated with this mosque have provoked heated controversies in the Bosnian public.

First, local Bosnian Muslims, who practice Islam according to the Hanafi madhhab (school of jurisprudence), are hostile to the proselytizing activities of the expatriate and domestic Wahabi groups, who also pray in the King Fahd mosque. Second, local Muslim intellectuals have been criticizing the Islamic community of Bosnia-Herzegovina for not maintaining the integrity of local Islamic tradition. For many secular and/or agnostic citizens of Bosnia-Herzegovina of all ethnic groups, the King Fahd Mosque stands for the intensification of religious life in the country. Finally, the mosque is politically instrumentalized in the media controlled by Serb and Croat nationalists, for whom conservative Muslims offer an easy target to spread anti-Muslim or anti-Bosniak propaganda in general.

In sum, post-socialist mosque architecture in Bosnia-Herzegovina reveals the many levels on which identity is produced through built forms and the contested relationship between culture and politics. The crux of the issue here is the negotiation of competing nationalist and religious ideologies in the realm of architecture, a competition carried out within the cultural sphere of a single democratic state, often in the context of the built form of the mosque.

6 While the entire minaret conflict has been extensively covered in the media, a comprehensive examination of the mosque's history, its previous demolition during the WWII, and the motivations for its controversial recent renovation have been mainly left out from reports.

7 The war-time adoption of the term "Bošnjak" as the official national denomination for Bosnian Muslims marked a turning point in a century-long political struggle for recognition of a denied national status. The crucial issue here is that the contemporary Bosniak nation was established on the basis of ethnicity, and the extent to which Islam represents one of its defining parameters is still unsettled.

8 It should be noted that not all of the donated mosques come with missionary communities. Moreover, not all donated mosques are architecturally alien or monumental; many are small, architecturally well integrated in their environments, often referring to both the local architectural heritage and modern architectural trends.

Mosques in Donji and Gornji Ahmići

Ruin of the Gornji Ahmići Mosque

Gornji Ahmići Mosque in the process of rebuilding

Ruin of the Donji Ahmići Mosque

On 16 April 1993, 116 Bosnian civilians were killed in a single day during a raid carried out by the Croatian militia. On the same day, 150 Bosnian houses and both mosques were destroyed as well.

Donji Ahmići Mosque rebuilt

The minaret of the rebuilt Donji Ahmići Mosque. The building of the Gronji Ahmići Mosque is in the back on the hill

The process of reconstruction started in the late 1990s, with the organized return of refugees.

The memorial in the courtyard of the Donji Ahmići Mosque, commemorating the 116 Bosnians killed on April 16, 1993.

Turhan Emin-beg Mosque in Ustikolina

Turhan Emin-beg Mosque (1448) in Ustikolina before the war

View of foundations and rubble at site of destroyed Turhan Emin Beg Mosque

Turhan Emin-beg Mosque in Ustikolina after reconstruction

Because of its importance as the oldest mosque in the country, the mosque was among the first targets of the Serbian military in April and June 1992, when it was looted, set on fire, and finally blown up.

Minaret of the Turhan Emin-beg Mosque in Ustikolina

Paradoxically, the mosque's status as a listed monument did not prevent its war-time destruction, or its inadequate post-war renovation and the reuse of the ruin's remains for local gardens and construction of a bridge by the SFOR.

Ciglane Mosque in Sarajevo

Ciglane Mosque
A team of Sarajevo-based architects, Aida Dajdžić and Namik Muftić, was commissioned to design a mosque suited to the surrounding modernist mega-housing blocks in Ciglane.

King Fahd Mosque in Sarajevo

King Fahd Mosque
The King Fahd Mosque and the King Fahd bin Abdul Aziz Al Saud Cultural Center (2000). This stylistically hybrid, marble-clad mosque is crowned with an Ottoman dome; two 49-meter-high minarets are a monumental signal of the presence of a pan-Islamic vision in Bosnia.

Acknowledgements

This book is the result of the activities of Archis Interventions in Southeastern Europe since 2005, which would not have been possible without the constant support of the ERSTE Stiftung; in particular, I would like to personally thank Christine Böhler, Knut Neumayer, and Filip Radunovic. The Archis SEE network project has been supported by so many of my colleagues that I cannot mention them all here. Still, I would like to thank Wilfried Hackenbroich, Florina Jerliu, Visar Geci, Cosmina Goagea, Constantin Goagea, Ştefan Ghenciulescu, Esra Can Akbil, and Giorgos Psaltis. I am very happy that I was able to meet so many interesting colleagues and become familiar with their initiatives and organizations in the past few years, and I am very grateful that they contributed their essays to this publication. Last, but not least, it was a Mercedes- Benz 200D, 1981 model, which brought Wolfgang Thaler, Thilo Fuchs, and me from Belgrade to Tirana in 2008, enabling me to start the Archis SEE network.

Biographies

Esra Can Akbil

is an architect, designer, and co-founder of Etika Architecture and Design Studio, which has been awarded several competition prizes. She also teaches design studios at the department of architecture, Eastern Mediterranean University, North Cyprus. As a designer and researcher, Esra Can Akbil has collaborated with a variety of partners on interdisciplinary and participatory projects related to spatial practices, and is co-founder of Archis Interventions_Cyprus Initiative.

Azra Akšamija

is a Sarajevo-born artist and architectural historian, and currently an Assistant Professor in the Visual Arts at MIT's Art, Culture and Technology Program. She received her PhD from MIT, Department of Architecture, in 2011. In her interdisciplinary practice, Akšamija investigates the representation of Islamic identities in the West, spatial mediation of identity politics, and cultural pedagogy through art and architecture. Her interdisciplinary projects have been exhibited in leading international venues, most recently at the Royal Academy of Arts London (2010), the Jewish Museum Berlin (2011), and the Fondazione Giorgio Cini as a part of the 54th Venice Biennial of Art.

Besnik Aliaj

is rector of the POLIS International School of Architecture and Urban Development Policies and a founding member of Co-PLAN. PhD in Urban Planning in 2006. Author of Tirana,the Challenge of Urban Development (2003; with Keida Lulo and Genc Myftiu).

Momcilo Arlov

is director of the Center for Civil Society Development (CCSD) in Mitrovica.

Branko Belaćević

is an architect who graduated from the University of Belgrade in 2008. Presently he is conducting research on the topic of transcriptions in architecture as part of his PhD studies at the Faculty of Architecture, University of Belgrade. Fully engaged in lecturing and research at Belgrade University from 2006 onward, and since 2011 he has worked as full-time lecturer at Polis University, International School of Architecture and Urban Policies in Tirana, Albania. He is a winner of several prizes in architecture competitions on national and international levels.

Cătălin Berescu

is an architect in Bucharest, Romania. He worked as an editor for several architectural journals, was involved in artistic projects, and has taught courses in new media and architecture, public space, and cartoons. During the last few years his main research field has been housing for the extremely poverty-stricken and housing discrimination, for which he did research in several European countries, carried out local intervention plans and ministerial methodologies in Romania, published and lectured extensively, and contributed to some international exhibitions. He is also an adobe buildings enthusiast.

Giulia Carabelli

is a PhD candidate in sociology at Queen's University Belfast, where she is currently writing her dissertation titled "Re(ad)dressing Mostar. Architecture and/ of Everyday Life as Part of the Conflict in Cities and the Contested State." She previously earned a Masters in Research Architecture from Goldsmiths College and a BA from Università Ca' Foscari di Venezia. Carabelli has been collaborating with Abart since 2009 and presented Abart's extensive research in several international conferences.

C.E.G.A. Foundation

is a non-profit organization registered under the Bulgarian Persons and Family Act in 1995 and re-registered in 2002, in accordance with the new act for legal entities with non-profit purposes, as an organization working for the benefit of the public. With its rich experience in developing solutions, operating research projects, identifying problems, and working side-by-side with young people from disadvantaged communities (the main target group), as well as with the Bulgarian government, local organizations, and groups, C.E.G.A. has been an important partner for the research phase and conceptualization of the project presented in this publication.

Slavica Chavdarovska

is an architect who graduated from the Faculty of Architecture, University of Skopje. Currently, she is working at a design and engineering company in Skopje. Her texts have been published in the first edition of Gradot ("The City," a series of books addressing the "Skopje 2014" project) and the architectural magazine Porta3. She is part of the informal group First Archi Brigade in Skopje.

Tina Ćorić

is a founding member and manager of the Abrašević Youth Cultural Center in Mostar.

Snezhana Domazetovska

is a student at the Faculty of Architecture, University of Skopje. She has been an intern for several architectural and urban planning studios across Europe. She is active in different citizens' organizations in Macedonia. She is part of the informal group First Archi Brigade in Skopje.

Boris Enev:

see fordewind architecture.

Thilo Fuchs

is a design strategist and creative director for numerous international projects in communication and exhibition design. Since 1997 his focus has been on brand communication in space, media design, and exhibition architecture. Former founding partner of unit-berlin, a design and communication agency. He is responsible for the communication design of Archis Interventions. Founding partner of TATIN Scoping Complexity, owner of TATIN Design Studio Berlin GmbH. He has taught at the Technical Universities of Berlin, Braunschweig, and Graz, and at the Donau University, Krems. Winner of numerous competitions and design prizes.

fordewind architecture

is a multidisciplinary studio founded in Vienna by Ephgenia Hodkevich and Boris Enev. The influence of architecture on the urban environment and the responsibility an architect holds toward social spaces is the focus of the studio. fordewind architecture ltd. deals with both architectural and interior design projects, as well as with theater productions, film projects, and installations.

Visar Geci

is an architect and co-founder of Archis Interventions_Prishtina.

Cosmina Goagea, Constantin Goagea, Stefan Ghenciulescu

are all architects, curators, and architectural critics living in Bucharest; they are partners in the Zeppelin Association and editors of Zeppelin magazine. Cosmina Goagea is program director of Zeppelin. Her research and curatorial practice is focused on urban activism, participative architecture, and public space rehabilitation, as well as political programs and urban development in former socialist countries. Constantin Goagea is director of the magazine and a practicing architect. His research work investigates the relationship of contemporary culture, accessible technology, and the human environment, and the innovative roles architecture can play in these and other social issues. Stefan Ghenciulescu is editor-in-chief of the magazine, a practicing architect, and a lecturer at the Ion Mincu University of Architecture and Urbanism, Bucharest (UAUIM). Author of The Transparent City. On Limits and Dwelling in Bucharest (2009).

Wilfried Hackenbroich

is the founder and principal of Hackenbroich Architekten in Berlin. Hackenbroich Architekten pursue various-scaled architectural and urban projects. Hackenbroich has curated exhibitions and written numerous articles on architectural and urban issues. He has edited various books on urban studies, most notably UN Urbanism (2010) and Transit Spaces (2006). Hackenbroich has taught at the Bauhaus Dessau Foundation, the University of Arts in Berlin, and the Architectural Association in London.

Ephgenia Hodkevich:

see fordewind architecture.

Şebnem Önal Hoşkara

is an architect in North Cyprus. PhD in Urban Design, 1994, from the University of Nottingham, U.K. Currently professor at the Department of Architecture, Faculty of Architecture, at the Eastern Mediterranean University, North Cyprus, and the dean of the faculty. Teaching involvement in architectural design studios, urban design studios, advance research methods, and conservation/revitalization of historic urban environments. She has more than 60 international and national publications to her credit, and is co-founder of Archis Interventions_Cyprus Initiative.

Valdete Idrizi

is the founder of Community Building Mitrovica (CBM) and winner of the International Women of Courage Award (2008) and the Soroptimist International Peace Award (2009).

Nina Ilieva

was born and raised in Sofia, Bulgaria. At age 19 she went to study architecture in Austria, then returned to Bulgaria to finish her architecture degree at the Sofia University of Architecture, Civil Engineering, and Geodesy. After that she moved to the United States, where her parents immigrated. In the United States Ilieva completed a master's degree in architecture and a postgraduate degree in City Design, Planning, and Policy from the Southern California Institute of Architecture in Los Angeles, CA. Currently Nina Ilieva works and lives in New York, where she is on the faculty of the New York Institute of Technology, as well as the Parsons New School of Design. She is a practicing architect and works in both the United States and Bulgaria. She recently contributed to the publication UNPLANNED: Research and Experiments on the Urban Scale, SUPERFRONT LA (2010).

Marta Ilievska

is an architect and a graduate of the Faculty of Architecture, University of Skopje. She is a co-founder of FORMIKA Plus - Studio for architecture and design, where she currently holds a position. Her other activities include working for the NGO IDnet (Regional platform for promotion of informal education) as a coordinator for the architectural program in Macedonia. She is part of the informal group First Archi Brigade in Skopje.

Florina Jerliu

is a founding member of Archis Interventions_Prishtina. She is an architect by profession, but has a strong background in NGO work. Throughout the 1990s she was involved with the Red Cross International Federation. In 1998/9 Jerliu worked as a special assistant for the US Kosovo Diplomatic Mission and also was part of the support staff to the Peace Conference in Rambouillet. After 1999, Jerliu engaged in the process of post-war urban development in Kosovo and was mainly focused on development strategies and the socio-economic prospects in Prishtina. From 2003–04 she was part of an international advisory team working on the new Vision 2020 for the municipality of Prishtina, and from 2007–10 worked for the mayor of Prishtina as an advisor on urban issues. Today, she manages her own architecture studio and teaches at the University of Prishtina.

Dragoş Lumpan

is a photographer and filmmaker. He graduated from the Academy of Theater and Film, Bucharest, Film Department, with an MFA in cinematography. He also has a BA in pastoral theology from the Christian Orthodox Theological University. His work has been exhibited internationally and he was the winner of several awards and prizes. His recent project, The Last Transhumance was released as part of the exhibition at the Romanian Peasant Museum, Bucharest, Romania.

Chara Makriyianni

is a founding member, former president (2006–2011), and currently honorary member of the inter-communal Association for Historical Dialogue and Research (AHDR) in Cyprus. She holds a Bachelor in Education (Hons), from the Faculty of Education, University of Nottingham; a Master of Arts in History in Education from the Institute of Education, University of London; and a PhD from the Faculty of Education, University of Cambridge. Makriyianni was elected to the board of EUROCLIO and served as the EUROCLIO Policy Officer (2004–2007). Currently, she is a member of the coordination committee in charge of the implementation of the new national curriculum in the Republic of Cyprus. She is the Coordinator Teacher Educator at the Cyprus Pedagogical Institute and in charge of implementing the new history curriculum in primary schools.

Vladimir Mitrović

graduated from the Department of Art History, Faculty of Philosophy, University of Belgrade (1989). He is the author of many studies, texts, and exhibitions of the history of architecture of the nineteenth and twentieth centuries in Vojvodina and Serbia. His articles have been published in national and international professional publications, art periodicals, and weekly and daily newspapers. As a curator, he works at the Museum of Contemporary Art of Vojvodina in Novi Sad (Vojvodine, Serbia). Selected books: The Architect Djordje Tabakovic (2005); Guidebook to Museums and Galleries of Vojvodina (2006); The Cityscape - Novi Sad in the Visual Arts from the Eighteenth through Twenty-first Centuries (2009); Architecture in Twentieth-century Vojvodina (2010).

Demet Mutman

is an architect whose main focus is on cities, urban development strategies, and possible alternative spatial transformations with the use of short-term activation. She has a PhD in architecture. In 2009 Mutman was responsible for the management of the 2009 Urban Age Award in Istanbul, which was part of the Urban Age Project. She is part of Archis Interventions' Divided Cities Network. Mutman currently works at the T. C. Maltepe University, Faculty of Architecture, as an assistant professor, where she teaches architectural design, urban design, and principles of city planning and urban design. Author of "Re-Animation and the European Space," Archilab Europe Strategic Architectural Exhibition Catalogue (2008, with Elke Mittmann).

Vlora Navakazi

is an architect and a lecturer at the Faculty of Architecture at the University of Prishtina. Founding member of Archis Interventions_Prishtina.

Münevver Özgür Özersay

is a founder and member of the Atelier-M Cyprus architectural office, and co-partner in Miro Designroom. Her PhD dissertation was titled "The Essential Structure of an Empowering Interaction in the Studio: The Students' Perspective."

Dinko Peračić

received an MAA from the Institute of Advanced Architecture of Catalonia (IAAC) and a degree in architecture and urban planning from the Faculty of Architecture, University of Zagreb. He is a founding member of Platforma 9,81, an association for architectural research, and a partner in the ARP architectural studio, with a focus on projects for culture, urban planning, and tourism. Winner of several architectural competitions in Croatia. Winner of the Salon of Architecture in Zagreb 2006 with R. Šilje, and in 2009 with M. Veljačić. He has taught at the Faculty of Civil Engineering and Architecture in Split since 2009.

Giorgos Psaltis

is an architect with an MSc in Sustainable Architecture in the Mediterranean Cities. His thesis was on divided Famagusta (CY); degree awarded from the University of Florence, 2011; thesis on divided Nicosia (CY); architecture degree (Laurea) awarded by the University of Rome, 'La Sapienza,' 2005. Currently working as an architect in both Cyprus and Italy; involved since the beginning of his studies in urban space and its transformation in relation to changes occurring in social contexts; particularly interested in the impact of the division in Cyprus on society and structures and the role of architecture and civil society in politically or socially conflicted contexts; involved in civil-society-led projects in Cyprus and Italy. Co-founder of Archis Interventions_Cyprus Initiative.

Tatjana Rajić

is an architect who has worked for EXPEDITIO since it was established in 1997. She is currently working as program manager, and her field of interest is green building and urban planning.

Marko Sančanin

studied political science and architecture in Zagreb. He is the founder and director of Platforma 9,81 – a not-for-profit Institute for Research in Architecture. The institute explores the spatial and urban implications of shifting political, economic, and cultural identities. Research, theoretical works, and designs all deal with concepts of spatial justice, socially sustainable development, and cultural heritage.

Dubravka Sekulić

is an architectural researcher, whose research mostly focuses on the issues of the transformation of public domain and contemporary cities. Other topics include Yugoslavian architecture in Africa. Her book Glotzt nicht so Romantisch!, about the relationship between roof extensions in Belgrade and laws, will be published in 2012 by the Jan van Eyck Academy. She often publishes texts, gives lectures, and exhibits her work.

Aneta Spaseska

is on the academic staff at Polis University in Tirana. Parallel to this, her position includes work at the Metropolis Architecture and Planning Studio. She graduated from the Faculty of Architecture, University of Skopje. During her studies she was involved in quite a number of international architectural and cultural projects. She is part of the informal group First Archi Brigade in Skopje.

Socrates Stratis

is an architect and urbanist with a doctoral degree in urbanism. He is Assistant Professor at the Department of Architecture, University of Cyprus. Stratis is one of the founding members of AA&U for Architecture, Art, and Urbanism. His research work is interdisciplinary, with a focus on the notion of the project as a constructive device if knowledge, aiming to investigate issues of connectivity, urbanity, and the public, especially in contested spaces. His work has been published internationally, and was shown at the Venice Biennale of Architecture in 2006 and 2008.

Wolfgang Thaler

is a photographer based in Vienna; his focus is on architectural documentaries in various fields. Recent publications cover a wide range, from the sixteenth century (Fürstenzimmer von Veldthurns, 2011) to The Looshaus, a new book on the famous building by Adolf Loos in Vienna, by Christopher Long (2011), to an upcoming publication on Yugoslavian architecture, Modernism In-between: The Syncretic Architectures of Socialist Yugoslavia (2012), a collaboration with Maroje Mrduljaš and Vladimir Kulić.

Miranda Veljačić, Dinko Peračić, and Marko Sančanin

founded Platforma 9,81 in 1999. Since 2000 she has organized and participated in many activist, research, competitive, architectural, urbanist, and art projects, as well as workshops , conferences, and lectures. In 2002 she graduated from the architectural department at the university of Zagreb. In 2006 she became a member of the Split Architects' Association and is also a member of the program committee for urban and youth culture at the Multimedia Cultural Center in Split. From 2007 until 2008 she was the editor of Oris. Winner of the Salon of Architecture in Zagreb, 2009, with Dinko Peračić.

Kai Vöckler

is an urbanist and publicist. Founding member of Archis Interventions; program director of the Southeastern Europe (SEE) Network. Urban development projects in Southeastern Europe. Urban research projects in Europe and Asia. Author, editor, exhibitions curator, and lecturer on art and urbanism themes. PhD in Art History, with a focus on urban spatial images. Currently Endowed Professor for Creativity in Urban Contexts at the Offenbach University of Art and Design, Germany. Author of Prishtina is Everywhere. Turbo Urbanism: The Aftermath of a Crisis (2008).

Srdjan Jovanović Weiss

is Assistant Professor at Temple University's Architecture Department, the founder of NAO, and a founding member of the School of Missing Studies. His books Almost Architecture, Lost Highway Expedition and Socialist Architecture: The Vanishing Act document new roles of spatial practitioners vis-a-vis emerging democratic processes in the former Yugoslavia and Southeastern Europe. Having coined the terms "turbo architecture," and the "architecture of Balkanization," Jovanović Weiss also practices design in the region. He is currently completing his PhD in Research Architecture at Goldsmiths University of London.

Mela Žuljević

is currently finishing her MA studies at the Academy of Fine Arts in Sarajevo, Department of Graphic Design. She is the project manager and designer at Abart/OKC Abrašević. At the moment she is coordinating two long-term projects: (Re)collecting Mostar and Amnezion - A Collaborative Course for Re-thinking the Public.

Archis Interventions – Project Credits

Archis Interventions is the not-for-profit branch of the Archis Foundation.
www.archis.org/interventions

Archis Interventions/Southeastern Europe

Program Director: Kai Vöckler
Design : Thilo Fuchs
Program Manager Mostar + Dip Karpaz/ Rizokarpaso 2011: Demet Mutman

Project Archis Interventions SEE network

The Archis SEE network was initiated 2008 by Kai Vöckler, on behalf of Archis, in cooperation with Srdjan Jovanović Weiss.

Supported by ERSTE Foundation

Project Prishtina 2006–2011

Archis Interventions_Prishtina
(Florina Jerliu, Visar Geci, Vlora Navakazi)
Archis Interventions_SEE
(Kai Vöckler, Thilo Fuchs, Cristina Antonelli)
Hackenbroich Architekten
(Wilfried Hackenbroich)

Collaborators:

representatives of the Municipality of Prishtina, Co-PLAN (Tirana), the Institute for Planning and Construction (EUP Engineering Prishtina), the Faculty of Civil Engineering and Architecture (University of Prishtina), the Kosovo Institute for Spatial Planning (MESP), architects from Prishtina and students of the Faculty of Civil Engineering and Architecture (University of Prishtina).

Supported by ERSTE Foundation. The Friedrich-Ebert-Stiftung (FES), the Kosovo Foundation for Open Society (KFOS) and the Municipality of Prishtina supported the workshops.

Project Bucharest 2009–2011

Zeppelin
(Cosmina Goagea, Constantin Goagea, Ştefan Ghenciulescu)
Point 4
(Justin Baroncea, Carmen Popescu)
Archis Interventions_SEE
(Kai Vöckler)
Hackenbroich Architekten
(Wilfried Hackenbroich)

Collaborators:

Teodora Răducă, Andra Stan, Radu Leşevschi, Gagyi Zsofi, Ioana Păvăluca, Tudor Elian. Initial workshop in 2009 in collaboration with ATU (Vera Marin), Space Syntax Romania (Esenghiul Abdul, Christian Beros) and Platforma 9,81 (Marko Sancanin). First intervention 2009 concept & production wooden bench for the Community Action Area: studioBASAR (Alexandru Axinte, Cristian Borcan). Interventions at selected chill points 2010 Justin Baroncea, Ştefan Ghenciulescu, Constantin Goagea, Cosmina Goagea, Radu Leşevschi, Teodora Răducă, Andra Stan, Cristian Niculici.

Photos: Dragoş Lumpan.

Supported by ERSTE Foundation, Union of Romanian Architects, The Administration of the National Cultural Fond, Goethe-Institut Bucharest, Austrian Cultural Forum Bucharest and the Embassy of the Kingdom of Netherlands in Romania.
www.e-zeppelin.ro

Project Cyprus 2010–2011

Archis Interventions_Cyprus
(Esra Can Akbil, Giorgos Psaltis, Şebnem Hoşkara)
Archis Interventions_SEE
(Kai Vöckler, Demet Mutman)

Collaborators:

Initial workshop in collaboration with the Urban Research & Development Center (URDC) of Eastern Mediterranean University, Gazimagusa/Famagusta.

Supported by ERSTE Foundation.

Project Divided Cities 2011

An initiative launched by Archis Interventions_SEE (Kai Vöckler, Demet Mutman) and Abart (Mela Žuljevic)

Supported by ERSTE Foundation.

Credits

ERSTE Foundation Series
Volume 2

SEE!
Urban Transformation in
Southeastern Europe

ERSTE Stiftung

DIE ERSTE österreichische Spar-Casse Privatstiftung
Friedrichstrasse 10, 1010 Wien

Cover Layout

Miriam Strobach, Collettiva Design

Edited by

Kai Vöckler

Design

Heimann und Schwantes, Berlin

Copy editing
Allison Moseley-Plath

Proofreading
Gilian Morris

Publisher

LIT Verlag GmbH & Co. KG Wien
A-1080 Wien, Krotenthallergasse 10/8
T: +43 (0)1 409 56 61 | F: +43 (0)1 409 56 97
LIT Verlag Berlin 2011
D-48159 Münster, Fresnostraße 2
T: +49 (0)251 620320 | F: +49 (0)251 231971
Mail: wien@lit-verlag.at | Web: www.lit-verlag.at

ISBN 3-643-90286-3

www.kai.voeckler.de

Photos/Illustrations

Kai Vöckler
p. 2, 8, 9, 14, 15, 16 (with Heimann + Schwantes), p. 46–49, 52-53, 60, 64, 105–107, 170–171.

Platforma 9,81
p. 20, 29–31.

Archis Interventions
p. 33/film stills by Luise Donschen, p. 65/film stills by Pixels Production + Visar Geci, p. 54–59 + 61–63 + 66–71 with Wilfried Hackenbroich, Cristina Antonelli, Anila Gjika (Co-PLAN), p. 82–83 with Mela Žuljević.

EXPEDITIO
p. 34–35, Perast photo p. 35 by Stevan Kordić.

Pulska Grupa
p. 37–39.

Zeppelin Association
p. 41.

Co-PLAN
p. 42–45.

Giorgos Psaltis
p. 75–79 (except p. 79 central square of Samanbahçe by Esra Can Akbil), p. 91 column 1, p. 93 column 1 + 3.

Münevver Özgür/Socrates Stratis
p. 86–88.

AHDR Archive
p. 91 column 2 + 3, p. 92, 93 column 2.

CBM/CCSD
p. 96–98.

Mela Žuljević
p. 100 column 2, 101.

Abart archive
p. 102–103.

Archis Interventions_Cyprus
p. 110, 111 (based on 'Revitalization of Dipkarpaz Project' report by Naciye Doratli, Sebnem Hoskara, Esra Can Akbil et al., 2008), p. 112 column 2.

Esra Can Akbil / Şebnem Hoşkara
p. 112 column 1 + 3.

Magic Blocks project team
p. 119–139 except photos p. 119–127 by Dragoş Lumpan (photo p. 127 column 1 above by Ştefan Tuchilă), photos p. 130–131 + 136–139 project team and Daniel Constantinescu.

Dragoş Lumpan
p. 140–146.

Dubravka Sekuli and Branko Belaevi
p. 149–151 (photos: Marija Strajni, Petar Stelki).

Wolfgang Thaler
p. 152–159, 195.

Dragan Krstevski
p. 161.

Marta Ilievska
p. 162–163.

Nina Ilieva
p. 166–169.

Cătălin Berescu
p. 172–175.

fordewind architecture
p. 178.

C.E.G.A.
p. 180–181.

Orfeas Skutelis
p. 184–185.

Miranda Veljačić/Dinko Peračić
p. 186–187.

Azra Akšamija
p. 191 (except column1 above + middle, column 3 above), p. 192 (except column 1 above + middle), p. 193.

Kemal Zukić
p. 91 column1 above + middle, column 3 above.

Helen Walasek
p. 192 column 1 middle.

Institute for Protection of Cultural Heritage of BiH
p. 192 column 1 above.